T0329933

NEOLIBERAL CONTENTIONS

Neoliberal Contentions

Diagnosing the Present

EDITED BY LOIS HARDER, CATHERINE KELLOGG,
AND STEVE PATTEN

UNIVERSITY OF TORONTO PRESS
Toronto Buffalo London

ISBN 978-1-4875-6088-1 (cloth)   ISBN 978-1-4875-6444-5 (EPUB)
ISBN 978-1-4875-6320-2 (PDF)

Library and Archives Canada Cataloguing in Publication

Title: Neoliberal contentions : diagnosing the present / edited by Lois Harder,
    Catherine Kellogg, and Steve Patten.
Names: Harder, Lois, 1966– editor. | Kellogg, Catherine, 1961– editor. |
    Patten, Steve, 1961– editor.
Description: Includes bibliographical references.
Identifiers: Canadiana (print) 20220437815 | Canadiana (ebook) 20220437858 |
    ISBN 9781487560881 (cloth) | ISBN 9781487564445 (EPUB) |
    ISBN 9781487563202 (PDF)
Subjects: LCSH: Neoliberalism.
Classification: LCC HB95.N46 2023 | DDC 330.12/2–dc23

We wish to acknowledge the land on which the University of Toronto Press
operates. This land is the traditional territory of the Wendat, the Anishnaabeg,
the Haudenosaunee, the Métis, and the Mississaugas of the Credit First
Nation.

University of Toronto Press acknowledges the financial support of the
Government of Canada, the Canada Council for the Arts, and the Ontario Arts
Council, an agency of the Government of Ontario, for its publishing activities.

Canada Council **Conseil des Arts**
for the Arts **du Canada**

ONTARIO ARTS COUNCIL
CONSEIL DES ARTS DE L'ONTARIO

an Ontario government agency
un organisme du gouvernement de l'Ontario

Funded by the   Financé par le
Government   gouvernement
of Canada   du Canada

Contents

Part Three: Happy, Resilient Individuals

Part Four: Producing Neoliberal Citizens

NEOLIBERAL CONTENTIONS

Introduction

LOIS HARDER, CATHERINE KELLOGG, AND STEVE PATTEN

Since the 1980s, neoliberalism has been a key animator of social life and, in turn, social science research. Emerging from the crisis of the Keynesian welfare state, neoliberalism describes a pervasive social transformation that has rewritten the terms of the relationships among citizens and the state; consumers and the market; and individuals and groups within a range of social forms. In broad outline, neoliberalism has advanced the adoption of competitive market principles throughout all aspects of our lives. The neoliberal prescription includes freeing markets from state regulation in the belief that unfettered competition will maximize profits, innovation, and well-being; emphasizing individual (rather than social or state) responsibility in order to ensure market access to a ready labour supply; and adopting private sector management principles and objectives by the public sector. Collectively, these prescriptions aimed to ensure flexibility, competitiveness, and efficiency (Brodie 1997, 224).

Observers and students of politics will immediately recognize the governing challenges, power, and resistance that inhere in such a wholesale rethinking of the terms of social interaction. Indeed, a plethora of theoretical and empirical analyses of neoliberalism have emerged over the last three decades. Studies have enquired into the success of neoliberal policy prescriptions, theorizing about the limits and possibilities posed by institutional structures and national cultures (Brenner, Peck, and Theodore 2010; Jenson 1989; 1997; Larner and Higgins 2017; Peck 2010a; Pierson 2011). Neoliberalism's internal contradictions have also risen to the fore. The tendency towards monopoly capitalism, predatory market practices, the social costs of low-wage, flexible employment, and the disproportionate effects of marketization and reduced social provision on racialized minorities, women, and people with disabilities have all emerged as significant consequences of neoliberalism's adoption (Bakan and Stasiulis 1997, Bakker 1996, Bakker and Silvey 2012; Brodie 2008, Cossman and Fudge 2002; Helleiner 2014, McKeen 2004, Vosko 2010). Further, scholars have observed the effects of neoliberalism on democratic engagement, on what counts as legitimate objects of struggle, and on efforts to undermine groups who resist neoliberal prescriptions and social costs (Brodie 2014; 2010; Brodie and Bakker 2008; Brown 2019; 2015).

Clearly, then, we are not at a loss for good thinking on neoliberalism. Yet due to its impressive adaptability and endurance, the need for on-going analysis of neoliberalism endures as well. It is this call to "diagnose the present," as Canadian political economist Janine Brodie encourages us to do, that provides the underlying motivation for the contributions to this volume. The intention is to mobilize the broad tenets of neoliberalism to understand, or take the measure of, contemporary politics and policy – focusing on Canada, but in a number of other jurisdictions as well. Context matters, as Brodie has so eloquently demonstrated. Regarding analyses of Canadian manifestations of neoliberalism, for example, we must be attentive to the country's resource-based, export economy and the regionalism to which it gives rise. As a settler-colony finally contending with its colonial foundations and articulating a sometimes triumphal, sometimes ambivalent multiculturalism; and a Western liberal democracy that, while not riven by populism itself, is nonetheless buffeted by its international manifestations, the complexity of the Canadian case offers rich examples of the malleability of neoliberalism, but also the limits of its explanatory force. Specific national, regional, and international conditions inflect the operation of neoliberal governance in every context – as the diverse chapters in this volume demonstrate. And given the rapidity and unpredictability of change – despite an overarching neoliberal logic – the obligation, or perhaps the compulsion, of diagnosis is on-going.

Stemming from a symposium honouring the career of Janine Brodie, the chapters in this collection use Brodie's scholarship as a springboard and inspiration, but each contribution offers its own distinct analysis and, like all fine scholarship, situates the research in the context of a wide range of contemporary scholarly and political debates. Brodie is centrally located in these analyses because of her long-standing and insightful contributions to understanding neoliberalism as a political, but especially (anti)-social phenomenon. Immediately recognizing both the magnitude of the change that neoliberalism represented as well as the contradictions that inhered within its governing logic, Brodie wrote prodigiously, describing neoliberalism as a state form, as an ideology, and – adopting Foucault – as a "mentality" of government (1994, 1995, 1997, 2002a, 2002b, 2007, 2008, 2010, 2014, 2015, 2018). Most importantly, Brodie was among the first scholars to observe the gendered dimensions of neoliberalism, outlining the processes through which an emphasis on individualization led, inexorably, to increased demands on families and the social care of women to fill the gaps that emerged as social services shrank. And when many scholars became enamoured of the moderating initiatives of "social investment," "social inclusion," and "social cohesion," Brodie saw, instead, the creativity and adaptability of neoliberalism as its agents sought strategies to ensure its continuation. The fact that "social" was a necessary modifier for investment, inclusion, and cohesion was a telling indicator of the extent to which collective well-being had been displaced as the central work of governing. Despite the projections of neoliberalism's demise in the wake of the 2008 financial crisis, it has trundled on, with intensifying crises now a central feature of this governing logic. Indeed, as John Clarke has argued, these are no longer crises *in* neoliberalism, but *of* neoliberalism (cited in Brodie 2018, 6). As a governing logic, neoliberalism is regularly forced to face its contradictions and limits and to adapt, taking different forms in different places and under different circumstances. It is this perpetual morphing and re-making, as well as Brodie's attention to neoliberalism as a form of governance and its impacts on "the social," that invigorate the neoliberal contentions that populate this volume.

How, then, does one contend with neoliberalism? In this introductory reflection, we engage this question from two angles. First, we consider the current status of neoliberalism, arguing that neoliberalism continues to inflect governance, policy-making, and a more general orientation to the realm of "the possible," even if we can also identify intensifying contradictions in governing practices and global circumstances. We then turn to exploring a number of approaches to the task of sense-making when the central concept is notoriously slippery and adaptable. Drawing from the touchstones that have informed the volume's contributors, we elaborate on Raymond Williams's residual, dominant, and emergent forces; the use of paradox; and the concept of assemblage. The idea of "the social" – of the ways we live together, mediate our disagreements, and envision our collective future – subtends this discussion. Indeed, this emphasis on "the social" is a distinctive feature of the analytic focus that animates this collection. Finally, we provide an overview of the chapters, highlighting shared approaches and themes as they track through distinctive geographic and policy contexts.

Is Neoliberalism Over?

This book is not a post-mortem, and we do not regard the current state of neoliberalism as a manifestation of the undead, even if contemporary Dracula and zombie analogies do have a certain resonance (Amar 2013, 249; Peck 2010b). Certainly, scholars have been heralding the end of neoliberalism for more than two decades. In the early 2000s, efforts to temper the worst effects of neoliberalism were evident in the discourse of social cohesion and social inclusion, noted above. Political projects envisioning a "third way" – a reconfiguration of social democracy that would navigate a path between hardcore neoliberalism and an ossified "old left" – signalled a desire to temper a single-minded economism, or at least to recast fiscal discipline as a necessary, but non-determinative, mode of governance (Giddens 1999). Ideas like the Tobin tax (to reduce stock market speculation), and Joseph Stiglitz's efforts, as head of the World Bank, to challenge the Washington Consensus on market fundamentalism (2002), were additional and coterminous harbingers of the end of neoliberalism. The 2008 financial crisis proffered another moment of reckoning, and when that did not come to pass, the ensuing rise of right-wing populism was heralded as the next signal for neoliberalism's demise. For some, this demise is apparent in the abandonment of liberalism altogether in the protectionist and moralistic policies of contemporary populist governments (Amar 2013, 239). For others, neoliberalism's end is evident in its abandonment of a promise for a brighter tomorrow through belt-tightening (Mitchell and Fazi 2017, 154). Austerity, it turns out, is a difficult policy to sell when the promised tomorrow never comes. And while it is true that our current context is marked by decidedly un-neoliberal elements – nationalism, populist anti-elitism (qua "drain the swamp"), authoritarianism (Brown 2019, 2) – such factors, along with neoliberalism's capacity for adaptation, attest to neoliberalism's co-existence with strange bedfellows, rather than its end. Moreover, neoliberalism's lingering impacts are especially evident in the tools we have available to address new crises – most notably the COVID-19 pandemic. The serious consequences of diminished policy and service capacity are starkly apparent, even as people are newly alive to the importance of substantive social connection and economic interdependence. Neoliberalism, we argue, has constrained our capacity to envision the social, of how we might set the terms of how to live together. As Brodie argues, whatever its failures and contradictions, neoliberalism has fundamentally reframed the relationship between the state and the market, transforming the "social literacies and grammars of post-war social citizenship" (2018, 16).

In her brilliant 2019 diagnosis of the state of neoliberalism in America, Wendy Brown argues that the popularity of far-right populism in the US, but also in the UK, Europe, Brazil, India, and elsewhere is not, in fact, a rejection of neoliberalism, but rather a logical result of neoliberalism's attack on democracy and its disregard for politics and the social. In Brown's analysis, the Trump era presents a kind of Frankensteinian emanation of neoliberalism – at least in relation to how neoliberalism was theorized by its primary architects – the German ordoliberals of the mid-twentieth century, and notable members of the Mont Pelerin Society – Milton Friedman, but especially Friedrich von Hayek. In Brown's analysis, neoliberalism's progenitors envisioned that capitalism and morality, left to their own internal dynamics – and thus unfettered by the designs and ambitions of various political meddlers – would produce the greatest freedom, order, and possibility for civilizational development (Brown 2019, 12–13). Yet neoliberalism in practice could not be left untouched by politics. Politicians, facing the vicissitudes of electoral politics, saw the advantages of a free-market message and the pitfalls of divisive moralism, with the result that the morality and tradition that Hayek imagined would moderate a free market were generally sacrificed in the pursuit of free trade and the unencumbered operation of financial capital markets. Indeed, this particularly market-centric version of neoliberalism has become so prevalent that the fact that there was a tradition/morality dimension to the founding theory is broadly unfamiliar (Brown 2019, 108). To be clear, politicians of a neoliberal cast embrace the claims of neutrality that neoliberalism offers even as they mobilize those processes for deeply political projects. By privileging measurement, orderliness, predictability, and forecasting, neoliberalism converts the economic analyst into the speaker of truth – seemingly neutral, objective, unbiased, depoliticized. The market becomes the domain where truth is produced, suffusing law and the juridical as the dominant expert knowledge.

With regard to morality, Hayek's formulation was envisioned as a check on the worst tendencies of the free market, yet this morality was to be expressed in highly privatized, patriarchal family relationships. Moreover, Hayek imagined that such relationships were formed and sustained through "voluntary conformity" (cited in Brown 2019, 99). Hayek fantasized the absence of power (and thus politics) from this formulation of the "personal, protected sphere," as well as from the market. The utter disdain for politics articulated by Hayek and his neoliberal brethren, and their ensuing failure to take politics seriously in the first instance, ensured that neoliberalism would be inherently crisis prone.

Hayek's disdain for politics leads directly to his assessment that the idea that people might form societies on the basis of their collective will was deeply mistaken and had to be undone (Brown 2019, 102). Clearly then, we have not travelled the full Hayekian distance, since collective, if also selective, understandings about how to live together remain the focus of lively debate. Nonetheless, neoliberalism's corrosive effects on democracy are abundantly clear. Waning support for public services, disengagement from the political process, and weakened participation in, and support for, labour unions are just a few of the indicators that our capacity for collective engagement has diminished. This is not to ignore important efforts of resistance and notable contradictions – such as public health leadership and citizen compliance (though variable) in addressing COVID-19. However, those resistances and contradictions must be understood within a vocabulary from which robust conceptions of the social have been vanquished. Individualism – tempered as it was by broad societal experiences of hardship and war – was rife for redefinition once those collective experiences and the sense of a "shared fate" were no longer first-hand experiences for large portions of national populations. It remains to be seen whether the 2020 global pandemic, or the more chronic condition of climate emergency, might reignite this sensibility. For now, however, neoliberalism persists because we have a weakened capacity to talk back to it.

What we face in our current moment then, is neoliberalism's latest adaptation. It is monstrous in its fealty to the judgments of bond-rating agencies at the expense of human well-being, and even when its sweeping ambitions encounter resistance – whether in the form of social justice causes or alt-right efforts to reinforce white, patriarchal privilege – they are refracted through neoliberalism's thorough undermining of democracy (Brown 2019, 8). Thus, we agree with Brown's assertion that "nothing is untouched by a neoliberal mode of reason and valuation and that neoliberalism's attack on democracy has everywhere inflected law, political culture, and political subjectivity" (2019, 8). Indeed, it is neoliberalism's distinct adaptive capacity; its ability to fail, to foment a state of continuous crisis, and yet to persist, that is its greatest strength. If anything, neoliberalism is resilient.

Approach

Given that we are persuaded that neoliberalism lives, unsurprisingly, we also want to advocate for the concept's continued usefulness. We certainly acknowledge that, in light of neoliberalism's crises, failures, paradoxes, and contradictions, its usefulness as an analytic tool might be dismissed altogether. Indeed, as Brenner, Peck, and Theodore observe, neoliberalism "has become something of a *rascal concept* – promiscuously pervasive, yet inconsistently defined, empirically imprecise and frequently contested" (2010, 184; emphasis in original). Nonetheless, to abandon the analytical lens of neoliberalism is to ignore significant consistencies and similarities across geographies and policy fields, even as specific historical and political contexts necessarily inflect its operation.

Following Brodie's lead, the chapters in this collection make the case for the ongoing usefulness of contending with neoliberalism by "diagnosing the present." The aim in this approach is two-fold: to situate contemporary phenomenon in a broader historical and political-economic context, and to observe the local and quotidian instances in which neoliberal rationality is both reinforced and resisted. The idea here is to discern how the elements of a social phenomenon have shifted over time, what has compelled those shifts, and with what effects – at macro, meso, and micro scales.

A number of contributors invoke Raymond Williams's discussion of the dominant, residual, and emergent elements of epochal cultural change, in the service of such analysis (Williams 1977). While Williams is interested in broad characterizations of epochs – in understanding the dominant cultural process that is taken up as a cultural system – he is also concerned with complex interactions that give historical moments a sense of movement and change (1977, 121). Residual elements are cultural phenomena formed in the past that continue to be active in the present context, though in an altered form as a result of their encounter with dominant forces (Williams 1977, 122). For example, Williams argues that the idea of "rural community" is a residual idea (in contemporary British society), offering both a limited alternative to urban, industrial capitalism, but largely as a fantasy escape – "a leisure function of the dominant order itself" (1977, 122).

As for the emergent, these are new practices, meanings, and values that are continually being created, yet without a strong sense of which ones will be of lasting consequence. In this context, Williams is careful to differentiate between "emergent in the strict sense, rather than merely novel" (1977, 123). Emergent cultural processes, like residual processes, must be understood in relation to the dominant, but because we have fewer points of reference through which to make sense of them, again, it can be challenging to determine whether they matter or not (Williams 1977, 123). Moreover, the more that emergent processes are oppositional (as distinct from merely alternative) to the dominant, the more likely that they will encounter strong efforts to incorporate them within dominant processes. Further complicating this process,

Williams notes, is the fact that the process of incorporation often "looks like recognition, acknowledgement, and thus a form of *acceptance*" (emphasis in original) (1977, 125). That said, Williams is at pains to point out that no dominant social order or dominant culture (or mode of production) can include all forms of human action. What gets excluded is often characterized as the personal, natural, or metaphysical – and the use of these terms generally offers a clue to identifying an excluded area, "since what the dominant has effectively seized is indeed the ruling definition of the social" (Williams 1977, 125). Feminist and sexuality scholars have noted, for example, how invocations of the natural have attempted to depoliticize the inequities of gendered caregiving and the ineffability of heterosexual marriage.

In late capitalism, the extent to which the market has infused itself into social and cultural life is so pervasive, Williams argues, that the possibility of emergence is increasingly challenging (1977, 125). Moreover, the distance between the alternative and the oppositional has significantly narrowed (Williams 1977, 126). Nonetheless, Williams offers some hope that change is possible: "The fact of emergent cultural practice is still undeniable, and … is a necessary complication of the would-be dominant culture" (1977, 126). The question of whether neoliberalism remains dominant or might be passing into the realm of the residual is one that a number of contributors to this volume engage. Observations regarding neoliberalism's ever-intensifying crises, and, relatedly, its penchant for failure, invite us to consider the conditions that arise as dominant cultural practices are undermined.

Two additional approaches to analyzing neoliberalism bear mentioning here: paradox and assemblage. In some senses these approaches are related, as they both point to a certain incoherence in neoliberalism. Further, these approaches work to counter a functionalist tendency in some neoliberal theorizing – a tendency to see neoliberalism itself as the explanation for all things: because neoliberalism. As Jamie Peck has so drily observed, "clearly, the principal tenets of neoliberalism were not handed down, as policy commandments, in tablets of stone from Mont Pelerin" (2010b, 106). Rather, neoliberal prescriptions have encountered local contexts and political dynamics, morphing accordingly. Peck argues, in fact, that neoliberalism adapts by learning from what it does wrong. "It fails, but tends to fail forwards" (Peck 2010b, 106). Thus, if neoliberalism's adaptive mode is "try, fail, try again," it is, perhaps unsurprising that both paradox and assemblage would prove especially useful in understanding neoliberalism's inner workings.

The identification of paradoxes illuminates how neoliberal logics, approaches, and policies produce contradictory outcomes, offering important clues as to where neoliberalism's crisis tendencies and failures are likely to emerge. As Bakker demonstrates, for example, the advocacy of "sound" macroeconomic policies by international financial institutions worsens gender inequality and generally creates greater financial hardship for the vast majority of people. The paradox of allegedly sound policies that nonetheless rely on the immiseration of women, a situation that COVID-19 made obvious, illuminates an important dimension of how power works in neoliberal policy prescriptions. Or stated differently, sound for whom? Similarly, Suzanne Ilcan's chapter notes how refugees in Nakivale, Uganda, are admonished to fulfil a neoliberal prescription of self-sufficiency through employment. However, employers in the local labour market are reluctant to hire these non-citizens, and Ugandans boycott the goods that they sell in local markets. In this context, the paradox of an expectation of economic independence in a situation where work is not otherwise enabled, renders moot neoliberalism's endorsement of individual responsibility. There is an abundance of evidence, then, that neoliberal prescriptions do not create more opportunities for more people, as neoliberal rhetoric promises, but rather concentrates wealth and life prospects in fewer and fewer hands. Situated in the midst of unrealizable expectations, despair makes sense – yet, as Catherine Kingfisher illuminates, we are, paradoxically, admonished to seek happiness.

Paradox also provides a means to understand how diametrically opposed policies can, nonetheless, share a neoliberal outcome. Elsewhere, Harder (2009, 649) has noted, for example, that both the legal recognition of same-sex relationships and the refusal to recognize those relationships can be justified in neoliberal terms. In the Canadian context, scholars have observed that the expansion of legally recognized relationship forms enabled the Canadian state to offload responsibility for care to more kinds of families, privatizing that responsibility and reducing the need for public provision (Cossman and Ryder, 2017). In the United States, the refusal to recognize same-sex marriages was justified on grounds that legal status would *increase* social costs – and thus should be resisted. In both cases, the neoliberal motivation of limiting social outlays forms the basis of the argument, but the policy response is diametrically opposed. Canada's welfare state provides benefits to individuals and then reduces those benefits when people form relationships (on the grounds that two can live cheaper than one); whereas marriage enhances entitlements in the United States (on the grounds that marriage produces social order and should be financially incentivized).

"Assemblage" thinking is also very much in evidence among these chapters, though at varying degrees of explicit engagement. Advocates of assemblage thinking urge us to pay attention to how heterogeneous elements come together with neoliberal effects, but also challenge the coherence of "neoliberal programs and forms of rule" (Higgins and Larner 2017, 2). As an assemblage, neoliberalism is an unstable constellation of heterogenous elements with varying degrees of consistency. Rather than insisting on "all neoliberalism, all the time," Vaughn Higgins and Wendy Larner, for example, urge us to focus on "the mundane practices through which neoliberal spaces, states, and subjects are being constituted in particular forms" (2017, 2–3). Like paradox, the value of assemblage lies in its capacity to detect contradictions and to observe moments of tension and weakness, while also alerting us to the factors that attract the attention of neoliberal true believers. Justin Leifso's chapter in this volume, for example, observes that the Japanese process of "Lean" management was not especially neoliberal in itself. Yet, its (variable) translation, first in a number of North American manufacturing contexts and then in a range of public sector agencies, was advanced as a neoliberal solution to crises of productivity and efficiency. It was an idea that was "lying around" in a specific moment, taken up by specific people in distinctive locations within decision-making structures, and subsequently put to neoliberal use. And while assemblage thinking has been critiqued on the basis that its attention to specific contexts obscures commonalities and patterns across jurisdictions and policy domains (Brenner, Peck, and Theodore 2010, 201), Leifso's deployment of the concept – as one example – suggests that assemblage can, indeed, be used for broader comparative purposes.

In short, neoliberalism is not dead, and it remains useful as a concept and an object of analysis – though that usefulness must be considered in light of a host of contradictions, failures, crises, and resistances. Moreover, while neoliberalism is not over, we would also argue that neoliberalism is not everything. There are many examples of policies, outcomes, and responses that do not neatly fit within a neoliberal framework. Brenner, Peck, and Theodore observe that "neoliberal institutional makeovers may sometimes be extreme, but they can never be complete (2010, 216). And as Isabel Altamirano notes in her contribution to this volume, neoliberalism is really beside the point in a context of on-going colonialism and dispossession. That said, neoliberalism has, undoubtedly, impacted how we think about how we live together and how to change the terms of our sociality, but it has not obliterated our capacity to also think otherwise. As we have learned so forcefully, there is nothing quite like a pandemic to remind us of our interconnection and our fundamental need for one another.

Chapter Overview

The works in this volume are largely disinclined to grand, over-arching theorizing. Instead, they focus on understanding the historical context that gave rise to contemporary political and social phenomena and explore the contradictions that emerge among social and political conditions and neoliberal policy prescriptions. Diagnosing the present is the central aim. We have arranged the chapters into four sections based around the scope of the contributions they entail. The first section presents three chapters (Clarke, Bakker, Altamirano) that set out the broad strokes of the interactions among neoliberal markets and socio-cultural conditions in the context of Brexit, macro-economic policy making, and Indigenous-settler interactions around resource extraction.

Section two includes three chapters (Leifso, Dobrowolsky, Epperson) that home in on specific policy tools in specific contexts (lean management broadly and in Saskatchewan; Canadian provincial immigration and settlement initiatives; American health care reform), finding that neoliberalism's orthodoxy is mobilized through a scavenger tendency. Its adherents are inclined to collect ideas from the contemporary zeitgeist and test them out with variable success, though more often failure.

In section three, the papers each examine a neoliberal keyword through which expectations of self-governance, contra social governance, are conveyed in more or less explicit and punitive forms (Kingfisher: happiness and housing; Phillips: resilience and mental health; Ilcan: self-reliance and refugee non-citizens).

Section four (DeGagne, Harder) engages the contradictions, tensions, and variegated usefulness of neoliberalism for understanding citizen-state interactions and conceptions of political community. DeGagne analyses LGBTQ+, Black Lives Matter, and the Toronto Police Service, while Harder explores Canadian citizenship law around international adoptions. Brodie rounds out the collection with her reflections on discipline and thinking neoliberalism as an academic vocation. Moderately elaborated chapter summaries follow.

John Clarke sets the stage for these neoliberal contentions. He conceptualizes neoliberalism as a conjuncture, a coming together of specific agents, forces, and historical particularities that entrenched neoliberalism as a broad social phenomenon even if it was also variable over space and time. Clarke notes a series of recent political events – Brexit, the rise of Trump, Russian revivalism, the rise of right-wing populism in Europe, India, Turkey, and Brazil – insisting that it is a mistake to understand these developments as all part of the same phenomenon. Instead, he argues, we should regard them as moments that are marked by "distinctive efforts to shift, rearrange, and redirect the balance of social and political forces with the aim of constructing new blocs and alliances ... [W]e are, [in short,] seeing new strategies in the field of politics." In the face of various tensions and contradictions in the neoliberal governing paradigm, manifest in specific national contexts, Clarke suggests that three key ideas can help us make sense of the present. First, drawing from Raymond Williams, Clarke advocates for a conjunctural analysis that attends to dominant, residual, and emergent social formations in historical context. Second, he notes the usefulness of the concept of articulation, which highlights both the process of assembling social forces and the speaking of politics culturally and ideologically. Third, Clarke focuses on the social, or how, despite the individualizing and marketized logics of neoliberalism, questions of how we live together are irrepressible. For readers interested in a masterclass on how to make sense of the present generally, and in making sense of Brexit in particular, Clarke's chapter will be especially illuminating.

Isabella Bakker takes up the task of making sense of neoliberalism by focusing our attention on three paradoxes: necessity, financialization, and austerity. Advancing a gendered analysis of orthodox economic policies, Bakker argues that the "sound" macroeconomic policies associated with neoliberalism have, in fact, created greater gender inequality. Failing to address the inadequacies of these so-called sound policies, and in particular, the failure to take social reproduction seriously, will have a lasting impact on economies and societies. Thus, as Bakker argues, "sound" macroeconomic policies create *false* economies, trading short term efficiencies for long term costs and consequences. After explaining social reproduction and its economic significance, Bakker sets out the three paradoxes, noting that the neoliberal "necessity" of freeing markets from the state in fact intensifies the need for state intervention to "stabilize the economy and to address social needs." The paradox of financialization increases wealth, but at the expense of workers and structures that support social reproduction, thereby undermining national economies and governments' capacities to address the consequences of increased inequality and the mobility of finance capital. Relatedly, the paradox of austerity emerges from decreased government revenues, constricting expenditures on public services and thus deepening crises. Women, in particular, bear the burden of this paradox, losing employment in the public sector and benefits. Ironically, and paradoxically, these losses have led to greater gender equality in some national contexts, as men's earnings have also decreased.

Isabel Altamirano examines the connections among colonialism, extraction, and neoliberalism in North America. She argues that the settler-colonial project of dispossession is not simply internal to the state, but also extends to external relations through global mining endeavours, an area in which Canadian firms are global leaders. Tracking the history of extractivism in the settler colonies of Canada, Mexico, and the United States, Altamirano elaborates on the resistances and refusals of Indigenous peoples whose lands have been expropriated, violated, and polluted in the service of global capital. This process has been exacerbated under neoliberalism, but it also predates it, and may well outlive it, with devastating consequences for Indigenous peoples and settlers who increasingly suffer the consequences of the environmental degradation that extractivism produces.

Having advanced these distinctive approaches to making sense of neoliberal governance, the second section of the volume examines three empirical examples of neoliberal government. Justin Leifso explores "Lean management," a Japanese approach to industrial organization, that has been widely adopted in the North American public sector. Leifso describes the adoption of Lean as a function of "groping" for ideas in the midst of crisis and, as noted above, choosing from among the possibilities that are "lying around." Leifso offers a compelling narrative of Lean's emergence, describing the role of Lean in Japan's economic success in the 1980s, and the perceived threat and inspiration that Japan's growing economic clout asserted, especially in North American industry. As North American industrial experts came to appreciate Japan's innovative "just in time" production model and focus on the elimination of wasteful activities in the production process, entrepreneurial researchers at MIT saw the possibility of translating the process to a range of sectors, or, indeed, everywhere. The public sector was seen as especially in need of transformation and lean experts were keen to impart their knowledge to neoliberal public sector reformers. Saskatchewan's health care system offers one example in this chapter. Thus, while put to neoliberal ends, Lean, like other governing technologies, has its own distinctive history and purposes that necessarily impact the process of translation and that require careful analysis.

Alexandra Dobrowolsky examines contradictory and contested developments in Canada's immigration policy sub-nationally, challenging dominant narratives around neoliberalism, and, ultimately, around the health of Canadian multiculturalism and equality. Examining immigration and settlement policy in BC and Manitoba primarily under the Harper government, her findings underscore neoliberalism's "differential instantiation across ... regions and sectors," and "its differential intersection with extant cultures and political traditions" (Brown 2016, 4). These case studies illustrate neoliberalism's contingency in the context of federalism, in light of the political economy and culture of two distinctive provinces. While both provinces sought immigrants who would contribute to the local economy, these contributions were necessarily distinctive, reflecting the specific social and market conditions in these two provinces. Provincial policies were also variably neoliberal, with Manitoba investing substantially in integration services to ensure the retention of newly recruited immigrants, while BC focused on issues of anti-racism and diversity. Moreover, despite the success of the provincial nominee system, the Harper Conservatives ultimately chose to reassert centralized authority over immigrant selection, revealing an important tension in neoliberal governance between innovation and control. This tale of two provinces thus provides a complicated story of rescaling, devolution, and neoliberal governance in immigration.

Working in a comparative vein, Brent Epperson investigates the adoption of health care reforms in Massachusetts and Utah, observing the various ways in which neoliberal policy prescriptions were advanced and resisted and the articulation of alternative modes for health care delivery, including the adoption of a single payer system. The paper draws from newspaper coverage of two state-level health reform efforts – the Massachusetts Health Reform Law (Romneycare) (2002–6) and the Utah Health System Reform (2004–11) at three key points in time: the preceding election campaign, the legislative debates surrounding the reforms, and the period following legislative passage. His analysis demonstrates that, while neoliberal narratives and framing metaphors of health were dominant within the state-based and national newspaper media, challenging narratives of the political right and left were present throughout the debates. Collectively, the state reform efforts that began in the period between the failed Health Security Act of 1994 and the Obamacare debates revealed greater political openness to health care policy change than was popularly portrayed. With that finding in hand, Epperson argues that the enduring presence of favourable narratives of single-payer health care offer hope for progressive reform advocates who continue to oppose the dominant neoliberal narratives animating health care reform.

The next set of chapters explicitly takes up the crisis of the social to which neoliberalism gives rise and its various individualized responses. Catherine Kingfisher takes up the "happiness" imperative, outlining its emergence in tandem with neoliberalism's focus on individualization and self-empowerment, but then examining urban collective housing projects in Vancouver and Tokyo as alternative and resistant "happiness" pursuits. Kingfisher notes that individual happiness and well-being have come to replace social welfare in policy design, based on the presumption that happiness is a universal desire and without reflection on its historical formation or situatedness in various traditions – religious and otherwise. Kingfisher is interested in happiness as both an artifact and technology of neoliberalism – both product and productive of proper neoliberal subjects. Like Bakker, she sees a paradox in happiness – while neoliberalism insists on personal happiness, it simultaneously creates the conditions of social isolation and alienation. This is not to presume that some "pure" form of sociality exists apart from neoliberalism or governing more generally, but rather Kingfisher's aim is to encourage readers to envision a scope of possibility beyond what neoliberalism narrowly prescribes.

Phillips's timely chapter offers an historical analysis of state responses to people with mental health challenges and, in particular, personal "resilience" as the neoliberal policy prescription for this contemporary crisis. Focusing on Ontario, Phillips tracks three broad, historical precursors, or programs, to addressing people living with mental health challenges: containment, medicalization, and deinstitutionalization. Each of these approaches was understood as progressive in its time, yet fell short. Phillips sees "resilience" as an emergent strategy, and one that, she predicts, will have a similarly unsatisfactory fate since it places the responsibility for one's mental well-being on people with the least capacity to cope. With an insistence on "recovery," people encountering mental health challenges are encouraged to "bounce back" even in the face of inadequate resources to support them. Further, mental illness is no longer a concept confined to the few, but rather mental health incorporates everyone. While potentially destigmatizing, this approach also risks obscuring the severity of mental illness for a subset of people, and the inadequacy of resilience and recovery for their conditions.

Suzan Ilcan is especially interested in the imposition of neoliberal governance on non-citizens. Despite the absence of state recognition that accompanies their lack of status, non-citizens do not escape governance. Rather they are subjected to prescribed modes of being – self-reliance schemes – without formal avenues for representation and with the expectation that they will simply be grateful for basic humanitarian aid. Further, Ilcan demonstrates that despite humanitarianism's association with care, generosity, and kindness, it too is impacted by neoliberal logics. Aid organizations are central actors in the promotion of individual empowerment and determining agents of deservingness. Self-reliance compels non-citizen refugees, in this case people located in the Nakivale Refugee Settlement in southwest Uganda, to integrate into the local market economy. Yet as Ilcan's research revealed, there was no guarantee that locals would purchase their goods or interact with their refugee neighbours in order to support this self-reliance scheme. Moreover, in the absence of formalized opportunities for resistance, refugees have become activists nonetheless, mobilizing against insecure conditions, lack of food, and inadequate support services.

Section four draws inspiration from Janine Brodie's work on the role of the state in creating citizens in its desired image. Examining the policing of intimacy, primarily in Toronto, Alexa DeGagne's chapter argues that neoliberalism works from both without and within the queer community to set the terms for appropriate sexual behaviour. She takes up three illustrative moments: the Toronto Police Service's apology for the 1981 bathhouse raids; the involvement of Black Lives Matter in the 2016 Toronto Pride March; and Project Marie, an undercover investigation of gay sex in a public park. DeGagne argues that efforts by mainstream LGBT activists to gain social and political recognition are driven by a conservative desire for normalcy, a desire that compels the transgressive elements of queerness into conformity with heterosexuality. The success of this project can be seen in a public display such as the bathhouse raid apology, or the increasing participation of public figures in Pride parades. But as DeGagne points out, the cost of this recognition is increased policing of LGBTQ2S+ folks who do not ascribe to, or are not seen to ascribe to, the pursuit of heteronormality. Racialized queer folks and people who, for various reasons, are unwilling to confine their sexual activity to the private, domestic sphere, thus find themselves subjected to criminalization, at the hands of the police and members of their own community.

Harder takes up the issue of citizenship in the context of inter-country adoptions, examining the complexities of neoliberal governance when family, nation, and national borders intersect. Canada's international adoption regulations are replete with assumptions about the proper relationship between family and nation, contestation about the form of the normative family, the work of kinship rules in policing national boundaries, and the relationship between race and nation. Moreover, even as the neoliberal state increasingly relies on families to provide care and ensure social reproduction, families' efforts to extend that care over national borders, and especially through relative adoptions, confront dynamics of nation-building that contradict such neoliberal prescriptions.

Janine Brodie gets the last word, offering a concluding chapter in which she reflects on her career as a social science scholar, on the concept of discipline, and its related cognates, disciple and disciplinarian, and the articulations of the chapters in this volume with her own work. This chapter should be required reading for all of us who aspire to, are interested in, or have the great good fortune to make a living in the social sciences. It is a profound description of the arc of an academic career and the benefits of curiosity as a guiding principle for scholarly pursuits. As Brodie describes, she began her career as a behaviouralist, enquiring into the role of women in political parties, and then encountered political economy, social theory, feminist theory, and poststructuralism, drawing from these ways of seeing to try to make sense of contemporary political phenomena. Brodie's contributions to our knowledge are instructive, not simply because of her substantive findings, but because of how she approaches the task of enquiry in the first instance. Her aim is to take up the contemporary political conversation, question or disrupt its assumptions, and consider the consequences, the incitements to change, and what might possibly come next. It is this approach to the study of politics that will surely endure in all of us who have had the opportunity to learn from her and with her.

The rise, evolution, character, and consequences of neoliberalism have been the subject of numerous scholarly volumes rooted in a range of disciplines across the social sciences and humanities. This volume offers a distinctly Canadian perspective influenced by political science and cognate social science disciplines. The chapters unpack the historical context of the contemporary moment, explore core contentions associated with neoliberalism's evolution, and provide a critical analysis of the lived consequences of neoliberalized social, political, and economic life. In a field of scholarship as crowded as studies of neoliberalism, it would be difficult to claim any volume fills a "gap" in the literature. We are confident, however, that this volume makes a unique and distinctive contribution and embodies an approach to the contemporary study of politics that readers will find illuminating and engaging.

As for the editors, we owe a debt of gratitude to each of our contributors for their generous participation in the book and in the editing process, and to Margot Challborn who undertook the fussy work of manuscript preparation. The Department of Political Science at the University of Alberta has been our intellectual home, made all the more congenial by Janine Brodie's leadership and vision. We are, of course, deeply indebted to her for the intellectual lives that we have been privileged to lead. Finally, we thank our respective spouses for their perspective, support, and good humour.

REFERENCES

Amar, Paul. 2013. *The Security Archipelago: Human-Security States, Sexuality Politics, and the End of Neoliberalism*. Durham, NC: Duke University Press.

Bakan, Abigail, and Daiva Stasiulis, eds. 1997. *Not One of the Family: Foreign Domestic Workers in Canada*. Toronto: University of Toronto Press.

Bakker, Isabella, ed. 1996. *Rethinking Restructuring: Gender and Change in Canada*. Toronto: University of Toronto Press.

Bakker, Isabella, and Rachel Silvey, eds. 2012. *Beyond States and Markets: The Challenges of Social Reproduction*. New York: Routledge.

Brenner, Neil, Jamie Peck, and Nik Theodore. 2010. "Variegated Neoliberalization: Geographies, Modalities, Pathways." *Global Networks* 10, no. 2 (April): 182–222. https://doi.org/10.1111/j.1471-0374.2009.00277.x.

Brodie, Janine. 2018. *Contemporary Inequalities and Social Justice in Canada*. Toronto: University of Toronto Press.

– 2015. "Income Inequality and the Future of Global Governance." In *Reimagining the Future: Critical Perspectives on Global Governance*, edited by S. Gill, 45–68. London: Palgrave.

– 2014. "Elusive Equalities and the Great Recession: Restoration, Retrenchment and Redistribution." *International Journal of Law in Context* 10 (4): 427–41.

– 2010. "Globalization, Canadian Family Policy, and the Omissions of Neoliberalism." *North Carolina Law Review* 88, no. 5: 1559–1592.

– 2008. "'We Are All Equal Now': Contemporary Gender Politics in Canada." *Feminist Theory* 9, no. 2: 145–64. https://doi.org/10.1177%2F1464700108090408.

– 2007. "Reforming Social Justice in Neoliberal Times." *Studies in Social Justice* 1, no. 2: 93–107.

– 2002a. "Citizenship and Solidarity: Reflections on the Canadian Way." *Citizenship Studies* 6, no. 4: 377–94. https://doi.org/10.1080/1362102022000041231.

– 2002b."An Elusive Search for Community: Globalization and the Canadian National Identity." *Review of Constitutional Studies* 7, no. 2: 153–77.

– 1997. "Meso-Discourses, State Forms and the Gendering of Liberal-Democratic Citizenship." *Citizenship Studies* 1 (2): 223–42. https://doi.org/10.1080/13621029708420656.

– 1995. *Politics on the Margins: Restructuring and the Canadian Women's Movement*. Halifax: Fernwood Publishing.

– 1994 "Gender, the State and Adjustment: The Strategic Silences of Restructuring." In *The Strategic Silence: Women and Global Economic Restructuring*, edited by I. Bakker, 52–65. London: Zed Books,

Brodie, Janine, and Isabella Bakker. 2008. *Where Are the Women? Gender Equity, Budgets and Canadian Public Policy*. Ottawa: Canadian Centre for Policy Alternatives.

Brown, Wendy. 2019. *In the Ruins of Neoliberalism: The Rise of Antidemocratic Politics in the West*. New York: Columbia University Press.

– 2015. *Undoing the Demos: Neoliberalism's Stealth Revolution.* Cambridge: MIT Press.

Cossman, Brenda, and Judy Fudge, eds. 2002. *Privatization, Law, and the Challenge to Feminism.* Toronto: University of Toronto Press.

Cossman, Brenda, and Bruce Ryder. 2017. "*Beyond* Beyond Conjugality." *Canadian Journal of Family Law* 30 (2): 227–63.

Giddens, Anthony. 1999. *The Third Way: The Renewal of Social Democracy.* Malden: Polity Press.

Harder, Lois. 2009. "The State and the Friendships of the Nation: The Case of Nonconjugal Relationships in the United States and Canada." *Signs* 34 (3): 633–58. https://doi.org/10.1086/593331

Helleiner, Eric. 2014. *The Status Quo Crisis: Global Financial Governance after the 2008 Financial Meltdown.* Oxford: Oxford University Press.

Higgins, Vaughn, and Wendy Larner, eds. 2017. *Assembling Neoliberalism: Expertise, Practices, Subjects.* New York: Springer.

Jenson, Jane. 1997. "Fated to Live in Interesting Times: Canada's Changing Citizenship Regimes." *Canadian Journal of Political Science* 30 (4): 627–44. https://doi.org/10.1017/S0008423900016450

– 1989. "'Different but not 'Exceptional': Canada's Permeable Fordism'" *Canadian Review of Sociology* 26 (1): 69–94.

McKeen, Wendy. 2004. *Money in Their Own Name: The Feminist Voice in Poverty Debate in Canada 1970–1995.* Toronto: University of Toronto Press.

Mitchell, William, and Thomas Fazi. 2017. *Reclaiming the State: A Progressive Vision of Sovereignty for a Post-Neoliberal World.* London: Pluto Press.

Peck, Jamie. 2010a. *Constructions of Neoliberal Reason.* Oxford: Oxford University Press.

– 2010b. "Zombie Neoliberalism and the Ambidextrous State." *Theoretical Criminology* 14 (1): 104–10. https://doi.org/10.1177/1362480609352784.

Pierson, Paul. 2011. *Politics in Time: History, Institutions, and Social Analysis.* Princeton: Princeton University Press.

Stiglitz, Joseph E. 2002. *Globalization and Its Discontents.* 1st ed. New York: W.W. Norton.

Vosko, Leah. 2010. *Managing the Margins: Gender, Citizenship, and the International Regulation of Precarious Employment.* Oxford: Oxford University Press.

Williams, Raymond. 1977. *Marxism and Literature.* Oxford: Oxford University Press.

PART ONE

Scoping Neoliberalism

1 Turbulent Times: Towards a Conjunctural Analysis of Neoliberalism and the Politics of the Present

JOHN CLARKE

I am preoccupied by the challenge of how to think about the politics of the present. Recently this question has centred on the turbulent politics associated with a variety of -isms: populism, nationalism, nativism, authoritarianism, and more. These developments appear in different forms across a global scale: from Putin's Russian revivalism to Modi's Hindu nationalism; from Bolsanoro's muscular Brazilian populism to Orbán's Hungarian nativism; from Trump's angry authoritarianism to the United Kingdom's rediscovery of imperial nationalism. All have been focused around political promises to make the nation "great again." The problem of how to think about such developments hinges on avoiding a pair of simplifications: on the one hand, there is the temptation to announce the novelty of these movements, identifying a new era (of populism, nationalism, rage, and more). The opposing temptation is to claim that they are merely the latest manifestation of forces that have a long and potent history (the long march of neoliberalism, globalization, or the era of financialized capitalism, for example). Instead, I want to explore a way of thinking about the present – the conjuncture – as combining different elements, old and new, transnational and local, and different -isms in distinctive forms.

Most of my examples are drawn from the UK and the turbulent politics that have surrounded Brexit: the British exit from the European Union. An unexpected victory for the Vote Leave campaign has proved extremely difficult to translate into political and governmental arrangements. An early claim (by then Prime Minister Theresa May) that "Brexit means Brexit" was a wildly optimistic piece of semantics, since making Brexit mean something in practice proved to be very difficult even after the UK's formal departure from the EU. However, Brexit marked a dramatic disjuncture that unsettled established political norms and expectations. It was a disruption that left many academics and other commentators feeling either that we had missed something significant, or that we had been right all along. I suggest that this division – the split between things being either all new or all too familiar – is not helpful for analyzing the politics of the present (whenever that present may be). My second starting point is that we should be very wary of treating Brexit, Trump, Orbán, and others as mere examples of something more general. That something may be an -ism (populism, nationalism, racism or even neoliberalism) or it may be a social force (the "white working class" is my current least favourite – a point I will return to later). Instead, I will argue that we should think about them as moments marked by distinctive efforts to shift, rearrange, and redirect the balance of social and political forces with the aim of constructing new blocs and alliances: that is, we are seeing new strategies in the field of politics. In order to develop this argument, I explore three ideas:

1. *Conjunctural analysis* – a central and recurring concern of work in cultural studies, that may also be approached through Raymond Williams's wonderful distinction between "epochal analysis" and "actual historical analysis" (1977). Like Janine Brodie, I have found Williams's insistence on thinking about the co-existence and entanglement of dominant, residual, and emergent formations in a historical moment both instructive and productive.
2. *Articulation* – understood as the practices of both assembling coalitions of social forces and creating political voice through discursive, ideological, or cultural representations. Both of these senses of articulation are visible in the new varieties of populism, nationalism, and authoritarianism. I will draw most obviously on the work of Stuart Hall who developed a rich and subtle approach to the politics of articulation – and the articulations of politics (this is discussed further in Clarke 2015).
3. *The social* – and its governing. Here, too, my interest has been a source of recurrent and productive intersections with Janine Brodie's work. Despite the individualizing and economizing logics of neoliberalism, the question of the social has not gone away. Indeed, it continues to cause problems of governing and is intimately linked to the current disruptions and dislocations.

Thinking Conjuncturally

The politics of this present have been marked by a variety of insurgent political movements, disrupting the processes of "politics as usual": the

UK, the US, India, France, Turkey, Hungary, and more have experienced political movements characterized by combinations of nationalist, populist, authoritarian, and autocratic tendencies. This certainly looks like the "shock of the new" and a seductive invitation to imagine a new era. Yet these same movements build on longer-running conditions, even as they disrupt or attempt to rearrange them. We might understand this longer framing in terms of neoliberalism, or the crises of neoliberalism, or perhaps the failures of neoliberalism. For some, it might be framed in terms of the end of neoliberalism, or at least the end of that strange hybrid "progressive neoliberalism" (Fraser 2019).

Although the temptation to use the neoliberal frame is always strong, it is worth thinking about other framings that identify other formations, settlements, and temporalities. So, we might treat the underlying conditions as the unresolved crises of Atlantic Fordism which, for a while, formed the stabilized regime of accumulation for twentieth century capitalism in the Global North. Bob Jessop, for example, has argued that Atlantic Fordism combined mass production and mass consumption in a "virtuous autocentric circle" sustained by a "mode of regulation'" centred on the Keynesian welfare state in distinctively national settings (2014). Whether a new regime of accumulation has been developed and stabilized through a new "spatio-temporal fix" is open to argument (see, for example, Jessop's own extensive explorations of this topic and Hayward 2014). For the purposes of this discussion, though, the frame of Atlantic Fordism and its crises changes our understanding of both the dynamics and temporalities that make sense of the present. In particular, it gives visibility to the questions of the "national economy" and the "core" Fordist working class, whose trajectory of remaking through processes of de-industralization and de-unionization dates from the original 1970s crises of Fordism.

An alternative framing, associated with a similar, but not exactly the same, periodization would be to link the contemporary disruptions to the political temporalities of (European) social democracy as the primary political articulation that secured consent for the development of Atlantic Fordism. It then mutated to become one of the key political means through which popular consent to the neoliberal program of constant innovation was managed. Some (e.g., Streeck, 2016 and Szombati, 2018 on Hungary) have argued that the exhaustion of left parties derives from their enrolment into this task of managing consent, while Jeremy Gilbert (2015) has suggested that the growing instability of consent – and particularly the rise of what he calls "disaffected consent" in the face of absent political alternatives – emerges from the limits and contradictions of this particular political articulation.

Nevertheless, while these framings bring different temporalities and formations into view, they operate largely within a Northern/Western spatial disposition. A rather different framing might be found in the unfinished dynamics of de-colonization and its "unfinished business" – what Gilroy (2004) calls "postcolonial melancholia." This field of disturbances makes us see the "nation" as configured in a different way, through its relation to empire, historically through the formation of imaginaries of the metropole and its Others and bearing on the present in the inability to address and reconcile the damage done by colonialism. In the moment of Brexit (echoed in a variety of other nativist/nationalist politics elsewhere), this legacy played out in hostility towards migrants that blurred and blended different images: colonial others, refugees from the Global South, Muslims, and the wrong sort of whites from the expanded EU (Romanians, in particular). The Leave campaigns demonized such others, building on and expanding the then Conservative government to create a "hostile environment" for those migrants who were illegal, not "genuine" or simply looked "out of place" (see, *inter alia*, Hiam et al. 2018; Humphris 2019). As Gary Younge, writing about Brexit, argued:

> For decades, the issue of race (the colour of people) and immigration (the movement of people) have been neatly interwoven, as though they are one and the same thing – as though "British" people are not also black and black people are not British.
>
> It has been profitable for politicians … to sow confusion about the difference between migration from the EU and elsewhere, or the distinction between economic migrants and asylum seekers. The argument that this was a vote about "economic" issues – since the hated European migrants were not brown or black – is belied by the deliberate commingling of every type of foreigner. (2016)

The potency of these devices is undeniable – and that long history of racialized divisions and inequality (in the UK and elsewhere) forms a critical focus for the political struggles to define and mobilize the nation. It is in the context of these multiple framings, and their diverse dynamics and temporalities, that I turn to the question of neoliberalism. The present conjuncture is, indeed, constituted by the dynamics of neoliberalism, or at least by the rise and proliferation of neoliberalisms (varying across time and space). But it cannot be only a question of neoliberalism in the singular, but of these proliferating neoliberalisms that are always entangled with, articulated with, and overdetermined by, all those other forces, dynamics, tendencies, antagonisms, and contradictions. Sometimes, these involve the terrain that neoliberal projects inherit (the crises of Atlantic Fordism, the complex antagonisms of post-colonial populations, etc.). At other times, they are the consequences of earlier neoliberal innovations, interventions, and strategies. In this respect, we should take note of Brodie's interest in neoliberalism's *failures:* its inability to overcome contradictions and antagonisms; its inability to generate stabilized settlements (Jessop's "spatio-temporal fixes"); and its uneven achievements in generating and sustaining popular consent. The constantly mutating character of neoliberalism has much to do with this history of failure. Jamie Peck has argued that we should attend, not just to the grandiose discourses of neoliberalism, but also the "turgid reality of neoliberalism variously failing and flailing forwards" (2010, 7). In this light we might treat the long temporality of the present conjuncture in a different way: not as the era of neoliberalism, but as the time of neoliberalism's failures. Here we would pay attention to its accumulating crises and antagonisms and its recurrent innovative efforts to find ways of managing or governing them, and then the failures of those managing and governing strategies: economically, politically, and socially. In short, we should be thinking about how these complicated dynamics of neoliberalism(s) are entangled with other forces.

This would be one way of "telling the time" of the present: looking at a landscape of failed (and discarded) neoliberal strategies, marked by a steady accumulation of crises, tensions, and antagonisms (always entangled with a desperate search for innovations that might resolve or at least contain them – from individuation to coercion to participation and more ...). But we need to understand a conjuncture as composed of multiple dynamics (not a singular line of development). So, not just neoliberalism, but how it is entangled with other dynamic forces and their trajectories, from the unsettled class formations that emerged from the ruins of Fordism, to the renewed racializations of the Global North (and their particular national trajectories) and the various disruptions of the family and gender orders that were central to the Fordist organization of mass production and mass consumption. These multiple dynamics are condensed into the making of a present – a "here and now" – that is simultaneously overdetermined and undetermined. It is overdetermined (in the Freudian/Althusserian sense) by the constitutive co-presence of multiple forces, tendencies, contradictions, and antagonisms. It is underdetermined in its multiple lines of possibility – the different resolutions of the current troubles that might be assembled and enacted. It is precisely this sense of multiplicity that resists simplistic or deterministic readings of the "crisis" or its resolution. On the contrary, the conjuncture has several crises in play which combine to create a terrain of possibilities. The present never has a singular route forward – there is no necessity of history that can guide us or doom us. Rather, there are different lines of flight from the present turbulence around which different social forces have to be mobilized, drawn into blocs and alliances to make one line of development come true. In the same moment, other possibilities have to be refused or denied ("simply unrealistic") and some forces have to be disrupted or demobilized, persuaded that change is not possible, that politics is a waste of time, or not for them (these arguments are developed more fully in Clarke 2010; and Clarke 2019). That is, we need to think about politics as the site of *articulation*: practices that make connections (and disrupt others).

Addressing Articulation

The concept of articulation was developed by Stuart Hall as a way of thinking about complex formations and was deployed by him in three ways. The first was his response to the problem of analyzing social formations where he followed Althusser in refusing the view of the base/superstructure distinction (and the internal relations of determination between the two parts) that had dominated much Marxist thinking. The idea of articulation addressed the complexity of social formations (as articulated unities) rather than simple, or expressive, totalities. This Althusserian view coincided with Hall's reading of critical parts of Marx, notably the 1857 "Introduction to the Critique of Political Economy," or *Grundrisse* (Hall 2003; Marx 1993). He took up Marx's description of the circuit of capital as a complex totality, composed of different moments (production, exchange, circulation, consumption, etc.) that combined to form a "unity in difference."

Second, this understanding of social formations as articulated structures was paralleled in his understanding of articulation as a way of describing the work of political mobilization or organization, in particular his Gramscian interest in the assembling of blocs or coalitions of social forces. As with social formations, the concept of articulation here draws attention to the contingent and multiple character of blocs and alliances, rather than a singular conception of the distinction between a ruling class and its subordinated other. At the same time, this conception of the mobilization (and de-mobilization) of sets of social forces was central to his attempt to develop a Gramscian focus on hegemony that addressed the organization of consent as a relation between the (would-be) leading bloc and sections of subaltern social groups. Here, it is possible to see the connections to the third usage of articulation in his work on discourse and ideology. In the development of articulation as an alternative to more reductive conceptions of ideology, we can see some of the characteristic formulations of his view of articulation, in particular, the understanding that the connections or links are not "necessarily given" as a fact of life or by law-like correspondences. Instead, he insisted on the importance of analyzing the specifics of particular articulations, giving attention both to their conditions of existence and the vital political-cultural work needed to make and sustain a particular articulation. No articulation – whether the combination of social instances in a social formation, a complex coalition of social forces, or a discursive alignment of meanings and politics – came with a "lifetime guarantee." Rather their distinctive configuration (involving the forms of connection as well as potential disjunctures) and their external conditions of existence created the possibility of both dis- and re-articulation. This understanding of articulation – which underlines both its contingency and the necessity of the labours of construction and maintenance – seems to me to be a vital tool for thinking about the current moment, precisely because it offers an alternative to thinking in terms of singularities. Jennifer Slack argues that articulation is one of the conceptual routes through which Hall "resists the temptation of reduction to class, mode of production, structure, as well as to culturalism's tendency to reduce culture to 'experience'" (1996, 122–3). In developing his work around the concept of articulation, Hall emphasized a double movement, in which the images of "giving voice to" and "connecting" are always in play. In an interview with Larry Grossberg, Hall noted:

> I always use the word "articulation," though I don't know whether the meaning I attribute to it is perfectly understood. In England, the term has a nice double meaning because "articulate" means to utter, to speak forth, to be articulate. It carries that sense of languageing, of expressing, etc. But we also speak of an "articulated" lorry (truck): a lorry where the front (cab) and back (trailer) can, but need not necessarily, be connected to one another. The two parts are connected to each other, but through a specific linkage, that can be broken. An articulation is thus the form of the connection that can make a unity of two different elements, under certain conditions. It is a linkage which is not necessary, determined, absolute and essential for all time. (Grossberg 1996, 142)

Hall insisted on this contingent character of articulation, both in terms of the discursive elements (which become provisionally coupled together) and the connections that are constructed between a specific discourse and the social forces spoken for by it – who discover themselves as political subjects through it. This seems particularly important as an orientation to the contemporary turbulence of populism, nationalism, racism, authoritarianism: elements that become coupled together and seek out their political subjects. As Hall insisted, this is a view of ideology that

> enables us to think how an ideology empowers people, enabling them to begin to make some sense or intelligibility of their historical situation, without reducing those forms of intelligibility to their socio-economic or class location or social position. (Grossberg 1996, 143)

Let me bring this abstract discussion back to the politics of the present, since it underlines the importance of thinking about contemporary political movements, not as instances of some more general principle – populism, nationalism, and the like – but as specifically articulated "unities in difference" that *selectively* draw on and connect elements from various pre-existing discourses: about the nation, the people and their others, power, place, and sovereignty, for example. Returning to Brexit as one instance of such politics, we might begin with the assembling of a new bloc (the Leave campaigns) involving some – but by no means all – fractions of both national and international capital, leading elements of several political parties (Conservatives, UKIP – the United Kingdom Independence Party – and Labour) with links to new technology and social media companies (Cambridge Analytica and Facebook), as well as being strongly embedded in key sections of traditional media (newspapers and magazines, especially). This bloc disrupted and reworked conventional lines of party political affiliation, building a cross-class coalition that drew in key segments of the middle classes (typically the occupationally and culturally "traditional" rather than "cosmopolitan" segments) and working classes (particularly in the older de-industrialized areas), creating what Cochrane (2019) has called an alliance of the post-imperial and post-industrial heartlands of the UK. This coalition was complexly stratified by age, with 45+ being the tipping point for anti-EU orientations.

This coalition – represented as the "British people" – was voiced as a resentful nation, taken for granted, or even abandoned by a cosmopolitan, Eurocentric elite. This was a nation whose vulnerability was being exploited by migrants, consuming valuable space and resources and leaving people feeling alienated from their "own" places. The Leave campaign drew on – and re-animated – well established nationalist, racist, and populist devices, linking them to a conception of sovereignty as a capacity that could be reclaimed (expressed in the promise to "take back control"). Here is one of several paradoxes of Brexit populism – the claim to restore national fortunes, politically, economically, and culturally (our way of life …) – in the face of its erosion by being in Europe, but where the future would be secured by being, in then Trade Minister Liam Fox's words, "open for business as never before" in a new global trading order: "We are essentially at the heart of the new campaign for global trade liberalization … We have a history as a great trading nation and, as we forge a new global role for ourselves we will carry the banner for free trade" (Hall 2017).

In discussions of Brexit and many other recent political developments, feelings of anger have been a central theme (see Mishra 2017 and Richards 2019 for two very different approaches). While accepting the greater visibility of such feelings in contemporary politics, there are two issues worth raising. The first is the problem of treating such feelings as marking an abrupt break with "normal politics," as if normal politics was entirely calculative, rational, and free of sentiment. Much of the discussion of populism treats those it mobilizes as an irrational "mob" or "crowd," echoing nineteenth century anxieties about popular movements: as Müller puts it, "[s]uspecting that the masses are up to no good has been the default position of liberalism since the early nineteenth century" (2019; see also Rancière 2011; Rudé 1964). The second concerns the challenge of dealing with affects, emotions, or "structures of feelings" (Williams 1977) as complex formations, rather than singularities. In the context of Brexit, many commentators have reflected on the anger that the Leave vote expressed, particularly among people who felt abandoned, forgotten, ignored, or dispossessed (see Koch 2017; McKenzie 2018, but also Knight 2017 on the emotions of Remain). I have argued elsewhere (Clarke 2019) that these structures of feeling are politically complex and conjuncturally specific. So, the sense of loss seen in many authoritarian-nationalist-populist movements typically weaves a sense of dispossession into xenophobic denunciations of those Others deemed to have taken possession, while the felt loss combines and condenses (waged) work, "ways of life," and systems of (relative) privilege, not least those of the hitherto secure sections of the Fordist middle and working classes. These feelings of loss are also entangled with racialized and gendered privilege that were embedded in those "ways of life" and which have occasionally manifested themselves as murderous rage. Given the growing interest in emotion and affect in the fields of politics and governing (e.g., Anderson 2016; Jupp, Pykett, and Smith 2017), it becomes important to tease out the different dimensions and dynamics that may be condensed in public voicings, perhaps especially those that claim to speak for the People (and its mood).

Second, the rejection of government, political elites, and "politics as usual" was perversely and paradoxically voiced through some of the most establishment figures it is possible to imagine – a network of politicians are educated at exclusive schools (including former Conservative ministers) proclaimed themselves on the side of the People and denounced the "enemies of the People" (see also Clarke and Newman 2017). Here we need to pay attention to the political-discursive work of articulation in the voicing of populist repertoires, what Hall has called "ventriloquism" to indicate its crafted quality. In a passage that might have been written about Brexit (but was about the arrival of Thatcherism) he wrote: "The press – especially those three popular ventriloquist voices of the radical Right, the *Mail*, the *Sun* and the *Express* – have played here a quite pivotal role" (1979, 18). The same voices – carefully calibrated with politicians such as Nigel Farage (former leader of the UK Independence Party), Michael Gove (Conservative MP, cabinet minister, and co-convenor of Vote Leave), and Prime Minister Boris Johnson – have been central to the work of Brexit populism.

I have offered this sketch of Brexit to emphasize its constructed quality as an articulated "unity in difference" both discursively and socially – a view that finds an echo in much of Janine Brodie's work. This orientation provides a basis from which to explore Brexit's problematic relationship with neoliberalism (or even the crises of neoliberalism). Brexit (like the moment of Trump) has been celebrated as a refusal of neoliberalism by its victims; those who have been deindustrialized, dispossessed, and disenfranchised in the global flows set in play by the deregulatory drives of neoliberal projects at national and international levels. Nevertheless, I would argue that the relationship between the current moment and neoliberalism demands analysis that is both more complex and more attentive to the dynamic of contradictions than such a simplifying view allows. The coalition and the articulations of Brexit were complex, stretching beyond the disconcerting celebration of the "white working class" that came in its wake. Here, we need to address the problems of class analysis, both in its rather static view of the working class (as if it did not contain young, zero hours contracted,* Europhile workers) and its problematic understanding of the relationship between racialized divisions and

---

* A zero-hours contract is a form of employment relationship in which the employer does not have to provide a guaranteed minimum number of hours to the worker.

class. (The "white working class" is too readily imagined as if its others are merely ethnic groups or "communities," rather than fractions of a working class that is formed both nationally and transnationally.)

Demanding a more complex account of the present is one thing; however, it also needs to be complemented with a more dynamic and complex understanding of neoliberalism that would account for its mutating quality. There are two key conditions for this mutability of neoliberalism that I want to observe. The first concerns the apparently empty political landscape in which neoliberalism is often theorized: there are plenty of neoliberal projects, politics, governments, strategies, devices, and practices that have supplanted past modes of governing, but little else. Instead, we may need to see this landscape as more cluttered, containing residual and emergent political and cultural formations alongside the dominant neoliberalism. When making these distinctions, Raymond Williams argued that it was important to note both their co-existence (rather than just attending to the dominant) and to examine the ways in which they were entangled. He argued that in "authentic historical analysis it is necessary at every point to recognize the complex interrelations between movements and tendencies both within and beyond a specific effective dominance" (1977, 121). In thinking about neoliberalism, I have argued elsewhere (Clarke 2008) that such an approach implies taking seriously the relationships between neoliberalism and those with whom it is obliged to "cohabit." It is a political-cultural project that has had to engage with other projects, working to displace, subordinate, or appropriate them. That implies thinking about the continued place of alternative political-cultural projects in a neoliberal dominated world.

In its multiple variations across time and space, then, we might see different articulations of neoliberalism as it negotiates the already occupied political-cultural terrain, engaging in what the linguist Alistair Pennycook calls "borrowing, bending, and blending" (2007, 47) cultural resources to make new utterances. So, I want to suggest that we might think of neoliberalism "never going out alone," as always hanging out with, and borrowing the ideas and the vocabularies of many different formations: social democratic, military authoritarian, nationalist, globalist, conservative, liberal, religious ... This echoes Catherine Kingfisher's distinction between what she calls the "preliminary grammar" of neoliberalism and its "disjointed, disjunctured articulations" in particular places (2002, 50). She argues that "it is, in fact, only in the circulation of neoliberal related meanings and their articulation with other meaning systems that neoliberalism takes on its multiple and contradictory lives" (Kingfisher 2002, 12). These articulations are not to be understood as fronts or facades behind which the "real" (and singular) neoliberalism is concealed, but points towards the second condition for thinking about the multiplicity of neoliberalism(s) and the landscapes that neoliberal projects – the will to neoliberalize, perhaps – have to negotiate. These are necessarily landscapes in the plural – the arrival of the neoliberal project in Pinochet's Chile encountered a political, economic, social, and cultural terrain very different from its appearance in Thatcher's Britain, and different again from its entry into the "liberation" of former socialist countries after the break-up of the USSR. But all of these landscapes contained pre-existing political-cultural formations; they were also rich in accumulated economic, social, and political contradictions and antagonisms – some of which, of course, neoliberalization promised to overcome, sweeping away residues, blockages, and obstructions (not unlike advertisements for toilet cleaners). In the process, such neoliberal projects have to build blocs and coalitions, begin to construct their desired populations, and find the ways – and voicings – through which to create consent.

If these complex (and messy) landscapes pre-exist the arrival of neoliberalizing projects, then they also have a habit of persisting alongside those projects, marked by varieties of resistance, refusal, and recalcitrance. The residual (and the residualized) sometimes come back to haunt these projects – as Brexit makes clear (albeit in a contradictory formation). But these landscapes are also transformed – reconstructed – by neoliberalization, in ways that involve the accumulation of new contradictions, antagonisms, and problems of governing (sometimes overlaid on the unfinished or unresolved antagonisms of earlier periods). To this we must add the consequences of neoliberal failures – creating more crisis-ridden, divided, contradictory, and antagonistic social formations, not least in the ways they reflect the problems of politically and governmentally *managing* neoliberalization and its effects. Despite neoliberalism's nominal anti-statism, it has reformed, restructured, and exploited state capacities – in both political and governmental terms – to try to manage its projects, to sustain popular consent to its regime of accumulation, and to organize the field of the social in appropriate ways. It has also looked to political parties to foster alternative ways of managing the project and its crises (despite not being averse to non-competitive political regimes, as evidenced by the Chilean experience). The struggles of national governments to manage both neoliberalization and its effects deliver the varieties of popular discontent visible in relation to Europeanization, internationalization, and globalization. Despite the (yet again) proclaimed end of neoliberalism discerned in the nationalist-populist-nativist-authoritarian-exclusionary varieties of contemporary political movements (both in and out of government), none of those coming to power through such articulations look like the pallbearers of neoliberal globalization. Indeed, as noted earlier, the UK Conservative government committed to administering Brexit announced their project as a new phase of globalization-as-free-trade. Whether they can manage the social and political consequences of such a process remains open to question; nevertheless, it matters to think of these as moments in which distinctive efforts are made to rearrange and solidify the political blocs and alliances necessary to stabilize the dominant project in the face of threats and dangers. Gramsci once argued that "the life of the state can be conceived as a series of unstable equilibria" (1973, 182) – an image that captures this dynamic of settling and unsettling perfectly. One of the key sites for the political stabilization and de-stabilization concerns the governing of the social: a field of recurrent turbulence, antagonisms, and contestations.

Governing the Social

There are several conceptual and conjunctural reasons for highlighting the question of the social. Conceptually, the social often appears as the poor relation of political economy. In both conventional and critical variants, the domain of the social is placed as residual, treated as a second order phenomenon whose character (if acknowledged at all) derives from the big forces and their dynamics. Fortunately, other conceptual and knowledge-making interventions from the margins (many margins …) have kept the social – its significance and its recurrent contestation – visible and productive. I have in mind feminism and especially the work of feminist political economists (including Janine Brodie and Isabella Bakker), geographers, sociologists, and cultural studies scholars. Rescuing the social has three aspects: first, understanding it as the (complex) site of relations and practices of social reproduction; second, seeing it as constituted and reformed by governmental practices that seek to secure the correct ordering of the population and its capacities (governments, as Foucault knew, always seek to make better people, or at least to make people better). Third, it is the domain through which people live "their imaginary relationship to the real conditions of existence" (Althusser 1970/1, 162). It offers the (imagined and material) grounding for their relationships to the economy, and the local, political, the national, and global scales. There is a growing interest in the role played by imaginaries or imagined domains and relationships in the organization and constitution of social formation. Here, though, I want to stress the way in which the social is traversed by different, and contending, imaginaries of how life is – and should be – lived. In her work on metropole-colony relations across England and Jamaica, Catherine Hall has argued the social is continuously engaged and reworked by projects seeking to map, reorder, and remake the social body:

> Marking differences was a way of classifying, of categorising, of constructing boundaries for the body politic and the body social. Processes of differentiation, positioning men and women, colonisers and colonised, as if these divisions were natural, were constantly in the making, in conflicts of power ... The mapping of difference, I suggest, the constant discursive work of creating, bringing into being, or reworking these hieratic categories, was always a matter of historical contingency. The map constantly shifted, the categories faltered, as different colonial sites came into the metropolitan focus, as conflicts of power produced new configurations in one place or another. (2002, 17, 20)

This is a profoundly suggestive view of the social as the focus of "conflicts of power" that produce different mappings – and it is certainly the terrain that governing projects seek to occupy, dominate, and direct, endlessly concerned with ordering the population (differentiating, hierarchizing) and with creating projects that aim to make the people who they should be. As Brodie has argued (2007 and elsewhere), neoliberalism has been a project committed to transforming the social through strategies of de-socialization and individualization that seek to create (or "release" in the naturalizing imagery of neoliberalism's advocates) those responsible, dynamic, and entrepreneurial selves and, of course, to discipline and punish (or make resilient – Phillips, this volume) those who fail the tests of responsibility. Yet the attention given to individualization (the latest incarnation of liberalism's obsession with "possessive individualism") has rather obscured the other dynamic in neoliberal projects towards what we might call possessive-competitive *familialism*. In the UK, for example, the summons to be hardworking and responsible was directed at families (projecting a nation of "hard working responsible families"). Similarly, it is worth remembering that Margaret Thatcher's famous observation that "there is no such thing as society" did not stop there but ended with "only individual men and women and their families." Indeed, it might be argued that the many varieties of liberalism, including neoliberalism, oscillate between the imagined individual and the imagined family as their basic unit of society. This familial conception has certainly facilitated political and discursive alliances between neoliberals and conservatives in many places, including the UK and the US.

This individual-familial nexus underpinned and legitimated the wider anti-social logics of neoliberalism, in particular the dismantling of collective or public institutions – public services, collective housing provision, the variants of the welfare state, and so on. I have argued elsewhere (in a discussion of "subordinating the social") that we need to address the processes that try to imagine – and institutionalize – new mappings of the social. These remakings of the social go well beyond its articulation with the economic to new assemblages of people, positions, and practices in multiple domains. Such changes construct new ways of life, elaborate new sets of distinctions and relations within a population, and aim to inculcate new habits and practices to deliver a "modern people" ready to take their place in a global world. Nevertheless, "[a]ttempts to subordinate the social have produced a profoundly uneven, contested and contradictory field in which the social refuses 'to go quietly.' It remains the focus of intense and unsettling desires – for security, improvement, success, solidarity and 'better ways of life' (of very different kinds)" (Clarke 2007, 984). Some aspects of this unruly social have been articulated in recent populist-nationalist movements and in opposition to the anti-social globalizing dynamics of neoliberalism. In this moment, though, exclusionary-authoritarian nostalgia for a lost way of life persists alongside, and in tense relationships with, versions of the social that imagine relations of solidarity across difference and that promote egalitarian conceptions of inclusion and participation.

It feels like a bad idea to neglect, or marginalize, the social, because that is where the dominant, residual, and emergent structures of feeling are most clearly, and most potently, entangled. It is in conceptions of the social that we can see the ways of life that are supposed to be "normal," the ways of life for which loss or nostalgia are felt, and the images of how we might live together, better, that bring into view future possibilities. These are imaginaries, combining plans, projects, desires, and doubts into structures of feeling that might become the conditions of possibility for future politics, especially if we understand politics as articulating the good sense of the many common senses in circulation:

this Gramscian view has recently been developed by Kate Crehan, who argues that

> Any effective, progressive political movement must speak a language and have a message that is recognized by the mass of those it seeks to reach. And this is certainly one reason why Gramsci saw the mapping of subaltern understandings of the world as so important. There is, however, another fundamental reason why he pays so much attention to collective subaltern common sense. Subaltern knowledge emerges in fragmented, often chaotic form, but the good sense embedded within it represents the embryonic beginnings of a genuine alternative to the existing hegemony; an alternative that is an indispensable element of a new economic and political order. (2016, 186–7)

For me, a key part of what makes the current moment different, yet familiar, is precisely the capacity of insurgent nationalist populist projects to voice these sentiments and selectively mobilize them and their bearers. These projects have been actively working on senses of loss, abandonment, social and political disenfranchisement, and perhaps especially the sense that "power" is always elsewhere, working its will in uncontrollable ways to transform the world and lives within it. It is here that the concept of articulation is important because it reminds us that speaking for the subaltern is always selective and constructive, not simply the reflection of popular feelings (see, by contrast, Judis 2016). This implies asking questions about what is being spoken, and what is being silenced. In whose name, in whose voice, are these representations being made? In this sense, populism is always a ventriloqual project. Nevertheless, these are varieties of populism in new articulations with forms of nationalism, versions of liberalism, registers of authoritarianism, and the potent, if selective, enrolment of residual sentiments about loss, exclusion, and the disappearance of "our way of life." These were turned into promises to make us great again or to "take back control" (Brexit), that produced support for right wing, authoritarian, nationalist (and nativist) political blocs who seem quite capable of keeping the neoliberal dreams and fantasies alive for a while longer, even if they are articulated in ever stranger forms.

However, there are other tendencies in play. For example, in the UK, an unexpected general election in June 2017 saw a Jeremy Corbyn-led Labour Party mobilize other disaffections – about austerity, public service cuts, authoritarian policies, anti-social government, increasing inequality, and more – to bring a new political coalition into being that denied Theresa May's Conservatives an overall majority in Parliament. In particular, Labour successfully animated and activated young voters. Subsequently many of these pro-social, pro-public sentiments crystallized in response to the disastrous fire at Grenfell Tower in the London Borough of Kensington and Chelsea. The fire, which burnt out a tower block of social/public housing, killed 72 people, and rendered many more homeless. Residents had warned of fire risks but had been ignored, while the exterior cladding and insulation, which proved highly flammable, had been fitted to a reduced specification to meet financial targets. Both the context of the fire, and the reaction of the local authority afterwards, revealed an extreme Conservative version of what Peck (2012) calls "austerity urbanism." The local authority had a very arm's-length relationship with its housing tenants (preferring prestige property development): a political-cultural orientation reflected in its failure to respond to the fire and the needs of tenants. In the aftermath, one local Member of Parliament, David Lammy (Labour, Tottenham), gave an interview in which he said, "I knew that appetite for the end of austerity existed in our cities," he says, "but the election proved it goes beyond that now. People want the social back. They are clear that you cannot contract everything out" (Adams 2017).

For me, this image combines both residual and emergent sensibilities of the social. It powerfully evokes a sense of the "lost social": what Lammy called the "civic glue" that held communities together with the state as a necessary element. But it is, I think, more than a residual or even nostalgic evocation, as it envisages a sense of community built around a state – an array of public services – that needs to be built, not just rediscovered, since the old state (at both national and local levels) was always more contradictory, conditional, and disciplinary than is being imagined now. Similarly, the "community to come" is committed to forms of solidarity across diversity, rather than a mono-cultural or exclusivist vision of community. But Lammy's image is most striking – and most strikingly emergent – because it is located in the practices through which "the community" around Grenfell Tower responded to the disaster, crafting intense mutual support, drawing on voluntary organizations, churches, and activists – as well as envisaging public services that would serve the public better. Both of these promises of emergent possibilities were stamped on by the general election called by the new Conservative leader, Boris Johnson, in 2019, in the name of getting "Brexit done." It produced a Conservative landslide as Johnson reanimated the Brexit bloc and Labour self-destructed (see, *inter alia*, Clarke, 2020; Spours, 2020). These shifts underline the turbulence of the current conjuncture and the difficulties of creating new moments of equilibrium (even before the pandemic arrived).

Conclusion

Conjunctural analysis's attention to multiplicities is both an analytic and political imperative. It enables us to avoid the simplifications of "epochal analysis" while making us look beyond singularities – populism, or nationalism, or neoliberalism – to consider the present in terms of articulated formations. It also enables us to consider the possible lines of movement in, and away from, the present. As the examples I have offered suggest, this implies considering elements of the "residual" that might be absent from, or silenced in, the currently dominant regressive formations. It also turns our attention to the emergent imaginaries or structures of feeling in which other ways of living may be glimpsed. Lammy's elegantly simple claim that "People want the social back" captures this possibility: articulating the "good sense" of current common sense against the continued neoliberal evisceration of the social. It also exemplifies how the three overarching themes of this argument come together. The idea of articulation makes productive sense in the context of conjunctural analysis – highlighting the political and cultural work that goes into mobilizing (and de-mobilizing) different social forces into political blocs and alliances. Articulation also leads us away from reductive assumptions about ideology and social location (especially class location) by asking how people come to imagine and understand themselves as political actors. In a moment when new political strategies summon people to find their voice – or at least respond to someone speaking in their voice – the urgency of thinking of politics as articulation should be evident. The field of the social – and its shifting and contested mappings – remains one of the critical sites for such political-cultural work. Recognizing this cluster of concerns – and the significance of their intersections – has been a vital and recurring thread in Janine Brodie's work and makes her a vital point of connection for the rest of us.

REFERENCES

Adams, Tim. 2017. "David Lammy: 'People Used to Ask, Blair or Brown? I Would Say, No, Just Black.'" *The Guardian*, July 2, 2017. https://www

.theguardian.com/politics/2017/jul/02/david-lammy-mp-grenfell-tower
-interview-blair-brown-black.

Althusser, Louis. 1970/71. "Ideology and Ideological State Apparatuses (Notes towards an Investigation)." In *Lenin and Philosophy and Other Essays*, 127–86. Translated by Ben Brewster. New York, NY: Monthly Review Press.

Anderson, Ben. 2016. "Neoliberal Affects." *Progress in Human Geography* 40 (6): 734–53. https://doi.org/10.1177%2F0309132515613167.

Brodie, Janine. 2007. "The New Social 'isms': Individualization and Social Policy Reform in Canada" In *Contested Individualization*, edited by Cosmo Howard. New York: Palgrave Macmillan.

Clarke, John. 2020. "Building the 'Boris' Bloc: Angry Politics in Turbulent Times." *Soundings: A Journal of Politics and Culture*, 74: 118–35. https://doi.org/10.3898/SOUN.74.08.2020.

– 2019. "A Sense of Loss? Unsettled Attachments in the Current Conjuncture." *New Formations*, no. 96/97: 132–46. https://doi.org/10.3898/NEWF:96/97.05.2019.

– 2015. "Stuart Hall and the Theory and Practice of Articulation." *Discourse: Studies in the Cultural Politics of Education* 36 (2): 275–86. https://doi.org/10.1080/01596306.2015.1013247.

– 2010. "Of Crises and Conjunctures: The Problem of the Present." *Journal of Communication Inquiry* 34 (4): 337–54. https://doi.org/10.1177/0196859910382451.

– 2008. "Living with/in and without Neoliberalism." *Focaal –Journal of Global and Historical Anthropology* 51: 135–47. http://doi.org/doi:10.3167/fcl.2008.510110.

– 2007. "Subordinating the Social? Neoliberalism and the Remaking of Welfare Capitalism." *Cultural Studies* 21 (6): 974–87. https://doi.org/10.1080/09502380701470643.

Clarke, John, and Janet Newman. 2017. "'People in This Country Have Had Enough of Experts': Brexit and the Paradoxes of Populism." *Critical Policy Studies* 11 (1): 101–16. https://doi.org/10.1080/19460171.2017.1282376.

Cochrane, Allan. 2020. "From Brexit to the Break-Up of … England?" In *Contested Britain: Brexit, Austerity, Agency*, edited by Marius Gunderjan, Hugh Mackay, and Gesa Steadman, 161–74. Bristol: Policy Press.

Crehan, Kate. 2016. *Gramsci's Common Sense*. Durham, NC: Duke University Press.

Fraser, Nancy. 2019. *The Old Is Dying and the New Cannot Be Born: From Progressive Neoliberalism to Trump and Beyond*. London: Verso.

Gilbert, Jeremy. 2015. "Disaffected Consent: That Post-Democratic Feeling." *Soundings: A Journal of Politics and Culture* 60: 29–41. https://doi.org/10.3898/136266215815872971.

Gilroy, Paul. 2004. *Postcolonial Melancholia*. New York: Columbia University Press.

Gramsci, Antonio. 1973. *Selections from the Prison Notebooks*. Edited by Geoffrey Nowell Smith and Quintin Hoare. London: Lawrence and Wishart.

Grossberg, Larry. 1996. "On Postmodernism and Articulation: An Interview with Stuart Hall." In *Stuart Hall: Critical Dialogues in Cultural Studies*, edited by David Morley and Kuan-Hsing Chen, 131–50. London: Routledge.

Hall, Catherine. 2002. *Civilising Subjects: Metropole and Colony in the English Imagination 1830–1867*. Chicago, IL: University of Chicago Press.

Hall, Macer. 2016. "Liam Fox Warns EU Risks Harming Itself if It Tries to Block British Trade after Brexit." *Express Online*, September 27, 2016. http://www.express.co.uk/news/uk/715030/Liam-Fox-EU-risks-harm -block-British-trade-Brexit-theresa-may-iain-duncan-brussels.

Hall, Stuart. 2003. "Marx's Notes on Method: A 'Reading' of the '1857 Introduction.'" *Cultural Studies* 17 (2): 113–49. https://doi.org/10.1080 /0950238032000114868.

– 1979. "The Great Moving Right Show." *Marxism Today* (January): 14–20.

Hayward, Mark, ed. 2014. *Cultural Studies and Finance Capitalism: The Economic Crisis and After*. London and New York: Routledge.

Hiam, Lucinda, Sarah Steele, and Martin McKee. 2018. "Creating a 'Hostile Environment for Migrants': The British Government's Use of Health Service Data to Restrict Immigration Is a Very Bad Idea." *Health Economics, Policy and Law* 13 (2): 107–17. https://doi.org/10.1017/s1744133117000251.

Humphris, Rachel. 2019. *Home-Land: Romanian Roma, Domestic Spaces and the State*. Bristol: Bristol University Press.

Jessop, Bob. 2014. "What Follows Fordism? On the Periodisation of Capitalism and Its Regulation." In *Phases of Capitalist Development: Booms, Crises, and Globalization*, edited by Robert Albritton et. al., 282–99. Basingstoke: Palgrave. https://bobjessop.org/2014/01/03/what-follows-fordism-on -the-periodisation-of-capitalism-and-its-regulation/.

Judis, John B. 2016. *The Populist Explosion: How the Great Recession Transformed American and European Politics*. New York: Columbia Global Reports.

Jupp, Eleanor, Jessica Pykett, and Fiona Smith, eds. 2017. *Emotional States: Sites and Spaces of Affective Governance*. London: Routledge.

Kingfisher, Catherine, ed. 2002. "Neoliberalism I: Discourses of Personhood and Welfare Reform." In *Western Welfare in Decline: Globalization and Women's Poverty*, 13–31. Philadelphia: University of Pennsylvania Press.

Knight, David. 2017. "Anxiety and Cosmopolitan Futures: Brexit and Scotland." *American Ethnologist* 44 (2): 237–42. https://doi.org/10.1111 /amet.12474.

Koch, Insa. 2017. "What's In a Vote? Brexit Beyond Culture Wars." *American Ethnologist* 44 (2): 225–30. https://doi.org/10.1111/amet.12472.

Marx, Karl. 1973 [1857]. "Introduction to a Contribution to the Critique of Political Economy." In *Grundrisse: Foundations of the Critique of Political Economy*, edited and translated by Martin Nicolaus, 81–114. Harmondsworth: Penguin.

McKenzie, Lisa. 2018. "'We Don't Exist to Them, Do We?' Why Working Class People Voted for Brexit." *London School of Economics* (Brexit Blog). January 15, 2018. https://blogs.lse.ac.uk/brexit/2018/01/15/we-dont-exist-to-them-do-we-why-working-class-people-voted-for-brexit/.

Mishra, Pankaj. 2017. *The Age of Anger: A History of the Present*. London: Penguin Books.

Müller, Jan-Werner. 2019. "Populism and the People." *London Review of Books* 41 (10): 35–7. https://www.lrb.co.uk/v41/n10/jan-werner-muller/populism-and-the-people.

Peck, Jamie. 2012. "Austerity Urbanism." *City: Analysis of Urban Change, Theory, Action* 16 (6): 626–55. https://doi.org/10.1080/13604813.2012.734071.

– 2010. *Constructions of Neoliberal Reason*. Oxford: Oxford University Press.

Pennycook, Alistair. 2007. *Global Englishes and Transcultural Flows*. London/New York: Routledge.

Rancière, Jacques. 2011. "Non, le peuple n'est pas une masse brutale et ignorante." *Liberation* 3 janvier 2011. https://www.liberation.fr/france/2011/01/03/non-le-peuple-n-est-pas-une-masse-brutale-et-ignorante_704326.

Richards, Barry. 2019. "Beyond the Angers of Populism: Towards a Psychosocial Inquiry." *Journal of Psychosocial Studies* 12 (1–2): 171–83. https://doi.org/10.1332/147867319X15608718111014.

Rudé, George. 1964. *The Crowd in History. A Study of Popular Disturbances in France and England, 1730–1848*. New York: Wiley & Sons.

Slack, Jennifer. 1996. "The Theory and Method of Articulation in Cultural Studies." In *Stuart Hall: Critical Dialogues in Cultural Studies*, edited by David Morley and Kuan-Hsing Chen, 112–27. London: Routledge.

Spours, Ken. 2020. "Shapeshifters: The Evolving Politics of Modern Conservatism." London: Compass. https://www.compassonline.org.uk/publications/shapeshifting-the-evolving-politics-of-modern-conservatism/.

Streeck, Wolfgang. 2016. "Social Democracy's Last Rounds: An Interview with Wolfgang Streeck." *Jacobin: Reason in Revolt*, February 25, 2016. https://www.jacobinmag.com/2016/02/wolfgang-streeck-europe-eurozone-austerity-neoliberalism-social-democracy/.

Szombati, Kristof. 2018. *The Revolt of the Provinces: Anti-Gypsyism and Right-Wing Politics in Hungary*. New York and Oxford: Berghahn Books.

Williams, Raymond. 1977. *Marxism and Literature*. Oxford: Oxford University Press.

Younge, Gary. 2016. "Brexit: A Disaster Decades in the Making." *The Guardian* June 30, 2016. http://www.theguardian.com/politics/2016/jun/30/brexit-disaster-decades-in-the-making.

2 Neoliberal False Economies and Paradoxes of Social Reproduction

ISABELLA BAKKER

Introduction

This chapter examines the continuities and ruptures in the false economies of social reproduction shortly after the 2008 global financial crisis and into the COVID-19 global health crisis. Economists refer to false economies as, in a sense, costs displaced into the future: a policy decision (or individual action) that saves money at the beginning but over the long run results in more money wasted than saved. False economies also present an opportunity cost – an effective choice to forgo a given alternative even if by default this may lead to greater and potentially unforeseen costs in the future.

This chapter will explore the false economies of austerity pursued after the 2008 global financial crisis in many countries as a strategy to rein in sovereign debt. These policies had uneven and highly unequal effects on countries and populations. Austerity measures also off-loaded many of the public cuts in health and social services onto households and largely women's unpaid labour, contributing to depletion costs in the sphere of social reproduction. Feminist economists have written a great deal about how measures of austerity that off-load many of the public cuts in health and social services onto households and largely women's unpaid labour create a false economy of short-term savings that results in larger costs accruing in the future. Furthermore, the 2008 financial crisis and the 2020 COVID-19 health crisis both helped to underscore and intensify the contradiction between the global accumulation of capital and the provision of stable and progressive conditions of social reproduction and life-making processes (Bakker and Gill 2003; 2019). The pandemic has revealed the opportunity costs in a crisis of social reproduction by highlighting the central importance of both the paid (globally women make up 70 per cent of the health and social care workforce, Oxfam 2021, 34) and the unpaid work of social reproduction, dramatically revealing the shortcomings of the capitalist political economy to ensure the basic human security and well-being of populations.

Yet, social reproduction today also remains variegated and uneven across scales, locations, and jurisdictions, despite being increasingly shaped by the power of capital in a global process of accumulation that is, in turn, premised on the intensified exploitation and commodification of labour, society, and nature (Bakker and Gill 2019). And we have seen that states that have sufficient resources and independence of action have responded to the more immediate needs of the dictates of public health and the ability of individuals and communities to meet basic needs through income supports. Yet few governments have addressed the increased demands of unpaid care and domestic work in their COVID-19 responses. According to the United Nations, using their COVID-19 Gender Policy Response Tracker, a mere 8 per cent of all existing social and labour market measures were focused on the domain of social reproduction (2020). This, I argue, has created a new false economy with future costs related to women's labour force participation, time, and income poverty and the depletion of human capacities among other factors.

While the two crises I explore reveal particular contradictions when it comes to current and future well-being, they also reinforce Fraser's, and others', argument,

> that every form of capitalist society harbors a deep-seated social-reproductive "crisis tendency" or "contradiction." On the one hand, social reproduction is a condition of possibility for sustained capital accumulation; on the other hand, capitalism's orientation to unlimited accumulation tends to destabilize the very processes of social reproduction on which it relies. (Fraser 2016, 100)

This chapter will consider three instances of false economy in relation to social reproduction. First, I will examine the fiscal austerity of so-called sound macroeconomic policies following the 2008 global financial crisis. After massive bailouts to the financial sector, austerity measures were brought in by many countries in an attempt to reduce public budget deficits and save costs on social and public health programs. What is paradoxical is that, according to UN research, in many parts of the world "sound" economic policies have resulted in greater gender inequality, as well as rising unemployment and lower growth, and, as we have seen, depletion of the public goods of health and care.

Second, non-investment in social reproduction can lead to future costs in terms of depletion of human capacities, time, and income poverty for those whose risks are downloaded and privatized. Those with higher incomes are able to meet their social reproduction needs through purchasing goods and services. Many of these future costs are often not measured by mainstream economics as they are not reflected in monetary terms in national income accounts.

Finally, the privatization and financialization of care, especially for the elderly in long-term care, creates a contradiction between investment for profit versus care in ways that can result in broader societal costs and, ultimately, neglect and death for the elderly in care institutions, to say nothing of the crass ethics of effectively abandoning the aged to the vagaries of market forces in the provision of care.

From Neoliberalism's "Sound" Policies to COVID-19 Fiscal Expansionism – Two Moments of False Economy

So-called sound macroeconomic policies emerged as a new dominant discourse in the 1990s wave of formal constitutional and quasi-constitutional changes in fiscal and monetary policy rules. Instituted at national and regional levels, these new policy rules effectively lock in a more market-oriented approach to economic policy-making that tends to prioritize the needs of investors over social needs (Bakker 2003; Brodie and Bakker 2008; Elson and Norton, 2002; Gill 1995). With respect to fiscal policy, balanced budget laws and stipulations as to the maximum size of budget deficits, as in the European Union Maastricht Agreements, are typical here: deficits are seen as linked to inflation (fuelled by too much of democratic politics) and the erosion of the value of capital and assets. Deficit reduction strategies typically do not entail tax increases, but instead involve fiscal austerity measures. Cuts in social expenditures are often made to balance budgets and finance interest payments on debt. Debt payments are especially large in many developing nations, in many cases taking up 25 per cent or more of annual budget outlays. By contrast, Oxfam notes that cancelling debts would release $3-billion dollars per month for poor countries that could be deployed to provide free health care for everyone (Oxfam 2021, 18). Research suggests that the fiscal austerity of "sound" macroeconomic policy tends to result in lower government expenditures in social and public health programs and more regressive and unequal tax systems. These effects, according to a recent study by the IMF, tend to hit the poor, and especially poor women, the hardest (Donald and Lusiani, 2017). Such austerity policies strike at the very heart of the public institutions associated with social reproduction. By contrast, evidence from the UN suggests that alternative frameworks of macroeconomic policy based on high levels of both revenues and public expenditure are more conducive to gender equality (UNRISD 2005).

With respect to monetary policy, during the 1990s, many nations moved to fully independent central banks or currency boards that cannot be made to fund government deficits. These institutions are committed to publicly specified inflation targeting as the centrepiece of monetary policy (as opposed to the promotion of full employment, which was the goal of central banks during the post-1945 welfare era), in many cases locking in the anti-inflation bias by statute (Gill 2002). This also explains why one of the most important purposes of these institutional changes is to insulate the making of economic policy from democratic accountability and control (e.g., legislative or popular accountability). Independence (with the governing boards of central banks staffed principally from economists within, or sympathetic to, the financial sector) is seen as a means to help enforce budgetary discipline and restraint on expenditures, particularly social expenditures, which might otherwise grow if economic policy were made more accountable to popular demands (Elson 2012). Partly as a result of these measures, the principal capitalist countries of the world, until recently, experienced minimal levels of inflation.

Changes of this type – which effectively cordon off monetary and fiscal policy from democratic accountability – can also occur indirectly through international agreements. For example, governments and the IMF may agree, often secretly, to programs of macroeconomic stabilization to deal with financial and balance of payments crises; or governments may agree to the conditions of World Bank structural adjustment programs (Floro and Hoppe 2005). Stephen Gill refers to this process as the new constitutionalism, a governance process involving mechanisms to regulate and extend the world market and lock in corporate and individual rights over collective and social rights (Gill 1995, 1998; Schneiderman 2000; Bakker and Gill 2003; Gill and Cutler 2014). New constitutionalism, and neoliberal governing practices more generally, treat the many and complex dimensions of social provisioning and care as externalities or as matters of private capacity and individual choice (Power 2004).

While the 2008 financial crash called into question the very survival of financialized capitalism, the mix of macroeconomic policies that have been adopted in the major capitalist countries in response to the crash involves a combination of very loose and expansionary monetary policy, followed by fiscal austerity measures occasioned by huge bailouts of troubled banks and corporations. In effect, the private debts and liabilities of large capitalist enterprises have been socialized. The large deficit spending caused by these bailouts has subsequently been transformed into sovereign debts and, typically, austerity policies in order to be able to satisfy creditors that these debts can be successfully serviced. In that sense, the post 2008 policies have been characterized as austerity for some – the majority of people – and cheap money policies for those able to borrow and invest in asset markets. By definition, only those who are credit-worthy can borrow large sums in these markets, resulting in an upward redistribution from the poor to the very rich. Brigitte Young is one of the few feminist political economists who has explored the distributional impact of central bank policy in rich countries. She argues that quantitative easing (unconventional monetary policy) – a policy used when the interest rate is close to zero and normal tools of monetary policy are no longer effective – was employed extensively in the post-2008 period (2021). Central banks buy financial assets adding new money to the economy and thereby providing banks with greater liquidity. She hypothesizes, through her quantitative research relying on results of the Household Finance and Consumption Survey of the ECB, "that since the rich own more assets than the poor, unconventional monetary policy benefits the wealthier quintile in the Eurozone countries (on average, comprised more of men) at the expense of the poorer strata of society (on average, comprised of more women)" (Young 2021).

Nevertheless, then, following the global financial crisis of 2008, many countries were driven by a politics of austerity for the majority and socialization of risk for the few. States acted quickly in response to banking failure through fiscal stimulus packages to support businesses and, to a lesser extent, workers. In response to rising fiscal and sovereign debts (e.g., due to financially induced crises and bailouts) cutbacks in public services were made with particularly adverse effects for the poor, including rising unemployment, falling wages, and a contraction of growth, thus deepening economic and social crises were intensified in many countries. Such a policy mix – perhaps inadvertently – tends to create what economists call a "fallacy of composition": namely, if all governments cut their expenditures, economic recession deepens at national and global levels. A second aspect – one that has gone largely unnoticed in the debates concerning global economic governance – is that a mixed picture is emerging with respect to patterns of gender inequality. In some countries, research indicates that women, overall, are faring worse due to austerity measures. In the United Kingdom, for example, public sector job cuts affected women more than men (57.5 per cent of job cuts affected women versus 42.5 per cent for men, based on 2012 data). Researchers found that changes to direct taxes and welfare benefits since 2010 have meant women will pay 74 per cent of the costs of reducing the UK budget deficit compared to 26 per cent for men (Elson 2013). More recent research provides an intersectional lens on the cuts to public services and tax and benefits changes in the UK finding that the poorest families have lost the most, with an average drop in living standards of around 17 per cent by 2020; lone mothers will experience a drop in living standards of 18 per cent (8,790 BP); and, Black and Asian households in the lowest fifth of incomes experience the biggest average drop in living standards of 19.2 per cent (8,407 BP) and 20.1 per cent (11,678 BP), respectively (UK Women's Budget Group 2017).

By contrast, in Greece, despite that fact that women were more affected than men by public sector cuts, paradoxically the social regression caused by high unemployment and deteriorating working and living conditions has actually narrowed gender gaps in employment, unemployment, and pay since 2008 through a general levelling down (Karamessini 2014). It is therefore vital to situate an analysis of changing conditions of gender equality within the broader dynamics of intergroup inequality to problematize "false" gains that may result from an overall harmonizing down of well-being (i.e., women may appear to be doing better but only because of a harmonizing down of wages/conditions for some men).

Social Reproduction Theory, Austerity, and COVID-19

Social reproduction theory – a term employed in feminist political economy to refer to daily and inter-generational reproduction of social institutions and labour (Picchio 1992) – and writings on the care economy, argue that care work advances human capabilities yet remains ignored or undervalued, especially in moments of austerity. Estimates of the contribution of care work and household production to GDP vary considerably across countries but are above 35 per cent in several countries generally considered affluent, such as Australia, New Zealand, and Japan, and below 20 per cent in countries with lower GDP, such as Mexico and the Republic of Korea (Ahmad and Koh 2011). Yet women's economic contributions are often erased if they take place outside of formal production, which means that current "measurements of economic performance, growth living standards and well-being are inaccurate" (Heintz 2019, 54). Also, the work of care is involved in producing not only services that supplement market and state efforts, but also produces the skills and people and the human capacities that will make the economy run in the future. This is what underpins all economies and what makes them sustainable (Heintz 2019, 82).

The COVID-19 pandemic has placed a focus on the home as more parents who are able or compelled to, stay home due to business and school closures.[1] The crisis has also revealed how neoliberal globalized economies depend on this non-market sphere of goods and services (such as childcare, learning, and food preparation) which have been displaced to this non-market sphere. This unpaid household labour carried out by some men but mostly women has served as an automatic stabilizer for household consumption and maintaining the conditions of social reproduction ("everyday life") (Heintz 2019). Closer scrutiny of the home – which is usually a black box in neoclassical economics – has refocused some of the discourse of crisis to caring labour (Bahn et.al. 2020). Studies of social reproduction have analyzed how paid employment and unpaid domestic labour – in all its facets – are part of the same interdependent processes of production and consumption that when combined, generate a household's livelihood (Bakker and Gill 2003, 2019; Himmelweit 1999, 2017). Generally, markets, states, and families are identified as the main institutional sites for social reproduction, but the allocation of responsibilities between them and the standard or quality of life they produce varies across historical periods in different societies based on struggles over social and economic priorities (Fraser, 2016; Luxton 2006; Mahon and Johnson 2004).

In the current moment of pandemic, richer states have resorted to a form of Keynesian expansionism to safeguard some aspects of social reproduction and capital accumulation by buffering the incomes of businesses and households in response to the necessary health lockdowns most societies experienced. However, the closure of schools has led to a downloading of care and learning responsibilities to parents, especially women. Due to the shutdown of non-essential activities, globally women are overrepresented in the sectors most impacted by the pandemic. The informal economy employs 740 million women, and in the first month of the pandemic, their income fell by 60 per cent (over $396 billion in earnings) (Oxfam 2021, 26). In Canada, at the beginning of the pandemic, women experienced disproportionate job loss, a disparity that was further intensified for minority women, as their employment is concentrated in low-paid services, retail, and personal services as well as the front line of care work. In terms of recovery, men returned to work sooner than women, and there is a significant consensus among researchers that recovery for women, as well as men, depends on a childcare strategy, suggesting that there is no return to pre-COVID (Yalnizyan 2020). A recent survey done by the Canadian Centre for Policy Alternatives into parental fees in regulated child care found that very high fees across the country (except in Quebec) are the driving force in whether parents will stop using child care especially during the pandemic period (Macdonald and Friendly 2021).

In sum, the paradox of "sound" macroeconomic policies and its political common sense often results in choices of austerity, reinforcing and extending systemic inequalities. This, in turn, creates what Brodie has called a "paradox of necessity": the dynamics of neoliberal globalization (the extension of market forces and capital flows with minimal government intervention) paradoxically give rise to the necessity for government intervention both to stabilize the economy and to address social needs (2003, 60). Brodie's paradox highlights the tension between maximal need for social protection and the shrinking of states' abilities to do so in the era of neoliberal globalism.[2] As she and a number of scholars have argued, neoliberal projects entail contradictions and have observed a diverse range of outcomes that suggest both closures and openings for potentially progressive agendas. This is very much in line with Polanyi's observation of the need for social protection and the requirement of a strong state to sustain a self-regulating market.

COVID has, out of necessity, moderated this paradox due to the wide-ranging nature of the public emergency and its direct effects on social reproduction and capital accumulation. A significant policy intervention in Canada (although not unique to Canada, see OECD 2020) is that of income support. The Canada Emergency Response Benefit (CERB) recognized that government has to go beyond a wage subsidy to employers to place income in the hands of individuals who either were able to stay home or had lost work hours (Yalnizyan, 2020). However, this was an emergency response. The question is whether neoliberalism will be revised through the contradictions revealed around the care economy, or whether the fiscal capacity of states in times of crisis will be extended through further fiscal stimulus in the form of income supports and service supports as part of recovery, to be followed by a period of extended austerity. As Adam Tooze notes, COVID may finally mark the death of the householder analogy about the limits of deficit spending,[3] a key element of the consensus of the 1990s (2020a). We see in this crisis that large economies with credible central banks are able to borrow on an epic scale without suffering, at least until now, financial-market disruption. At the same time, very large holders of private capital have had to invest their money somewhere and have done so by "putting it in government debt because that's the safest port in a storm" (Tooze 2020a).

This interregnum between the 1990s consensus and a potential new moment for policy-makers will greatly depend on how coronavirus debt is handled in the post-pandemic period. How debt will be repaid will be a political, and ultimately class, issue with conservatives ramping up new campaigns of austerity. Such a response would fuel the vicious cycle of creating ever more false economies, especially if issues of care and social reproduction are not addressed directly through supportive policies. The next section will offer some examples of past false economies of austerity, linking these to the conditions of social reproduction.

False Economies, Hidden Costs, and Depletion

Mainstream economists use the term "false economy" to refer to an attempt to save money in the short run, resulting in a greater expense in the long run. Feminist researchers and scholars have written extensively about the cuts to social reproduction in health and education and the undervaluing of child care as prime examples of a false economy of savings. As costs are off-loaded to the unpaid sector of social provisioning, various knock-on effects accrue to women in their roles as primary care givers, including erratic labour force participation, health deterioration, and old age poverty due to lower levels of literacy and skills and, thus, lifetime earnings. Rai, Hoskyns, and Thomas have pointed to the crisis in care as manifested in depletion through social reproduction which they define as "the level at which the resource outflows exceed resource inflows in carrying out social reproductive work over a threshold of sustainability, making it harmful for those engaged in this unvalued work" (2014, 3–4). The production of labour power and human capacities (physical, technical, social) involves expending work and energy that require replenishment by states and the private sector (Elson 2012). Rai et. al. suggest that depletion in the realm of social reproduction could potentially be reversed through three channels: (1) *Mitigation*, whereby individuals pay someone else or share tasks of social reproduction; (2) *Replenishment* by state or private bodies (e.g., through benefits, tax breaks, work conditions, wages); (3) *Transformation*, which involves structural changes including accounting for depletion by measuring the contribution of social reproduction to the macro economy (Rai et. al. 2014).

Overall, research has shown that not investing in social reproduction may be a false economy from the public finance perspective, as money not spent now will require that more be spent at a later stage in the criminal justice, health, or benefits systems. In the UK, for example, league tables that collate the incidence of issues such as crime, mental health, and obesity compared to European numbers, find that doing nothing or indeed cutting back will amount to almost £4 trillion in the next 20 years. By contrast, an investment package that would include targeted interventions, universal childcare, and paid parental leave could help address as much as £1.5 trillion worth of the cost of these social problems (Kersley n.d.).

In this sense, the economist's prescription of a false economy may be postponed, or offset, by the hidden economy of unpaid care work and social reproduction. This "strategic silence" (Bakker 1994) about the "fleshy, messy and indeterminate stuff of everyday life" and "unpaid" labour (Katz 2001) obscures its function as a safety valve to stall the social and economic effects of the paradox of necessity.

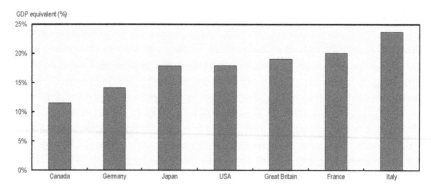

Unpaid care work's contribution to GDP in OECD countries
Source: Ferrant, G. and A. Thim (2019), "Measuring women's economic empowerment: Time use data and gender inequality," *OECD Development Policy Papers*, No. 16, OECD Publishing, Paris, https://doi.org/10.1787/02e538fc-en.

This false economy of savings, which this graph shows, remains largely hidden and buried by the broader narrative that calls ever more women into the workforce, invoking their "underutilized" human capital while affirming the two-earner household model. Yet even the two-earner family model is having difficulty meeting its social reproduction needs, given, for instance, the sharp rise in household debt before the pandemic (OECD 2017).

Indeed, households are increasingly being drawn into financial markets through relations of debt and pension plans investing in stock markets, for instance. If we use Gerald Epstein's broader interpretation of financialization as the increasing dominance of financial motives, financial institutions (including financial markets) and financial interests including in regulation (2005), we can link it directly to a range of institutional structures including firms, governments, and households. And, as a number of feminist political economists have done, we can link it directly to the changing conditions of social reproduction, as financialization has entailed the greater integration of individuals and households into financial markets, especially through the new centrality of debt (Roberts 2015). The financialization of social reproduction – the increasing mediation of social reproduction through financial markets and interest-paying financial transactions – has, according to Roberts,

become increasingly important in mediating the social relations of housing (e.g., through privatised and securitised mortgage financing), forms of consumption (e.g., by using credit cards to pay for food), education (e.g., through student loans, and in the US, loans to pay for all levels of schooling), security in old age (e.g., through the privatisation of pension plans), and so on (2015, 11).[4]

Another aspect of financialization related to social reproduction is the outsourcing of care services. In the UK, social care has been one of the targets of austerity since 2010, and in the US and other countries long-term care has been under siege despite the rising need for such care (Horton 2017). Increasingly, states have withdrawn, and private investors have stepped into this growing market circumventing public responsibility for funding care. However, financial ownership of many care companies has been driven by their real estate assets and the availability of debt financing rather than the needs of care. Financialization of care has been enabled by the undervaluing of care, but it has also been resisted by a recognition of the human relationships embedded in care (Horton 2017). As a recent report on financial ownership of chains of residential care homes points out: "The problem is that the chain owners have developed business models which aim to turn the sector into a high return activity through a combination of financial engineering and political lobbying while shifting the risks and costs onto others including residents, staff, the state and private payers" (Burns et al. 2016, 2).

The appalling record of deaths in long term care homes in Canada (and other countries) during the COVID-19 pandemic reveals striking differences between for-profit and non-profit homes. A study published in the *Canadian Medical Association Journal* found that the poor design standards of older long-term care facilities were particularly susceptible to high rates of COVID transmission in Ontario. For-profit chains run the highest proportion of older facilities, and thus, "for-profit [long-term care] homes have larger COVID-19 outbreaks and more deaths of residents from COVID-19 than not-for-profit and municipal homes ..." (Stall et. al 2020). Research has shown that for-profit facilities offer comparatively substandard care and the Canadian Medical Association, as early as 1984, recommended the transition away from private facilities (see https://healthydebate.ca/opinions/crisis-privatized-care-in-ontario/). This example is perhaps the most extreme result of a false economy of cost cutting and downloading of risk.

Feminist Responses to COVID-19 Recovery – The End of False Economies?

Brigitte Young has recently asked why, in the European context, the issue of gender inequality is largely absent from high-level recovery plans. She surveys plans from the European Union, the OECD, and

Chatham House illustrating the gender blindness of these reports (2023). Young also interrogates how traditional macroeconomists neglect the gender lens due to their reliance on gender-blind data. Young is also critical of feminist economics and its neglect of the macro economy, arguing that most accounts focus on the micro level of the care economy and the shift of burdens to women's unpaid labour.

In Canada, income support programs began early and were a boost for both individuals and businesses. These were largely universal and gender blind with little or no intersectional analysis, either in terms of policy design or assessment of impacts (GATE/YWCA 2020). However, many of the jobs in which women are concentrated – the "5 Cs" of caring, clerical, catering, cashiering, and cleaning (Scott 2020) – were severely impacted by the pandemic creating the first "she-cession" in history (Yalnizyan 2020). Further, it is racialized women who are over-represented in these service jobs.

Recognizing some of the effects of lockdowns and job losses for many women, the Government of Canada introduced, beginning October 2020, the Canada Recovery Caregiving Benefit (CRCB) for employed and self-employed people who cannot work because they must care for their child under 12 years old or a family member who needs supervised care. The CRCB has been extended in early 2021 from 26 weeks to 38 weeks and provides $500 per week ($450 once taxes are withheld) and represents a stopgap measure rather than a structural shift in financing care. In addition, the government announced $100 million in funding to women's groups covering three areas: ending violence against women and girls; improving women's and girl's economic security and prosperity; and encouraging women and girls to pursue leadership and decision-making roles. While funding for grassroots women's organizations is a welcome turn, a comprehensive national plan grounded in alternative macroeconomic thinking is warranted, as a return to the pre-pandemic normal will further entrench the inequalities heightened through the pandemic.

Two ambitious recovery plans have been developed by the Feminist Alliance for International Action (FAFIA) and by the Gender and Economy Institute at the University of Toronto (GATE), both in conjunction with the YWCA. To what extent do these alternative plans engage with the macroeconomic context?

Macroeconomic policies consist of fiscal and monetary policies. Fiscal policies relate to how governments gather resources and how they spend their monies. Fiscal policies also relate to deficit financing and how public debts are managed. Monetary policies are exercised through central banks affecting the supply of credit and resources available to a range of financial institutions. They also involve interest and exchange rates. All of these macroeconomic policies are mainly conducted in what is considered a gender-blind fashion, focusing on narrow goals such as raising economic growth rates rather than "… more fundamental objectives such as human development, well-being and the enjoyment of rights" (Heintz, 2015, 1). Yet gender-blind policies are not gender neutral (Bakker 1994). Both monetary and fiscal policy "changes the macroeconomic environment and interacts with structural features of the economy to produce different outcomes for women and men" (Heintz, 2019, 19). For instance, the distribution of paid and unpaid work between the state, the private sector, the household, women, and men is a pre-determined structural feature of any economy, as is the segregation of women and men into different types of employment.

A Feminist Economic Recovery Plan for Canada: Making the Economy Work for Everyone

This plan provides an intersectional lens to recovery and focuses on investing in good jobs; recognizing care work as essential work; bolstering small business; strengthening infrastructure for recovery; and diversifying voices in planning and assessment of policy impacts. There is a consideration of revisions in the tax system to pay for these measures and also a brief discussion of the need to revise fiscal and monetary policies to address intersectional inequities. A key point is the call to address investment in critical services and social infrastructure, noting the economic and social benefits. Indeed, from the viewpoint of general frameworks of accumulation, growth, and investment, a seven-country report cited by the World Economic Forum found that government investment in social infrastructure, including education, health, and care work, will produce more "bang for the buck" than physical infrastructure projects like bridges and highways. For example, in the US, research has shown that an investment of 2 per cent of GDP in social infrastructure raises employment by about 3.4 per cent compared to 1.2 percentage points for similar investment in physical infrastructure. The logic behind these findings is that social infrastructure is much more labour intensive than physical infrastructure, and care jobs are much more likely than construction jobs to employ women (Schmitt 2016).

In sum, this recovery plan does touch on the macro framing of spending and taxation initiatives directed at recovery. It does not, however, set proposals within the context of the changes brought by financialized capitalism and how these have shifted the macroeconomic environment

(Young 2023). In particular, how do these proposed measures tackle the false economy of sound macroeconomic policies and the austerity response to sovereign debt management?

A Feminist Economic Recovery Plan for Canada: Human Rights Approach

A twin study by FAFIA and the YWCA employs key human rights obligations such as equality and non-discrimination as a normative guide to the recovery response focusing on the right to an adequate standard of living, health, adequate housing, the right to social security, and childcare (Misra and Ward 2020). It is interesting that several human rights principles that have been related to how governments spend and tax within the context of their human rights obligations are not singled out. A key budget-focused obligation of governments under international human rights treaties is to make full use of the country's maximum available resources to realize human rights obligations of respect, protection, and fulfillment (CESCR 1999, para. 15). Each of these obligations has two dimensions: conduct and result. The obligation of conduct means the government is obliged to behave in a way that reasonably can be expected to realize the enjoyment of the particular right. The obligation of result means the government is obliged to achieve outcomes that enhance the enjoyment of specific rights. For example, does public expenditure on health represent "action reasonably calculated to realize" the right to health in a way compliant with obligations of non-discrimination and equality? Findings of unequal health expenditure across different social groups might suggest a case of failure to meet obligation of conduct if we find the group with the lowest share of expenditure has the lowest health status (Balkrishnan and Elson 2007, 9). The principle of maximum available resources could be applied in a powerful way to assess whether economic recovery proposals address existing false economies to meet obligations that avoid retrogression, or a step back, in the level of protection of enjoyment of rights already realized.

Conclusion

Over the past 25 years, research suggests that responsibility for social reproduction has shifted away from states and towards families and individuals who must meet those needs increasingly through markets or through labour performed largely by women in the domestic sector (some hired by other women). This shift has been uneven and variegated across societies depending on their resources and previous socialized commitments to welfare and care. For example, the Nordic countries have tended to socialize such provisions, whereas in other countries, such as the US, their provision is more privatized and market based. This dual shift can be linked to what I have previously called "the reprivatization of social reproduction" (2003). Reprivatization implies that, due to shrinking welfare states and social investments in wealthy countries of the Global North ("sound" policies), social reproduction will once again be assigned to the private sphere of households and women's unpaid work. Social reproduction can also be shifted to domestic workers within the household or substituted through market services and commodities depending on income and class.

This separation of the social from the economic reflects a shift in economic governance that suggests individual rather than society-wide responsibility for these essential activities, a phenomenon discussed in several other chapters in this volume (Ilcan, Kingfisher, Harder, Phillips). As Suzan Ilcan illustrates, the demise of social responsibility and its replacement by individual endeavour even extends to refugee camps. Each of these alternative forms of capitalist development suggests different outcomes related to income and gender inequalities.

In conclusion, I offer several points that allow us to raise questions concerning the future and, indeed, whether capitalism is the problem or the solution.

An immediate question concerns the future of macroeconomic policy insofar as governments actually overcome the present economic and health emergency. The financing of emergency measures to promote economic recovery in 2020/1 was made possible by the lowest ever interest rates worldwide, which allowed for massive, and possibly unprecedented, government borrowing on the financial markets. This shows that when capitalism is at stake, governments – partly led by the independent central banks whose leaders are drawn from the private financial sector – will do "whatever it takes" to preserve the existing socio-economic system. So what happens in the future? These debts will need to be serviced, setting up a massive class struggle over the future of policies connected to that servicing: Will the policy choice be to download those costs to the working poor in particular and the economically and socially marginalized more generally, via long term austerity measures?

A related question is whether it could be plausibly claimed that the pandemic and its related economic emergency is endogenous to the very mechanisms of capitalism, including the ideology and practice of "sound" economics. Generally speaking, capitalist systems socialize the risk of the powerful and privatize risk for the many.

Finally, one possible answer to the question of capitalism in the future has been provided by the Nordic countries, and particularly by Finland, which is an exemplar of successful strategies to deal with the COVID economic emergency. Finland has one of the highest human development indices in the world and is known for its first-class health care and education and social systems. Often overlooked in the Finnish case, however, is the fact that more than 60 per cent of Finnish workers are unionized (compared to a 16 per cent average in the OECD in 2017) and with 89 per cent having collective bargaining coverage (see OECD 2021).[5] Indeed, the unions and their pension funds are major holders of capital and big investors in the economy. As a result, the working and professional classes in Finland are very broad-based. They have enormous structural power in the determination of corporate and political choices and, therefore, in defining and evaluating the opportunity costs facing Finland both in the present and the future.

So, this example shows that one form of capitalism – possibly the exception rather than the rule – can be a sustainable solution that provides meaningful and progressive social reproduction. On the other hand, the value contribution of social reproduction in terms of the reproduction of life and of capitalist relations, that is of both labourers and labour power, needs to be brought into the equation to underscore the interdependence of production and social reproduction (Mezzadri 2019).

Whether this is likely to the case in Canada or in other wealthy countries, or indeed throughout the world, rests upon the mobilization of political and social forces not simply to countervail but also wrest power from the commanding heights of capital. And the ethics of this perspective are very simple: public health and care should be public goods that are socialized and universal and not subject to intensified exploitation and treated as commodities.

NOTES

1 Informal workers have long dealt with the home as a place of both paid work and care.
2 Public spending during the neoliberal era has been hollowed out through consecutive regimes of lowered taxes on the rich and corporations. Between 1985 and 2019, the global statutory corporate tax rate fell from 49 per cent to 23 per cent and countries may be losing $427 billion each year to international corporate tax abuse and private tax evasion (Oxfam 2021, 21–2).

3 The household analogy of debt as a moral burden and of profligate spending beyond one's means may be apt in some situations such as is the case for many poorer countries who are dependent on foreign creditors who only lend in the currency of another country (e.g., US dollars). As Tooze points out advanced economies can borrow in their own currencies and from their citizens, none more so than the US (2020b).
4 Wall Street has taken advantage of the collapse in the housing market, for example, where many families have lost their homes as a result of foreclosures, by buying up properties at fire-sale prices. Indeed, former US Secretary of Treasury Steve Mnuchin, seems to be one of the beneficiaries of this practice at Goldman Sachs.
5 Union membership rates, the number of trade union members who are employees as a percentage of the total number of employees in a given industry or country, are normally lower than collective agreement coverage rates which refer to all workers whose terms of work are collectively negotiated.

REFERENCES

Ahmad, Nadeem, and Seung-Hee Koh. 2011. *Incorporating Estimates of Household Production of Non-market Services into International Comparisons of Material Well-Being*. Working Paper No. 42, OECD Statistics Directorate.

Bahn, Kate, Jennifer Cohen, and Yana van der Meulen Rodgers. 2020. "A Feminist Perspective on COVID-19 and the Value of Care Work Globally." *Gender, Work, & Organization* 27 no. 5: 695–9. https://doi.org/10.1111/gwao.12459.

Bakker, Isabella. 2003. "Neo-liberal Governance and the Reprivatization of Social Reproduction." In *Power, Production and Social Reproduction: Human In/security in the Global Political Economy*, edited by Isabella Bakker and Stephen Gill, 66–80. New York, Palgrave Macmillan.

– 1994. *The Strategic Silence: Gender and Economic Policy*. London: Zed Press.

Bakker, Isabella, and Stephen Gill. 2019. "Rethinking Power, Production and Social Reproduction: Toward Variegated Social Reproduction." *Capital & Class* 43 (4): 503–23. https://doi.org/10.1177%2F0309816819880783.

– eds. 2003. *Power, Production and Social Reproduction: Human In/security in the Global Political Economy*. New York, Palgrave Macmillan.

Balakrisnan, Radhika, and Diane Elson. 2007. "Auditing Economic Policies in the Light of Economic and Social Rights." *Essex Human Rights Review* 5 (1): 1–19.

Bezanson, Kate, and Meg Luxton. 2006. *Social Reproduction: Feminist Political Economy Challenges Neo-Liberalism*. Montreal: McGill-Queen's University Press.

Brodie, Janine. 2003. "Globalization, In/Security, and the Paradoxes of the Social." In *Power, Production and Social Reproduction: Human In/security in the*

Global Political Economy, edited by Isabella Bakker and Stephen Gill, 47–65. New York, Palgrave Macmillan.

Brodie, Janine, and Isabella Bakker. 2008. *Where Are the Women? Gender Equality, Budgets and Canadian Public Policy*. Ottawa: Canadian Centre for Policy Alternatives.

Burns, D., L. Cowie, J. Earle, P. Folkman, J. Froud, P. Hyde, S. Johal, I.R. Jones, A. Killett, and K. Willimas, K. 2016. *Where Does the Money Go? Financialised Chains and the Crisis in Residential Care*. Manchester: Centre for Research on Socio-Cultural Change.

CESCR. 1999. "International Covenant on Economic, Social and Cultural Rights." https://www.ohchr.org/EN/ProfessionalInterest/Pages/CESCR.aspx.

Donald, Kate, and Nicholas Lusiani. 2017. "The Gendered Costs of Austerity: Assessing the IMF's Role in Budget Cuts Which Threaten Women's Rights." https://socialprotection-humanrights.org/resource/gendered-costs-austerity-assessing-imfs-role-budget-cuts-threaten-womens-rights/.

Elson, Diane. 2013. "Financial Crisis, Austerity and Gender Equality in UK." Presentation to GEM-IWG Seminar, Jagiellonian University, Krakow, July 2013.

– 2012. "Social Reproduction in the Global Crisis." In *The Global Crisis and Transformative Social Change*, edited by P. Utting, S. Razavi, and R. Varghese Buchholz. Geneva: UNRISD.

Elson, Diane, and Andy Norton. 2002. "What's Behind the Budget? Politics, Rights, and Accountability in the Budget Process." https://gsdrc.org/document-library/whats-behind-the-budget-politics-rights-and-accountability-in-the-budget-process/.

Epstein, Gerald. 2005. *Financialization and the World Economy*. Cheltenhem: Edward Elgar Publishing.

FAFIA/YWCA. 2020. *A Feminist Economic Recovery Plan: Human Rights Approach*. Ottawa: FAFIA.

Floro, Maria, and Hella Hoppe. 2005. *Engendering Policy Coherence for Development*. Berlin: Firedrich Ebert Stiftung. https://library.fes.de/opus4/frontdoor/index/index/docId/5287.

Fraser, Nancy. 2016. "Contradictions of Capitalism and Care." *New Left Review* 100. (July/August): 99–117.

GATE/YWCA. 2020. *A Feminist Economic Recovery Plan: Making the Economy Work for Everyone*. Toronto: GATE, Rotman School of Management, University of Toronto.

Gill, Stephen. 2002. "Constitutionalizing Inequality and the Clash of Globalizations." *International Studies Review* 4 (2): 47–65. http://doi.org/10.1111/1521-9488.00254.

– 1998. "New Constitutionalism, Democratisation and Global Political Economy." *Pacifica Review: Peace, Security & Global Change* 10 (1): 23–38. https://doi.org/10.1080/14781159808412845.

– 1995. "Globalisation, Market Civilisation and Disciplinary
Neoliberalism." *Millennium* 24 (3): 399–423. https://doi.org/10.1177
%2F03058298950240030801.

Gill, Stephen, and Claire Cutler, eds. 2014. *New Constitutionalism and World
Order*. Cambridge: Cambridge University Press.

Heintz, James. 2019. *The Economy's Other Half: How Taking Gender Seriously
Transforms Macroeconomics*. Newcastle: Agenda Publishing.

– 2015. *Why Macroeconomic Policy Matters to Gender Equality*. UN Women
Policy Brief No. 4. New York: UN Women. https://www.unwomen.org
/en/digital-library/publications/2015/12/macroeconomic-policy-matters
-for-gender-equality.

Himmelweit, Susan. 2017. "Changing Norms of Social Reproduction in an Age
of Austerity." The Open University. http://iippe.org/wp/wp-content/uploads
/2017/01/suegender.pdf.

– 1999. "Caring Labor." *The Annals of the American Academy of
Political and Social Science* 561 (1): 27–38. https://doi.org/10.1177
%2F000271629956100102.

Horton, Angela. 2017. October. "Finacialisation of Care: Investment and
Organising in the UK and US" PhD diss., Queen Mary, University of London.

Karamessini, Maria. 2014. "Structural Crisis and Adjustment in Greece: Social
Regression and the Challenge to Gender Equality." In *Women and Austerity:
The Economic Crisis and the Future of Gender Equality*, edited by Maria
Karemessini and Jill Rubery, 165–85. Abingdon and New York: Routledge.

Katz, Cindi. 2001. "Vagabond Capitalism and the Necessity of Social Reproduction."
Antipode 33 (4): 709–28. https://doi.org/10.1111/1467-8330.00207.

Kearsley, Helen. 2010. "A False Economy: Undervaluing Childcare." *Child
Poverty Action Group* Issue 135 (Winter 2010): 10–13. http://www.cpag.org
.uk/sites/default/files/false_economy_undervaluing_childcare.pdf.

Luxton, Meg. 2006. "Feminist Political Economy in Canada and the Politics
of Social Reproduction." In *Social Reproduction: Feminist Political Economy
Challenges Neo-liberalism*, edited by Kate Bezanson and Meg Luxton, 11–44.
Montreal and Kingston: McGill-Queen's University Press.

Macdonald, David, and Martha Friendly. 2021. *Sounding the Alarm: Covid-19's
Impact on Canada's Precarious Child Care Sector*. Ottawa: CCPA.

Mahon, Rianne, and Richard Johnson 2004. "NAFTA, the Redesign and Rescaling
of Canada's Welfare Regime." http://www.carleton.ca/spa/Publication
/NAFTA%20Johnson%20and%20Mahonrevised.pdf.

Mezzadri, Alessandra. 2019. "On the Value of Social Reproduction," *Radical
Philosophy* 2 (Spring): 33–41.

Misra, Shivanghi, and Tara Ward. 2020. "*A Feminist Economic Recovery Plan
for Canada: Human Rights Approach*." Ottawa: The Feminist Alliance for
International Action and YWCA Canada. Online: www.feministrecovery.ca.

Organisation for Economic Co-operation and Development. 2021. *Collective Bargaining Coverage*. Paris: OECD; February 22, 2021.

– 2020. *Tax and Fiscal Policy Response to the Coronavirus Crisis: Strengthening Confidence and Resilience*. Paris: OECD.

– 2019. *Measuring Women's Economic Empowerment: Time Use Data and Gender Inequality. OECD Development Policy Papers, No. 16*. Paris: OECD.

– 2017. "Economic Outlook." http://www.oecd.org/eco/outlook/Resilience-in-a-time-of-high-debt-november-2017-OECD-economic-outlook-chapter.pdf.

Oxfam. 2021. *The Inequality Virus*. Great Britain: Oxfam. www.oxfam.org.

Picchio, Antonella. 1992. *Social Reproduction: The Political Economy of the Labour Market*. Cambridge: Cambridge University Press.

Power, Marilyn. 2004. "Social Provisioning as a Starting Point for Feminist Economics." *Feminist Economics* 10 (3): 3–19. https://doi.org/10.1080/1354570042000267608.

Rai, Shirin, Catherine Hoskyns, and Dania Thomas. 2014. "Depletion: The Cost of Social Reproduction." *International Feminist Journal of Politics* 16 (1): 86–105. https://doi.org/10.1080/14616742.2013.789641.

Roberts, Adrienne. 2015. "Gender, Financial Deepening and the Production of Embodied Finance: Towards a Critical Feminist Analysis." *Global Society* 29 (1): 107–27. https://doi.org/10.1080/13600826.2014.975189.

Schmitt, John. 2016. "Can Investing in Social Infrastructure Jump-Start Economies?" *World Economic Forum*. April 15, 2016. https://www.weforum.org/agenda/2016/04/can-investing-in-social-infrastructure-jump-start-economies.

Schneiderman, David. 2000. "Investment Rules and the New Constitutionalism." *Law and Social Inquiry* 25 (3): 757–87. http://doi.org/10.1111/j.1747-4469.2000.tb00160.x.

Scott, Katherine. 2020. "COVID-19 Crisis Response Must Address Gender Faultlines." *The Monitor*, March 20, 2020. https://monitormag.ca/articles/covid-19-crisis-response-must-address-gender-faultlines.

Stall, Nathan M. et. al. 2020. "For-Profit Long-Term Care Homes and the Risk of COVID-19 Outbreaks and Resident Deaths." CMAJ 192 (33): E946–E955. https://doi.org/10.1503/cmaj.201197.

Tooze, Adam. 2020a. "A Historian of Economic Crisis on the World After COVID-19." *New York Magazine*, August 7, 2020.

– 2020b. "Should We Be Scared of the Coronavirus Debt Mountain?" *The Guardian*, April 27, 2020.

UK Women's Budget Group. (2017). *Intersecting Inequalities: The Impact on Black and Minority Ethnic Women in the UK*. London: Women's Budget Group.

United Nations Research Institute for Social Development (UNRISD). 2005. *Gender Equality: Striving for Justice in an Unequal World*. Geneva: UNRISD.

UN Women. 2020. "Whose Time to Care? Unpaid Care and Domestic Work during Covid-19." https://data.unwomen.org/publications/whose -time-care-unpaid-care-and-domestic-work-during-covid-19.

Yalnizyan, Armine. 2020. "Recovery Depends on Childcare Strategy to Get Women Back to Work." First Policy Response Project, Toronto Metropolitan University. https://policyresponse.ca/recovery-depends-on-childcare-strategy-to-get-women-back-to-work/.

Young, Brigitte. 2023. "Covid-19 and the Gender Dilemma: Shortcomings in both Macroeconomics and Feminist Economics." In *Handbook on Critical Political Economy and Public Policy*, edited by Christoph Scherrer and Joscha Wullweber. Cheltenham and Camberley: Edward Elgar.

– 2021. "The Distributive Impact of Central Banks' Quantitative Easing Program." February 10, 2021. *Just Money* (Harvard blog). https://justmoney .org/the-distributive-impact-of-central-banks-quantitative-easing-program/.

Young, Brigitte, Isabella Bakker, and Diane Elson, eds. 2011. *Questioning Financial Governance from a Feminist Perspective*. New York: Routledge.

3 Neoliberalism and Resource Extraction: Colonial Continuities

ISABEL ALTAMIRANO-JIMÉNEZ

Introduction

Taking inspiration from Janine Brodie's analytical emphasis on the historically contingent relations between the state and the market, this chapter maps the relationship between neoliberalism and colonialism and examines how they operate together in the North American context. Drawing on critical Indigenous studies and critical political economy, I argue that current capitalist expansion of natural resource extraction connects colonialism to neoliberalism, demonstrating how the devaluation of Indigenous peoples and ways of life and the dispossession of land are not phenomena of the past, but contemporary processes. Focusing on capitalism rather than on neoliberalism, Byrd et. al. note there is no separation between the practices of primitive accumulation that institute and expand capitalist development and those associated with colonialism and Indigenous dispossession (2018). Although settler colonial studies have been preoccupied with land-making practices and the constitution of the settler home and settler subjectivities (Veraccini 2010; Wolfe 2006), concomitantly, this area of studies has contributed to the erasure of "the making and unmaking" of Indigenous and Black humanity (Lethabo King, 2019, 39). Thus, in looking at the relationship between colonialism and neoliberalism I am interested in the complex processes through which both Indigenous land and bodies have been constructed as lacking. Land dispossession relied on a hierarchical understanding of humanity, and on power to enforce and sustain it (Lethabo King 2019, 46).

(Settler) Colonialism, Land, and Race

Scholars have characterized settler colonialism as a specific ongoing colonial formation mainly concerned with land and resources. However, land dispossession was constituted through the interplay between possessing land and racial hierarchies, which construct Indigenous land as "wasteland" that only acquires value through settlers' interventions (Voyles 2015, 7) and bodies as less than. This teleology justified a wide range of legal, cultural, conceptual, and administrative measures mobilized to characterize Indigenous peoples' forms of relations to land and economic activities as inferior, underutilized, and underdeveloped (Bhandar 2018). Such a characterization culminated with the primacy of Anglo-European political and property relations, which were seen as capable of maximizing the value of land and resources. The logic of settler colonialism becomes operationalized through the "ideology of improvement" (Bhandar 2018, 4). European liberal ideologies of property and entitlement justified dispossession through the depiction of Indigenous peoples as savages and their lands as empty (Moreton-Robinson 2017). In this sense, value is not concerned with the form of property but with the racial habitation of land. It is white-European control over land that renders resources valuable.

The connection between race, land, and value legally codified the doctrine of *terra nullius*, embraced throughout Canada and the United States. Narratives of *terra nullius* prefigured Indigenous lands as empty lands that could only acquire value through property-making practices (e.g., agricultural activities, fencing, expansive cattle foraging) and free mining principles. While colonial entitlement to land has been central to the Canadian and the US economies, the collaborative deployment of public and private money facilitated capitalization, natural resource extraction, and cross-border trade. The colonial state was simultaneously committed to facilitating the free flow of capital and intervening in everyday life to preserve its rule. Free mining, for example, was formally enshrined in the British Columbia Gold Fields Act of 1859 in Western Canada and in the American General Mining Law of 1872 (Hoogeveen 2015, 126). Free mining allowed private companies and individual prospectors to stake a mineral claim without the consent of, or in consultation with, private owners and Indigenous peoples. Encouraged by an emergent English geological science that emphasized the purity of minerals, and supported by the dynamics of industrial capitalism, the dispossession of Indigenous lands accelerated in the nineteenth century in both Canada and the US. As I detail later, free mining and the ideology that underpinned it were subsequently imposed in other jurisdictions, as Canada became the largest player in global mineral exploration through the 1980s and 1990s.

In the nineteenth century, as news of the discovery of gold spread, thousands of settlers, miners, and prospectors encroached upon Indigenous peoples' lands, altering their ecosystems, their relations to territory, and their relations to each other. The cumulative dispossession of

Indigenous peoples in Anglo North America has taken form through a bundle of processes including law-making, removal, treaties, starvation, settlements, surveys, residential schools, forced enfranchisement, and the spread of disease. Land dispossession and resource extraction thus relied on a structure of violence that was shaped by hierarchical understandings of humanity, and, indeed, these processes remain central to colonial expansion (Clogg 2013, 9). Later, as rich petroleum deposits were found in Alberta, more people were drawn into the industry. In the violent, toxic history of natural resource extraction, contested interpretations of scientific evidence, degraded ecologies, health concerns, and gendered violence continue to shape the racialized experience of extracting minerals (McLahan 2014; NYSH 2016; Wiebe 2016).

Similar to Canada, in the US, the federal government and Indigenous peoples developed various treaties through which the latter were forced to cede huge portions of their territories in exchange for self-government and sovereignty over the lands set aside as tribal reservations. As mineral resources were identified, the American government abrogated treaties in order to provide settlers opportunities for mining, further reducing the size of tribal reservations in the process. Moreover, in 1919 the US government prohibited the creation of new tribal reservations but provided 5 per cent of the net value of extracted resources for the benefit of Indigenous communities (Lewis et al. 2017). Indigenous lands were subjected to intensive natural resource extraction that has left a toxic legacy.

In the nineteenth century, prior to the American Civil War, the hunger for land became the driving force for the doctrine of Manifest Destiny through which Indigenous nations, and other nations as well, would be forced to surrender to racially superior American settlers (Perea 2001). Writing about the movement of empire, Byrd contends that US expansionism was, and continues to be, facilitated by the "transit of Indianness" (2011, 10). From Byrd's perspective, making countries or peoples of the Global South into "Indians" facilitates imperialist expansion (2011, 11). For example, the Mexican government's failure to control Indigenous nations at the northern border became an indication of its incapacity to put land to its most valuable use (Perea 2001, 144). The United States eventually invaded and gained control over nearly half the territory claimed by the Mexican state. As a former colony of Spain, Mexico embraced the system of split mineral and surface ownership after its independence in 1810. In 1884 and 1892, the Mexican mining law was modified to substitute the Spanish colonial code with a property regime that granted ownership of the subsoil to land owners. As well, the adoption of free mining in Mexico produced a number of *fundos mineros,* or mining estates, in different regions of the country, as American mining companies capitalized on newly opened opportunities. By the early 1900s, 81 per cent of Mexican mining property was concentrated in foreign hands. However, foreign investment was initially unrewarding as gold and silver mines were in disarray after the Independence movement (Brown 2012, 101–2). The Mexican government was also pressured by the American government to negotiate the McLane-Ocampo Treaty, or the Treaty of Transit and Commerce 1859. This treaty would have given the US perpetual rights of transit to the Isthmus of Tehuantepec. This geopolitical hotspot shortens the distance between the Pacific Ocean and the Gulf of Mexico, easing the movement of goods and enhancing their profitability. However, the United States Senate failed to ratify this treaty as internal political divisions between northern and southern states prevented the American government from carrying out its plan (Sexton 2011, 135).

The processes briefly described here broadly reveal the ways in which colonialism operates, subjugating and dispossessing Indigenous peoples and transforming their land and resources into property. As I explain in the next section, colonial practices of accumulation were not just a precondition of capitalist development but remain indispensable to the neoliberal expansion of natural resource extraction.

Neoliberalism, Indigenous Peoples, and Colonial Continuities

Although the goals of settler colonialism remain relatively constant, the mechanisms through which settler states have dispossessed Indigenous land and devalued Indigenous ways of life and bodies are not uniform across space and time. In most analyses of neoliberalism in Anglo settler contexts, neoliberalism's connection to colonialism has been obscured. Elsewhere, I have noted that how neoliberalism unfolds in practice cannot be separated from the specific colonial, social, political, cultural, and economic contexts which shape its locally contingent form (Altamirano-Jiménez 2013). Thus, it is useful to observe how state discourses have changed, while paying attention to colonial continuities and broader patterns of the expansion of natural resource extraction. In this sense, I am interested in making connections between how neoliberalism and colonialism operate together, within and beyond the boundaries of the state.

Indigenous and critical scholars have insisted on the need to consider the continuity of colonial land dispossession under historically changing capitalist forms of accumulation (Altamirano-Jiménez 2013; Coulthard 2014; Pasternack 2015; Stanley 2016). Glen Coulthard argues that looking at land dispossession exclusively from a capitalist perspective erases the fact that dispossession structures colonial relations (2014, 59). With neoliberalism, state discourses and modes of governing have shifted towards a stronger reliance on market mechanisms, self-regulation, privatization, individualizing practices, and forms of Indigenous recognition that are exercised through the market (Altamirano-Jiménez 2004; 2013; Bargh 2011). Under these forms of recognition, the dispossession of Indigenous peoples is anchored in privatization and the normalization of property relations (Pasternack 2015), and through the separation of land claims from self-governance (Altamirano-Jiménez 2004). Thus, dispossession occurs through a range of strategies that include exchanging colonial regulatory control in favour of a more market-oriented practice (Pasternack 2015), land claim agreements and re-regulation of land (Altamirano-Jiménez 2004; 2013), and municipalization (Schmidt, 2022). These strategies reproduce colonial ideologies and reinforce the authority of the state while delegating limited powers (granted by the state) to Indigenous communities (Starblanket 2019, 451).

As I discuss below, using the governance rationales of eliminating public debt and/or producing wealth for the public good, these new and aggressive grabs of lands and water continue to violate Indigenous treaty rights and environmental protection programs. At the same time, these strategies are coupled with the state's structural disinvestment in Indigenous communities (Blackstock 2015; Pasternack 2015) and circumscribed opportunities through which Indigenous peoples are invited to participate in the market (Altamirano-Jiménez 2004; 2013). Neoliberal state policies not only blame Indigenous peoples for surviving colonization, but also discipline them for the purpose of managing the deepening and intensification of land dispossession. Under neoliberalism, dispossession continues to operate through racialized lines that underpin the accumulation of wealth for economic and political projects that subordinate Indigenous self-determination. The intensification of natural resource extraction exacerbates Indigenous confrontation with unmoderated, deregulated, mobile industries.

While settler states' efforts to access Indigenous land and resources continue within their borders, they have also extended and naturalized their power in other jurisdictions. As Scott Morgensen writes, "By the twentieth century – amid a formal demise of colonial empires, putative decolonisation of the global South, and global capitalist recolonisation – the universalisation of Western law as liberal governance was ensured by the actions of settler states" (2011, 53). Thus, "Indianness" also moves through a range of political, social, administrative, and economic strategies that function to control land and natural resources abroad. The neoliberal rationalities justify inter-jurisdictional negotiations, knowledge sharing and the adoption of desirable norms. The reality, however, often reveals struggles over who can control natural resources, unequal access to resources, and specific economic and political interests (Perreault 2014, 39). Colonial racialization and neoliberalism coalesce, resulting in the expansion of resource extraction with unjust and colonizing outcomes for different countries and Indigenous peoples.

Neoliberalism with a North American Flavour

Thinking through neoliberalism not only requires engaging with different inter-jurisdictional scales of analysis but explicitly exploring its relation to colonialism. In this section, I discuss the state-society relationship and the liberalization of the economy, specifically, the North American Free Trade Agreement (NAFTA). This agreement not only created the legal and administrative structures to facilitate economic integration, but also legitimated the imposition of Anglo-property regimes and natural resource use practices to expand resource extraction. Corporations are given the "right" to exploit Indigenous lands and public lands, accelerating dispossessions (Melamed 2015). Privatization and new land-management practices became central to commodifying previously untradeable entities such as Indigenous communal lands and resources (Altamirano-Jiménez 2013).

In Canada, neoliberal restructuring involved a radical, political economic experiment that restructured the Keynesian welfare state. Neoliberal policies focused simultaneously on resource extraction and encouraging Indigenous peoples to become entrepreneurs by building their own local economies (Altamirano-Jiménez 2004; Young 2008). Private corporations and governments aligned themselves to create a stable business environment. Unresolved land claims were seen as a problem that limited the state's ability to act unilaterally (Egan and Place 2013, 131). In this context, land claim agreements became a mechanism to extinguish Indigenous title, encourage Indigenous people to take their place in the economy, and resolve their precarious citizenship. Indigenous peoples were encouraged to integrate into the global economy and realize their newly recognized collective rights through self-government and the market. Individualization, self-care, and pathologizing discourses functioned to rationalize Indigenous communities' precarious living conditions as a product of dysfunctional cultural traditions and lifestyles, and not as a result of ongoing processes of dispossession (Altamirano-Jiménez 2013; Lindroth 2016; Strakosh 2015).

If NAFTA paved the way for the intensification of natural resource extraction, the consolidation of neoliberalism throughout the 1990s contributed to deepening and intensifying its scope. Tax incentives contributed to the intensification of high-volume, rapid extraction of oil and gas and mining. In 2006, Stephen Harper was elected prime minister of Canada with a minority government. His Indigenous policy focused on the acceptance of everyone's responsibilities to alleviate poverty and improve one's personal circumstances. This policy, however, ignored the fact that Indigenous peoples' living conditions have been actively produced through decades of colonial policies. Harper's minister of Indian Affairs, for example, suggested that the federal government would never be able to meet the housing needs of First Nations and it was time they used their reserve land to combat poverty (Canada, Department of Indian and Northern Affairs 2010). The government subsequently insisted on empowering those Indigenous citizens who were "ready" to assume their place in the economy (Pasternak 2014, 6), attempting to interpolate Indigenous people into a project of self-policing. At the core of this policy was the creation of new legal mechanisms to privatize property on reserve. With the support of prominent Indigenous leaders, Bill C-63, the First Nations Property Ownership Act (FNPOA) was introduced in the House of Commons in December 2009, with the aim of enabling First Nations communities to request that the Government of Canada make regulations respecting the establishment and operation of a system for the registration of interests and rights in reserve lands (Canada Department of Indian and Northern Affairs 2009).

Besides privatizing Indigenous land, in 2012, after securing a majority government, Harper introduced the controversial Economic Action Plan aimed at increasing the economy's "competitiveness" and "resilience" (Canada 2012). The plan, billed as "responsible development" for all Canadians, not only ignored Canada's legal obligations to Indigenous peoples but also obscured ongoing dispossession and the environmental violence unfolding on their lands. Indigenous leaders and the Idle No More movement rejected the plan for aggressively overriding legal obligations while enabling extractive industries' activities. For Idle No More activists, this plan constituted a "First Nations land grab" (Lameman 2014) that cemented their opposition and ignited their efforts to educate people about the scope of this initiative.

In the 2015 election, Justin Trudeau's Liberals came to power promising to redress the injustices of the Canadian state's relationship with Indigenous peoples – a direct response to the "rock the Indigenous vote" campaign in many communities (Gerster 2019). However, the Liberal government quietly maintained the Harper plan. Despite promising a new relationship with Indigenous peoples, the Liberal government continues to support controversial resource extraction projects.

In response, Indigenous communities have mobilized. In August 2018, for example, the Federal Court of Appeal found that Canada did not adequately consult the six First Nations opposing the controversial Trans Mountain pipeline, running from Alberta to the west coast of British Columbia and, in a unanimous decision, quashed the pipeline approval.* However, both the federal and Alberta governments continued efforts to generate support for the project among Canadians, mobilizing discourses of economic rationality that justify resource extraction as a key driver of Canada's continued prosperity.

This is similar to what happened in Mexico in the early 1990s. In 1989, Mexico ratified the International Labor Organization 169 Convention. The convention legitimized the concept of free, prior, and informed consent that had been demanded by the global Indigenous movement (Sawyer and Gomez 2012). In order to meet NAFTA commitments, however, the Salinas government introduced a series of constitutional changes aimed at liberalizing Indigenous and peasants' control over their lands and other resources. Article 27 of the Mexican Constitution, for example, made it possible to buy land and fishing grounds and coastal land for aquaculture purposes. The Electricity Public Service Law was changed to enable wind energy development under the framework of a self-supply regime through which corporations became simultaneously users and generators of their own electricity. To synchronize national laws with the 169 Convention, in 1991 the federal government modified Article 4 of the constitution to recognize the "pluricultural" nature of the Mexican state and the right of Indigenous peoples to self-determination. A year later, the legal basis for free entry mining was also formally established in the Mexican Constitution, fully opening the mining sector to foreign investment (Tetreault 2016, 645). Since then, the Canadian mining industry has aggressively extended its presence throughout Mexico and Latin America. In subsequent developments, municipalities were prevented from imposing taxes on mining corporations, and limits to foreign investment in the industry were removed. With these changes, concession holders could even demand that land occupied by towns be vacated to facilitate their economic endeavours (Bacon 2013, 44).

Effectively, these legal changes produced a situation in which the recognized territorial jurisdiction of Indigenous peoples, national law, and NAFTA rules became dissonant. On the one hand, the federal government must now grant concessions to subsurface resources. On the

---

* Tsleil-Waututh Nation v. Canada (Attorney General), 2018 FCA 153 (CanLII), [2019] 2 FCR 3.

other, resource extraction cannot be performed without having access to the surface, which continues to be owned by Indigenous communities. As a result, territorial conflicts exploded.

Unlike Canada and the US, in Mexico the energy sector was controlled by the state and had constituted one of the central pillars of Mexican nationalism. This changed in December 2013, when then President Enrique Peña Nieto fast-tracked a reform package that included over 80 changes to the Mexican Constitution aimed at privatizing and providing foreign investors with access to the energy sector. Importantly, these modifications included the privatization of once state-controlled oil and electricity industries. These changes authorized the private sector to pursue oil and gas exploration and generate, transmit, and distribute electricity anywhere within the national territory. Although the law requires that the energy company first negotiate directly with property owners, it takes away the owners' rights to refuse land expropriation. Like the Harper government, President Peña Nieto justified these changes in the name of "better development." The changes were enthusiastically celebrated by the US energy industry and investors waiting to have access to these resources (Financier 2017; Harlow 2016).

Although neoliberalism has not figured centrally in discussions of economic development in the US, Indigenous participation in the economy was heralded as a way to build nationhood and self-determination in the early 1980s. The Leasing Mineral Act of 1920 had created the legal basis to increase resource extraction on public lands and reservation lands held in trust. In the context of the oil embargo of the Organization of Petroleum Exporting Countries (OPEC) and, specifically, with the Indian Mineral Development Act of 1982, members of Indigenous reservations gained the right to extract their own resources (Frantz 1999, 260). However, the state set significant limits to Indigenous peoples' ability to develop politically and economically. The search for minerals had played a significant role in the history of the colonization of the American West, and the pursuit of mineral and oil and gas resources, wind, solar, and biomass found on Indigenous peoples' lands had, once again, put pressure on these communities. In a 2011 report, the Revenue Watch Institute had warned that any long-term energy policy in the US had to include Indigenous communities as partners (Grogan, Morse, and Youpee-Roll 2011). However, in 2015, the McKeon National Defense Authorization Act was used to transform hundreds of thousands of acres of Indigenous land into private property. As was the case in Mexico, this dramatic change was not debated or voted on, but was realized through budget bills.

During his time in office, US President Donald Trump proposed privatizing Indigenous reservation lands, representing this move as an opportunity to ease restrictions on energy investment and gain access to oil-rich reserves (Pierce 2016). Although Indigenous communities have the usufruct right to the land, they do not own it. They can drill and extract resources, but they are subject to harsher regulations than those applied to private investors. Certainly, some communities welcomed the opportunity to transform 56-million acres of Indigenous land held in trust into private property; after all, privatization defines the terms in which Indigenous peoples can participate in social and economic life. From industry's perspective, privatization also ensures access to land and resources beyond the land itself, making it possible to deregulate drilling and the exploitation of coal reserves.

In both the US and Canada, governments have enlisted the support of members of the Indigenous business class to legitimize privatization. These alliances demonstrate the complexity of Indigenous peoples' positions regarding the future of their lands. While the Indigenous aspiration to participate as equal players in the market economy is a legitimate one, the question remains whether the terms of such participation enable the broader goal of self-determination (Pasternack 2015). According to Byrd et al., the recurring pattern of land dispossession is the Anglo settler colonial condition itself, which materializes in complex geographies of capital accumulation, violence, devaluation of Indigenous life, and property relations (Byrd et al. 2018).

Towards the End of Neoliberalism?

After nearly four decades, the move towards monopoly, financialization, land dispossession, racialization, predatory market practices, and recurrent global economic crises have highlighted neoliberalism's endurance, contradictions, and adaptability. In 2016, the election of Trump was simultaneously seen as reflective of the crisis of neoliberalism and as a radical departure from the standard operating principles of a democratic society. Trump did not invent white supremacy, but he celebrated it loudly and clearly. He did not create anti-immigration sentiments, but he certainly capitalized on them. Trump's presidency was represented as an exception, as an anomaly in US history. Such a representation, however, ignores the country's legacies. What made Trump different was that he did not refrain from promoting a white nationalist vision of the country. "Make America great again" was meaningful to disenchanted citizens experiencing a decline in their standard of living and who felt cheated by an economic system that no longer spreads wealth to its middle class. The flow of executive orders to ban Muslims from entering the country, revoke the Affordable Care Act, build a wall on the US-Mexican border, and approve the construction of two of the most controversial pipelines, the Keystone XL and Dakota Access pipelines, without consultation, signalled a shift. It hinted at a new configuration of forces, alliances, and relationships with the transnational capitalist class and reactionary political power.

The approval of pipelines, the fast-tracking of environmental reviews, and privatization were central to the American energy plan under the Trump administration. The goal was to eliminate obstacles to the exploitation of natural gas, coal, and oil. For example, in approving the construction of the controversial Dakota Access and Keystone XL pipelines, Trump not only overturned former President Barack Obama's decision to halt the projects, but also created expectations in Canada. Not surprisingly, the decision to advance the Keystone XL Pipeline from the Alberta oilsands to the Gulf Coast was celebrated by both the federal and Alberta governments, only to lament its cancellation under the newly elected Biden administration.

The tense renegotiation of NAFTA concluded in 2018 with the United States-Mexico-Canada Agreement (USMCA). This agreement resembles the previous one, but with some important changes. For example, it deepens investment in oil and gas, mining, and the energy sector. The legislation modified to fit free trade agreements can no longer be reversed. In addition, dispute resolution has now been extended to extractive industries, energy generation, and telecommunications. USMCA also establishes a general exception to protect Indigenous interests. For example, the provisions now stipulate a tax exception for Indigenous crafts and recognizes the importance of the environment for Indigenous peoples and their role in conservation. However, it also preserves NAFTA provisions that limit Indigenous interests only to handicrafts, harvesting of natural resources, and conservation (Barrera 2018; Schwartz 2018). Although these changes were celebrated for being progressive, in reality they fell short with regard to the proposal submitted by the International Inter-Tribal Trade and Investment Organization to the Canadian government in 2017. This proposal called for cooperation to build capacity and improve Indigenous peoples' living conditions in the three countries through engagement in cross-border trade. It also suggested stronger reservations to effectively protect Indigenous rights and their interest in land, free movement of Indigenous peoples across the Canada-US border, and greater protection of Indigenous cultural property and traditional knowledge (International Inter-Tribal Trade and Investment Organization 2017). UMSCA focused, instead, on expanding the scope of business.

In the spring of 2020, the COVID-19 pandemic created unprecedented global challenges. Although many economic activities stopped, natural resource extraction continued, spotlighting what was deemed essential and who was worth protecting. Despite Indigenous communities' efforts to shield themselves, ongoing large-scale resource extraction exacerbated the threat posed by COVID-19 as workers continued to move in and out of extraction sites. Governments also loosened regulations, environmental reporting, and consultation processes for industries. Simultaneously, though, the pandemic, Indigenous-led resistance, and calls for just transitions and greener, more egalitarian public investment seem to have gained currency.

American President Joe Biden came to power in the middle of an economic and political disaster in the US. Moving away from his predecessor, Biden campaigned on the promise of a Green New Deal for meeting the challenges of climate change. He recognized that the US needs to "embrace greater ambition on an epic scale to meet the scope of this challenge" and that the "environment and our economy are completely and totally connected" (Biden, nd). Biden quickly advanced a temporary expansion of the social safety net and proposed more climate spending than any other American president. His American Job Plan included investment in clean energy and prioritized climate change mitigation. Biden also promised to make US electricity production carbon-free by 2035 and to have the country achieve net zero emissions by 2050.

Emulating Biden, Prime Minister Trudeau has also taken steps towards climate change mitigation. He announced that Canada will enhance its emissions reduction target to below 2005 levels by 2030. He has highlighted the importance of working with other global leaders to address climate change while creating growth and improving the well-being of all people. Similarly, Mexico is expected to meet specific targets by 2040.

These changes would appear to suggest a move away from resource extraction and towards a greener economy. Climate change is, no doubt, the greatest challenge we face as a global community. Climate change also represents the greatest contemporary economic opportunity. Alliances among government, civil society, and corporations have been key to adopting green technologies and decarbonization. However, neither the development of renewable energy nor greener technologies and decarbonization occur in a vacuum. The latter require access to strategic raw materials such as lithium and other rare minerals. Almost immediately after taking office, Biden pledged to address the country's strategic vulnerability on critical materials (United States Secretary of Defense, 2022). The expected growth in solar panels, wind turbines, electric vehicles, and rechargeable batteries will, no doubt, increase demand for metals and minerals needed to produce green technologies.

This is the important caveat to climate change. In the Global North, governments' efforts to secure critical materials and transition to renewable energy have uncomfortable echoes of past energy control. Actions to transition to a low carbon economy not only manifest in securing sources within the boundaries of the state but also abroad. For example, the Biden administration expressed concern regarding Mexican President Andrés Manuel López Obrador's proposal to limit private investment in the renewable energy industry. As noted earlier, USMCA opened Mexico's energy sector to foreign investment. In a visit to Mexico, the US Secretary of Energy affirmed the need for Mexico to maintain and enhance open and competitive markets and to develop its renewable energy for export (US Mission to Mexico, 2022). This, in my mind, not only highlights that energy transitions are never just about solving the problems of our time but also the transnational, unequal power relations and contexts in which they unfold.

Canada's continuous exploitation of natural resources within its borders couples with the vigour with which it controls mining activities abroad. The Mining for Clean Energy report, for example, highlights this country's rich deposits of 14 of 19 metals and minerals needed to produce solar energy (Mining Association of Canada). Yet these domestic riches are seemingly insufficient, as Canadian firms continue to have a stronghold in global mining. What kind of energy transitions are envisioned when land dispossession remains a continuity? Scholars have warned of the high social, environmental, and political costs of the new rush to secure rare minerals needed for decarbonization (Riofrancos 2020) and energy transition (Altamirano-Jiménez 2017; 2020; Dunlap 2019; Howe and Boyer 2015). Extractive industries have been fraught with social, political, and environmental conflicts and have come under scrutiny for their connection to human rights abuses, land dispossession, violence, environmental contamination, and exploitative working conditions. There is a tension between the need to address climate change and capital accumulation, raising the question of how decarbonization will be achieved and at what cost. Importantly, it requires us to reflect on the imperative of capital accumulation, who benefits, and who bears the burden of protecting the environment.

Indigenous Refusal on Turtle Island

Audra Simpson argues that if there is a structure of settler colonialism that is identifiable through time, there is also a structure of refusal. Refusals are symptoms of the structure of colonial power manifested in governance practices, policies, and the manufacturing of consent affecting the everyday lives of Indigenous peoples (Simpson 2017, 21). Refusal is a political stance, a theory, and a practice. The Indigenous refusal to die, to let go of their sense of collective self-determination, and to consent to dispossession expose the continuous operation of the colonial structure.

In Mexico, the beginning of NAFTA and the legal changes to accommodate it were marked by the Zapatista uprising. USMCA and Mexican president López Obrador are, once again, confronting Indigenous refusal of resource extraction and the expansion of economic zones in the Tehuantepec Isthmus and Oaxaca, as well as the development of the Mayan Train that would traverse six Mexican states, and many other mega development projects. In his first speech in Congress, President López Obrador said, "We will do everything we can to abolish this neoliberal regime" (Webber, 2018). However, his plans to intensify resource extraction and development in Indigenous territories are, in fact, consistent with the consolidation and deepening of neoliberalism. In enacting their right to say no, Indigenous and Zapatista communities have turned away from the state, generating and embodying everyday practices that act upon their own legal traditions and communal practices. In doing so, they have declared their territories free of mining and other extractive processes. By refusing, Indigenous communities have made clear that it does not matter who is in power when the laws, the rules, and the racial ideologies that make colonial dispossession possible are kept intact.

Besides USMCA, the controversial wall that Trump promised to build along the Mexico-US border not only sparked opposition, heated exchanges, and diplomatic tensions between the two countries, but also alienated Indigenous peoples. The Kumeyaay and Kickapoo, among others, occupy land along the US-Mexico border and have enacted practices to oppose state border control. The Tohono O'odham, a nation whose reservation spans 75 miles on the US-Mexico border, opposed the construction of the wall. They accused Trump of signing an executive order without consulting the Indigenous peoples affected. The Tohono O'odham have long struggled with the militarization of a border that divides their traditional lands, which stretch south to Sonora, Mexico (Hamilton 2017). Narratives supporting the proposed wall not only erase the border as a product of the US invasion of Mexico but also disregard its everyday effects on people and communities. In addition, such narratives conceal the fact that free trade agreements have not only failed to stop migration but exacerbated the need for Mexican nationals to pursue economic opportunities in the US. Dispossession is not only about land and resource grabbing but also about the bodies that are dispossessed, displaced, or rendered irrelevant to the economy. Jody Byrd notes that in a world of increasing capital accumulation and environmental changes, the influx of people of the Global South into the Global North reflects the fact that dispossession involves being forced to move (2011). While settler states are concerned with the influx of people and attempt to contain them, Indigenous motion is survival and an active refusal of the borders that cut across past and present Indigenous roads and routes throughout Turtle Island.

In both Canada and the US, current struggles against resource extraction are also located in a history of refusals that seek to disrupt forms of capital mobility and accumulation (Coulthard 2014, 35). Idle No More, for example, brought people together in towns and cities across Canada and other parts of North America. The images of Indigenous peoples drumming and round dancing in malls, demonstrating, and taking direct actions disrupted both the economy and hegemonic assumptions about the disappearance of Indigenous peoples. Importantly, Idle No More also forged new forms of relationality and embodied practices, through which people are constituting alternative ways of living together.

In 2016, Indigenous nations signed the continent-wide Treaty Alliance to oppose five pipelines awaiting approval, including the Enbridge Northern Gateway, Kinder Morgan's Trans Mountain Pipeline, and the Keystone XL Pipeline (McSheffrey 2016). Grand Chief Steward Phillips from the Union of British Columbia Chiefs noted, "Based on our sovereignty, inherent right to self-determination, we have collectively decided that we will pick up our sacred responsibilities to the land, waters, and people. We come in solidarity to protect our territory from the predations of big oil interests" (McSheffrey 2016). The Tiny House Warriors opposing the Trans Mountain Pipeline also embody refusal. Acting upon their responsibilities and asserting Secwepemc laws and jurisdiction they strategically build tiny houses along the 518 kilometres of pipeline (Secwepemcul'ecw Assembly 2018).

Similarly, in the US, the fight against the Dakota Access Pipeline that would have been built through the waters of the Sioux tribe reservation, garnered support for Standing Rock beyond North America. In 2015, the Standing Rock Sioux Tribe, operating as a sovereign nation, passed a resolution opposing the Dakota Access Pipeline for posing a threat to their very survival as a people. Through their struggle, this community has exposed that land seizure involves the dispossession of water and interconnected waterways. Indeed, "water is life" has become a ubiquitous slogan across the hemisphere, reactivating water as a terrain of struggle and an agent of decolonization. Indigenous land and water defenders link Indigenous bodies, water, and land within a network of life that refuses to disappear (Yazie and Baldy 2018, 1). These are refusals that embody a vision of relationality and interdependence that stands in sharp contrast to the devaluation of Indigenous life and the dispossession of Indigenous land.

Conclusion

Inspired by Janine Brodie's analytical method of mapping the historical and contingent relations between the market and state forms (2015; 2010; 2006), I have argued that any examination of neoliberalism requires that we pay attention to the broader historical connection with colonialism. Racialization and land dispossession are continuous, though their means of expression may shift. By highlighting the connection between the structure of colonialism and the ways in which resource extraction is expanded, I complicated discussions of settler colonialism as a process exclusively concerned with the state and land acquisition. I emphasized the ways in which settler states move along imperialist imperatives for the purposes of capital accumulation. In doing so, I argue that neoliberalism is a moment of a much larger colonial trajectory of capital accumulation. Whether or not it is morphing into something else is, in my mind, irrelevant if the colonial structure remains.

If there is a colonial structure, there is Indigenous refusal both historically and at present. Indigenous peoples refused and continue to refuse colonialism; they continue to defend their territories and different ways of inhabiting the world that do not rest upon the devaluation of Indigenous life and the dispossession of land. Indigenous refusals, however, are not only about rejecting natural resource extraction, dispossession, or capital accumulation, but rather about building alternative Indigenous life projects that draw on Indigenous legal traditions, stories, and the practices of being with one another in reciprocal, affective relationships.

REFERENCES

Altamirano-Jiménez, Isabel. 2020. "Possessing Land, Wind and Water in the Isthmus of Tehuantepec, Oaxaca," *Australian Feminist Studies* 35 (106): 321–35. https://doi.org/10.1080/08164649.2021.1919989.
– 2017. "The Sea Is Our Bread: Interrupting Green Neo-liberalism," *Marine Policy* 80: 28–34. http://doi.org/10.1016/j.marpol.2017.01.015.
– 2013. *Indigenous Encounters with Neoliberalism. Place, Women and the Environment in Canada and Mexico*. Vancouver: UBC Press.

– 2004 "North American First Peoples: Slipping up into Market Citizenship?" *Citizenship Studies* 8 (4): 349–65. https://doi.org/10.1080/1362102052000316963.

Bacon, David. 2013. *The Right to Stay Home: How US Policy Drives Mexican Migration*. Beacon Press.

Bargh, Maria. 2011. The Triumph of Maori Entrepreneurs or Diverse Economies? *Aboriginal Policy Studies* 1 (3): 59–69. https://doi.org/10.5663/aps.v1i3.12560.

Barrera, Jorge. 2018. "New Trade Agreement a 'Step Up' from NAFTA on Indigenous Rights," CBC, October 1, 2018. https://www.cbc.ca/news/indigenous/usmca-trade-deal-indigenous-rights-1.4846073.

Bhandar, Brenna. 2018. *Colonial Lives of Property. Land, Law and Racial Regimes of Ownership*. Durham: Duke University Press.

Biden, Joe. n.d. "The Biden Plan for a Green Energy Revolution and Environmental Justice." https://joebiden.com/climate-plan/.

Blackstock, Cindy. 2015. "Should Governments Be Above the Law? The Canadian Human Rights Tribunal on First Nations Child Welfare." *Children Australia* 40 (2): 95–104. http://doi.org/10.1017/cha.2015.6.

Brodie, Janine. 2015. "Constituting Constitutions: The Patriation Moment." In *The Patriation Negotiations*, edited by Lois Harder and Steve Patten, 25–46. Vancouver: University of British Columbia Press.

– 2010. "Globalization, Canadian Family Policy and the Omissions of Neoliberalism." *North Carolina Law Review* 88 (5): 1559–92.

– 2006. "North American Deep Integration: Canadian Perspectives." *Asia-Pacific Panorama* 4 (1): 1–25.

Brown, Kendal W. 2012. *A History of Mining in Latin America: From the Colonial Era to the Present*. Albuquerque: University of New Mexico Press.

Byrd, Jodi et al. 2018. "Predatory Value: Economies of Dispossession and Disturbed Relationalities." *Social Text* 36 (2): 1–18. https://doi.org/10.1215/01642472-4362325.

Byrd, Jodi et al. 2011. *The Transit of Empire*. Minneapolis: University of Minnesota Press.

Canada. 2012. "Economic Action Plan. Jobs, Growth, and Long-Term Prosperity." https://www.budget.gc.ca/2012/plan/pdf/Plan2012-eng.pdf.

Canada. 2009. "Bill C-63: First Nations Certainty of Land Title Act." https://lop.parl.ca/staticfiles/PublicWebsite/Home/ResearchPublications/LegislativeSummaries/PDF/40-2/c63-e.pdf.

Canada. Department of Indian and Northern Affairs Canada. 2010. "Family Homes on Reserves and Matrimonial Interests or Rights Act." laws-lois.justice.gc.ca/eng/acts/F-1.2/.

Clogg, Jessica. 2013. "Modernizing BC's Free Entry Mining Laws for a Vibrant, Sustainable Mining Sector." *Fair Mining Collaborative*. http://wcel.org/sites/default/files/publications/WCEL_Mining_report_web.pdf.

Coulthard, Glen Sean. 2014. *Red Skin, White Masks: Rejecting the Colonial Politics of Recognition*. Minneapolis: University of Minnesota Press.

Dunlap, Alexander. 2019. *Renewing Destruction: Wind Energy Development, Conflict and Resistance in a Latin American Context*. London: Rowman and Littlefield.

Egan, Brian, and Jessica Place. 2013. "Minding the Gaps: Property, Geography, and Indigenous Peoples in Canada." *Geoforum* 44: 129–38. http://doi.org/10.1016/j.geoforum.2012.10.003.

Financier Worldwide Magazine. 2017. "Investment Opportunities in the Mexican Oil Industry," September 2017. https://www.financierworldwide.com/investment-opportunities-in-the-mexican-oil-industry#.XR4nOyMrIy4.

Frantz, Klaus. 1999. *Indian Reservations in the United States. Territory, Sovereignty, and Socioeconomic Change*, Chicago: University of Chicago Press.

Gerster, Jane. 2019. "Trudeau's Liberals Benefited from Record Indigenous Voter Turnout in 2015. Can They Again?" *Global News*, September 14, 2019. https://globalnews.ca/news/5887701/indigenous-voter-turnout/.

Grogan, Maura, Rebecca Morse, and April Youpee-Roll. 2011. *Native American Lands and Natural Resource Development*. New York: Natural Resource Governance Institute.

Hamilton, Dawchelle. 2017. "Trump's Border Wall Could Carve Path Through Native American Lands." *NBC News*, September 16, 2017.

Harlow, Simon. 2016. "Why Mexico's Oil Reform is a Huge Opportunity for Investors." *Oil Price*, November 21, 2016. https://oilprice.com/Energy/Energy-General/Why-Mexicos-Oil-Reform-Is-A-Huge-Opportunity-For-Investors.html#.

Hoogeveen, Dawn. 2015. "Subsurface Property, Free Entry Mineral Staking and Settler Colonialism in Canada" *Antipode* 47 (1): 121–38. https://doi.org/10.1111/anti.12095

Howe, Cymene, and Dominic Boyer. 2016. "Aeolian Extractivism and Community Wind in Southern Mexico." *Public Culture* 28 (2): 215–35. http://doi.org/10.1215/08992363-3427427.

International Inter-Tribal Trade and Investment Organization. 2017. "Submission by the International Inter-Tribal Trade and Investment Organization to the Government of Canada for the Renegotiation and Modernization of NAFTA." IITIO. https://iitio.org/nafta/.

Lameman, Crystal. 2014. "Right to Self-Determination." World Oceans Day Anti Tar Sands Pipeline Rally. June 12, 2014. https://www.youtube.com/watch?v=NGsVfWlur3Q.

Lethabo King, Tiffany. 2019. *The Black Shoal. Offshore Formations of Black and Native Studies*. Durham: Duke University Press.

Lewis, Johnny, Joseph Hoover, and Debra MacKenzie. 2017. "Mining and Environmental Health Disparities in Native American Communities."

Current Environmental Health Reports 4 (2): 130–41. https://doi.org/10.1007 %2Fs40572-017-0140-5.

Lindroth, Marjo. 2016. "The Biopolitics of Resilient Indigeneity and the Radical Gamble of Resistance." *International Policies, Practices and Discourses* 4 (2): 130–45. https://doi.org/10.1080/21693293.2015.1094243.

Melamed, Jodi. 2015. "Racial Capitalism." *Critical Ethnic Studies* 1 (1): 76–85. https://doi.org/10.5749/jcritethnstud.1.1.0076.

McLahan, Stephane. 2014. "Health Study in Fort Chipewyan Full Report." https://www.dropbox.com/sh/nu0lftnz521nm46/AABXa8S3TJOWSs _cH2js3b3ua.

McSheffrey, Elizabeth. 2016. "First Nations across North America Sign Treaty Alliance against the Oil Sands." *The National Observer*, September 22, 2016. http://www.nationalobserver.com/2016/09/22/news/first-nations -across-north-america-sign-treaty-alliance-against-oilsands.

Mining Association of Canada. n.d. "Canada's Mined Materials Provide the Building Blocks for Green Technology." https://mining.ca/mining -stories/canadas-mined-materials-provide-the-building-blocks-for-green -technology/.

Moreton-Robinson, Aileen. 2017. *The White Possessive. Property, Power, and Indigenous Sovereignty*. Minneapolis: University of Minnesota Press.

Morgensen, Scott. 2011. "The Biopolitics of Settler Colonialism: Right Here, Right Now." *Settler Colonial Studies* 1 (1): 52–76. https://doi.org/10.1080 /2201473X.2011.10648801.

Native Youth Sexual Health Network and Women's Earth Alliance. 2016. "Violence on the Land, Violence on Our Bodies. Building an Indigenous Response to Environmental Violence." http://landbodydefense.org /uploads/files/VLVBReportToolkit2016.pdf.

Pasternack, Shiri. 2015. "How Capitalism Will Save Colonialism: The Privatization of Reserve Lands in Canada." *Antipode* 47 (1): 179–96. https:// doi.org/10.1111/anti.12094.

Perea, Juan F. 2011. "Fulfilling Manifest Destiny: Conquest, Race, and the Insular Cases," In *Foreign in a Domestic Sense: Puerto Rico, American Expansion, and the Constitution*, edited by Christina Duffy Burnett and Burke Marshall, 140–66. Durham: Duke University Press.

Perreault, 2014. "What Kind of Governance for What Kind of Equity? Towards a Theorization of Justice in Water Governance." *Water International* 39 (2): 233–45. https://doi.org/10.1080/02508060.2014.886843.

Pierce, Charles. 2016. "Will Trump Years Benefit Native American Tribes?" *Squire*, December 6, 2016. https://www.esquire.com/news-politics /politics/news/a51289/trump-native-american-lands-energy/.

Riofrancos, Thea. 2020. *Resource Radicals: From Petro-Nationalism to Post-Extractivism in Ecuador*. Durham: Duke University Press.

Sawyer, Suzana, and Edmund Terence Gomez, eds. 2012. *The Politics of Resource Extraction: Indigenous Peoples, Multinational Corporations, and the State*. New York: Palgrave Macmillan.

Schmidt, Jeremy. 2022. "Dispossession by Municipalization: Property, Pipelines, and Divisions of Power in Settler Colonial Canada." *Environment and Planning C: Politics and Space*. https://doi.org/10.1177%2F23996544211065654.

Schwartz, Emma. 2018. "Unpacking Equity: The Fight for Indigenous Rights under USMCA." *The Public Policy and Governance Review*, November 28, 2018. https://ppgreview.ca/2018/11/28/unpacking-equity-the-fight-for -indigenous-rights-under-usmca/.

Secwepemcul'ecw Assembly. 2018. "Tiny House Warriors Reclaim Land, Block Trans Mountain Expansion Pipeline Route." July 11, 2018. https://www .secwepemculecw.org/.

Sexton, Jay. 2011. *The Monroe Doctrine. Empire and Nation in Nineteenth Century America*. New York: Hill and Wang.

Simpson, Audra. 2017. "The Ruse of Consent and the Anatomy of 'Refusal': Cases from Indigenous North America and Australia." *Postcolonial Studies* 20 (1): 18–33. https://doi.org/10.1080/13688790.2017.1334283.

Stanley, Anne. 2016. "Resilient Settler Colonialism: Responsible Resource Development, 'Flow-Through' Financing, and the Risk Management of Indigenous Sovereignty in Canada." *Environment and Planning A: Economy and Space* 48 (12): 2422–42. https://doi.org/10.1177%2F0308518X16660352.

Starblanket, Gina. 2019. "The Numbered Treaties and the Politics of Incoherency." *Canadian Journal of Political Science* 52 (3): 443–59. https://doi .org/10.1017/S0008423919000027.

Strakosch, Eizabeth. 2015. *Neoliberal Indigenous Policy: Settler Colonialism and the "Post-Welfare" State*. London: Palgrave Macmillan.

Tetreault, Darcy. 2016. "Free-Market Mining in Mexico." *Critical Sociology* 42 (4–5): 643–59. https://doi.org/10.1177%2F0896920514540188.

U.S. Mission to Mexico. 2022. Statement by US Secretary of Energy Jennifer M. Granholm on Travel to Mexico City, Mexico. January 22, 2022. https:// www.energy.gov/articles/statement-us-secretary-energy-jennifer -m-granholm-travel-mexico-city-mexico.

United States Secretary of Defense. 2022. "Securing Defense-Critical Supply Chains: An Action Plan Developed in Response to President Biden's Executive Order 14017." February 2022. https://media.defense.gov/2022 /Feb/24/2002944158/-1/-1/1/DOD-EO-14017-REPORT-SECURING -DEFENSE-CRITICAL-SUPPLY-CHAINS.PDF.

Veraccini, Lorenzo. 2010. *Settler Colonialism. A Theoretical Overview*. Cambridge: Palgrave Macmillan.

Voyles, Traci B. 2015. *Wastelanding: Legacies of Uranium Mining in Navajo Country*. Minneapolis: University of Minnesota Press.

Webber, Jude. 2018. "Mexico: AMLO's 'People Power' Rattles the Markets. *Financial Times*, November 24, 2018. https://www.ft.com/content /8e1a0d40-ee36-11e8-89c8-d36339d835c0.

Wiebe, Sarah. 2016. *Everyday Exposure: Indigenous Mobilizations and Environmental Justice in Canada's Chemical Valley*. Vancouver: UBC Press.

Wolfe, Patrick. 2006. "Settler Colonialism and the Elimination of the Native." *Journal of Genocide Research* 8 (4): 387–409. https://doi.org/10.1080 /14623520601056240.

Yazie, Melanie K., and Cutcha Risling Baldy. 2018. "Introduction: Indigenous Peoples and the Politics of Water." *Decolonization: Indigeneity, Education & Society* 7 (1): 1–18.

Young, Nathan. 2008. "Radical Neoliberalism in British Columbia: Remaking Rural Geographies." *Canadian Journal of Sociology* 33 (1): 1–36. http://doi.org/10.29173/cjs1525.

PART TWO

Neoliberalism Meets Policy

4 Lean on Everything? Lean Management's Awkward Place in Neoliberalism

JUSTIN LEIFSO

Introduction

In graduate seminars and meetings with her students, Janine Brodie was fond of referring to a quote from the preface to the 1982 edition of Milton Friedman's *Capitalism and Freedom*. "Only a crisis – actual or perceived – produces real change," Friedman wrote, adding that "when that crisis occurs, the actions that are taken depend on the ideas that are lying around" (Friedman and Friedman 1982, ix). Straightforward and succinct, the quote reveals much about the deliberate political project of neoliberal scholars such as Friedman and Hayek (see Mirowski and Plehwe 2009; Stedman-Jones 2012). More than that, though, it serves as an entry point for the students' lesson on how ideas and practices are deployed and redeployed as components of shifting forms of governance. The lesson that follows typically involves a discussion about how governance and the Canadian state are inexorably tied to crises and state actors "groping" for solutions to those crises. The lesson is drawn from Brodie's own work, where she has offered an insightful interpretation of Canada's political economic history. Explaining the origins of Canada's National Policy, Brodie observes that, after Great Britain moved towards free trade in the nineteenth century and dismantled the set of preferential policies in place to prop up the political economies of its colonies, "the colonial elite searched 'gropingly' for a new development strategy" (Brodie 1990, 92). This search led to a series of policy interventions under the umbrella of John A. MacDonald's National Policy, or what Brodie refers to as the First National Policy (Brodie 1990, 97–105). When the era of the First National Policy came to an end in the 1920s, she writes, "state actors would once again have to 'grope' towards a national development strategy" (Brodie 1990, 135), a process that would be repeated in the face of crisis in the 1970s (Brodie

1990, 182). In times of crisis, decision-makers cast about for solutions in the form of ideas, necessarily grasping those that fall within their ambit. In her conclusion to this volume, she approaches the simultaneous social, political, economic, and cultural catastrophes of COVID-19 with the same analytical focus on change, calling into question the presumptive eulogies for neoliberalism while also remaining vigilant in watching for what comes next.

In this chapter, I expand on Brodie's pedagogy and scholarship by exploring how ideas and practices are taken up and deployed as part of emerging and shifting forms of rule. Like John Clarke's approach, I am interested in the contingency of ideas, even when bounded by a prevailing conception of governing, such as neoliberalism. More particularly, I explore how Lean Management (Lean), a manufacturing and management approach with its roots in post-war Japan, came to be "lying around," waiting to be found and deployed by decision-makers as part of assemblages of neoliberal technologies. I examine what the genealogy of Lean, from Toyota's shop floors to operations in various agencies of the contemporary Canadian state, says about neoliberal rationality, its corresponding forms of rule, and their ability to shape-shift and morph by adopting and deploying practices and technologies that, while complementary, have histories quite separate from neoliberalism.

Lean Bureaucracies

Lean is endemic in Canadian public bureaucracies. Lean practices and initiatives are present in the federal government, each provincial government, the administration of each of the country's twenty largest cities, in universities, hospitals, schools, and non-profits. It is exceedingly common for expertise in Lean, including Lean iterations such as "agility," or the various watered-down practices of Lean such as "continuous improvement" to be included in the "required competencies" section of public service job advertisements.

Notably, Saskatchewan offers North America's primary exemplar of Lean's introduction into state institutions. Between 2005 and 2015, the province deployed Lean into its health care system and provincial bureaucracy in a thoroughgoing and intensive application of public sector Lean. Following a serendipitous visit to Seattle by a regional health executive from the province, Lean emerged in the province and grew under the stewardship of Lean consultants drawn from a sprawling and loosely connected network of experts. Before the initiative fell out of favour (and was subsequently mobilized in other jurisdictions), thousands of public servants and health practitioners in the province were trained, practices were implemented, and existing institutional infrastructure was reconfigured for the sole purpose of eliminating waste.

Lean's emergence in bureaucratic spaces is plainly consistent with neoliberal rationality and, in particular, the problematization of the state and public institutions that underwrote the work of Von Mises (1944) and the public choice scholars (i.e., Niskanen 1971; Buchanan 1977). This lineage of neoliberal thought casts public bureaucratic institutions in the role of hopelessly inferior cousins to their private sector counterparts. Lacking a price motive, public institutions are presumptively inefficient since their operations are not exposed to the disciplining forces of the market. In Saskatchewan, for example, Lean was deployed as a solution to the governing Saskatchewan Party's vexing problem of meeting a 2007 election promise to reverse previous cuts to health care while delivering more efficient government. Lean offered the chance to realize this paradoxical platform by allowing Premier Brad Wall to pledge to "do more with less" by eliminating the inefficiencies that his neoliberal ideology posited as endemic in bureaucracies. As the Saskatchewan case shows, Lean's emergence as a technology of neoliberal governance is not particularly surprising (Leifso 2021).

It would be, however, both an empirical and theoretical mistake to suggest that Lean is *merely* a neoliberal technology or neoliberal project. Brodie's lessons remind us to resist the urge to adopt essentialist, sweeping categorizations without an appreciation for nuance. As such, I now turn to telling the story of how Lean's genealogy intersected with that of neoliberalism. I use Miller and Rose's (2008) concept of problematization to bring structure to the story, tracing the history of Lean being offered as a solution to a shifting series of problems, mobilized in sites where its focus on efficiency was understood to be a panacea for whatever ailed specific epistemic or industrial settings. Ultimately, I argue that the emergence of Lean in public sector institutions speaks to neoliberalism's extraordinary adaptability. Drawing from Brown (2019), the editors of this volume have pointed out that neoliberalism in recent years has taken on new nationalist and populist components that may, on their surface, seem inconsistent with neoliberalism's technical, economic veneer. Surely, there are many more examples of "nonneoliberal" things being used in "neoliberal ways." I use the concept of assemblages to offer one account of how this takes place, arguing that at any point, dominant rationalities and forms of rule like neoliberalism can inherit, abandon, redeploy, and reform a seemingly limitless number of discourses and practices such as Lean as part of a shifting constellation of what we understand to be "neoliberal."

The Problem of Japan's Success

Miller and Rose's (2008) concept of problematization provides a useful approach to understanding change. In short, they describe a cycle of identifying problems and finding solutions. For Miller and Rose, "the history of government might well be written as a history of problematizations, in which politicians, intellectuals, philosophers, medics, military men, feminists, and philanthropists have measured the real against the ideal and found it wanting" (Rose and Miller 2008, 61). Equally important to identifying problems is the process by which solutions to them are sought and implemented. Li (2007) describes this process as "rendering technical." Problems are stripped of socio-political context, generating technical and scientific solutions that are then available for implementation in settings across a diverse landscape of contexts.

Here, I use problematization to help trace the genealogy of Lean before it was picked up by states and deployed as part of neoliberalizing reforms. The story begins in post-war Japan and the reaction by North American industry and popular culture to Japanese industrial and commercial success. By the 1970s, Japanese industry had become the envy of their competitors. In 1962, *The Economist* ran a story entitled "Consider Japan," laying out the argument that the economic growth being experienced in Japan was only a sign of things to come. Indeed, between 1946 and 1976, the Japanese economy grew exponentially, eventually accounting "for about 10 per cent of the world's economic activity though occupying only 0.3 per cent of the world's surface and supporting about 3 per cent of the world's population" (Johnson 1982, 7). The growth of Japan's political economy was extraordinary; as political economist Sven Steinmo (2010, 108) remarks, "Japan grew from a country devastated by nuclear war and firebombed cities in 1945 to the second richest country in the world in less than 40 years."

In North America, Japan's post-war success was viewed, as the *Harvard Business Review* described at the time, as "both an impressive and puzzling achievement" (Drucker 1981). This response took form in different ways depending on context but reflected a collective concern with the state of domestic industry in an increasingly global economy. For North Americans, Japan's success became alarming when Japanese corporations began acquiring assets that they understood to be symbols of their own success, culture, or exceptionalism. Radio City Music Hall, MGM Pictures, 7-Eleven, and physical landmarks such as hotels and skyscrapers, provoked special consternation. In popular culture, the trend of Japanese takeovers and expansion of corporate Japan into the United States was cast into the future, a future in which Japanese business interests dominated the American private sector. Motion pictures such as *Die Hard* and *Back to the Future II* included references to the rise of Japanese business. Popular novels, including Michael Crichton's *Rising Sun* (1992) and Tom Clancy's *Debt of Honor* (1994) referenced the apparently increasing likelihood of Japan's eventual takeover of the United States (Fandino 2016). In the press, the perceived rise of Japanese corporations and their dominance over their North American counterparts played itself out through bleak predictions. Local dailies bemoaned that Japan was "buying" the US with "our money" in what amounted to an "economic Pearl Harbour" (Harvey 1988). Others warned of the "Japanning of America today" (Schweisenberg 1982). Sentiments in national publications were less transparently parochial but still alarmed over the prospects of the Japanese takeover. A columnist in the *Washington Post* remarked that the "Japanese now own almost everything in America" (Kornheiser 1990).

Books appeared to warn of the existential threat of Japan's emergence. Pascale and Athos (1982, 201) cautioned that the reputation of American industry "increasingly weakened even while our self-satisfaction remained the same." Ouchi's (1981, 12) damnation was more severe: "Japan has somehow managed to maintain a work ethic," while their North American counterparts had "become soft, lazy, and feel entitled to the good life without earning it." Pegels (1984) lamented that "Japan's industrial might has passed the West," going on to predict that it "appears that Western industry will have to be satisfied with the second-place position it now holds." Most famously, Vogel's *Japan as Number One* (1984) issued dire warnings, suggesting that it was "highly unlikely" that Americans, Canadians, and others in the West would be able to catch up to Japan in the "foreseeable future," but with "total effort," their manufacturers would be able to "remain reasonably close to Japan." Without such "total effort," Vogel warned, those Western producers would "soon discover that the gap between themselves and Japan in productivity [would] widen even more" (1984, 13–14).

Depictions of a surely Japanese future and the press's inflammatory language reflected and amplified public opinion at the time. By 1990 anti-Japanese sentiment began to rival anticommunism in the United States (Heale 2009). Industrial areas dependent upon manufacturing were especially prone to ugly demonstrations. In Michigan – long dependent on the auto sector – Japanese vehicles were vandalized, Detroit parking lots sported signs that said "no Japanese cars allowed," and an Asian-American man was beaten to death by two white unemployed auto workers (Heale 2009, 24). Japan was "presented as a dangerous 'other' to 'the West' on the basis of its alleged differences from a normative but vaguely defined Western model, thus demonstrating the endurance of negative Western stereotypes of the 'Orient'" (Morris 2011, 3).

While these passionate condemnations of the "Japanese Miracle" – often steeped in racialized xenophobia – served as a form of problematization, broad distrust of another country's success is not a specific enough problem to solve through technical fixes. For the introduction of operationalizable, practical technologies to be possible, a more specific and well-defined problem needed to be identified. In the United States and Canada, identifying the precise secret to Japan's success became a paramount priority. Political science was, unsurprisingly, searching for state-centred answers to the question of the "Japanese Miracle," with Chalmers Johnson's influential *MITI and the Japanese Miracle* (1984) setting the stage for a spirited academic debate about the role of the "developmental state." Business leaders, meanwhile, were much more interested in understanding the practices that Japanese companies were using to produce high-quality goods so efficiently. One executive argued that in the coming decade, the key issue would be how their businesses "respond to one fact – the Japanese know how to manage better than we do" (quoted in Ouchi 1981, 3). The executive's peers apparently agreed, and North American companies in the 1980s and 1990s diligently studied the practices of their Japanese counterparts. General Motors, Ford, Chrysler, Hewlett-Packard, General Electric, Westinghouse, IBM, and others began focussing on understanding what made the rise of corporate Japan possible (Ouchi 1981, 291). Convinced that Japanese corporations had captured the market on the means to more efficient manufacturing, these representatives of industry looked for "the secret" to Japan's success.

As academics, engineers, and executives studied the differences in manufacturing techniques, they identified a problem that was more refined than the broader attacks on Japan's rise: the practices of North American industry were inefficient, inflexible, and uncompetitive in the face of their Japanese counterparts. One set of researchers "concluded that the auto industries of North America and Europe were relying on techniques little changed from Henry Ford's mass-production system and that these techniques were simply not competitive with a new set of ideas pioneered by the Japanese companies" (Womack, Jones, and Roos 1990, 3). Auto manufacturing in North America was characterized by bulky, large-scale, mass production that had been innovated in Detroit by Ford and his rivals before being exported throughout the world as the standard model for auto manufacturing. This model "buffered" against risk: large inventory supplies mitigated the possibility of parts shortages. Assembly lines had "built in buffers" to ensure that production continued if equipment broke down. And "legions of utility workers were kept on the payroll to buffer unexpected periods of high absenteeism, repair areas were huge in order to buffer against poor quality, and so on" (Krafcik 1988, 43–4). Such large-scale redundancies, according to the researchers, meant that the operations remained stale and unable to innovate in a way that would allow them to remain competitive. Analysts (e.g., Pegels 1984, Alston 1986) often focussed on particular dynamics of Japanese manufacturing, including inventory, human resource management, and the attitude of Japanese managers and workers as key factors in the rise of Japanese industry.

This characterization of the "Japan problem" was much different from the version of problematization that had been offered by politicians and the mainstream press. The new articulation of the problem did not reflect a dangerous foe utilizing unfair tactics. Instead, the manufacturing and economic malaise being felt in the 1980s was a symptom of an inability to compete with a more efficient and innovative counterpart. North American industry was inflexible, inefficient, and bloated. In a word, it was *bureaucratic*. Indeed, while the problematization of North American industry was specific to the practices that were taking place on factory floors, it echoed those neoliberal critiques being launched at state institutions. In Canada, one Royal Commission bemoaned that the federal government had grown bloated, and state institutions had "been under little compulsion" to ensure that public funds "were being employed with the greatest possible efficiency and effectiveness" (Canada 1979, 24). Seven years later, another Royal Commission warned of "big government" (Canada 1985, 24), which was characterized by a byzantine collection of "countless subsidies, guaranteed loans, quotas, tax provisions, technical and research assistance, environmental regulations, and other instruments and policies too numerous to mention" (Canada 1985, 26). The critiques facing North American industry undeniably resembled those facing state institutions. Industry, like government, was bloated, inflexible, and inefficient. Clearly, that was a problem.

Finding Solutions: The Toyota Production System

With a problem identified, it was now possible to find solutions. For many, the obvious response was to emulate those practices that had made Japan's auto manufacturing sector so innovative. Schonberger (1982) argued that Japanese practices could simply be studied in the West, making a grand call to action centred upon his belief that the

"Japanese have had little trouble learning our techniques, and we will have little trouble learning theirs" (Schonberger 1982, 14). In a more tempered tone, Alston argued that Americans "should study the Japanese and adapt what we see as useful," and that while "Japanese culture contains many elements and concepts that are different from ours, some can clearly be adapted to the American scene." As such, North American industry moved to emulate Japanese practices and soon after, "the wraps were off. Western manufacturers, academics, and consultants [were] joining study missions to Japan by the planeload" (Schonberger 2007, 403).

Many researchers seeking answers to the success of Japanese industry looked to the Toyota Production System. The production system had remained insulated within the boundaries of Toyota's manufacturing system and supply chain for much of the mid-twentieth century, remaining almost entirely unknown in the West until a small number of academic papers and articles in the business press began to advocate for a number of practices developed at Toyota (Emiliani 2006; Schonberger 2007). The design of the production system had begun with Sakichi Toyoda, the inventor of an automatic loom that detected manufacturing flaws and shut down production when threads broke. Toyoda founded the Toyoda Group in 1918, eventually expanding into automobile production in the 1930s (Holweg 2007, 421). Upon his death, Toyoda passed control of his company to his son Kichiiro, who focused on auto manufacturing rather than the loom business that his father had founded (Holweg 2007, 421). With the nascent Japanese auto market dominated by local branch subsidiaries of Ford and General Motors (Holweg 2007, 421), Toyoda made it a priority to catch up to his international competitors, ultimately travelling to Detroit to study the Ford automobile factories. Impressed with the scale of the production but certain it was both unfeasible in the space available in Japanese factories, and unable to offer variety in models or trims, the Toyodas and engineers such as Taiichi Ohno set to creating an improved system for Toyota.

The Toyota Production System, as it would come to be known, would emerge as the result of the efforts of these engineers' and factory staff to modify Detroit-style, large-scale auto manufacturing processes and accommodate the limited space afforded by Japanese factories. In particular, Toyota's engineers worked to make the company's production methods more flexible than its Western counterparts. Manufacturers in the United States and Europe, with the luxury of enormous economies of scale, could deploy relatively rigid processes. Parts for cars, for example, were typically stamped out of sheets of metal using large dies.

The steel, pressed between two dies using hundreds of kilograms of pressure, took the shape of fenders, bumpers, and the like. With each individual die weighing multiple tonnes, changing the equipment on the assembly line to make, for instance, a different model, or to make adjustments when equipment was misaligned or broken down, required entire days. For engineers such as Ohno, however, this process only made sense at those Western factories that were producing tens of thousands of cars at a time – an unrealistic scale at that point in Japan. Through experimentation and trial-and-error, the Toyota engineers devised a system for changing the casts much more rapidly, allowing equipment to be changed over in a matter of hours and allowing plants to produce a wider variety of products over a shorter period than their Western counterparts (Womack, Jones, and Roos 1990, 52–4).

Other components of the Toyota Production System included the practice of only producing those parts that were needed for the next step of the process, fabricating as many fenders or doors as were needed for cars that were being assembled at the time. This system, in which the components for finished products were produced just in time for its final assembly, became known as "Just-in-Time" production. *Kanban,* an inventory process that included mechanisms by which depleted inventory was identified for additional production or ordering, was a similarly important dimension of the model. Such practices were not only primary components of the Toyota Production System, but also elements that were identified by those researchers in academia and industry who were looking for lessons (e.g., Schonberger 1982; Pegels 1984; Pascale and Athos 1981). Cumulatively, these practices represented the company's dedication to eliminating waste – or *muda* in Japanese – through committed effort to experimentation and improvement; what the company would eventually call *kaizen,* or continuous improvement. The Toyota Production System that existed in the 1970s was thus one that had evolved over decades in the mid-twentieth century, through experimentation, trial and error, and what Holweg (2007, 422) calls "continuously iterating learning cycles." As North American manufacturing was critiqued for being inflexible, inefficient, and bloated, the Japanese Production System's central focus on eliminating waste and creating a nimbler method for producing goods offered an attractive alternative.

The Toyota Production System had emerged in response to a particular context. Facing challenging circumstances in post-war Japan, Toyota's management and engineers adapted the manufacturing practices used in North American auto factories to suit their local conditions. Out of the tedious and decades-long work of these engineers came a series of practices appropriate for the time and place. While these practices had been identified by multiple Western writers and researchers, however, the Toyota Production System remained a disarticulated set of practices that had yet to be adopted on a wide scale by Western industry. It would not be until a set of MIT researchers put a concise name to Toyota's practices and announced to their Western audience that they could be implemented essentially anywhere, that "Lean" would emerge as an answer to the problem of the West's lagging competitiveness.

From the Toyota Production System to Lean: A Story of Translation

The term "Lean" was not used to describe the Toyota Production System, either within Toyota or outside of it, until the 1980s. There were, in fact, few written descriptions of how Toyota conducted its business until the 1970s, when Japanese authors began to describe the system for outside audiences. The name "Lean" emerged in 1988 when John Krafcik, a former engineer at a California factory owned jointly by General Motors and Toyota (Emiliani 2006, 172), coined the term in a paper published in MIT's *Sloan Management Review* (Krafcik 1988). Krafcik described the "superiority" of Lean production over the traditional mass production utilized by manufacturers such as Ford or General Motors. Krafcik's paper was an early product of the work of the International Motor Vehicle Program (IMVP), a research project in which he worked as a research assistant and that would become crucial in the emergence of Lean in North America (Womack, Jones, and Roos 1990). The IMVP was comprised of researchers at the Massachusetts Institute of Technology (MIT) who, spurred by the oil price spike and funded with a small grant, set out with the mandate to explore "the future of the automobile" (Holweg 2007, 423). By 1985, the project's researchers had turned their attention from broad questions of the future of the automobile to the more specific task of understanding how and why Japanese auto manufacturers had gained so much of the international auto market, largely at the expense of their American competitors. The IMVP was structured much as other large-scale academic investigative projects, with primary investigators at MIT coordinating the efforts of collaborators from a diverse set of institutions and firms across the US, Europe, and Japan. The project's investigative methodology included visiting factories in these countries, interviewing executives, managers, engineers, and front-line staff on the shop floor to determine and compare the practices, not only of Japanese factories, but also those in North America and Europe.

In addition to publications such as Krafcik's, IMVP researchers produced working papers and briefing documents for the government and industry stakeholders who helped fund their work, honing their understanding both of the newly named "Lean" production system as well as how to describe the system to Western audiences (IMVP 1994). This work culminated in the publication of the enormously influential book *The Machine That Changed the World,* authored by IMVP leaders James Womack, Daniel Jones, and Daniel Roos (1990). Womack, Jones, and Roos examined how the practices that they called Lean Production emerged within Toyota before reviewing the various facets of how Japanese firms such as Toyota conducted their business, from customer relations to inventory control, to management of the factory operation. In their book, Womack, Jones, and Roos introduced the Lean label to a wider audience, arguing that it fit the Japanese system because it uses "less of everything compared with mass production – half the human effort in the factory, half the manufacturing space, half the investment in tools, [and] half the engineering hours to develop a new product in half the time" (Womack, Jones, and Roos 1990, 11). More importantly, though, they reframed the Toyota Production System, not only by assigning it a label, but also by making it accessible for a wide audience. They insisted that Lean practices could be adopted without limitations: "Our conclusion is simple: Lean production is a superior way to make things … It follows that the whole world should adopt lean production, and as quickly as possible" (Womack, Jones, and Roos 1990, 231).

It is important to note that there had been other attempts to sell Toyota's practices to Western audiences. By the time Womack, Jones, and Roos' book was published in 1990, there were myriad books, chapters, and articles, some of them written by engineers who had worked in Japanese firms, that identified Just-in-Time production, Kanban inventory, and the like (e.g., Ohno 1978; 1982; Shingo 1989). Yet with its dramatic title and new, concise label, Lean production, and the authority bestowed upon them by their prestigious location at MIT, *The Machine That Changed the World* established its authors as authorities over the subject that they were translating for Western audiences. Some within the Lean industry have worked to demonstrate the extent to which Toyota Production System practices were being implemented in North American industry independent of the work and publications of the IMVP researchers (e.g., Emiliani 2016). Nonetheless, it was the Lean name that stuck, and it was the purveyors of the Lean moniker who became among the first Lean experts, and who continue to be referred to as the "founders" of Lean (Spence 2013).

The original Lean authors thus sought to *translate* the specific practices of the Toyota Production System into a universal template, under the name "Lean." Beyond assigning English nomenclature and descriptions to the practices they observed in Japanese factories, however, the early Lean authors' translations were rendered so as to be appropriate for implementation across a wide variety of activities. Clarke et al. (2015) describe translation both in terms of literal translation between languages – surely present in this process – as well as making knowledge and practices understandable in different contexts and settings. They describe translation as the process of "making a meaning (or set of meanings) move from one linguistic or cultural context to another" (Clarke et al. 2015, 35). Translation thus represents the process by which something – in this case the practices and approaches observed in the Toyota Production System – is made understandable and implementable in settings that have little (or nothing) to do with its original context. In the case of Lean, the academic researchers and industry insiders, most notably the authors of *The Machine That Changed the World*, framed the translated version of the Toyota Production System – Lean – as the solution to the problem of corporate North America's newfound laggard status in the global marketplace.

Stripped of the mid-century Japanese context in which Lean was developed, the authors of *The Machine That Changed the World* could turn Lean's tenets into a product that could be implemented anywhere. Indeed, with the publication of their tome, Womack, Jones, and Roos (1990, 14) proclaimed that Lean would, "as it inevitably spreads beyond the auto industry... change almost everything in almost every industry – choices for consumers, the nature of work, the fortune of companies, and, ultimately, the fate of nations." They worked quickly to ensure that their grand predictions would be realized. Womack and Jones would go on to write a collection of additional books (e.g., Womack and Jones 1996; Womack and Jones 2005; Womack 2011; Jones and Womack 2011) to promote Lean's tenets to a growing audience. They founded "research institutes," the Lean Enterprise Institute in the United States, the Lean Enterprise Academy in the UK, and additional non-profit institutes in other countries that came to belong to the "Lean Global Network" (Jones and Womack 2016, 29) to serve as institutional nodes and repositories of research and guidance for those looking for new solutions to various problems.

Through their books, articles, and research institutes, these early Lean advocates would become central figures in an enormous industry. Indeed, their Lean creation has grown to be remarkably popular and successful. As Liker, Fruin, and Adler (1999, 5) point out, "since the publication of *The Machine That Changed the World*," Lean has become "the standard reference point for many American firms." Never shy to celebrate the success of their creation, Jones and Womack (2016,

27) have called Lean "the most successful approach to business improvement in our generation." And with Lean's popularity has come a sprawling, loosely (if at all) connected network of "experts" in the form of consultants, authors, and gurus. Myriad publications espouse Lean solutions for problems in a seemingly infinite series of activities: accounting (Maskell and Baggaley 2004; Stenzel 2007), construction (Shang and Low 2014; Santorella 2011), human resources (Jekiel 2011; Harris and Harris 2007), health care (Black 2016; Aij and Lohman 2016; Graban 2012), information technology (Bell and Orzen 2011; Williams and Duray 2013), and government and state institutions (Price and Elliotte 2011; Teeuwen 2011). Blogs, podcasts, YouTube videos, pamphlets, and presentations trumpet the benefits of Lean for any organization; certification in Lean or one of its derivatives (e.g., Lean Six Sigma) find their way into job descriptions. This network of experts makes it its job to ensure that Lean is found "lying around." For problems in any industry, in any sector, Lean has solutions.

Lean's (Awkward) Neoliberalism

As I described above, Lean's focus on the elimination of waste makes it a comfortable fit in neoliberalized bureaucracies, where the belief that waste and inefficiency abound in public sector institutions has underwritten a long series of public sector reforms in Canada going back to New Public Management-inspired *Public Service 2000* (Canada 1990). Yet, to argue that Lean is somehow inherently neoliberal means ignoring its own rich and dynamic history. Neither Toyota's engineers nor the MIT researchers who worked so hard to turn the Toyota Production System into Lean were invested in a neoliberal project. Lean has its own story, one whose contours have been shaped by processes parallel to, though sometimes resembling, neoliberalization.

So how, then, to proceed with studying and theorizing how these disparate and "non-neoliberal" things come to populate what we understand to be neoliberalism. Is it neoliberalism at all? I, like Janine Brodie and the editors of this volume, believe in the concept's ongoing utility. But such awkward questions do require analytical tools that can accommodate these challenges. I suggest that *assemblage* is one promising option. Assemblage, a concept of growing popularity in critical geography, refers to "some form of provisional socio-spatial," (Anderson and McFarlane 2011, 124; quoted in Higgins and Larner 2017a, 4), an "unstable constellation" (Ong 2007, 5) or an ensemble "of heterogeneous elements" (Ong and Collier 2004, 5). Assemblages are, in short, collections of ideas, logics, discourses, and technologies brought together

in conditional arrangements that best reflect the abstract ideal of a political rationality. While those deploying assemblages as a concept often
do so when studying intersections of these disparate elements in very
specific sites, the emergence of Lean as a technology of neoliberalized
bureaucracy is an example of how we can think of neoliberalizing assembling practices, institutions, and discourses in broader patterns and
formations. As neoliberal rationality forms and reforms, shifts, and
shapeshifts, new components can be added while existing components
are rearranged to accommodate them.

Brodie and critical scholars who share her observation of the contingency of neoliberalism, have provided the tools for painting a nuanced picture of neoliberalism. It is much more than a set of policies,
including deregulation and privatization, which privilege the market
over the state (Larner 2000). Treating neoliberalism as an assemblage
means rejecting the notion that it is a *thing* and conceptualizing it as an
uneasy, shifting aggregate of components with varying degrees of consistency with one another. As Higgins and Larner write, the challenge
for critical scholars is "to know what to do with complexity and contradictions – particularly when the result is that their cases do not fit into
the parsimonious explanations that might allow for the tidy packaging
under labels such as 'neoliberal projects,' 'neoliberal eras' and the like"
(Higgins and Larner 2017b: 308). This approach affords the flexibility to
confront "awkward assemblages" and the ambiguous (and not always
neoliberal) effects they entail.

In light of these critical perspectives, Lean should not be considered
a result, derivative, or inherent part of neoliberalism. Its story is too
rich, with its own history of shifting pathways, contexts, and agencies
to reduce its emergence in state institutions merely "because of neoliberalism." It should, rather, be understood as a set of practices that
has been (relatively) recently brought into the neoliberal fold. Moving
through networks of experts and insiders, Lean was translated and redeployed in a wide range of settings, each with its own particular problem for which Lean offered the solution. Then, as states faced crises of
governance, the technologies and logics of Keynesian rationality were
problematized, and Lean was presented as a solution to those problems as well. Through problematization and solution finding, through
experimentation in different settings and travels through a growing
network of expertise, Lean now finds itself as the solution for a wide
array of problems vexing policy practitioners. As such, Lean provides
an instructive lesson for researching neoliberalism. Higgins and Larner
(2017a, 5) call for scholars to place "analytical emphasis on the process of assembly, rather than the resultant formation" of neoliberalism,

arguing that it is "important to recognize *how* heterogeneous elements may come together in ways that have neoliberal effects and the challenges and contestations that limit the possibilities of coherence in neoliberal programs and forms of rule" (2017a, 2). Accordingly, I argue that studying individual cases such as Lean, reveal the trajectory of practices, discourses, policies, and technologies of governance that converge with others to form patterns that we recognize as broader forms of rule. This approach helps us continue the work of Janine Brodie, whose career has been marked by an unwillingness to accept simplistic or essentialist accounts of governance and power. Understanding technologies, such as Lean, as components of shifting and provisional assemblages will also help mitigate against the risk of waiting for "big shifts," marked by large-scale crises that signal the end of one form of governance and the beginning of another. Lean's practices existed far before the ascendance of a neoliberal form of rule and became a part of it well after. The processes of problematization, solution-finding, and network-building that marked its inclusion into a neoliberal assemblage suggests that critical scholars can and should keep a careful lookout for those ideas and practices that might be found lying around, having travelled through their own convoluted trajectories towards new patterns that can, or will, become recognizable as emergent forms of rule.

REFERENCES

Aij, Kjeld H., and Bas Lohman. 2016. *Practical Lean Leadership for Health Care Managers: A Guide to Sustainable and Effective Application of Lean Principles.* Baton Rouge, FL: CRC Press.

Anderson, B., and McFarlane C. 2011. "Assemblage and Geography." *Area* 42: 124–7. https://doi.org/10.1111/j.1475-4762.2011.01004.x.

Alston, Jon P. 1986. *The American Samurai: Blending American and Japanese Managerial Practices.* Berlin: De Gruyter.

Bell, Steve, and Michael A. Orzen. 2011. *Lean IT: Enabling and Sustaining Your Lean Transformation.* Boca Raton: CRC Press.

Black, John. 2016. *The Toyota Way to Healthcare Excellence: Increased Efficiency and Improve Quality with Lean,* (2nd ed.). Chicago: Health Administration Press.

Brodie, Janine. 1990. *The Political Economy of Canadian Regionalism.* Toronto: Harcourt Brace Jovanovich.

Brown, Wendy. 2019. *In the Ruins of Neoliberalism: The Rise of Antidemocratic Politics in the West.* New York: Columbia University Press.

- 2015. *Undoing the Demos: Neoliberalism's Stealth Revolution*. Cambridge, MA: MIT University Press.

Buchanan, James M. 1977. "Why Does Government Grow?" In *Budgets and Bureaucrats: The Sources of Government Growth*, edited by Thomas E. Borcherding. Durham, NC: Duke University Press.

Canada. 1990. *Public Service 2000. (PS2000)*. Ottawa: Privy Council Office.

Canada. 1984. "Report of the Royal Commission on the Economic Union and Development Prospects for Canada." (MacDonald Commission.) Ottawa: Privy Council Office.

Canada. 1979. "Report of the Royal Commission on Financial Management and Accountability." (Lambert Commission) Ottawa: Supply and Services Canada.

Clancy, Tom. 1994. *Debt of Honor*. New York: Berkley Books.

Clarke, John, Dave Bainton, Noémi Lendvai, and Paul Stubbs. 2015. *Making Policy Move: Towards a Politics of Translation and Assemblage*. Bristol: Policy Press.

Crichton, Michael. 1992. *Rising Sun*. New York, NY: Alfred A. Knopf.

Drucker, Peter F. 1981. "Behind Japan's Success." *Harvard Business Review*, January 1981. https://hbr.org/1981/01/behind-japans-success.

The Economist. 1962. "Consider Japan." *The Economist*, September 8, 1962.

Emiliani, Robert. 2017. "Is Lean the Same as TPS?" *Bob Emiliani's Lean Leadership Blog*, January 31, 2017. https://bobemiliani.com/comparing-tps-and-lean/.

- 2006. "Origins of Lean Management in America: The Role of Connecticut Businesses." *Journal of Management History* 12 (2): 167–84. http://doi.org/10.1108/13552520610654069.

Fandino, Daniel. 2016. "Die Hard: Nakatomi Plaza and the Fear of a Rising Japan." *Wired*. http://wiredhistory.com/2016/12/die-hard-nakatomi-plaza-and-the-fear-of-japan/. Retrieved July 2017.

Friedman, Milton, and Rose D. Friedman. 1982. *Capitalism and Freedom / Milton Freedman, with the Assistance of Rose D. Friedman; with a New Preface by the Author*. Chicago: University of Chicago Press.

Graban, Mark. 2012. *Lean Hospitals: Improving Quality, Patient Safety, and Employee Engagement*. 2nd ed. Boca Raton, FL: CRC Press.

Harris, Chris, and Rick Harris. 2007. *Developing a Lean Workforce: A Guide for Human Resources, Plant Managers, and Lean Coordinators*. New York: Productivity Press.

Harvey, Paul. 1988. "Japan Buys US with Our Money." *Kentucky New Era*, September 6, 1988.

Heale, M.J. 2009. "Anatomy of a Scare: Yellow Peril Politics in America, 1980–1993." *Journal of American Studies* 43 (1): 19–47. http://doi.org/10.1017/S0021875809006033.

Higgins, Vaughan, and Wendy Larner. 2017(a). "Introduction: Assembling Neoliberalism." In *Assembling Neoliberalism: Expertise, Practices, Subjects,* edited by Vaughan Higgins and Wendy Larner, 1–21. New York, NY: Palgrave Macmillan.

– 2017(b). "Conclusion: Awkward Assemblages." In *Assembling Neoliberalism: Expertise, Practices, Subjects,* edited by Vaughan Higgins and Wendy Larner, 305–12. New York: Palgrave Macmillan.

Holweg, Matthias. 2007. "The Genealogy of Lean Production." *Journal of Operations Management* 25 (2): 420–37. http://doi.org/10.1016/j.jom.2006.04.001.

International Motor Vehicle Program (IMVP). 1994. "The International Motor Vehicle Program Online Publications: 1994 Research Papers." https://web.archive.org/web/19970607112120/http://web.mit.edu:80/ctpid/www/imvp/94pub.html. Retrieved July 2017.

Jekiel, Cheryl M. 2011. *Lean Human Resources: Redesigning HR Processes for a Culture of Continuous Improvement.* New York: Productivity Press.

Johnson, Chalmers A. 1982. *MITI and the Japanese Miracle: The Growth of Industrial Policy, 1925–1975.* Stanford: Stanford University Press.

Jones, Daniel T., and James P. Womack. 2011. *Seeing the Whole Value Stream.* Cambridge: Lean Enterprise Institute.

Jones, Daniel T., and James P. Womack. 2016. "The Evolution of Lean Thinking and Practice." *The Routledge Companion to Lean Management,* edited by Torbhorn H. Netland and Daryl J. Powell, 26–32. New York: Taylor and Francis.

Kornheiser, Tony. 1990. "Japan's Big Gulp." *The Washington Post,* March 25, 1990. https://www.washingtonpost.com/archive/lifestyle/1990/03/25/japans-big-gulp/0fd26b39-9659-44df-8fda-495adc2eb745/?utm_term=.a390f875c2b9.

Krafcik, John. 1988. "Triumph of the Lean Production System." *Sloan Management Review* 30 (1): 41–52.

Larner, Wendy. 2000. "Policy, Ideology, Governmentality." *Studies in Political Economy* 63 (1): 5–25. https://doi.org/10.1080/19187033.2000.11675231.

Leifso, Justin. 2021. "Moving and Resisting Lean: Saskatchewan's Contested Implementation of Lean Healthcare." *Canadian Public Administration* 64 (4): 611–30.

Li, Tania. 2007. *The Will to Improve: Governmentality, Development, and the Practice of Politics.* Durham: Duke University Press.

Liker, Jeffrey K., W. Mark Fruin, and Paul S Adler. 1999. *Remade in America: Transplanting and Transforming Japanese Management Systems.* New York: Oxford University Press.

Maskell, Brian H., and Bruce Baggaley. 2004. *Practical Lean Accounting: A Proven System for Measuring and Managing the Lean Enterprise.* New York, NY: Productivity Press.

McTiernan, John. 1988. *Die Hard*. Los Angeles: Twentieth Century Fox.

Miller, Peter, and Nikolas Rose. 2008. *Governing the Present: Administering Economic, Social, and Personal Life*. Malden, MA: Polity Press.

Mirowski, Peter, and Dieter Plehwe. 2009. *The Road from Mont Pèlerin: The Making of the Neoliberal Thought Collective*. Cambridge: Harvard University Press.

Morris, Narelle. 2011. *Japan-Bashing: Anti-Japanism Since the 1980s*. New York: Routledge.

Niskanen, William. 1971. *Bureaucracy and Representative Government*. Chicago: University of Chicago Press.

Ohno, Taiichi. 1982. "How the Toyota Production System Was Created." *Japanese Economic Studies* 10 (4): 83–104. https://doi.org/10.2753/JES1097-203X100483.

– 1978. *The Toyota Production System*. New York, Productivity Press.

Ong, Aihwa. 2007. "Neoliberalism as Mobile Technology." *Transactions of the Institute of British Geographers* 32 (1): 3–8. https://doi.org/10.1111/j.1475-5661.2007.00234.x.

Ong, Aihwa, and Stephen Collier 2004. "Global Assemblages, Anthropological Problems." In *Global Assemblages: Technology, Politics and Ethics as Anthropological Problems*, edited by A. Ong and S.J. Collier, 3–21. Malden, MA: Blackwell.

Ouchi, William G. 1981. *Theory Z: How American Business Can Meet the Japanese Challenge*. London: Addison-Wesley Publishing Company.

Pascale, Richard T., and Anthony G. Athos. 1982. *The Art of Japanese Management: Applications for American Executives*. New York: Warner Books.

Pegels, C. Carl. 1984. *Japan vs. the West: Implications for Management*. Boston: Kluwer-Nijhoff.

Price, Mark, Walt Mores, and Hundley M. Elliotte. 2011. *Building High Performance Government Through Lean Six Sigma: A Leader's Guide to Creating Speed, Agility, and Efficiency*. New York: McGraw-Hill.

Rose, Nikolas, and Peter Miller. 1992. "Political Power Beyond the State: Problematics of Government." *The British Journal of Sociology* 43 (1): 173–205. https://doi.org/10.2307/591464.

Santorella, Gary. 2011. *Lean Culture for the Construction Industry: Building Responsible and Committed Project Teams*. New York: Productivity Press.

Schonberger, Richard J. 2007. "Japanese Production Management: An Evolution – With Mixed Success." *Journal of Operations Management* 25: 403–19. https://doi.org/10.1016/j.jom.2006.04.003.

– 1982. *Japanese Manufacturing Techniques: Nine Hidden Lessons in Simplicity*. New York: Free Press.

– 1982. "The Japanning of America Today." *Durant (OK) Daily Democrat*, October 17, 1982.

Shang, Gao, and Sui Pheng Low. 2014. *Lean Construction Management: The Toyota Way*. Singapore: Springer.

Shingo, S. 1989. *The Toyota Production System*. New York: Productivity Press.

Spence, Rick. 2013. "Top Misconceptions of the Lean Movement, According to Founder Jim Womack." *Financial Post*, October 24, 2013. http://business .financialpost.com/entrepreneur/top-misconceptions-of-the-lean-movement -according-to-founder-jim-womack/wcm/44d599ce-5095-4856-8af0-763f722fee31.

Stedman-Jones, Daniel. 2012. *Masters of the Universe: Hayek, Friedman, and the Birth of Neoliberal Politics*. Princeton: Princeton University Press.

Steinmo, Sven. 2010. *The Evolution of Modern States: Sweden, Japan, and the United States*. Cambridge: Cambridge University Press.

Stenzel, Joe. 2007. *Lean Accounting: Best Practices for Sustainable Integration*. Hoboken, N.J.: John Wiley & Sons.

Teeuwen, Bert. 2011. *Lean for the Public Sector: The Pursuit of Perfection in Government Services*. Boca Raton, FL.: CRC Press.

Vogel, Ezra F. 1984. *Japan As Number One: Lessons for America*. New York, NY: Harper & Row.

Von Mises, Ludwig. 1944. *Bureaucracy*. Glasgow: W. Hodge and Company.

Williams, Howard, and Rebecca Duray. 2013. *Making IT Lean: Applying Lean Practices to the Work of IT*. Boca Raton, FL: CRC Press.

Womack, James P. 2011. *Gemba Walks*. Cambridge, MA: Lean Enterprise Institute.

Womack, James P., Daniel T Jones, and Daniel Roos. 1990. *The Machine That Changed the World: Based on the Massachusetts Institute of Technology 5-Million Dollar 5-Year Study on the Future of the Automobile*. New York: Rawson Associates.

Womack, James P., and Daniel T. Jones. 2005. *Lean Solutions: How Companies and Customers Can Create Value and Wealth Together*. New York, NY: Free Press.

– 1996. *Lean Thinking: Banish Waste and Create Wealth In Your Corporation*. New York: Free Press.

Zemeckis, Robert. 1989. *Back to the Future II*. Los Angeles: Universal Pictures.

5 Puzzles in Neoliberalism and Problems for Multiculturalism and Equality: Repatriating Immigration Policy – A Tale of Two Provinces

ALEXANDRA DOBROWOLSKY

Problematics, Puzzles, and Parameters

This chapter examines contradictory and contested developments in, and assessments of, Canada's immigration policy sub-nationally, challenging dominant narratives around neoliberalism and, ultimately, around the health of Canadian multiculturalism and equality. My analysis pays homage to several key dimensions of Janine Brodie's oeuvre vis-à-vis neoliberalism, governance, and equality. Moreover, because it is grounded in an appreciation of distinctive, sub-national, political economic norms and practices, this chapter also benefits from Brodie's pivotal work on regionalism (1990) and shares certain affinities with Brent Epperson's chapter on American health care reform in this volume. Here I underscore what Wendy Brown describes as neoliberalism's "differential instantiation across ... regions and sectors," and "its differential intersection with extant cultures and political traditions" (2016, 4) through two case studies that illustrate neoliberalism's contingency in the context of federalism. A consideration of the political-economy and culture of two distinctive provinces – Manitoba and British Columbia (BC) – and their implications vis-à-vis immigration policy, provide a more complicated story of rescaling, devolution, and neoliberal governance. Nonetheless, this tale of two provinces does not auger well for multiculturalism and equality.

With advanced neoliberalism, the patterns of decentralization in federal states and devolution onto the private and third sectors are common. In Canada, the field of immigration has been no exception. While under its constitution, immigration is a responsibility held jointly by national and provincial governments, the former had historically taken the lead role in this area. This changed in the mid-1990s with the proliferation of provincial and territorial nominee programs (PTNPs) – expedited immigration pathways designed by provinces and territories to meet their particular economic needs. Manitoba and BC were the first to sign these agreements, and, after most other provinces and territories (except for Quebec and Nunavut) followed suit, they were also widely viewed as having the most "successful" programs, albeit for markedly different reasons. They were also unique (along with Quebec) for their series of bilateral agreements with the central government through which they acquired responsibility for the design and delivery of immigration settlement and integration services.

PTNP decentralization and immigrant service delivery devolution took place in a period of neoliberal consolidation and epitomized the federal government's efforts to wash its hands of costly and often messy immigration matters (Dobrowolsky 2011, 2012). Central government immigration services were "cut back, deregulated, or privatized, while local institutions and actors [were] given 'responsibility with power' through a process of 'regulatory dumping'" (Lewis 2010, 5). While these trends manifested themselves in the Chrétien Liberals' immigration policy preferences (Abu-Laban 2009), they intensified under Stephen Harper's Conservative governments, and the basic norms became those of limiting federal immigration program expenditures, "increasing emphasis on economic potential in the selection of applicants" and "devolving settlement responsibilities to communities and non-state organizations" (Lewis 2010, 5). What becomes puzzling is that the Conservatives then proceeded to assert more control over PTNPs and rescinded their settlement service agreements with Manitoba and BC, thereby "repatriating" the national government's role in these areas. In both cases, this was inconsistent and somewhat paradoxical, given neoliberal tenets.

This chapter queries why these shifts took place, particularly if Manitoba and BC were indeed successes, and assesses the repercussions of these policy shifts for equality and multiculturalism, before, during, and after repatriation. I argue that the explanation lies in the complexities that come with a federal system, particularly with the dynamics of different provincial political economies and cultures, and neoliberalism, as it is "neither singular nor constant in its discursive formulations, policy entailments, and material practices" (Brown 2016, 4).

These fluctuations are examined through a grounded (Gravelle, Ellermann, and Dauvergne 2013), scalar lens, drawing on primary and secondary sources, as well as qualitative interviews with government officials, scholars in the field, settlement service providers, and provincial nominees in Manitoba and BC. So-called successes will be evaluated in light of their impact on equality and multiculturalism in

Canada, and with an intersectional analysis. The first section briefly reviews key debates around federalism. Next, I examine the similarities and differences in the two provinces' PNP experiences and problematize both provinces' purported policy successes. I then detail how experiments with rescaling did result in certain innovations in settlement service delivery and programming, but then evaluate the fallout from the federal government's repatriation of this sector. I conclude by making sense of these challenging immigration policy developments in the context of advanced neoliberalism and assess their significance for federalism and multi-level governance, as well as multiculturalism and equality in Canada.

This analysis demonstrates that while neoliberalism has had an impact on all scales, there have been moves at meso and micro levels to work around federal economic constrictions that epitomized macro-level neoliberalization. Thus, while provincial "successes" were more limited than commonly perceived, due to the constraints of econocentric PTNPs, neoliberal disruptions occurred nonetheless, with short-lived, creative settlement programs more oriented towards the social, and in tune with micro-scale community needs.

Federalism and Neoliberalism: Questions and Conundrums

Debates around federalism and the merits/demerits of sub-state legislative autonomy are legion. Jennifer Wallner neatly encapsulates them, however, by identifying two "rival interpretations ... that we can loosely (and albeit imperfectly) divide between federal skeptics and optimists" (2014, 11). Canadian skeptics are often found on the left and worry about the implications of lacking a strong central government to uphold national social programs. They concur with Harold Laski who wrote, not long after the Great Depression, "by dividing power and authority among different orders of government, federalism creates weak governments and prevents the emergence of critical standards of policy uniformity that are necessary for a society to flourish" (1939, 367). In contrast, Wallner's optimists, and typically liberals, view Canadian federalism as a means of recognizing not only provincial, but multi-national and cultural identities (Kymlicka 1998; Gagnon 2014, 32), acting as a catalyst for "autonomous decision making to create distinctive policy packages" (Wallner 2014, 13). There can also be "contagion" effects (Charles and Mackay 2013) both positive, as in the emulation of innovative approaches, and negative. In relation to the latter, for instance, neoliberalism can also impede new program development as interprovincial "races to the bottom" on taxation rates can translate into less revenue and capacity for creative policy development at the provincial level. Moreover, as Banting cautions: "Divided jurisdiction raises the level of consensus required for innovation, and thereby complicates the process of introducing new programs" (1987, 174) or, as McGrane notes, can stymie the reform of established programs (2014, 43).

Tammy Findlay references feminist critiques of federalism and its capacity to "stall progressive policy change" (2015, 33) due to opaque and elitist intergovernmental negotiations (Sawer and Vickers 2010; Grace 2011) that act as barriers to equality seekers. Yet here too the assessments are mixed. Some have considered the pragmatic "multiple crack hypothesis": equality seekers can shift their focus of attention from one level of government to another depending on which level is most receptive. Whether such an approach is viable, however, pivots on the capacities of the political actors involved, and the ideas and economic contexts at play (Dobrowolsky 2000).

Neoliberalism, as has been well established by Brodie and others, changes over time and across space, and similarly, federalism needs to be placed in a "social, political and economic context" (Findlay 2015, 3). When this is done, it becomes apparent that multi-level governance can both perpetuate, but also potentially forestall, neoliberal policy shifts (Collier 2009). The devolution of immigration was seen as an opportunity for policy creativity, and one that contributed to the purported successes of the MPNP and BC-PNP. But how and why were they "successful," and according to whom? And again, if Manitoba and BC selection and settlement programs received accolades, what accounts for the federal government's seemingly paradoxical re-assertion of its authority in these areas, and with what consequences? In particular, how has this immigration policy expansion and retraction affected Canada's much vaunted multiculturalism and equality? To answer these questions, a closer look at the two provinces is required.

Manitoba and BC Similarities: PNP Successes?

Manitoba became the "first province to adopt and use" the PNP and then was largely "saluted for its successful immigration attraction and settlement strategies" (Bucklaschuk, Moss, and Annis 2009, 64). The Canada-Manitoba Immigration Agreement (CMIA) was struck in 1996 and the "PNP annex was approved in 1998, along with a second annex providing for the devolution of settlement services" (Seidle 2013, 9). The MPNP program fit well with both Manitoba's New Democratic Party-led government's efforts at policy creativity under Howard Pawley (1981–8), and its Progressive Conservative government's (Premier

Gary Filmon 1988–99) neoliberal preferences, including efforts to give an economic boost to areas beyond Winnipeg. From 1999 onward, under a succession of NDP governments, we see both the growth and fine-tuning of the MPNP, reflecting their moderate centre-left attempts to marry economic and social priorities by both expanding the program and working on service provision.

In 1999, Manitoba received federal approval to increase nominees. The numbers more than tripled, from 4,610 in 2000 to 15,963 in 2011, and in that year "77 per cent of all immigrants to Manitoba came through the PNP" (Seidle 2013, 8, 9). However, the Harper government's decision to begin limiting Canada's overall immigrant intake abruptly halted this phenomenal growth. After 2010, Manitoba's share of principal applicants was set at 5,000 and, as a result, "total landings [began] to level off" (Clement, Carter, Vineberg 2013, 17). This dramatic reversal occurred even when the MPNP had been widely lauded by both federal and provincial officials across Canada, especially those in what was then the Department of Citizenship and Immigration Canada (CIC).

Indeed, various indicators are marshalled to highlight the MPNP's achievements (Carter, Morrish, and Amoyaw 2008). As its initial nominee target intake of 200 (Nakache and D'Aoust 2012, 169) swelled into the thousands (Carter, Pandey, and Townsend 2010, 8), the province was able to meet its objectives of counteracting population aging and decline and the central government's desire to lessen "pressure on federal immigration programs" and disperse immigrants "across Canada" (Lewis 2010, 243). Manitoba also had the most comprehensive program (Carter 2012, 186), as it incorporated more flexibility and scope for the "social" in what was fundamentally an economic immigration pathway. From 2004 to 2013, the MPNP had five streams: General; Family Support; Employer Direct; International Students and Strategic Initiatives (Seidle 2013, 10). Significantly, not all PTNPs contained categories for families (e.g., in 2010 BC, Ontario and Nova Scotia did not). Beyond having more open-ended streams, Manitoba was exceptional in examining "the 'entire package' of characteristics of applicants when assessing applications" (Carter 2012, 186), and in its concerted efforts to work with communities (Kukushkin 2009). All this led Premier Selinger to declare, in reaction to federal repatriation: "Manitoba's program has been a model for the rest of Canada and should not be tampered with" ("Manitoba politicians spar" 2012).

BC's program, launched in 1998, contrasted sharply with Manitoba's approach, as the former had just two basic streams: Strategic Occupations and Business (Seidle 2013, 12). Because BC was already an immigrant destination and did not face the same demographic challenges as Manitoba, its success came in its selectivity. The BC-PNP, launched under a tactical "Third Way" NDP government, exemplifies efforts to respond to a competitive global market by using immigration levers to consolidate trade and business links to Pacific Rim countries, and to fill key skill shortages in the province. Subsequent changes dovetailed with the BC Liberals' neoliberal proclivities for strategic investment and entrepreneurialism. Thus, BC's PNP "successes" came in producing optimum economic returns, with the Liberals especially targeting wealthy businessmen [sic], particularly from China, to invest in the province and promote trade with the Asia Pacific (BC-PNP official interview on file with author).

While most provinces have various iterations of business immigrant streams, BC's PNP included the following subcategories: (i) Business Skills, (ii) Regional Skills, and (iii) Strategic Projects. BC's selectivity was even more apparent in its Strategic Occupation Stream given its particular areas of focus: Skilled Workers; International Graduates; International Postgaduates; Designated Health Professionals; and Entry-Level/Semi-Skilled Workers in Select Occupations (Seidle 2013, 12). Unlike Manitoba, BC did not have a Family Support Stream. Such specificity combined with the reality that BC is a draw for immigrants, has meant that the BC-PNP has been able to meet its prime objective of attracting investors and select workers, and it has had little difficulty with retention.

Overall, nominees residing in BC were situated in a significantly higher average earning bracket than those of nominees in most other provinces (save for Alberta; CIC, 2011, 41). From the establishment of the first-time business stream in 2002 to March 2010, the BC government proudly tallied the following successes: "571 nominee candidates have been approved, committed over $600 million in new investment and created 2,550 jobs" (British Columbia, 2011, 1). Here, success clearly lies in exclusivity and economic dividends. Again, both the MPNP and BC-PNP were considered successes by their respective provincial governments, by other provinces, and, for a time at least, by the federal government, "as something of a model to be emulated elsewhere" (Clement, Carter, and Vineberg 2013, 58). However, when these programs are assessed from the "bottom up," the nature and effects of such successes are called into question.

Nominees in Manitoba did find work and did stay, but these achievements obscure the trade-offs involved. In one study, 58 per cent of the Manitoba nominees interviewed "expressed a reasonably high level of job satisfaction"; however 89 per cent also indicated they had difficulty finding work and only 36 per cent were working in their fields (Carter 2012, 196). Among the problems were credential recognition, along with mismatches between nominees' skills, fluctuating job markets, and lack of information about small-centre labour demands (Lewis 2010, 250). Having been chosen for their skills, nominees, in general, tend to fare better on the employment front than other immigrants (Pandey and Townsend 2010, 17). However, because they are often encouraged to settle in less well-resourced and networked areas, adverse effects, such as de-skilling, can hit nominees and their families hard, both financially and psychologically (Ley 2010; Dobrowolsky 2011, 2012; Dobrowolsky, Bryan, and Gardiner Barber 2015). Manitoba nominees "with lower levels of educational attainment saw the largest advantage in earnings in the first full year of landing" (Pandey and Townsend 2010, 16), again suggesting that the best and brightest do face challenges that are often overlooked. In addition, and more broadly, "the issue of economic integration should properly involve a comparison of immigrant performance relative to native-born Canadians with equivalent characteristics" (Hum and Simpson 2002, 126).

Manitoba made significant inroads in settlement service provision (discussed below), and has "the highest percentage of immigrants using services (41.9 per cent)" (Wilkinson and Bucklaschuk 2015, 14), but because of their sheer magnitude, nominees across Manitoba carry most of the burden of application and settlement, and the response to needs like housing, health care, schooling, and child care services is insufficient.

Moreover, the proportion of immigrants settling outside of Winnipeg grew considerably after 2009 (Clement, Carter, Vineberg 2013, 5). This development was held up as a marker of success, and yet in these areas, immigrant organizations, social supports, and established ethnocultural communities and social networks are limited (Bucklashuck, Moss, and Annis 2009, 66). In rural areas in particular, settlement has a "mixed history" in that for "some communities, especially those with a strong employment base, proactive employers and strong municipal governments" the processes could be "progressive and responsive" but in others "the challenges have gone beyond a lack of settlement services" and include "the lack of economic champions, or limited housing options, limited services in schools or health care facilities" (Clement, Carter, and Vineberg 2013, 49).

Manitoba's immigration minister rated the MPNP as a "'tremendous success'" in that it "'enriches cultural diversity' and provides a 'tool' to assist in the maintenance of Francophone communities" (Lewis 2010, 253). But what do immigrants receive in return, especially beyond

Winnipeg, where cultural imbalances are more likely to emerge since the vast majority of residents are of British or European origin and "[f]ew residents claim visible minority status" (Bucklaschuk, Moss, and Annis 2009, 65)? In addition, when community organizations have worked with the government to influence selection, they have often matched "like with like," seeking out nominees who share the same ethnic, religious, or linguistic makeups of particular parts of Manitoba. (Lewis 2010, 253). Immigration consultants have been known to recruit German nominees to come to Steinbach, a German-speaking settlement, and community associations work to stream newcomers to existing ethnocultural communities, such as Mennonites in Winkler and Filipinos in Winnipeg, because this is presumed to be "the best route to long term retention of newcomers" (Lewis 2010, 253). While this may contribute to social cohesion, it can also lead to a pecking order of preferred groups, and the possibility of various forms of geographic racism. In addition, such formal and informal mechanisms privilege "communities that have been in the province longer and that have a larger pool of collective resources," thereby favouring established groups (Lewis 2010, 253). Such practices therefore constitute not just a discriminating, but a potentially discriminatory, slippery slope.

Unlike Manitoba, BC has little trouble attracting immigrants, and especially business immigrants to urban areas. More than half of all investors in the first federal government investor-class program chose BC as their destination (Wood 2015). Vancouver and its environs have become infamous for their "millionaire migrants" (Ley 2010) and BC became a PTNP success story because of its appeal to certain types of wealthy investors and its gains in attracting immigrants to meet specific labour demands. For example, the BC-PNP initially targeted business immigrants with $2 million in net worth and at least $1 million to invest in the BC economy (Huynh 2004, 9). When applications remained low, amendments were made to reduce this amount ("Business Immigration" 2008), but still a high economic bar ruled out those with less access to resources. Such specificity can then be interpreted as reinforcing classism, cultural selectivity, and perpetuating a gendered division of labour.

In both BC and in Manitoba, nominees were initially disproportionately male, but this was also category dependent. Because some BC PNP subcategories featured professions that tend to be female dominated, such as nursing and midwifery, its gender mix was slightly better than Manitoba's. Nonetheless, BC's econocentric specificity, combined with a lack of a family category, perpetuated both gendered streaming, and exclusions. For instance, in BC, 63 per cent of principal applicants were male, but this rose to 73 per cent for its skilled worker subcategory. In contrast, in the first phase of its PNP, 81.4 per cent of Manitoba's principal applicants were male, but with increased category diversification between 2004–6, this dropped to 75.6 per cent (British Columbia 2011, 16).

Government policy analysts have not considered the repercussions of BC's "successes." As one illustration, wealthy business owners, and highly skilled and educated immigrants, in general, tend to be drawn to metropolitan areas. Here, higher costs of living, combined with prevalent problems such as lack of credential recognition and deskilling, can have an impact on class positioning (Ley 2010). For those launching business ventures, they face challenges of greater competition, and even market saturation, particularly when setting up in pre-existing and longstanding "ethnic enclaves" (interviews 2015). Thus, Bauder has argued that immigrants in smaller BC communities actually earn more than they would in Vancouver (2003, A13). BC's Regional Business stream and its 2004 pilot project, the Regional Immigration Initiative (RII), are examples of efforts to retain immigrants in smaller communities, with the communities identifying and developing the resources to do so (Nolan, McCallum, and Zehtab-Martin 2009). Of course, immigrants in these rural areas face the same challenges in BC as they do in Manitoba, including credential recognition, difficulties obtaining work in their field, and challenges around finding affordable and safe housing. Concomitantly, Henin and Bennett's study revealed employment discrimination and racism (2002) were more apt to occur in less diverse, rural areas.

At the same time, however, even in BC's larger cities, new sets of old concerns around racialization have resurfaced. Stevenson encapsulates the problem as follows:

A great many people with wealth and entrepreneurial skills left Hong Kong for other countries, and particularly to Canada, immediately prior to British withdrawal from the colony in 1997. This phenomenon led to complaints, particularly in Vancouver, that Chinese immigrants were building "monster houses" and driving up real estate prices...More recently, there have been expressions of concern in British Columbia about the increasing prominence of the Chinese language. (2014, 91)

For example, in Richmond, a city known for its high Chinese-Canadian population, "complaints over lack of integration has City Hall presently undertaking a public consultation process on non-English signs throughout the community and their perceived threat to 'community harmony'" (Wood 2015). These troubling expressions of Sinophobia in the media and in other public domains (Ley 2010), undercut PNP successes and any gains that have been made around multiculturalism and equality.

Ironically, PTNP successes (i.e., becoming a hugely popular pathway for immigrants, and resulting in skyrocketing numbers of nominees) put pressure on federal immigration programs. In the first year of PNPs there were only 477 admissions, whereas by 2010, "36,428 new permanent immigrants gained entry through provincial nomination" (Bloemraad 2012, 3) and, by 2009, there were more than 50 categories of PTNPs (Seidle 2010, 50). The federal government under Stephen Harper thus responded by "repatriating." This process began in 2009 when "CIC implemented annual limits for PNP principal applicants," and by November 2012, then Immigration Minister Jason Kenney stated that "the federal government does not want to 'completely cede [its] role in selecting immigrants'" (Seidle 2013, 188), resulting in pressure to align PTNP streams with federal programs.

Federal enthusiasm for PTNPs was waning, and this took place in the context of increasingly conflictual federal-provincial relations more generally. Harper's "open federalism," which was meant to be province-friendly, turned out to be "disengaged federalism," a dynamic in which the prime minister eschewed meetings with individual premiers and acted unilaterally. To be sure, "frequent intergovernmental meetings and conference calls ... occur within the immigration sector provid[ing] the opportunity to raise particular issues" but there is still "no ongoing committee or working group with a specific mandate with regard to PNPs" (Seidle 2013, 19).

The central government began reasserting its role in immigration matters, ostensibly ensuring that there was more policy uniformity, while enacting the Harper government's command and control tendencies. The provinces were not happy, but as far as Jason Kenney was concerned, "we can't have 10 provinces arbitrarily setting their own goals, because ultimately there's one pipeline for immigration, and that runs through the Government of Canada" (quoted in Maher 2010).

In addition to reducing overall immigration targets, the Harper Conservatives' repatriation plans also sent earthquakes and aftershocks through the federal government's settlement service agreements in BC and Manitoba, to which we will now turn.

Further "Repatriation" Dilemmas: Lessons and Losses around Settlement Services

A wide range of federally funded programs exist across the country to support newcomers in their first years in Canada, although such programming and services are usually provided through third parties, including immigrant service providers (SPOs). After striking a deal with Quebec (Banting 2012), and following the prevailing neoliberal rationale, the Liberal federal government was keen to make similar deals with other provinces to off-load its delivery of settlement programming. However, only two provinces would take up this offer, Manitoba and BC, and they did so with the proviso that they would receive the entire amount that the federal government would save with devolution (Banting 2012). Manitoba initiated in 1998 (Leo and August 2009), and BC followed suit. Beyond Quebec, then, only BC and Manitoba adopted the devolved model for delivery of services, but unlike Quebec, BC and Manitoba were required to report to the CIC annually on their provision of settlement and integration services (Seidle 2010, 53). All this would change in April 2012 when the Harper government cancelled the funding for these types of agreements.

The response from Manitoba and BC was shock, and in some cases outrage ("Manitoba politicians spar" 2012). The May 1998 Canada-British Columbia Co-operation Agreement on Immigration had devolved responsibility for immigration settlement and integration to the province. The agreement clearly epitomized neoliberal logics, as it included "an emphasis on reducing overlap and duplication, and the growing interest of the federal and provincial governments in results and outcomes" (Dickson et al, 2013, 7). Yet less consistent with a neoliberal approach, funding levels to BC increased over the course of this and two subsequent accords. BC received $23.37 million for 1998–99; by the 2004 agreement this increased to $36.4 million and by 2012, "the third agreement indicated that $120.7 million would be allocated in support of design, administration, delivery and performance measurement and evaluation, plus $7.3 million for administration in 2009–10" (Dickson et al, 2013, 9).

With such substantial funds, the province was able to launch a range of pilot programs and new initiatives that could incorporate more social considerations. Labour market outcomes were a prime consideration, to be sure, but other major objectives included increased attention to vulnerable populations; greater emphasis on youth in the school system; more variety in language training provision; and greater concern with family offerings and supports" (Dickson et al. 2013, 12). In terms of governance, new bodies and programs were established within the BC government, and there was work across ministries, as well as with local governments, businesses and public sector organizations (Dickson et al. 2013, 13). These collaborations were "widely recognized as a strength of the BC model" (Dickson et al. 2013, 23). BC government efforts "evolved considerably from 1998–2013" and programs such as WelcomeBC "moved from a relatively stable period, through a very dynamic, innovative and experimental period, to one focused on learning and implementing a more sustainable, consistent, and system building approach to programs" (Dickson et al, 2013, 16).

Experimentation by a range of community organizations in the settlement sector occurred, such as the Affiliation for Multicultural Societies and Service Agencies' (AMSSA) "Safe Harbour" program promoting diversity in workplaces and organizations, and the Building Welcoming and Inclusive Neighbourhoods program to deal with issues of racism, diversity, and inclusion.

The federal government's "repatriation" signalled the end of such pilots, programming, and program delivery models. Predictably, this course correction had a devastating impact on the settlement sector and community organizations, but it also impacted the BC government, requiring the vacating of positions, offices, and even branches of the provincial government engaged in immigration and diversity issues. This meant a loss of expertise around immigration and multiculturalism issues. In true neoliberal fashion, the provincial government hollowed out and community organizations found themselves taking up the slack, all the while scrambling, and even competing, for limited federal funding.

In Manitoba, the federal government initially transferred $3,550,000 in settlement funding and $200,000 in associated funding, including the salaries of four full time positions. By 2012–13, "the amount had grown to over $36,000,000 and Manitoba Settlement staff numbered about 25" due to both "a significant investment by the Government of Canada (roughly tripling the national settlement funding envelope in this period) and also to growth resulting from the federal allocation formula, matching settlement funding to individual provinces with their landing numbers" (Clement, Carter, Vineberg 2013, 4). When Jason Kenney announced, in April 2012, that the federal government was cancelling the agreement, Manitoba had only one year's notice to cope with this drastic realignment (whereas BC had two).

For a smaller province, the substantial funding boost provided by the settlement agreements added focus to core settlement needs, but also forged strong interpersonal connections across sectors. Because it was also easier to take risks on this smaller scale, there was more leeway for creativity in Manitoba. With repatriation, service providers and community associations worried that relationships would be eroded, beginning with "the flexibility of provincial staff and their encouragement on innovation and creativity in the service sector" (Clement, Carter,

Vineberg 2013, 55). They also spoke of personal connections that built "trust and led to solutions that matched local needs" and feared the consequences of "an approach that blanketed regions and communities with the same program options and requirements" (ibid., 56). They felt that core funding had "left agencies in a better position to focus their effort on delivery to the benefit of newcomers" (ibid.).

In April 2014, Local Immigration Partnerships or LIPs became the preferred federal funding model whereby the federal government, through CIC (and its Liberal incarnation as Immigration, Refugees and Citizenship Canada), effectively contracted out services to settlement organizations. The federal government effectively enacted a command-and-control approach, engaging in streamlining through "one size fits all models" and reducing funds. Groups were compelled to apply for money to provide services and did not receive grants to develop new projects. Whereas, under the previous model, funds could be transferred to different Ministries and programs, with LIPs, funds were tightly micromanaged. This resulted in greater competition between groups, more time spent on obtaining funding, fewer resources, and less innovation.

Conclusions: What This Means for Federalism, Immigration, Multiculturalism, and Equality

This tale of two provinces is a complex story of rescaling, devolution, and governance in immigration, and its repercussions for federalism, multiculturalism, and equality. Despite the success claims of both Manitoba and BC, the ending is not cheery. In fact, on multiple fronts and for different reasons, these case studies are troubling for Canadian multiculturalism and equality, and point to a vulnerable future. Nonetheless, the various program shifts can also provide important insights, particularly when we make use of scalar and governmentality analyses.

First, and most obviously, this study reveals that neoliberalism's impact can be felt at all scales. Global marketized immigration norms are evident at macro, meso, and micro levels, as the logic around service delivery "streamlining" and their repercussions attest. Both types of immigration agreements reviewed in this paper are typical of neoliberal models in the sense that both download federal responsibilities to provincial and non-governmental parties. Nominees become "ideal" migrants because they epitomize archetypal neoliberal "entrepreneurs." They are the best economic "investments" in terms of their capital: financial, human, and social. The presumption is that with nominees' money and/or their know-how, they can contribute to provincial economies, and do so at minimal expense, as they are likely to integrate quickly and easily. In choosing these particular immigrants, both levels of government appear oblivious to not only class biases, but also the implications in terms of gender, race, and ethnicity. And, because these programs are more about take than give, the real-life sacrifices involved for the nominees in question are seldom fully countenanced.

Neoliberal streamlining and downsizing are also prime considerations at different points in the story, when, for instance, federal funding for immigrant services "shrank about one-fifth between 1997–2004" (Lewis 2010, 5). Increased funds for service delivery were allocated, and program innovation occurred in the mid 2000s, but these developments were accompanied by neoliberal logics in the form of devolution, and the intent to minimize duplication and overlap. The Harper government's subsequent "repatriation" was an exercise in econocentric control that has hollowed out the provincial immigration sector and its more imaginative efforts around diversity, relegating community organizations' scope to tightly managed service delivery.

At the same time, however, this analysis also illustrates that while neoliberalism is omnipresent, it is not omnipotent and unchanging. In fact, it highlights that a range of choices is being considered at multiple scales. Of course, these choices are constrained, given the intricate power relations involved at every turn. However, it is important to note the fact that diverse political actors are engaging in decision-making; that neoliberalism is not an immutable force.

Federal governments' (both Liberal and Conservative) immigration policies were certainly affected by global trends as they attempted to attract "designer" migrants, as well as cost-cut, decentralize, and devolve immigration policy. But just as decisions were made to roll out neoliberalism, there were also agreements that allowed for, and even supported, provincial experimentation that created more room for the social. Granted, immigration matters at both levels are increasingly in private hands (e.g., employer-driven models), attenuating state accountability, but this too reflects choices taken by the governments in question. The Harper government chose not to closely supervise the private sector, and yet it engaged in oversight, and even micromanagement, of provincial governments' and settlement organizations' programming. Its cookie-cutter approach to PTNPs and LIPs consolidated a minimal marketized governance model, but again this was a choice, one that reversed earlier trends.

The case studies considered in this chapter also show how provincial government decisions can be made and unmade. The fact that there were variations in nominee programs across the country underscores that provincial governments have had the power to innovate with programming of different kinds. As we have seen, BC chose a narrow, rigid, economic approach, but Manitoba opted for a broader, more flexible take on its PNP. Both "successes" have been called into question, but they do illustrate that provincial governments have the capacity to change the direction of policy, evident in expanding PNP streams as well as the attempts to bolster the most economically focussed programs with some creative social supports. Federalism, then, can both open up and close down policy possibilities over time, but an understanding of policy decisions is crucial.

This analysis also demonstrates the need for a deeper understanding of provincial contexts, socioeconomically, politically, and culturally. With respect to socio-economic shifts, beyond the rise of neoliberalism, it is important to consider upswings and downturns in provincial political economies. This paper highlights how modern-day socio-economics are bound up with immigration politics and the handling of multiculturalism and equality, as they have been throughout Canada's history.

Concomitantly, while a federal system can accommodate and foster innovation, there is also the question of the resources of the participating governments, particularly given that the circumscribed tax base of the subnational level necessarily constricts their capacities (fiscal, institutional, and human). BC and Manitoba's creativity took place when there was more federal money and when there could be more provincial personnel to administer the programs. Therefore, when we consider PTNPS as a whole, it is important to remember that not all provinces and territories have the same capacity, and poorer provinces may either be unwilling or unable to experiment or emulate innovations in other provinces.

In terms of partisan politics, by delving more deeply into the distinctive contexts of two provinces, it becomes evident that governments and their bureaucracies (Paquet 2015) matter. While the differences between parties have no doubt lessened with the consolidation of neoliberalism, there are nonetheless ideological variations between parties of the left and the right, as well as among parties of the same name in different provinces (i.e., between the NDP in BC versus the NDP in Manitoba), or between the federal and provincial levels (e.g., the PCs in Manitoba versus the federal Conservatives, or the BC Liberals and the national Liberals), the latter reflecting Canada's confederal party system. Clearly, there are also differences in political leadership at both levels that can impact intergovernmental relations, and federalism cannot be divorced from party conflicts and powerful political and economic interests (Gray 2010, 27).

Political choices in a federal system must also be put into cultural context. Constitutional and legislative commitments to multiculturalism and equality, as well as multicultural nationalism at the federal level, make Canada unique. But the cultural histories of provinces and their immigration pasts also impact political and cultural decisions. Incidences of Sinophobia in BC, or Manitoba's efforts at integration by matching "like with like," have deep resonance in the provinces in question and can undercut Canada's purported multicultural and equality commitments.

On the micro scale, it is critical to acknowledge that nominees are also making choices. In fact, many immigrants chose Canada because of its reputation for multiculturalism and equality (my interviews). They strategically weigh different immigration routes, and most opt for PTNPs in order to enter Canada more expeditiously. However, this approach can be adversely affected by politics and policy decisions at the federal level. Concomitantly, nominee choices are not unconstrained, given the challenging gender, race, and class dynamics they experience on the ground. For nominees experiencing downward class mobility and racial and gender discrimination, having their hopes and dreams dashed around equality and multiculturalism may not only have devastating financial, physical, and emotional effects, but may also have a detrimental intergenerational impact. For those considering Canada, changed circumstances around multiculturalism and equality may indeed lead immigrants to opt against this country, given its tarnished reputation.

In the final analysis, macro and meso scale measures have painted a rosier picture than the realities experienced at the micro level, and so success clearly depends on how and who measures it, and where. PTNPs use particular kinds of immigrants as quick fixes to provinces' and territories' economic and demographic dilemmas, while inadequately addressing the long-term social and cultural needs of nominees. However, provinces are distinct, as are the regions within them, and they will react differently to new arrivals. When the social and economic supports are lacking, transitions and integration, not surprisingly, are difficult. This will not bode well for the immigrants in question, nor for Canada's celebrated equality and multiculturalism. Comprehensive strategies that factor in the political economies and cultures of provinces, that harness their creative and innovative possibilities, that feature greater collaboration among multiple scales, and with the immigrants in question, are some elements that can lead to a happier ending to these tales of two provinces and, hopefully, more tangible and long-lasting successes.

While this chapter focuses on intergovernmental immigration policy changes unfolding primarily in the Harper era, I write this postscript in 2021, under a purportedly "sunnier" Justin Trudeau Liberal government, albeit one that has not been as distanced from its predecessor on immigration and citizenship matters as is commonly assumed (see Dobrowolsky 2017). I am also writing in the thick of the COVID-19 crisis, one in which multiple social and economic challenges, the result of decades of neoliberal-instigated underfunding, have become all too real, for far too many.

In response, extraordinary levels of spending on pandemic-related fiscal supports have occurred, federally and provincially. At present, Manitoba has "one of the largest per capita expenditures on stimulative infrastructure" of all the provinces and its COVID-19 measures have amounted to the equivalent of $9,400 worth of supports per person, with $8,400 picked up by the federal government (MacDonald 2021, 34). BC has the second highest level of spending on direct measures (after Alberta and its higher amount here reflect far more federal support), and its government "stands out as providing the highest per capital individual supports, worth over $800 a person – eight times higher than the next highest province, Quebec" (MacDonald 2021, 39).

Yet, the disparate impacts of COVID-19 on the communities of concern in this chapter have also become painfully apparent. (Im)migrants, racialized communities, and women are among the most vulnerable populations. They are adversely affected by the pandemic as they work in areas deemed essential, and on the front lines. This includes not only health care workers and first responders, but also employees in meat plants that have been hit hard with coronavirus outbreaks and high death tolls (Dryden 2020). In the summer of 2020, Migrante Manitoba wrote an open letter "'crying for help'" due to an out-of-control outbreak that took place in Brandon's Maple Leaf meat plant (Thompson 2020). Migrants are doing the most dangerous, and often the lowest paying jobs, and they are not even able to access basic health care and income supports.

Furthermore, in Winnipeg, "People from the city's Filipino and West Asian populations experienced higher job loss and a greater reduction in hours than white residents at the height of the lockdown" and the "employment rate for men is recovering faster than women" (Kavanagh 2021). Immigrant women, especially, are falling further behind (Hari and Nardon 2020), simply because they are found "in the retail, restaurant and hospitality sectors" that have been hit the hardest by pandemic (Kavanagh 2020).

In addition to these challenges, pandemic-associated incidents of anti-Asian racism have spiked across Canada, with more women targeted than men. Notably, the highest numbers of anti-Asian attacks have taken place in BC, with Vancouver experiencing a 707 per cent increase in anti-Asian hate crimes (Karamali 2021). These jaw-dropping numbers may also reflect the fact that more people are willing to report these abuses in the current context.

And so, in closing, this postscript underscores that the COVID-19 crisis has served to expose, more starkly and vividly, the tangible repercussions of robust neoliberalism, the profound inequities and racism in Canadian society, despite discourses, at multiple scales, of a welcoming, open-door, and diverse Canada (Dobrowolsky 2020), as well as the limitations of narratives of immigration policy success in Manitoba and BC.

REFERENCES

Abu-Laban, Yasmeen. 2009. "The Welfare State Under Siege?: Neo-liberalism, Immigration and Multiculturalism." In *Women and Public Policy in Canada: Neo-liberalism and After?*, edited by Alexandra Dobrowolsky, 146–65. Don Mills: Oxford University Press.

Banting, Keith. 2012. "Remaking Immigration: Asymmetric Decentralization and Canadian Federalism." In *Canadian Federalism: Performance, Effectiveness and Legitimacy*, edited by Herman Bakvis and Grace Skogstad, 261–81. Don Mills: Oxford University Press.

– 1987. *The Welfare State and Canadian Federalism*, 2nd ed. Montreal and Kingston: McGill-Queen's University Press.

Bauder, Harald. 2003. "Newcomers: Get Rich, Go Rural." *The Globe and Mail*, September 2, 2003, A13.

Bloemraad, Irene. 2012. "Understanding 'Canadian Exceptionalism' in Immigration and Pluralism Policy." Transatlantic Council on Migration. July 2012.

British Columbia. 2011. "Ministry of Jobs, Tourism and Innovation." *BC Provincial Nominee Program Evaluation Report*.

Brodie, Janine. 1990. *The Political Economy of Regionalism*. Toronto: Harcourt, Brace, Jovanovich.

Brown, Wendy. 2016. "Sacrificial Citizenship: Neoliberalism, Human Capital, and Austerity." *Constellations* 23 (1): 3–14. https://doi.org/10.1111/1467-8675.12166.

Bucklaschuk, Jill, Alison Moss, and Robert C. Annis. 2009. "Temporary May Not Always Be Temporary: The Impact of 'Transitional' Foreign Workers and Increasing Diversity in Brandon, Manitoba." *Our Diverse Cities* 5: 64–70.

Carter, Tom. 2012. "Provincial Nominee Programs and Temporary Foreign Worker Programs: A Comparative Assessment of Advantages and Disadvantages in Addressing Labour Shortages." In *Legislating Inequality: Temporary Labour Migration in Canada*, edited by Christine Straehle and Patti Lenard, 178–201. Montreal and Kingston, McGill-Queen's University Press.

Carter, Tom, M. Morrish, and B. Amoyaw. 2008. "Attracting Immigrants to Smaller Urban and Rural Communities: Lessons Learned from the Manitoba Provincial Nominee Program." *Journal of International Migration and Integration* 9 (2): 161–83. http://doi.org/10.1007/s12134-008-0051-2.

Carter, Tom, Manish Pandey, and James Townsend. 2010. "The Manitoba Provincial Nominee Program: Attraction, Integration and Retention of Immigrants." IRPP Study No: 10 (October).

Charles, Nickie, and Fiona Mackay. 2013. "Feminist politics and framing contests: domestic violence policy Scotland and Wales." *Critical Social Policy* 33(4): 393–615. http://doi.org/10.1177/0261018313483488.

Citizenship and Immigration Canada (CIC). 2011. *Evaluation of the Provincial Nominee Program*. Ottawa: Evaluation Division, CIC.

Clement, Gérard, Thomas Carter, and Robert Vineberg. 2013. *Case Study: The Realigned System of Settlement Service Delivery in Manitoba 1999 to 2013.* Report Prepared for the Western Canadian Consortium on Integration, Citizenship and Cohesion (WCCICC), 1–161.

Collier, Cheryl. 2009. "Violence against Women or Violence against 'People'? Assessing the Impact of Neoliberalism and Post-neoliberalism on Anti-Violence Policy in Ontario and British Columbia." In *Women and Public Policy: Neoliberalism and After?*, edited by Alexandra Dobrowolsky, 166–86. Don Mills: Oxford University Press.

Dickson, Heather, Evert Lindquist, Ben Pollard, and Miu Chung Yan. 2013. "Devolving Settlement Funding from the Government of Canada: The British Columbia Experience, 1998–2013." Report Prepared for the Western Canadian Consortium on Integration, Citizenship and Cohesion (WCCICC).

Dobrowolsky, Alexandra. 2020. "A Diverse, Feminist 'Open Door' Canada? Trudeau-Styled Equality, Liberalisms, and Feminisms." In *Turbulent Times and Transformational Possibilities? Gender and Politics Today and Tomorrow*, edited by Fiona MacDonald and Alexandra Dobrowolsky, 23–48. Toronto: University of Toronto Press.

– 2017. "Bad versus Big Canada: State Imaginaries of Immigration and Citizenship." *Studies in Political Economy* 98 (2): 197–222. https://doi.org/10.1080/07078552.2017.1343001.

– 2012. "Nuancing Neoliberalism: Lessons Learned from a Failed Immigration Experiment." *Journal of International Migration and Integration* 14 (2): 197–218. http://doi.org/10.1007%2Fs12134-012-0234-8.

– 2011. "The Intended and Unintended Effects of a New Immigration Strategy: Insights from Nova Scotia's Provincial Nominee Program." *Studies in Political Economy* 87 (1): 109–41. https://doi.org/10.1080/19187033.2011.1 1675022.

– 2000. *The Politics of Pragmatism: Women, Representation and Constitutionalism in Canada*. Don Mills: Oxford University Press.

Dobrowolsky, Alexandra, Catherine Bryan, and Pauline Gardiner Barber. 2015. "Choices, Calculations, and Commitments that Help to Create a Home Away from Home." In *The Warmth of the Welcome: Is Atlantic Canada a Home Away from Home for Immigrants?*, edited by Evangelia Tastsoglou, Alexandra Dobrowolsky, and Barbara Cottrell, 60–79. Sydney: CBU Press.

Dryden, Joel. 2020. "Filipino workers at Meatpacking Plant Feel Unfairly Blamed for Canada's Biggest COVID-19 Outbreak." *CBC News*. April 26, 2020. https://www.cbc.ca/news/canada/calgary/cargill-high-river-jbs -brooks-deena-hinshaw-1.5545113.

Findlay, Tammy. 2015. *Femocratic Administration: Gender, Governance and Democracy in Ontario*. Toronto: University of Toronto Press.

Gagnon, Alain. 2014. *Minority Nations in the Age of Uncertainty: New Paths to National Emancipation and Empowerment*. Toronto: University of Toronto Press.

Grace, Joan. 2011. "Gender and Institutions of Multi-Level Governance: Child Care and Social Policy Debates in Canada." In *Gender, Politics, and Institutions: Towards a Feminist Institutionalism*, edited by Mona Lena Krook and Fiona Mackay, 95–111. Basingstoke: Palgrave Macmillan.

Gravelle, Matthew, Antje Ellermann, and Catherine Dauvergne. 2013. "Studying Migration Governance from the Bottom-UP." In *The Social, Political, and Historical Contours of Deportation*, edited by Bridget Anderson, Matthew Gibney, and Emanuela Paoletti, 59–77. New York: Springer.

Gray, Gwendolyn. 2010. "Feminism, Federalism and Multilevel Governance: The Elusive Search for Theory?" In *Federalism, Feminism and Multilevel Governance*, edited by Melissa Haussman, Marian Sawer, and Jill Vickers, 19–36. Burlington: Ashgate.

Hari, Amrita, and Luciara Nardon. 2020. "Immigrant Women Falling behind During Pandemic." *Winnipeg Free Press*, November 10, 2020. https://www .winnipegfreepress.com/special/coronavirus/immigrant-women-falling -behind-during-pandemic-573024941.html.

Henin, Bernard, and Michelle R. Bennett. 2002. "Immigration to Canada's Mid-Sized Cities: A Study of Latin Americans and Africans in Victoria, BC."

RIIM Working Paper Series No. 02-22. Vancouver, BC, Metropolis British Columbia.

Hum, Derek, and Wayne Simpson. 2002. "Selectivity and Immigration in Canada." *Journal of International Migration and Integration* 3 (2): 107–27. https://doi.org/10.1007/s12134-002-1005-8.

Huynh, Vien. 2004. *Closer to Home: Immigration Policy in Western Canada.* Canada West Foundation, Building the New West Report #3.

Karamali, Kamil. 2021. "Anti-Asian Racism in Canada More 'Frequent' as Report Tallies Hundreds of Attacks During Pandemic." *Global News*, March 23, 2021. https://globalnews.ca/news/7715260/ant-asian-racism-report-pandemic/.

Kavanagh, Sean. 2020. "Indigenous Winnipeggers, Visible Minorities, People with Disabilities Hit Harder by Pandemic: City Economist." *CBC News*, September 10, 2020. https://www.cbc.ca/news/Canada/Manitoba/economist-pandemic-impact-1.5719068.

Kukushkin, Vadim. 2009. "Immigrant-Friendly Communities: Making Immigration Work for Employers and Other Stakeholders in Small-Town Canada." Conference Board of Canada. Presentation for Leader's Roundtable on Immigration, Chatham-Kent, Ontario, April 23, 2009.

Kymlicka, Will. 1998. "Multinational Federalism in Canada: Rethinking the Partnership." In *Beyond the Impasse, Toward Reconciliation*, edited by Guy Laforest and Roger Gibbins, 15–50. Montreal: Institute for Research on Public Policy.

Laski, Harold. 1939. "The Obsolescence of Federalism." *New Republic* 98 (3): 367–79.

Leo, Christopher, and M. August. 2009. "Multilevel Governance of Immigration and Settlement: Making Deep Federalism Work." *Canadian Journal of Political Science* 42 (2): 491–510. http://doi.org/10.1017/S0008423909090337.

Lewis, Nathaniel M. 2010. "A Decade Later: Assessing Successes and Challenges in Manitoba's Provincial Immigrant Nominee Program." *Canadian Public Policy* 36 (2): 241–64. https://doi.org/10.3138/cpp.36.2.241.

Ley, David. 2010. *Millionaire Migrants: Trans-Pacific Life Lines*. Oxford: Wiley-Blackwell.

Maher, Stephen. 2010. "N.S. Faces Uphill Battle on Immigration." *The Chronicle Herald*, December 9, 2010. http://nexuscanada.blogspot.com/2010/12/ns-faces-uphill-battle-on-immigration.html?m=0.

"Manitoba Politicians Spar over Immigration Changes." 2012. *CBC News*, April 19, 2012. http://cbc/news/canada/manitoba/story/2012/04/19/mb-immigration-showdown-legislature-manitoba.html.

Macdonald, David. 2021. "Picking Up the Tab: A Complete Accounting of Federal and Provincial COVID-19 Measures in 2020." Canadian Centre for

Policy Alternatives. https://policyalternatives.ca/sites/default/files
/uploads/publications/National%20Office/2021/01/Picking%20up
%20the%20tab.pdf

McGrane, David. 2014. *Remaining Loyal: Social Democracy in Quebec and
Saskatchewan*. Montreal and Kingston: McGill-Queen's Press.

Nakache, Delphine, and Sarah D'Aoust, 2012. "Provincial and Territorial
Nominee Programs: An Avenue to Permanent Residency for Low-Skilled
Temporary Foreign Workers?" In *Legislating Inequality: Temporary Labour
Migration in Canada*, edited by Christine Straehle and Patti Lenard, 158–201.
Montreal and Kingston, McGill-Queen's University Press.

Nolan, C., K. McCallum, and Anisa Zehtab-Martin. 2009. "Regionalization BC
2008: Regionalization and Rural Immigration in British Columbia." Working
Paper Series no. 09 (06), Metropolis British Columbia.

Pandey, Manish, and James Townsend. 2010. "Provincial Nominee Programs:
An Evaluation of Earnings and Retention Rates of Nominees." Department
of Economics Working Paper Number 2010-01. Winnipeg: University of
Winnipeg.

Paquet, Mireille. 2015. "Bureaucrats as Immigration Policy-Makers: The Case
of Subnational Immigration Activism in Canada, 1990–2010." *Journal of
Ethnic and Migration Studies* 41 (11): 1815–35. https://doi.org/10.1080/13691
83X.2015.1023185.

Sawer, Marian, and Jill Vickers. 2010. "Introduction: Political Architecture
and Its Gender Impact." In *Federalism, Feminism and Multilevel Governance*,
edited by Melissa Haussman, Marian Sawer, and Jill Vickers, 3–18. London:
Ashgate.

Seidle, F. Leslie. 2013. "Canada's Provincial Nominee Immigration Programs.
Securing Greater Policy Alignment." IRPP Study No. 43.

– 2010. "Intergovernmental Immigration Agreements and Public
Accountability." *Policy Options* (July–August): 49–53.

Stevenson, Garth. 2014. *Building Nations from Diversity: Canadian and American
Experience Compared*. Montreal and Kingston: McGill-Queen's University
Press.

Thompson, Sam. 2020. "Migrant Workers at Brandon Maple Leaf Plant Seek
Shutdown, Increased Health Measures." *Global News*, August 24, 2020.
https://globalnews.ca/news/7295412/maple-leaf-foods-brandon
-covid-19-outbreak/.

Vancouver Sun. 2008. "Business Immigration Falls Short of Target." May 5,
2008. Online: www.canada.com/vancouversun/news/business/story
.html?id=730014e0-36ba-4788-82d7-7fddb62c82d7.

Wallner, Jennifer. 2014. *Learning to School: Federalism and Public Schooling in
Canada: New Paths to National Emancipation and Empowerment*. Toronto:
University of Toronto Press.

Wilkinson, Lori, and Jill Bucklaschuk. 2014. "What Are the Settlement
    Experiences of Newly Settled Newcomers to Western Canada: An Interim
    Report." Draft Report Prepared for the Western Canadian Consortium on
    Integration, Citizenship and Cohesion (WCCICC), March 31, 2014: 1–30.
Wood, Graeme. 2015. "Refugees Reporting Higher Earnings in Canada than
    Investor Immigrants." *National Post*, March 2, 2015. http://www
    .nationalpost.com/m/wp/blog.html?b=news.nationalpost.com/2015/03/02
    /refugees-reporting-higher-earnings-incanada-than-investor-immigrant.

6 Challenging Narratives to Neoliberalism in Media Representations of American Health Reform: Lessons from the United States

BRENT EPPERSON

Introduction[1]

The range of neoliberal policy narratives and their social consequences in the United States are arguably clearest in the health sphere. The myth of market efficiency and the promise that market competition and choice can replace a publicly funded and universally accessible health care system left millions of Americans uninsured and without access to quality health care. Hook and Markus (2020) argue that narratives of choice and personal responsibility have contributed to worse health outcomes and shorter life expectancy in the US than in comparable developed countries. Currently, even modest public health care expansions encounter challenge and vulnerability. Analysis of ongoing health reform debates exposes a spectrum of neoliberal policy narratives that coexist in contention both within, and between, the Republican and Democratic parties. It further reveals narratives of resistance on the margins that seek to reify and reintegrate "the social" – or in this case, articulate a sense of social care in the relationship between the state and citizens.

Resistance to neoliberalism in American health care policy has taken on new urgency following persistent Republican attempts to repeal, replace, or undermine Obamacare – the 2010 federal Patient Protection and Affordable Care Act (ACA). While full repeal efforts failed during the Trump presidency, the administration weakened tax regulations to stop enforcement of the individual insurance mandate (Gostin 2019). The Trump Administration expanded limited-duration private insurance plans that exclude coverage of pre-existing medical conditions, reduced funding for ACA enrolment campaigns, and relaxed rules for states to apply for waivers to offer insurance plans that do not meet ACA standards (Oberlander 2018; Scott 2019). Examining three national surveys from 2016–19, Gaffney et al. (2020) estimate that 2.3 million Americans lost health insurance during the Trump presidency. The growth in uninsurance was particularly concentrated in Republican-controlled states that rejected the ACA Medicaid expansions and relied more heavily on the private insurance market (Skopec et al. 2020). While the Biden administration reversed the Trump-era reforms in March 2021 (Luhby 2021) and mooted the possibility of reinforcing the ACA with a public insurance option (Sotomayor 2021), the Trump years demonstrated that the ACA is vulnerable to targeted rollbacks through executive orders or future congressional repeal.

This ongoing struggle reveals discursive continuity in American health policy debates, including conflicts and overlap between mainstream Democratic and Republican proposals. Neoliberal emphasis on individual responsibility, choice, efficiency, and competition continues to shape American health care policy and delineate political possibility. Analysis further reveals that the Affordable Care Act fundamentally altered the architecture of the American health care system and further entrenched a particular neoliberal narrative that remains dominant in the Democratic Party.

Recent research has demonstrated that the neoliberal health care narratives were equally present in White House and congressional offices where key decisions were made. Through extensive interviews with senior policy staffers who developed and implemented the ACA, Genieys, Darviche, and Epperson (2020) demonstrate that its policy architects were committed to maintaining the market-oriented features of the health care system, while preserving Medicare and Medicaid as parallel public systems to buttress the private insurance market. They viewed single payer proposals as politically unfeasible and a threat to consensus. Their leading priorities throughout the reform effort were cost control and maintaining the largest possible political coalition to ensure legislative success (Genieys, Darviche, and Epperson 2020). While Republicans maintain their desire to dismantle the ACA in favour of an even more market-fundamentalist system, and progressive Democrats continue to advocate for single-payer or other models of universal insurance coverage from the margins of their party, Obamacare and the favoured health policy narratives of Democratic Party elites will not be easily displaced.

Trumpian criticisms of Obamacare were well rehearsed. Far-right Republican and libertarian critics have consistently disparaged the individual and employer insurance mandates to expand health insurance coverage as federal government overreach. They have emphasized states' rights arguments to demand the devolution of health care policy-making (for example, regarding Medicaid funding and private health insurance regulations that benefit low-income Americans and those who would otherwise be too sick to access the private insurance market). In the American context, the focus on states' rights simultaneously reflects a conservative tradition of trusting lower levels of government to cleave more closely to their values, the history of conservative resistance to the expansion of federal powers, and acceptance of social inequality (Epperson 2017, 37–78).

Emphasizing states' rights as a means to oppose federal efforts to improve conditions for marginalized people is a long-standing tradition on the American right. States' rights arguments harken back to anti-abolitionists in the 1850s, as well as civil rights opponents in the 1960s (Diamond 1995, 66–90; Nelson 1999, 114–15). In the health sphere, objections to federal government policies to help the uninsured were already present during the Medicare debates of the 1960s (Zelizer 2015). Beyond states' rights arguments, narratives of resistance to increased government regulation of the insurance industry and health insurance mandates were present in the Utah Health System Reform (UHSR) from 2004 to 2011, and the Massachusetts Health Reform Law debates from 2002 to 2006 (Epperson 2017). Importantly, and much like the Obamacare debates, counter narratives in Utah and Massachusetts that favoured universal access were also part of these state-level efforts and have remained part of the American health care reform story. Thus, there has been consistency in the competing narratives during several state and federal reform cycles.

In some ways, it is surprising that opposition to Obamacare has remained such a galvanizing issue for the American right. After all, the reform left tens of millions of Americans uninsured and was far more limited in its expansion of public health care than the Medicare and Medicaid reforms of the 1960s. However, the ACA lacked a supportive groundswell fuelled by narratives of social solidarity. Instead, it was an elite-driven reform effort. Tuohy (2018) writes:

> It was the fate of the United States that, were it finally to achieve universal health care coverage, it would have to do so in an era dominated not by grand epic narratives of national solidarity or universal rights but by an expert discourse of market-oriented redesign. (440–1)

Tuohy explains that the technocratic, economic-oriented language of the policy elites who designed the ACA lacked "an epic narrative of public purpose" and seemed disconnected from President Obama's grandiose rhetoric that promised to solve big national problems (including health care). The most effective policy narratives, Tuohy argues, reconcile the discourses of experts with public cultural discourses (Tuohy 2018, 428–9). A key lesson from the ACA story, of course, is that future health policy reformers need to get the policy narrative right if they want to resolve the ongoing crises of uninsurance and under-insurance in the United States. Yet because American health policy experts largely remain committed to neoliberal narratives of piecemeal, market-oriented reform (Genieys, Darviche, and Epperson 2020), the ACA is an easy target for Republican opponents.

Building from Raymond Williams's keywords, Janine Brodie (2007) notes that the "residual" social policy narratives of past regimes and "emergent" new progressive narratives, as well as unanticipated social risks and political divisions, challenge the neoliberal status quo in different political contexts. Despite the dominance of neoliberal narratives and metaphors of health care, when existing public programs are grounded in legislation – e.g., Medicare, Medicaid, the State Children's Health Insurance Program (CHIP), the Veterans Health Administration (VHA), and even government regulations of the private insurance industry – they act as residual references and as public safeguards against market expansion. As prior research has shown, these residual references are significant, since citizens become deeply invested in universal public health and social programs (Ferree 2009; Lazar and Church 2013, 279; Tuohy 1999, 102).

Brodie (2007) has argued that the neoliberal policy regime seeks to solidify its place through individualization of responsibility and the establishment of a new vision of social justice founded upon mass adherence to a myth of choice. This vision rejects prior notions of equity, the welfare state, collective responsibility, and social progress (Brodie 2007, 100–05). The dominant position, however, never stands unopposed: other ways of imagining health care are available. Massachusetts and Utah provide examples of the implementation of neoliberal health policy, as well as narratives that challenge it. As this chapter demonstrates, the media plays an important role in these debates by mobilizing and favouring market-oriented policy narratives (Brodie 2015, 12).

Media Representations of Health Care Reform and the Meso-narrative of Neoliberalism

For most observers, the media filters their interpretations of health care reform debates. Media narratives and frames define issues and assign meaning to events, contextualizing policy proposals (Chandler 2007, 2–9, 217–20; Chomsky and Herman 1988; Hall 1997, 1–12, 13–73, 223–90;

Keren 2011; Orgad 2012). Policy narratives are always present in the media; however, the frequency of coverage "waves" across time in reaction to surrounding events. A "media wave" can be understood as sustained increase in coverage of an issue. An initial event draws media attention, and then competition for public attention extends the wave duration (Giasson and Brin 2010; Giasson et al. 2010; Vasterman 2005). The announcement of a major health care reform effort may serve as the pivotal event that a wave of media reporting follows.

Peter Vasterman's (2005) "media hype" framework and Janine Brodie's (1997) conceptualization of "meso-narratives" assist interpretation of competing policy narratives and media representations. Vasterman (2005) examines the curiosity that the media generates about policy debates, as well as the role of journalists in amplifying issues. More frequent reporting on an issue can sustain stories, as media outlets follow one another's coverage. Brodie (1997) defines a meso-narrative as "the periodic rewriting of stories about the modernity story." In different eras, dominant political-economic logics are effectively communicated through stories that define some policy proposals as modern and reasonable, while others are excluded as either anachronistic or radical. Grounded in particular national histories and complex power relations, Brodie explains further:

> Meso-narratives are an historical consensus about what is understood to be rational, progress, emancipation, justice, and so on. As such, they act as historically defined templates which underlie a policy field, shaping the content and delivery of public goods, and allowing for a certain measure of coherence in state activities, identity formation and forms of political contestation. (Brodie 1997, 227)

During media coverage of the Massachusetts and Utah debates, and later Obamacare, neoliberal health policy proposals were regularly articulated as rational. These proposals included preserving the private insurance system, corporate actuarial practices that led to care rationing and outright exclusion, and the legitimacy of profit-seeking. Proposals that challenged the neoliberal vision received much less favourable media attention.

A Health Reform Debate That Never Ended

Many years after the passage of the ACA, contention surrounding the reform remains lively. The first Republican effort to overturn the legislation took place on 23 March 2010 – the day that President Obama signed the ACA into law. On that day, the attorney general of Utah and his counterparts in twelve conservative states filed a lawsuit to challenge Obamacare (*New York Times* 2010). Since then, court challenges and dozens of congressional efforts to "repeal and replace" the ACA have continued (O'Keefe 2014). In a much-publicized Texas decision in December 2018, a judge ruled that the individual insurance mandate within the ACA is unconstitutional, arguing that the entire ACA must be struck down (Goodnough and Pear 2018, Gostin 2019). Subsequently known as *Texas v. United States*, seventeen Democratic-controlled states challenged the decision, and the case has continued to make its way through the courts (Gostin 2019; Keith 2019).

Notably, the schism between the centre-right, far-right, and libertarian factions within the Republican Party's ranks on the direction of health reform can be traced back to earlier state-level debates in Utah and Massachusetts (Associated Press 2017; Lee et al. 2017; Roy 2017). Mitt Romney supported individual insurance mandates as a moderate Republican governor after the idea was conceived by the Heritage Foundation (Appleby 2005; Haislmaier 2006; Romney 2006; Roy 2011). Utah's moderate Republican governor, Jon Huntsman, initially supported insurance mandates until he was outflanked by more conservative Republicans (Cherkis 2011; Cherkis and Ward 2011). Meanwhile, the libertarian and most conservative elements of the Republican Party have opposed mandates consistently. In the context of the Romneycare debates, this division within Republican ranks was aptly described as "free-market purity vs. a sort-of-free-market pragmatism" (Fitzgerald 2005). However, while these health care policy factions have existed since the Romneycare debates (Fitzgerald 2005; Ross 2006), the Republican balance of power in Washington during the Trump era favoured a hard-right perspective on health care reform – specifically, opposition to insurance mandates, reduced support for means-tested health care programs, fewer public protections from insurance company abuses, fewer insurance industry regulations, and more devolution of health policy-making power to the states (Krieg 2017; Watson 2017).

On the left of the neoliberal spectrum, leading congressional Democrats and state attorneys general towed the line to defend the ACA in the courts (Ollstein 2019). If we understand the 2010 ACA as a continuation of left neoliberalism, tracking from the Clintons' failed 1994 Health Security Act, and the legislative success of the Massachusetts Health Reform Law of 2006, the underlying principles are clear: save the for-profit health care system from itself. Obamacare preserved health care as a commodity, implementing a new regulatory framework that put an end to unpopular pre-existing condition exclusions and lifetime limits for insurance payments to treat costly medical conditions. It expanded Medicaid (means-tested social insurance for the poor) and provided subsidies to help low-income people purchase private insurance (Epperson 2017). Yet, in keeping with the dominant neoliberal orthodoxy in the Democratic Party, Obamacare did not fundamentally challenge the employment-based private insurance system.

In opposition to the Affordable Care Act, and on the right of the political spectrum, the 2017 Graham-Cassidy bill offered, arguably, the most developed of the Republican repeal-and-replace efforts. Graham-Cassidy aimed to drastically reduce federal ACA outlays and to eliminate both individual and employer insurance mandates, weaken consumer protections from insurance rate increases due to age or pre-existing conditions, and increase individual reliance on private Health Savings Accounts (HSAs) (Soffen 2017). While the Graham-Cassidy bill did not succeed in repealing Obamacare in 2017, these central policy proposals, which, in part, have roots in the Utah Health System Reform, still underpin conservative Republican narratives. The reform logic presumes that the health insurance market will work better and serve everyone, without government subsidies or increased oversight.

Finally, outside of the neoliberal policy frame, a number of 2020 Democratic presidential candidates expressed support for the ambiguous "Medicare-for-all" slogan, which amounted to a social investment state (SIS) narrative in favour of a single-payer system to guarantee universal coverage. In practice, however, Medicare-for-all means different policy proposals to different candidates (Kurtzleben 2019). Medicare-for-all is the equivalent to "repeal and replace" for progressives. Since none of these narratives is new, and each persists in contemporary debates, it remains valuable to examine their place in earlier state-level reforms.

The Meso-narrative of Neoliberalism in the Media – Examples from the Utah and Massachusetts Health Care Reforms

The media's coverage of Obamacare largely missed the fact that the dominant narratives of the federal debates were already present in earlier and parallel state-level reform efforts. Most notably, the cases of the Massachusetts Health Reform Law and the Utah Health System Reform demonstrate the diversity of competing narratives in state reform efforts.

The Romneycare initiative in Massachusetts largely served as the blueprint for the Affordable Care Act. For its part, the Utah Health System Reform served as a counter example for ACA critics. Obama's successes – requiring the health insurance industry to accept more government regulation; expanding health insurance coverage through investments in Medicaid; mandating that individuals purchase health insurance; obliging large companies to provide health insurance to their workers; and providing subsidies to help lower-income people (those not poor enough to qualify for Medicaid) to purchase private health insurance – all imitated the Romneycare strategy at the state level. Similarly, the legislative failures of progressive Democrats in the federal ACA debates – abandoning single-payer social insurance; renouncing the so-called public option to compete with private health insurance companies – reinforced the dominance of the market-oriented Romneycare model. Once Obamacare was implemented, and despite the cries of socialism emitting from its critics, the new policy architecture affirmed a prevailing neoliberal vision of health care delivery.

To grasp the significance of this new policy architecture, it is helpful to understand how neoliberal governmentalities aim to redefine citizenship practices (Brodie 2007; Rose 1999; Dean 1999). Advancing values of individualism, entrepreneurialism, and resilience, neoliberal governmentality increases social precariousness through the implementation of market-oriented social policies that redefine the "relationship between citizenship and social justice" (Brodie 2007, 94). This redefinition of citizens' relationship to social justice, in practice, individualizes responsibility for navigating social risks, repudiates systemic explanations for poverty and other societal problems, and rejects collective responsibility to find solutions (Brodie 2007). Thus, Utah's and Massachusetts' reforms differed along a neoliberal scale, yet both policy approaches rejected collective responsibility for risk and extensive new social investments.

Perhaps one of the clearest articulations of the neoliberal health care narrative came from Dr. Norman Thurston, the Utah Health Reform Implementation Coordinator and a key adviser to the Utah Governor's Office. In his "Brief History of the Utah Health System Reform," Thurston wrote:

> The invisible hand of the marketplace, rather than the heavy hand of government, is the most effective means whereby reform may take place … Utah's approach to health system reform is to move toward a consumer-based system, where individuals are responsible for their health, health care, and health care financing. A major step in that direction is the development of a workable defined contribution system … Utah's approach to health system reform relies on the fundamental principles of personal responsibility, private markets, and competition. To promote competition in the health care system, consumers need three things – accurate and

relevant information, real choice, and the opportunity to benefit from making good choices. The exchange model enhances private competition in the health care system by providing all three elements of increased competition. (Thurston 2011)

Thurston starts with a familiar Adam Smith reference, then moves to condemn government intervention with a broad brush, treating patients as consumers, and reductively describing the health care system as a market. He celebrates competition, and frames Utahans as rational consumers who can make the best choices for themselves if they have accurate information.

This narrative clearly appeals to a Republican political base. It was notably less frequent during the Massachusetts health reform, which was built on delicate alliances between a Republican governor, a Democratic legislature, well-organized progressive social activists, and the powerful insurance and pharmaceutical lobbies. In Utah, conservative Republican rhetoric pervaded the official narrative throughout the UHSR's implementation, in large part, because Republicans held a super majority in the state legislature. Conservative state lawmakers were eager to appeal to Utah's business community, which was opposed to insurance mandates or any tax increases to support the expansion of coverage. Compared to Massachusetts, pressure from social movements and patient advocacy groups was less significant. The Utah reform took place in large part because Governor Huntsman wanted to prove that he could do better than Governor Romney, and Utah Republicans wanted to prove that they could develop an even more market-oriented alternative to the ascendant neoliberal orthodoxy that underpinned the 1994 Clinton plan, Romneycare, and later Obamacare as it developed parallel to the Utah effort (Epperson 2017, 245–50).

Media representations of health care during these state reforms often included tales of triumphant neoliberalism. Governor Romney himself wrote an op-ed in the *Wall Street Journal* to carefully frame the Massachusetts legislation:

Only weeks after I was elected governor, Tom Stemberg, the founder and former CEO of Staples, stopped by my office. He told me that "if you really want to help people, find a way to get everyone health insurance." I replied that would mean raising taxes and a Clinton-style government takeover of health care. He insisted: "You can find a way." I believe that we have. Every uninsured citizen in Massachusetts will soon have affordable health insurance and the costs of health care will be reduced. And we will need no new taxes, no employer mandate and no government takeover to make this happen ... One great thing about federalism is that states can innovate, demonstrate and incorporate ideas from one another. Other states will learn from our experience and improve on what we've done. That's the way we'll make health care work for everyone. (2006)

Romney's message was clear. He represented the legislation as a conservative, business-community inspired proposal to control costs and expand access to private health insurance. Romney aimed to set his plan apart from the Clintons' 1994 HSA, a plan he criticized as a "government takeover." He creatively framed the state's health care crisis (skyrocketing health care outlays, and rising numbers of uninsured) as a "personal responsibility" issue. In the op-ed, he further emphasized bipartisanship as a foundation for legislative success and as a sign of the merits of the plan. He acknowledged the role of the conservative Heritage Foundation in developing the plan, and outlined his administration's efforts to find efficiencies (Romney 2006). It is possible that Romney's carefully framed representation of the legislation was intended to appeal to conservative political sensibilities, without alienating undecided political moderates, perhaps in light of his political objectives in the approaching Republican presidential primaries. It is equally possible that he was trying to strike the delicate balance he needed to maintain the bipartisan coalition that supported health care reform. In either case, the framing effectively represented the appeal to neoliberal policy logic – corporate endorsement, policy entrepreneurship, faith in the market to meet the needs of consumers with limited oversight, a rejection of employer insurance mandates and tax increases, and a positive reference to policy devolution and state-level innovation.

Challenging the Neoliberal Meso-narrative: Libertarian Critiques

Both the political left and right challenged health policy narratives in Massachusetts and Utah. While both libertarian and SIS narratives appeared less frequently in newspaper coverage than the dominant neoliberal narratives, the challenging narratives comprised an important part of the overall media representation of these debates. On the political right, libertarian narratives that opposed any government regulation of the private health care market were key in challenging neoliberalism. It is important to note that the label "libertarian" (like the term "liberal," for that matter) has a unique meaning in the United States. In the American case, Noam Chomsky has described libertarianism as a type of anarcho-capitalism that favours markets without government regulations or restraints (Chomsky et al. 2002, 200; Chomsky and Sedlak 2011).

With the support of think tanks such as the Cato Institute, the American libertarian ideology sanctifies private property, disparages public welfare programs, and rejects most forms of taxation (Chomsky et al. 2002, 200; Chomsky and Sedlak 2011). The libertarian challenging narratives in newspaper media coverage of the Massachusetts and Utah debates were principally used to oppose Romneycare *and* Obamacare reforms. Libertarian columnists viewed insurance mandates and government-regulated insurance exchanges as infringements on free markets and violations of individual rights.

In one of the best examples of a libertarian critique during the Massachusetts debates, a *Boston Herald* piece entitled "Critics slam insurance plan as intrusive and unwieldy," noted:

> Conservatives bashed the law as an unwarranted government intrusion that will fail to achieve universal coverage or widespread public support. "It represents an unprecedented level of interference with personal decision-making," said Michael Tanner of the Cato Institute, a libertarian think tank. "Simply by breathing in Massachusetts they're saying you must buy the product they say you should have" ... The law's lack of built-in cost controls will quickly result in higher premiums, new taxes and larger fines. Barbara Anderson of Citizens for Limited Taxation applauded Romney's core goal of encouraging personal responsibility for medical costs, but she said the law is going to "end up accomplishing a lot less than they're saying and it's going to cost a lot more." (Ross 2006)

The Ross article backhandedly praised the individual responsibility aspects of Romneycare while condemning health care regulations and insurance mandates.

Libertarian critiques were also present during the UHSR; however, it was more common for these pieces to focus on Obamacare or even to pejoratively compare Romneycare to the UHSR reform, which was more tolerable to libertarians. For example:

> Government-run health care has been tried in Massachusetts ... and it's a disaster. According to Peter Suderman, Associate Editor at *Reason* magazine, "since 2006, the cost of the state's insurance program has ballooned by 42 per cent, or almost 600 million. According to an analysis by the Rand Corporation, 'in the absence of policy change, health care spending in Massachusetts is expected to nearly double to $123 billion in 2020,

increasing 8 per cent faster than the state's gross domestic product.' Insurance costs in Massachusetts are the highest in the nation and double-digit rate increases are expected again this year. Yet, President Obama claimed Saturday that under the Democrats' plan, rates would go down. How is this possible? The only reason Massachusetts hasn't become insolvent is because of large transfusions of cash from Washington, which perpetuates the illusion the program works." (Thomas 2010)

Libertarian pieces accounted for a small, yet noteworthy part of media representations in the Massachusetts and Utah cases, but criticism of these state reforms was not limited to the libertarian right.

The Cracks Where the Light Gets In: Challenging Social Investment State (SIS) Narratives of Health Care Reform

In the Democratic-leaning media, challenging narratives were based primarily on the SIS perspective that favourably represented socialized insurance, socialized medicine, or government-regulated mandatory private health insurance. The SIS perspective amounts to "a fundamental break from the neoliberal view of social policy as a cost and a hindrance to economic and employment growth" (Morel, Palier, and Palme 2012, 2). In health care policy, a SIS perspective urges governments to provide "universal access to safe, high-quality, efficient health care services, better cooperation between social and health care services, and effective public health policies to prevent chronic disease [which can] make an important contribution to economic productivity and social inclusion" (European Commission 2013, 20). It holds that governments should aim to "guarantee universal access and increase the quality of health care" (European Commission 2013, 20) through a socialized insurance system, a socialized medicine system, or a regulated and subsidized mandatory private insurance system (Palier 2009). The SIS perspective can be clearly distinguished from neoliberal conceptualizations that subjugate health care to market forces (Jenson 2011, 73). The United States is frequently identified as a policy outlier in which SIS reforms have struggled to gain traction (Sipilä 2008). Nonetheless, the pro-single payer narrative appeared in newspaper coverage of the Massachusetts and Utah reforms, and it was clearly grounded in the SIS perspective.

The notion of a single-payer system as a logical alternative to the inefficient American employment-based insurance model was a common argument that emerged in both state reforms. Indeed, in some examples of the pro-single payer narrative, journalists who had formerly criticized the Canadian health care system had come to celebrate it as a superior option. For example, a *New York Times* columnist declared in 2005, in the lead up to the passage of Romneycare:

> Of course, there are a lot of other compelling reasons to support a single-payer plan besides helping the auto industry. Although it is by far the most costly in the world, our health care system still leaves 43 million people uncovered. The latest World Health Organization rankings listed America's system 33rd, below Costa Rica and only two notches above Cuba. Most advocates of universal health care focus on the opposition of Republicans and insurance companies. But perhaps the most important factor keeping an overhaul off the national agenda is one that few Democrats acknowledge: most of Mr. Gettelfinger's [of the UAW union] fellow labor leaders don't support a single-payer system either. The reason comes down to simple self-interest. The United Auto Workers is one of the few private-sector unions that doesn't run its own health plan. Rather, most have created huge companies to administer their workers' plans, giving them a large and often corrupt stake in the current system. (Fitch 2005)

The Fitch (2005) article was notable in framing health care reform as an issue of national pride, and its reference to the intersection between health reform and labour politics. This piece was indicative of the creative framing that journalists sometimes used to demonstrate the positive aspects of single-payer.

Leading public intellectuals, such as Paul Krugman, also regularly extolled the benefits of single-payer. Writing in the *New York Times*, Krugman stated:

> Many pundits see red at the words "single-payer system." They think it means low-quality socialized medicine; they start telling horror stories – almost all of them false – about the problems of other countries' health care. Yet there's nothing foreign or exotic about the concept: Medicare is a single-payer system. It's not perfect, it could certainly be improved, but it works. So here we are. Our current health care system is unraveling. Older Americans are already covered by a national health insurance system; extending that system to cover everyone would save money, reduce financial anxiety and save thousands of American lives every year. Why don't we just do it? (Krugman 2006)

Krugman was not only advocating single payer (socialized insurance) as the best model for reform. He was advocating the expansion of the existing Medicare program – *Medicare-for-all*, which later became a policy catch phrase for progressives – to cover all Americans as the most direct route to accomplish the systemic transition.

Americans already trusted and relied on socialized medicine; many of them simply did not understand and too frequently bought into anti-single payer reform rhetoric. However, this argument that single-payer is already integrated into the American health policy framework encounters the problem that, with the exception of military veterans who *earned* access to the Veterans Health Administration (VHA) through service, and senior citizens who *earned* access to Medicare after retirement from decades of productive employment, other Americans who access means-tested socialized medicine through Medicaid or the CHIP program are suspect, under neoliberal logic, because of their poverty. The long association of public health insurance programs like Medicaid and CHIP with means-testing arguably has the perverse effect of undermining public support for socialized insurance since the beneficiaries of these programs are not perceived as ideal – independent, entrepreneurial, consumerist, and active in the labour market – neoliberal citizens.

In another piece, Krugman summarized the political failure of the Clinton administration's 1994 Health Security Act (HSA), mixing praise with criticism in what amounted to calls for universal health care:

> Bill Clinton's health care plan failed in large part because of a dishonest but devastating lobbying and advertising campaign financed by the health insurance industry – remember Harry and Louise?[2] And the lesson many people took from that defeat is that any future health care proposal must buy off the insurance lobby. But I think that's the wrong lesson. The Clinton plan actually preserved a big role for private insurers; the industry attacked it all the same. And the plan's complexity, which was largely a result of attempts to placate interest groups, made it hard to sell to the public. So I would argue that good economics is also good politics: reformers will do best with a straightforward single-payer plan, which offers maximum savings and, unlike the Clinton plan, can easily be explained. We need to do this one right. If reform fails again, we'll be on the way to a radically unequal society, in which all but the most affluent Americans face the constant risk of financial ruin and even premature death because they can't pay their medical bills. (2005)

The arguments of Krugman and other academics were important in outlining a case for single-payer. However, public intellectuals were not the only proponents.

The pro-single payer narrative was particularly poignant when health care providers penned the editorials. For example, a physician writing in the *New York Times*, Dr. Robin Cook, declared:

> Although I never thought I'd advocate a government-sponsored, obviously non-profit, tax-supported, universal access, single-payer plan, I've changed my mind: the sooner we move to such a system, the better off we will be. Only with universal health care will we be able to pool risk for the entire country and share what nature has dealt us; only then will there be no motivation for anyone or any organization to ferret out an individual's confidential, genetic makeup. (2005)

Similarly, in perhaps the most concise and articulate critiques of market-oriented health care, the *Boston Herald* quoted the Massachusetts Nurses Association: "We believe the free-market, deregulated, and corporatized approach to the delivery of health care in the commonwealth ... is an abject failure, and it is the primary cause of the crisis we now face." The Massachusetts Nurses Association proceeded to call for a phased transition to a single-payer social insurance system (Heldt-Powell 2002).

The pro-single payer narrative of the Massachusetts and Utah reform debates gives cause for hope in future reforms. These articles offered anecdotal stories about ordinary patients and facts about single-payer systems (e.g., lower costs and greater efficiency), which reminded readers that market-based health care was not the only option for managing health care. They demonstrated that the prioritization of profit often undermines the quality of health care, and helped readers to see that they could expect more from their health care system. In contesting the national myth that market-oriented health care is superior, columnists emphasized the benefits of socialized insurance, socialized medicine, or regulated mandatory insurance systems in other countries. Other writers advocated for the expansion of existing American public health care programs such as Medicare or the Veterans Health Administration (Heldt-Powell 2002; Kowalczyk 2005; Woolhandler and Hochman 2006). While the SIS narratives are emergent ideas, they provide valuable discursive building blocks to challenge neoliberal primacy in health policy-making.

Conclusion

Previous research has shown that both existing public health care programs and dissenting voices in health and social policy debates are central to resisting neoliberalism. Janine Brodie (2007) underscores the role of "residual" and "emergent" policy narratives. The residual programs of post-Second World War social liberalism are remnants from a time of greater social investment and solidarity. Social liberalism emphasized equality between citizens and called for more universal conceptualizations of social rights. Brodie refers to this as the "social citizen" identity and makes the case that it can still inspire progressive movements (Brodie 2007). In addition to residual policies, Brodie (2007) emphasizes the value of emergent narratives to challenge neoliberal logics of governance. New narratives of contestation – however marginal they may seem initially – are often visible in media analyses.

The neoliberal policy outcomes in the Massachusetts and Utah reforms should not dismay those who advocate for a more equitable health care system. Instead, these cases remind us that no matter how dominant neoliberal narratives appear, there are, as Leonard Cohen reminds us, always cracks where the light gets in. In any polemic, *how* someone represents an issue often proves more important than the content or truth of arguments. The intense and often hyperbolic American health reform debates offer extensive examples of competing media representations that emerge in the struggles to sway public opinion and reform policies. The lessons from these battles – knowing the policy narratives that dominated media representations, knowing the contesting narratives, and contemplating ways to improve resistance discursively – can inform future resistance.

Comparative data shows that in 2017, the United States was still spending more than twice as much as other developed countries on health care per capita, without achieving universal access (Sawyer and Cox 2018). While reforms on the left of the neoliberal policy spectrum, such as Romneycare and Obamacare, admittedly improved the lives of millions of Americans through the expansion of access to health insurance and regulations that curtail some of the worst insurance industry abuses, neoliberal governance has failed to control costs or expand access to care. A staggering 27 million Americans still lacked health insurance in 2017 (Lee 2018). While this was an improvement over the 44 million who lived without health insurance in 2013, the experience of the Trump presidency showed that a hostile president could partially undermine the ACA through executive orders without sweeping legislation.

Knowing how egregiously neoliberal health policy orientations have failed, there is a duty to reject complicity in the neoliberal project. Addressing socially engaged researchers and policy-makers, Janine Brodie (2011) eloquently warned:

Conformity takes on a far less benign aura, however, when we fail to interrogate policy ideas and processes that fail to measure up to their promise,
when we further privilege those already privileged, and when we violate fundamental principles of fairness and social justice. In these cases,
conformity slides into the realm of complicity, when, unwittingly or not,
we become accomplices in the propagation and reproduction of social
injustices.

We can refuse complicity and conformity, in part, by helping to ensure
that voices of contention in past debates are heard, and that their ideas
and lessons inform future reform efforts. The minority voices in the
Massachusetts and Utah cases, such as those that passionately argued
for single-payer health care, offer us the roadmap to developing a more
inclusive, equitable, and compassionate health care system. In the spirit
of what Foucault called "hyper and pessimistic activism" in which "we
always have something to do" (Foucault 1997, 256), we should remember that America remains immersed in an ongoing struggle for fairness and justice in health care. Resisting neoliberal conceptualizations
of health care as a market sphere, and even more menacing libertarian proposals, is an uphill battle. Yet, despite adverse political circumstances, we must remember that the situation can be reversed. In health
care reform, media framing and policy narratives will always matter.
Taking inspiration from the residual and the emergent, the best story-
tellers have the power to help shape future reform outcomes.

NOTES

1 This section and parts of subsequent sections are largely based on my
   doctoral dissertation: "Media Representations of State-Level Health Care
   Reforms in the United States (2002–11): Policy Narratives, Media Frames,
   and Legislative Outcomes in the Massachusetts and Utah Cases," (PhD dissertation, University of Alberta, 2017).
2 The Harry and Louise advertisements portrayed conversations between
   two stereotypically "normal" Americans – a married, white, middle-class
   couple – during the 1993–4 health reform debates. The frame and narrative sought to appeal to middle-class and affluent voters, creating fear that
   "Hillarycare" would take away their high-quality insurance and force them
   into a substandard, government-managed plan. The punch line was: "They
   [the government] choose, we [people with high quality, private health
   insurance] lose." The Health Insurance Association of America financed
   the campaign. It appeared on national networks, was credited to a front

organization for the insurance industry, the "Coalition for Health Insurance Choices" (Holmberg 1999; Scarlett 1994; West et al. 1996).

REFERENCES

Appleby, Julie. 2005. "Mass. Gov. Romney's Health Care Plan Says Everyone Pays." *USA Today*, July 5, 2005. Sec. Money. Factiva.

Associated Press. 2017. "Koch Brothers' Political Network Says Senate GOP Healthcare Bill Is Insufficiently Conservative." *Los Angeles Times*, June 24, 2017. http://www.latimes.com/nation/nationnow/la-na-koch-healthcare-20170624-story.html.

Brodie, Janine. 2015. "Income Inequality and the Future of Global Governance." In *Critical Perspectives on the Crisis of Global Governance*, edited by Stephen S. Gill. 45–68. Palgrave Macmillan, London.

– 2011. "On Courage, Social Justice, and Policymaking." *Federation for the Humanities and Social Sciences* (blog). June 21, 2011. https://www.ideas-idees.ca/blog/courage-social-justice-and-policymaking.

– 2007. "Reforming Social Justice in Neoliberal Times." *Studies in Social Justice* 1 (2): 93–107. http://doi.org/10.26522/ssj.v1i2.972.

– 1997. "Meso-Discourses, State Forms, and the Gendering of Liberal Democratic Citizenship." *Citizenship Studies* 1 (2): 223–39. https://doi.org/10.1080/13621029708420656.

Chandler, Daniel. 2007. *Semiotics: The Basics*. New York: Routledge.

Cherkis, Jason. 2011. "Who Really Killed Utah's Healthcare Mandate?" *Huffington Post*, June 9, 2011. http://www.huffingtonpost.com/2011/06/09/huntsmanhealthcare_n_874423.html.

Cherkis, Jason, and Jon Ward. 2011. "Huntsman Was for Health Care Mandate before He Was against It." *Huffington Post*, May 20, 2011. http://www.huffingtonpost.com/2011/05/20/huntsman-was-for-health-care-mandate_n_864838.html.

Chomsky, Noam, and Edward S. Herman. 1988. *Manufacturing Consent: The Political Economy of Mass Media*. New York: Pantheon Books.

Chomsky, Noam, Peter Mitchell, and John Schoeffel. 2002. *Understanding Power: The Indispensable Chomsky*. New York: The New Press.

Chomsky, Noam, and Tom Sedlak. 2011. "Noam Sayin'? The High Times Interview with Noam Chomsky." *High Times*, July 29, 2011. Accessed on Chomsky.info: https://chomsky.info/20110729/.

Cook, Robin. 2005. "*Decoding Health Insurance*." *New York Times*, May 22, 2005. Sec. 4. Factiva.

Dean, Mitchell. 1999. *Governmentality: Power and Rule in Modern Society*, 1st Ed. London: Sage Publications.

Diamond, Sara. 1995. *Roads to Dominion: Right-Wing Movements and Political Power in the United States*. New York: Guilford Press.

Epperson, Brent. 2017. "Media Representations of State-Level Health Care Reforms in the United States (2002-2011): Policy Narratives, Media Frames, and Legislative Outcomes in the Massachusetts and Utah Cases." PhD diss., University of Alberta.

European Commission. 2013. "Investing in Health: Commission Staff Working Document, Social Investment Package." February 2013. https://ec.europa .eu/health/sites/health/files/strategy/docs/swd_investing_in_health.pdf.

Ferree, Myra Marx. 2009. "An American Roadmap? Framing Feminist Goals in a Liberal Landscape." In *Gender Equality: Transforming Family Divisions of Labor*, edited by Janet Gornick and Marcia Meyers, 284–97. London: Verso Press.

Fitch, Robert. 2005. *"Big Labour's Big Secret." New York Times* December 28, 2005. Sec. A. Factiva.

Fitzgerald, Jay. 2005. "Conservatives Debate Romneycare Insurance Plan." *Boston Herald*, June 27, 2005. Sec. Finance. Factiva.

Foucault, Michel. 1997. "On the Genealogy of Ethics: An Overview of Work in Progress." In *Michel Foucault: Ethics, Subjectivity, and Truth. The Essential Works of Michel Foucault*. Vol. I, edited by Paul Ranibow, translated by Robert Hurley. 253-80. New York: The New Press.

Gaffney, Adam, David Himmelstein, and Steffie Woolhandler. 2019. "How Much Has the Number of Uninsured Risen Since 2016 – And At What Cost to Health and Life?" *Health Affairs*. October 29, 2020. https://www .healthaffairs.org/do/10.1377/hblog20201027.770793/full/.

Genieys, William, Mohammad-Saïd Darviche, et Brent Epperson. 2020. "Les gardiens des politiques de santé face à la réforme Obama." *Gouvernement et action publique* 9 (3): 59–79. https://doi.org/10.3917/gap.203.0059.

Giasson, Thierry, Colette Brin, et Marie-Michèle Sauvageau. 2010. "La couverture médiatique des accommodements raisonnables dans la presse écrite québécoise: Vérification de l'hypothèse du tsunami médiatique." *Canadian Journal of Communications* 35 (3): 431–53. http://doi.org/10.22230 /cjc.2010v35n3a2309.

Giasson, Thierry, Colette Brin, et Marie-Michelle Sauvageau. 2010. "Le Bon, la Brute, et le Raciste : Analyse de la couverture médiatique de l'opinion publique pendant la « crise » des accommodements raisonnables au Québec." *Revue canadienne de science politique* 43 (2): 379–406. http://doi .org/10.1017/S0008423910000090.

Goodnough, Abby, and Robert Pear. 2018. "Texas Judge Strikes Down Obama's Affordable Care Act as Unconstitutional." *New York Times*, December 14, 2018. https://www.nytimes.com/2018/12/14/health /obamacare-unconstitutional-texas-judge.html.

Gostin, Lawrence. 2019. "Texas v. United States: The Affordable Care Act Is Constitutional and Will Remain So." *Journal of the American Medical Association (JAMA)* 321 (4): 332–3. https://doi.org/10.1001/jama.2018.21584.

Haislmaier, Edmund F. 2006. "The Significance of Massachusetts Health Reform." The Center for Health Policy Studies at The Heritage Foundation. https://www.heritage.org/health-care-reform/report/the-significance -massachusetts-health-reform

Hall, Stuart. 1997. *Representation: Cultural Representations and Signifying Practices*. London: Sage Publications.

Heldt-Powell, Jennifer. 2002. "Panel, Critics Want Health Reform; Health System Is Questioned." *Boston Herald*, January 28, 2002. Sec. Finance. Factiva.

Holmberg, Susan Lee. 1999. "Confronting Value Strain: Press Coverage of Health Care Reform in Sweden and the United States." Ph.D. diss., University of Washington. https://digital.lib.washington.edu /researchworks/handle/1773/10729.

Hook, Cayce J., and Rose Markus. 2020. "Health in the United States: Are Appeals to Choice and Personal Responsibility Making Americans Sick?" *Perspectives on Psychological Science* 15 (3): 643–64. https://doi.org /10.1177/1745691619896252.

Jenson, Jane. 2011. "Redesigning Citizenship Regimes after Neoliberalism: Moving towards Social Investment." In *Towards A Social Investment Welfare State?: Ideas, Policies and Challenges*, edited by Nathalie Morel, Bruno Palier, and Joakim Palme, 61–88. Oxford: Oxford University Press.

Keith, Katie. 2019. "Texas v. United States Oral Arguments in July." *Health Affairs* (blog), April 12, 2019. https://www.healthaffairs.org/do/10.1377 /hblog20190412.997469/full/.

Keren, Gideon. 2011. *Perspectives on Framing*. New York: Psychology Press.

Kowalcyzk, Liz. 2005. "Two BU Scholars to Criticize Romney Health Plan." *Boston Globe*, July 20, 2005. Sec. Metro/Region. Factiva.

Krieg, Gregory. 2017. "Comparing the Senate Health Care Bill to Obamacare and the House Proposal." *CNN Politics*, June 23, 2017. http://www.cnn .com/2017/06/22/politics/comparing-obamacare-ahca-senate-health-care -bill/index.html.

Krugman, Paul. 2005. "One Nation, Uninsured." *New York Times*, June 13, 2005. Sec. A. Factiva.

– "Death by Insurance." 2006. *New York Times*, May 1, 2006. Sec. A. Factiva.

Kurtzleben, Danielle. 2019. "Beyond 'Bumper Sticker' Slogans: 2020 Democrats Debate Details of Medicare-For-All." *National Public Radio (NPR)*, February 25, 2019. https://www.npr.org/2019/02/25/697095749/beyond -bumper-sticker-slogans-2020-democrats-debate-details-of-medicare-for-all.

Lazar, Harvey, and John Church. 2013. "Verifying the Reliability of Research Results." In *Paradigm Freeze: Why It Is So Hard to Reform Health-Care Policy in Canada*, edited by Harvey Lazar, John N. Jarvis, Pierre-Gerlier Forest, and

John Church, 253–82. Montreal and Kingston: McGill-Queen's University Press.

Lee, Chris. 2018. "The Number of Uninsured People Rose in 2017, Reversing Some of the Coverage Gains Under the Affordable Care Act." *Kaiser Family Foundation*. December 10, 2018. https://www.kff.org/uninsured/press -release/the-number-of-uninsured-people-rose-in-2017-reversing-some-of -the-coverage-gains-under-the-affordable-care-act/.

Lee, M.J., Tami Luhby, and Deirdre Walsh. 2017. "First on CNN: Details of Rand Paul, Mark Sanford Obamacare Replacement Bill." *CNN Politics*, February 15, 2017. http://www.cnn.com/2017/02/14/politics/rand-paul -mark-sanford-obamacare/inde.html.

Luhby, Tami. (2021) "Biden's Moves on Obamacare Attract New Signups – and a Second Look from Red States." *CNN Politics*, March 23, 2021. https:// edition.cnn.com/2021/03/22/politics/biden-health-care-trump-affordable -care-act/inde.html.

Morel, Nathalie, Bruno Palier, and Joakim Palme. 2011. "Beyond the Welfare State as We Knew It?" In *Towards a Social Investment Welfare State?: Ideas, Policies and Challenges*, edited by Nathalie Morel, Bruno Palier, and Joakim Palme, 1–32. Oxford: Oxford University Press.

Nelson, Lynn. 1999. *States' Rights and American Federalism: A Documentary History*. Greenwood Publishing Group.

New York Times. 2010. "Is the Affordable Care Act Unconstitutional?" *Room for Debate* (blog), March 28, 2010. https://roomfordebate.blogs.nytimes .com/2010/03/28/is-the-health-care-law-unconstitutional/.

Oberlander, Jonathan. 2018. "The Republican War on Obamacare – What Has It Achieved?" *New England Journal of Medicine* 379 (8): 703–5. https://doi .org/10.1056/nejmp1806798.

O'Keefe, Ed. 2014. "The House Has Voted 54 Times in Four Years on Obamacare: Here's the Full List." *The Washington Post*, March 21, 2014 . https://www.washingtonpost.com/news/the-fi/wp/2014/03/21 /the-house-has-voted-54-times-in-four-years-on-obamacare-heres-the -full-list/?noredirect=on&utm_term=.e1fdd0f31ef1.

Ollstein, Alice Miranda. 2019. "Court Allows House Democrats to Join Obamacare's Defense." *Politico*, February 14, 2019. https://www.politico .com/story/2019/02/14/democrats-obamacare-1170699.

Orgad, Shani. 2012. *Media Representation and the Global Imagination*. Cambridge: Polity Press.

Palier, Bruno. 2009. *La réforme des systèmes de santé*. Paris: Presses Universitaires de France.

Romney, Mitt. 2006. "Healthcare for Everyone? We Found a Way." *Wall Street Journal*, April 11, 2006. Section J.

Rose, Nikolas. 1999. *Powers of Freedom: Reframing Political Thought*. Cambridge: Cambridge University Press.

Ross, Casey. 2006. "Critics Slam Insurance Plan as Intrusive and Unwieldy." *Boston Herald*, April 13, 2006.

Roy, Avik. 2017. "The New Senate Republican Bill Will Transform American Health Care." *Forbes (The Apothecary)*, June 23, 2017. https://www.forbes .com/sites/theapothecary/2017/06/23/the-new-senaterepublican-bill-will -transform-american-health-care/#346b61024318.

– 2011. "How the Heritage Foundation, a Conservative Think Tank, Promoted the Individual Mandate." *Forbes (Pharma and Healthcare)*. October 20, 2011. http://www.forbes.com/sites/theapothecary/2011/10/20/how-a -conservative-think-tank-invented-the-individual-mandate/.

Sawyer, Bradley, and Cynthia Cox. 2018. "How Does Health Spending in the U.S. Compare to Other Countries?" Health System Tracker. Kaiser Family Foundation. December 7, 2018. https://www.healthsystemtracker.org /chart-collection/health-spending-u-s-compare-countries/#item-start.

Scarlett, Thomas. 1994. "Killing Health Care Reform." *Campaigns and Elections* 15 (10): 34–7.

Scott, Dylan. 2019. "Why Democrats Aren't Taking Up a Bill to Neutralize Obamacare's Latest Legal Threat: The Wonky Debate over How Far Democrats Should Go to Protect Obamacare, Explained." *Vox*, February 13, 2019. https://www.vox.com/policy-and-politics/2019/2/13/18222149 /texas-judge-obamacare-house-democrats-trump-sabotage.

Sipilä, Jorma. 2008. "Social Investment State: Something Real or Just a New Discourse?" Paper prepared for presentation at the 2nd Annual RECWOWE Integration Week. Oslo, June 10–14, 2008. http://recwowe.vitamib.com /publications-1/papers/wp04/ploneefile.2008-06-04.6491796649 /preview_popup.

Skopec, Laura, John Holahan, and Joshu Aarons. 2020. "Health Insurance Coverage Declined for Nonelderly Americans between 2017 and 2018, Leaving Nonexpansion States Further Behind." Urban Institute. https:// www.urban.org/sites/default/files/publication/102532/health-insurance -coverage-declined-for-nonelderly-americans-between-2017-and-2018 -leaving-nonexpansion-states-further-behind_0.pdf.

Soffen, Kim. 2017. "There's One Obamacare Repeal Bill Left Standing. Here's What's in It." *Washington Post*, September 6, 2017. https://www .washingtonpost.com/graphics/2017/politics/cassidy-graham-explainer /?utm_term=.360227f66627.

Sotomayor, Marianna. 2021. "What's in, and out, of Biden's Health Care Plan?" *NBC News*, March 14, 2021. https://www.nbcnews.com/politics/meet -the-press/blog/meet-press-blog-latest-news-analysis-data-driving-political -discussion-n988541/ncrd1030086#blogHeader.

Thomas, Cal. 2010. "Health Care Bill a Bunch of Expensive Baloney." *Salt Lake Tribune*, March 22, 2010. Sec A. Factiva.

Thurston, Norman K. 2011. "The Utah Health Exchange: A Look in the Rearview Mirror." Avenue H. http://www.avenueh.com/images/PDFs/health%20reform%20history/Rearview_Mirror_on_the_Utah_Health_Exchange__4_.pdf.

Tuohy, Carolyn Hughes. 2018. "Welfare State Eras, Policy Narratives, and the Role of Expertise: The Case of the Affordable Care Act in Historical and Comparative Perspective." *Journal of Health Politics, Policy and Law* 43 (3), 427–53. https://doi.org/10.1215/03616878-4366172.

– 1999. *Accidental Logics: The Dynamics of Change in the Health Care Arena in the United States, Britain, and Canada.* New York: Oxford University Press.

Vasterman, Peter L. 2005. "Media Hype: Self-Reinforcing News Waves, Journalistic Standards, and the Construction of Social Problems." *European Journal of Communication* 20 (4): 508–30. https://doi.org/10.1177%2F0267323105058254.

Watson, Kathrun. 2017. "How the Senate GOP Health Bill Differs from the House Bill and Obamacare." *CBS News Online*, June 24, 2017. http://www.cbsnews.com/news/how-the-senate-gop-health-bill-differs-from-the-house-bill-and-obamacare/.

West, Darrell M., Diane Heith, and Chris Goodwin. 1996. "Harry and Louise Go to Washington: Political Advertising and Health Care Reform." *Journal of Health Politics, Policy, and Law* 21 (1): 35–68. https://doi.org/10.1215/03616878-21-1-35.

Woolhandler, Steffie, and Michael Hochman. 2006. "Healthy Skepticism." *Boston Globe*, October 28 2006. Sec. Op-Ed.

Zelizer, Julian. 2015. *The Fierce Urgency of Now: Lyndon Johnson, Congress, and the Battle for the Great Society.* New York: Penguin.

PART THREE

Happy, Resilient Individuals

7 Happiness and Governance: Some Notes on Orthodox and Alternative Approaches[1]

CATHERINE KINGFISHER

> Scholarship for an uncertain world demands a marketplace of ideas that ignites social imaginaries about the possibilities of politics broadly defined.
>
> (Brodie 2012, 146)

Introduction

In this chapter, I synthesize the insights provided by critiques of the contemporary obsession with happiness and well-being in two linked discussions.[2] I begin by situating the contemporary orthodox approach to happiness as both an artifact of the crises of neoliberalism *and* a key technology for the production of proper neoliberal subjects. The neoliberal disassemblage of the social and the resulting economic, political, and environmental precariousness provide the broad frame for the discussion, within which I focus on the isolation and alienation engendered by neoliberal individualization, on the one hand; and the obsession with being happy, as individuals, on the other.

In the second half of the chapter I turn to a discussion of alternative ways of thinking about and practising well-being. I begin with an overview of approaches that theorize and investigate happiness as *simultaneously social and subjective,* focusing on emergent research in anthropology and cultural psychology. This work expands the perspectives of positive psychology and happiness economics to include more possibilities for the location, genesis, and practice of well-being. I illustrate the potential of this wider framework by means of an analysis of urban collective housing communities. Unique among intentional communities in their efforts to make space for both the subjective and the social, urban collective housing communities participate in global networks through which non-neoliberal, non-individualizing approaches to the good life circulate. They thus represent a form of resistance that moves beyond refusal to offer a potential "yes" – that is, a direction in which we might want to go (Klein 2017).

I focus on two communities: Quayside Village, in North Vancouver; and Kankanmori, in Tokyo. Both are located in countries that have undergone processes of neoliberalization and are witnessing the negative impacts of individualization, including social isolation among the elderly, alienation among youth (such as *hikikomori*, "social withdrawal," in Japan), and increasing problems with interpersonal violence, suicide, and mental health more generally (Allison 2013; Chang et al. 2013; Cleveland 2014; Goodman 2012; Horiguchi 2012; Keefe et al. 2006; Kitanaka 2012; Leheny 2014; Sugimoto 2014; Toivonen 2012;). Significantly, Tiefenbach and Kohlbacher (2013a, 2013b), in analyzing the Japanese government's National Survey on Lifestyle Preferences between 2010 and 2012, discovered that a key determinant of happiness and well-being in Japan is loneliness.

Together, the two sections of the chapter answer Janine Brodie's call to place into relief the cultural and historical specificity of commonsensical formulations in order to open up the possibility of exploring alternative frameworks (2002, 2007a, 2007b, 2012). Where do orthodox models of happiness come from? What are the conditions of their emergence? What do they assert as commonsense, or natural, and to what effect? My subsequent analysis of the alternative offered by urban collective housing communities also speaks to Gibson-Graham's project (1996, 2006) of highlighting what sits outside of dominant political and economic formations – in this case, a kind of post-individualization that does not erase the individual, but rather situates the self in the context of relationships of interdependence. My goal in the chapter is thus to bridge two strands of analysis that have tended to remain disarticulated: on the one hand, the turn to what Sherry Ortner (2016, 49) refers to as "dark anthropology," with its focus on "the harsh and brutal dimensions of human experience, and the structural and historical conditions that produce them," in particular, neoliberalism; and, on the other, the turn to anthropologies (or sociologies) of the good, focused on happiness, well-being, and morality/ethics (58–9). As Brodie would argue, the two strands are inextricably tied – not only in terms of their historical emergences (Ortner positions the latter as a kind of push-back against the former), but also as necessary for the doing of good social research; that is, research with potential for engagement and intervention. As Ortner (2016, 60) asks, "What is the point of opposing neoliberalism if we cannot imagine better ways of living and better futures?"

The Happiness Imperative in Historical, Theoretical, and Cultural Context

The "contemporary obsession with happiness" refers to the culture of happiness that emerged in the 1970s, following Bhutan's introduction of a Gross National Happiness Indicator to replace Gross National Product as a measure of prosperity and well-being. Subsequently, the United Nations has instituted an International Day of Happiness and now releases an annual World Happiness Report. Thus, happiness and well-being have become increasingly prominent in the policy orientations of governments across the globe, in most cases based on the insights produced by happiness economics and positive psychology. This confluence of academic, policy, and popular orientations has created the conditions of possibility for the emergence of a paradigm shift in approaches to governance – to how we organize and regulate our lives at all levels, ranging from state policies to our own projects of self-improvement and fulfilment. In this paradigm shift, "welfare," an expansive concept that "can only be imagined, and put into practice, in the context of a very clear social whole," is supplanted by "well-being," a discursive frame focused more narrowly on individual selves (James 2008, 69–70). Individual happiness, taken for granted as a primordial, universal desire, is now positioned as a solution to a number of what were formerly considered to be *social* problems, including alienation among youth, social isolation among the elderly, economic hardship, and the negative social impacts of environmental degradation.

Why happiness has emerged as a central concern at this particular historical juncture is generally not considered. Nor are dominant theorizations and practices of well-being situated as culturally and historically specific. On the contrary, proponents of the orthodox view, including academics, policy-makers, and the self-help and pharmaceutical industries, treat them as transparently and universally self-evident. The subject and location of happiness – the individual – is similarly assumed to be universal and fixed. The orthodox project, in other words, is marked by a poverty of reflexivity.

In the last decade or so, however, a number of scholars and social commentators have begun to challenge the hegemony of this new paradigm. Historian Darren McMahon (2006), for instance, situates happiness historically by tracing temporal shifts in conceptualizations and practices of well-being in Euro-American philosophical, religious, and political traditions (see also Kingwell 1998). Critical feminist and anti-racist theorist Sarah Ahmed (2010) analyzes the power relations informing current efforts to promote happiness, in the process exposing its ugly underbelly: the obligations and coercions, the blamings, and the exclusions. More generally, anthropologists and cultural psychologists have pointed to the culturally specific nature of orthodox models (e.g., Christopher and Hickinbottom 2008; Joshanloo and Weijers 2014; Uchida and Ogihara 2012; Jiménez, 2008; Johnston et al. 2012; Kingfisher 2013; Mathews and Izquierdo 2009; Thin 2012); while others, writing from the perspective of critical psychology and political economy, have explored the linkages between orthodox approaches to happiness and neoliberal forms of governance (Ehrenreich 2009; Ferguson 2007; Kingfisher 2013; McDonald and O'Callaghan 2008). Some of this work, most notably that in political economy, builds on the insights of Sen (1999) and Nussbaum (2011), whose "capabilities" approach, oriented to developing societies, firmly situates possibilities for well-being in social, cultural, and political context. Together, these critiques indicate that while the culture of happiness represents a reiteration of a concern that has deep historical roots in a number of philosophical and religious traditions, this iteration takes unique shapes, articulating in significant ways with other contemporary cultural and political formations. One might also note its resonance with discourses of resilience in mental health, discussed by Janet Phillips in this volume. Thus, what we are witnessing is not simply another turn in the *longue durée* of a key human conversation, but rather, a conversational turn that entails fundamental reconceptualizations and repositionings – of objects, persons, and processes – in the context of particular sets of power relations. Happiness, like Lean Production (discussed by Leifso in this volume), has been lying around, usefully repurposed for neoliberal aims.

To simplify a long and complicated history, in general, in Euro-American contexts, happiness has been transformed from an experience gifted to humans by the gods, as articulated in Greek philosophy, to something that humans have control over. In the contemporary context, happiness is something all humans should have by way of right, as well as something that we are personally responsible for and even obliged to achieve (McMahon 2006; see also Ahmed 2010; Davies 2015; Kingwell 1998) – what I refer to as the happiness imperative. This move from happiness as happenstance – as something outside of human agency – to post-Enlightenment constructions of happiness as an artifact of human agency, and thus a human responsibility, is reflected in the overwhelming emphasis on *the internal* and *the emotional* in the narrative of contemporary happiness studies. This transition from the external to the internal runs parallel to a shift from a two-tiered to a one-tiered system of personhood. Whereas in the former model, selves were firmly embedded in shared cosmological and ethical frameworks of meaning and value, in the latter, cosmological and ethical frameworks have become increasingly optional and relative to individual desire (Taylor 1989; see also Christopher and Hickinbottom 2008). Together, these unfolding reconceptualizations and repositionings comprise the social production of a particular form of personhood, creating the conditions of possibility for the *individualization* and *desocialization* of well-being.

It is in this context that positive psychology has come to dominate the conversation. Emerging in the late 1990s, positive psychology asserted that psychology as a discipline had suffered from an over-emphasis on what is wrong (mental illness, distress, crisis), and an under-emphasis on what is right (strengths and capacities) (Argyle 1987; Carr 2004; Csikszentmihalyi 1990, 1997; Gable and Haidt 2005; Linley et al. 2006; Seligman 2002, 2006; Seligman and Csikszentmihalyi 2000). The result was a call to focus on enhancing the positive instead of fighting the negative. A key method in this process was work on the self by means of therapy, meditation, medication, and various other techniques for developing positive thoughts – all with the goal of producing a positive attitude, itself positioned as a form of happiness (see, e.g., Ben-Shahar 2007; Dolan 2014). In theoretically, diagnostically, and therapeutically orienting to what goes on inside people's heads, the relevance of what happens between people, and of how societies, economies, and political systems are organized, were left by the wayside. While orthodox happiness studies have broadened in recent years to emphasize the importance of social relationships and engagement in the wider society, via, for instance, voluntarism (Seligman 2012; Layard 2005; Vaillant 2015), for the most part, it is still the case that this framework positions collective enterprises less as activities worthy in and of themselves, and more as mechanisms for individuals to augment their own personal sense of well-being.

The orientation of orthodox models to internal states and positive emotions is also culturally specific. The individual pursuit of happiness is not, in fact, valorized in all contexts (Mathews 2012; see also Manzenreiter and Holthus 2017). Indeed, in many societies the individual per se is not of central importance, and an orientation towards others and towards the group more widely holds primacy of place. There are enough ethnographic examples to indicate that it is precisely the contemporary Euro-American construct of the self that is unique – not the other way around (e.g., Geertz 1975; Kingfisher 2002; Lutz 1988; van Uchelen 2000). Nor are emotional satisfaction and positive affect universally valorized. Feelings of dependence, subservience, and dissatisfaction are in some contexts valued more than independence and "feeling good" (e.g., Christopher and Hickinbottom 2008; Mageo 1998; Joshansloo and Weijers 2014). Indeed, the pursuit of personal pleasure – in the form of positive psychology's emotional satisfaction and positive affect – is considered socially dangerous in some societies, since it can turn people away from the community; and in others it is simply inconceivable (Izquierdo 2009; Lutz 1988; Throop 2015). Similarly, personal achievement, considered a key determinant of well-being in Euro-American contexts, is de-emphasized relative to intersubjectivity and a self-other balance in East Asian societies (Uchida and Kitayama 2009; Uchida and Ogihara 2012; Uchida, Ogihara, and Fukushima 2015). The point is that happiness – what it is, how and where it is generated, and its relative importance – is a profoundly cultural construct.

Given the salience of well-being in governmental arenas, to what extent do the distinctively contemporary, Euro-American assumptions informing orthodox approaches infuse state and international efforts to incorporate well-being into official policy-making processes? Policy orientations to well-being have not been limited to Euro-American states but have also been take up in non-Western countries – for example, in Thailand, the United Arab Emirates, and Japan, among others (Barameechai 2007; Dolan, Peasgood, and White 2006; Keenan 2016; Stiglitz, Sen, and Fitoussi 2010; Uchida, Ogihara, and Fukushima 2015; United Nations 2011; see also Moore 2011; Walker and Kavedžija 2015). Uncritical adoption of orthodox perspectives entails positioning the individual as the locus of well-being and thus as the primary focus of investigation and intervention, leading, in turn, to policy initiatives designed to create the conditions of possibility for the *individual* pursuit of particular *internal* states. This would serve to buttress the universalization of possessive liberal individualism (Ahmed 2010; Christopher and Hickinbottom 2008; Joshanloo and Weijers 2014; Kingfisher 2002; McMahon 2006; Zevnik 2014), representing a form of cultural imperialism that extends, as Suzan Ilcan demonstrates in this volume, even to refugees.

Of course, not all governments taking up well-being as a policy concern have adopted orthodox approaches without question or modification. Japan, which established a Commission on Measuring Well-Being in 2010, provides a case in point. Among its five key orientations, the Commission included recognition that, "[t]o ensure that we achieve a sustainable society, we should examine well-being not only at the individual level but also at a collective level. In addition, we should focus on inequity within societies" (Uchida, Ogihara, and Fukushima 2015, 826). In locating well-being in the interpersonal as well as the intrapersonal, and in highlighting issues of social structure and political economy, the Commission provided a corrective to the ethnocentrism of mainstream happiness studies. The Commission was disbanded by the Abe administration in 2013, however, jeopardizing the influence of its broader approach to well-being, with all indicators pointing to increasing individualization in Japanese society as a whole (Coulmas 2008; Mathews 2017).

It is here that dominant policy orientations to happiness reveal their politics of neoliberal forms of governance entailing the erosion of state supports and the devolution of responsibility for well-being to individuals. Orthodox approaches to happiness thus both reflect and serve to further neoliberal projects of governance (Abbinnett 2013; Ahmed 2010; Bruckner 2010; Ehrenreich 2009; Fernández-Ríos and Cornes 2009; McDonald and O'Callaghan 2008; Zevnik 2014). It is important to note that we are *all* enjoined to work on ourselves in order to become happier and more fulfilled. Certainly, the work of governance that gets done at the margins – the policing and regulation of welfare recipients, the homeless, the "others" to the market, and the inmates of carceral society, for instance – is essential to this project. But the work that gets done in the so-called centre, in the taken-for-granted, mundane, everyday lives of proper middle- and upper-class subjects, is equally crucial. There is a plethora of technologies-of-self devoted to this enterprise, ranging from the state-sponsored to the individually purchased – all designed to enable us to craft ourselves into the kinds of persons most valued in our society (Ahmed 2010; Ehrenreich 2009; Ferguson 2007; Fernández-Ríos and Cornes 2009; Kingfisher 2013; McDonald and O'Callaghan 2008; Zevnik 2014). It comes as no surprise, then, that the most valued self of positive psychology and the ideal neoliberal subject are one and the same: self-examining, self-governing, "active," entrepreneurial (in the widest sense), and autonomous. In this sense, the current obsession with happiness, and the oppressions of the happiness imperative, are simultaneously diagnostic of neoliberalism as a set of governing practices *and*, perhaps, a response to the crises of precariousness engendered by decollectivization. We are faced with a kind of desperate attempt to feel good in isolation, and, perhaps, to deresponsibilize ourselves for the care of others at the very moment that we are overwhelmed with being responsibilized for our own well-being.

In being held (and holding ourselves) responsible for our own happiness, analysis of our lives is channelled away from political economy and structures of inequality and towards a particular form of destructured, non- or post-social personhood. "Rather than assuming that happiness is simply found in 'happy persons,'" then, we could think more carefully about "how claims to happiness make certain forms of personhood valuable" (Ahmed, 2010, 11). In working to transform ourselves into such valuable persons, we can become so engrossed in monitoring ourselves for negativity and working to cultivate positivity that we fail to attend to what is happening outside of ourselves. We remove ourselves from collective engagement, thereby contributing to the decollectivization that Bourdieu (1998) claimed is one of the biggest dangers of neoliberalism (see also Mathews 2017). And if, as Foucault (1979, 1980) noted, power operates best via its own erasure, here is a perfect example: the diversion of attention from structure to the self, and the self-assertion of power vis-à-vis one's own self in ways that erase structure.

In her discussions of privatization – a hallmark of neoliberalism – Janine Brodie (2002, 100) makes the insightful point that privatization is not just about moving things from one arena to another. Rather, as she puts it, "[i]t is a profoundly cultural process in which the thing moved is itself transformed into something quite different. Objects become differently understood and regulated." The privatization and individualization of happiness thus instantiate a particular governmental move that involves simultaneous redefinitions of the self and displacements of the social. In this context, it becomes useful to refer to the contemporary culture of happiness as a "regime of happiness" (Zevnik 2014, ix), inextricably tied to governmental attempts to create proper depoliticized, consuming subjects – a kind of happiness/market/governance complex.

Working from the Social In: An Alternative

What happens if we take a different entry point, starting with the social and working inwards to the individual? Certainly, as Mathews (2017, 231) points out, "the experience of happiness is individual." But does that mean that happiness and well-being are produced *solely* by individuals? Is happiness an exclusive characteristic of the person (Cieslik 2017, 31), or is this reading, perhaps, an artifact of the methodological individualism of positive psychology?

Anthropological and sociological approaches open up possibilities for explorations of well-being that are not exclusively individualistic in orientation. Eschewing methodological individualism in favour of a broad range of holistic qualitative methods designed to capture nuance and specificity, such approaches work to relocate the genesis and practice of happiness, at least partly, in the space between people and in social structures and institutions. Happiness is thus conceptualized as an inherently *social* and *collaborative* process (Cieslik 2017; Markus and

Kitayama 1991; Manzenreiter and Holthus 2017; Calestani 2013; Fischer 2014; Jiménez 2008; Kingfisher 2013; Jackson 2011; Johnston et al. 2012; Lambek 2015; Mathews and Izquierdo 2009; Robbins 2013, 2015; Thin 2012; Throop 2015; Walker and Kavedžija 2015). As performance ethnographer William Peterson (2016, 2, 11) puts it, "what is inside the body ... [is] plotted out through the coordinates of culture.... When we experience happiness, it is in the world in which our bodies are located."

For its part, cultural psychology, drawing attention to "the critical role of culture in explaining psychological functions and behaviors" (Uchida, Ogihara, and Fukushima 2015, 823), contributes the concept of *interdependent happiness* (Hitokoto and Uchida 2015). This concept permits theoretical and methodological movement beyond positing collective enterprises as mere mechanisms for augmenting a personal sense of well-being, towards broader understandings of where happiness is located (perhaps in between persons as much as inside of them), and of how it might be produced (perhaps socially as much as individually).

The emergence of these approaches to understanding happiness represents one instance of the development of what Brodie (2012, 129) refers to as social literacy. They embody a first step in recognizing the historical, cultural, and power-laden parameters within which orthodox theorizations and practices of happiness are currently confined. This is not to engage in the wholesale rejection of what can be learned from positive psychology and happiness economics. Nor is it to deny that alternative approaches to happiness also instantiate forms of governance. Rather, it is to expand the conversation to include "different choices about what is equitable, politically possible, and socially responsible" (Brodie 2012, 116), in the context of an overall desire to make our worlds better.

The Alternative of Urban Collective Housing Communities: Kankanmori and Quayside Village

Urban collective housing communities provide fruitful sites for exploring models of well-being that expand the myopic orientations informing mainstream happiness studies. Increasingly popular across the globe, urban collective housing communities participate in an international network of intentional communities, comprising a social movement that challenges heteronormative nuclear family formation and rigid practices of private property ownership. Thus, alongside (or underneath) elite government and academic circuits for the global travel of orthodox approaches to happiness sits another circuit, comprised of web communities, conferences, and site exchanges designed to spread knowledge of the "best practices" of intentional community.

Urban collective housing communities are unique among intentional communities in two respects. First, as forms of utopic practice that simultaneously articulate claims about what is wrong with society and desires for "something better," they critique while remaining fundamentally engaged with dominant cultural formations (Levitas 2013; see also Cooper 2014; Sargisson 2007, 2012. See Hage 2011; Harvey 2000; Jackson 2011; Moore 1990; Robbins 2013, 2015; and Turner 2012 on the anthropology of utopia). Thus, unlike other types of intentional community – rural ecovillages and spiritual communes, for instance – they are integrated with, rather than segregated from, society at large, thereby transcending with/against, inside/outside binaries. Indeed, many such communities see themselves as serving an educative function, working *within* existing social systems to model feasible alternative possibilities. In addition, in explicitly providing space for both the personal and the social, they transcend individualist/collectivist binaries, providing an opportunity to map constructions of happiness as a *simultaneously social and subjective process*. This in-betweenness reveals an approach to the good life that challenges the radical individualism of dominant regimes of happiness without being exclusively collectivist in orientation.

Kankanmori, in Tokyo, and Quayside Village, in North Vancouver, are the first purpose-built urban collective housing communities in their cities, located just outside of their respective urban cores. Each was several years in the planning, entailing multiple meetings of would-be residents and collaborations with architects. They are of roughly similar size (at this writing Kankanmori has 36 residents living in 28 units, while Quayside Village has 29 residents in 19 units). Each is deliberately cross-generational in composition, and both are oriented to the amelioration of social isolation and alienation via the co-production of forms of sociality that balance interdependence and independence. They also work to address economic and environmental issues via the sharing of resources (e.g., vegetable gardens, laundry rooms, and equipment, such as vacuum cleaners and ironing boards). Located in societies in which mainstream approaches to happiness have gained traction in recent years, both communities also participate in global networks through which alternative approaches to the good life circulate. Accordingly, in their own policy formation,[3] they draw on orthodox models, but also on a range of models from the "core" of collective housing movements (most notably Sweden and the US), as well as from local imaginaries of more socially cohesive pasts. In Tokyo, this includes *nagaya*, a form of pre-Meiji era architecture and community organization (Schulz 2014), and, in Vancouver, counter-culture era experiments in communal living (Aronson 2010).

Kakanmori and Quayside Village include private apartments, complete with kitchen and bathroom, as well as shared spaces, most notably, a common kitchen and dining area, gardens, laundry room, and play areas for children. Although both communities are involved in cross-community networks, they are completely self-governing, to which end they have a number of sub-committees that report at monthly meetings, during which decisions about a range of endeavours (such as garden usage, community expenditures, and social events) are made collectively.

Kankanmori's mission statement articulates three core intentions:

1. share space and time with others
2. have independent and private space as well as communal space
3. spend time in common activities

In addition, there are five principles:

1. everyone needs to cherish their own independent life as well as sharing
2. everyone from single people to large families can enjoy Kankanmori
3. living at Kankanmori needs to be both practical and ecological
4. life needs to be open to the outside world
5. there needs to be a focus on communication and diversity: we need to grow and learn from each other

For its part, Quayside Village articulates the following goal:

> To have a community which is diverse in age, background and family type, that offers a safe, friendly living environment which is affordable, accessible and environmentally conscious. The emphasis is on quality of life including the nurture of children, youth, and elders.

Despite their loosely similar orientations to community and space, Quayside Village and Kankanmori are situated in dramatically different societies. Thus, my focus on these two communities is designed to trace both the travel of intentional community models of well-being across cultural and national space, and their translation and assemblage in specific contexts – in this case, in societies stereotyped as traditionally individualistic, on the one hand, and collectivist, on the other.

Below, I outline how members of Quayside Village and Kankanmori envision their communities and the ways in which the communities represent a response to some of the crises generated by neoliberalism. My goal is to provide insight into how the two communities operate as practical thought experiments – instantiating what Ruth Levitas would call utopia as method, and illustrating what Davina Cooper would refer to as everyday utopias (Levitas 2013; Cooper 2014).

Conceptualizing and Experiencing Kankanmori and Quayside Village: A Brief Description

Without exception, residents report that their decisions to join Quayside Village and Kankanmori stemmed from dissatisfaction with lives they experienced as isolating, leading to a desire for social connection. A number of Kankanmori residents see their community as an explicit political and policy-relevant intervention designed to address the problems generated by post-war social fragmentation (such as childcare shortages and increases in domestic violence), as well as issues associated with a rapidly aging population. Some also position collective housing as an antidote to a post-war redefinition of "the good life" (*ikigai*) in which commitments to work and extended family began to take on an increasingly negative valence in relation to valorizations of privacy, individualism, and consumerism (see Mathews 1996). The shift in recent years towards an emphasis on individual development and fulfillment, accompanied by a loosening of social and institutional strictures on individuals (Mathews 2017), thus sits alongside a longing for community and connection. Members of Quayside Village similarly expressed desires to ameliorate loneliness and to benefit from "community," which they describe as having people to spend time with and depend on for support in tight situations, sharing resources, creating safe spaces for children – and enjoying all this while maintaining privacy.

In both cases, there is an attempted recreation of traditional nuclear and extended family ties, but in altered form, since diversity – of age, background, profession, and philosophical orientation – is considered a keystone. As one person at Kankanmori put it, residents are neither friends nor family, but "something different, something new." The key frame here is thus not only nostalgia, but also – and perhaps more importantly – an orientation to grafting historical imaginaries with contemporary realities and aspirations.

As already noted, Quayside Village and Kankanmori are spatially and organizationally designed to balance interdependence and independence. Significantly, this does not translate into a desire to participate in community simply in order to boost one's own personal level of happiness. It is not about conceptualizing relationships in self-serving, instrumental terms, as "investments." Rather, the goal is to build a healthy community with a capital "C" – that is, the community that, as one Kankanmori resident put it, is a "basic characteristic of humanity." Nor is community with a capital "C" about the dissolution of the autonomy or integrity of the individual. Neither the community nor the individual cannibalize the other; rather, they are constructed, and practised, as inextricably tied. Ikuko Koyabe, one of the architects of Kankanmori and widely known as the "mother" of collective housing in Japan, told me that while collective communities need to start at the level of the individual, individual desires are only ever accomplished via engagement with a community, via learning how to live with difference and how to communicate.

Their responses to the COVID-19 pandemic illustrate how Kankanmori and Quayside Village residents work to collaboratively balance individual health and safety with the need for connection. In exacerbating loneliness, the pandemic has prompted all of us to recognize how interdependent we are, how much we need – and want – each other. Like so many, residents of Kankanmori and Quayside Village have made extensive use of electronic forms of contact, holding meetings via Zoom, and relying more on email than on face-to-face encounters for information and social connection. But they also maintained physical co-presence, albeit in scaled-down forms. At Kankanmori, for instance, small groups of residents gather for tea-at-a-distance in the common room, just as groups of two or three continue to meet in the courtyard at Quayside Village. Quaysiders also began a new tradition: beginning in spring 2020, at 9:30 each morning residents brought chairs to the third-floor walkway in order to enjoy morning coffee and conversation together, even while sitting well apart. They have also had the occasional balcony singalong. When one resident told the community that she would have to self-isolate for two weeks because someone on the hospital ward she visited had tested positive for COVID-19, a roster of volunteers was set up within hours to help her with her dinners. In the meantime, at Kankanmori, 27 people, including six children, enthusiastically signed up for the first (physically spread out) common meal after their self-imposed lockdown was lifted. And everyone was excited about the impending birth of the one resident's third child: new life and new energy for everyone to enjoy and nurture as they endeavour, together, to provide mutual enjoyment and support in these times. In these ways, and in community agreements about mask wearing in shared spaces, residents of Quayside Village and Kankanmori were able to remain together while practising the public health measures that keep them physically separated.

This is not to say that Quayside Village and Kankanmori are completely harmonious environments. Residents' participation in community endeavours waxes and wanes, and everyone struggles to navigate the relationship between what they mark as the social and what they mark as the private. Members have spoken to me at length about the pressures they have experienced in meeting their obligations to the community while also fulfilling their obligations to work and their immediate families. There are, in addition, personality clashes, decisions that disappoint some people, and so on. As one woman in another intentional community I visited put it, "this is not paradise." Nonetheless, members see these struggles as part of collective living and consider the benefits to far outweigh any drawbacks or inconveniences.

Recognizing the struggles and conflicts involved in living in an intentional community serves as a corrective to any desire to romanticize the non-neoliberal (Kingfisher and Maskovsky 2008) and/or the "non-Western." Instead, it invites us to attend to the forms of governance practised in communities such as Quayside Village and Kankanmori. What is required of residents? What tensions might be involved in negotiations between connection and personal freedom? How is the relationship between philosophy and reality negotiated – in other words, how are ideas mobilized through practice, and what bumps are encountered along the way? Conceptualizing urban collective housing communities as examples of utopia-as-method means that, like orthodox approaches to happiness, they are *policies*, in the sense of charters for social perception and action (Malinowski 1926). They authorize and work to instantiate particular kinds of persons and particular kinds of sociality. In this sense, urban collective housing communities represent nexuses of utopic desire, culture, and governance, and need to be explored as such. As participants in these communities move objects – in this case, happiness and well-being – from the exclusive arena of the private and individualized to an arena that is simultaneously social and subjective, how are persons and sociality reconfigured? In other words, philosophies of intentional community require unpacking and specification no less than neoliberal orthodoxies.

The play of similarity and difference in relation to cultural context is also crucial to consider. Despite the roughly similar philosophies and built environments outlined above, there are dramatic differences between Kankanmori and Quayside Village in their uses of space, communicative practices, decision-making processes, and approaches to conflict. Comparing across contexts thus reveals a rich array of imaginaries and practices that we – scholars, policy-makers, and members of society – can engage as we contemplate where we want to be heading.

Conclusion

At the foundation of social literacy lies recognition of the social, beginning with the reality that humans are a biosocial species, that we are not autonomous monads, and that we live enmeshed in, as both products and producers of, social systems. It entails exploring the conditions of possibility for hegemonic governing philosophies, which, in positing themselves as universal, timeless, and commonsensical, "resist public debate and the exploration of alternative ways of thinking" (Brodie 2002, 91; 2012). It involves, in other words, undertaking a history of the present, asking both how things are now, relative to other times, and how things are here, relative to elsewhere. It is an exercise, then, in making the familiar strange, and in positing the here-and-now as a profoundly social and political production. In relation to my focus for this chapter, orthodox approaches to happiness and well-being, and their articulation with the twinned neoliberal processes of disassembling the social and relocating social problems to individuals, are thereby denaturalized, their politics and power relations placed into relief.

Recognizing the specificity, temporality and, therefore, vulnerability of a particular governing philosophy – seeing it *as* a governing philosophy and not as a natural inevitability – opens up possibilities for exploring where a governing regime is tenuous, interrupted, resisted outright, or simply not in operation (Gibson-Graham 2006). A critical happiness study (Cieslik 2017) takes into account the cultural and historical specificity of dominant approaches, with particular attention to their ties to power relations. Challenges from within the discipline of psychology – as represented by cultural psychology – as well as from without – as represented by anthropology, but also including the work of sociologists (e.g., Cieslik 2017) – reveal the power-laden and cultural/historical specificities of orthodox models. At the same time, these challenges broaden our perspective to include a range of ways of thinking about and practising well-being. Given their ties to neoliberal forms of governance, mainstream approaches to happiness will not solve the crises of isolation and alienation created by neoliberalism, but instead will exacerbate them. It is only by expanding the parameters of conceptualization, theorization, and practice that a better what-next to neoliberalism can be imagined. Again, this is not to romanticize the non-neoliberal; nor is it to deny that non-orthodox approaches to happiness also instantiate forms of governance. Rather, it is to extend the scope of our scholarly viewing and therefore of possibility. And, in terms of practice, it is to recognize that the "global cultural super-market" (Mathews 2012) is the means by which a range of "products" might circulate – not only neoliberal cultural formations, including or-thodox approaches to happiness, but also alternative approaches. The marketplace of alternative approaches may not be as flashy and it may be a low-budget enterprise, as many counter-hegemonic movements are. But it exists, and our engagement with it, as people dedicated to imagining better societies (Brodie 2012), can only serve to increase its traction in both policy arenas and public culture, thereby providing a better and more varied "tool-kit" (Fischer 2014, 216) for well-being ac-tivists and policy-makers.

Urban collective housing communities provide just one example of an alternative, non-neoliberal approach to happiness: always already imperfect and unfinished yet reflexive and always striving – one at-tempt, simultaneously critical and hopeful, fantastical and realistic, to address some of the ravages of this era and point in the direction of something better. Significantly, in creating co-membership, they pro-vide a counter to the crisis of decollectivization engendered by neolib-eralism, creating opportunities for further mobilizations and alliances in the service of social justice. They are not the end-all and be-all, but rather an example of the formations that a critical and cross-cultural social literacy can bring into view and nurture.

ACKNOWLEDGMENTS

I am indebted to Lois Harder, Catherine Kellogg, Steve Patten, and the anonymous reviewers of this volume for their insights and suggestions. I also thank John Clarke for his comments, and for presenting a version of this chapter on my behalf at the Janine Brodie *Festschrift* conference. Last but not least, I thank Janine Brodie for her deep and enduring inspiration.

NOTES

1 This chapter draws on my book *Collaborative Happiness: Building the Good Life in Urban Cohousing Communities*, Berghahn Books, 2021.
2 Throughout this chapter I use the terms "happiness" and "well-being" sometimes together and sometimes interchangeably. This mirrors patterns of usage in the literature, and also serves to highlight the importance of

openness and imprecision, particularly in the context of cross-cultural analysis.

3 I use "policy" here to refer not only to official government programs, but also to encompass unofficial charters for social perception and action (Malinowski 1926).

REFERENCES

Abbinnett, Ross. 2013. *Politics of Happiness: Connecting the Philosophical Ideas of Hegel, Nietzsche, and Derrida to the Political Ideologies of Happiness*. New York: Bloomsbury.

Ahmed, Sara. 2010. *The Promise of Happiness*. Durham and London: Duke University Press.

Allison, Anne. 2013. *Precarious Japan*. Durham: Duke University Press.

Argyle, Michael. 1987. *The Psychology of Happiness*. London: Methuen.

Aronson, Lawrence. 2010. *City of Love and Revolution: Vancouver in the Sixties*. Vancouver: New Star Books.

Barameechai, Juthamas. 2007. "The Green and Happiness Index." Paper presented at the International Conference on Happiness and Public Policy, Bangkok, Thailand. July 2007.

Ben-Shahar, Tal. 2007. *Happier: Learn the Secrets to Daily Joy and Lasting Fulfillment*. New York: McGraw Hill.

Bourdieu, Pierre. 1998. *Acts of Resistance: Against the Tyranny of the Market*. New York: The New Press.

Brodie, Janine. 2012. "Social Literacy and Social Justice in Times of Crisis." *Trudeau Foundation Papers* 4 (1): 117–46.

– 2007a. "The New Social 'isms': Individualization and Social Policy Reform in Canada." In *Contested Individualization: Debates about Contemporary Personhood*, edited by Cosmo Howard, 153–69. New York: Palgrave Macmillan.

– 2007b. "Reforming Social Justice in Neoliberal Times." *Studies in Social Justice* 1 (2): 93–107. http://doi.org/10.26522/ssj.v1i2.972.

– 2002. "The Great Undoing: State Formation, Gender Politics, and Social Policy in Canada." In *Western Welfare in Decline: Globalization and Women's Poverty*, edited by Catherine Kingfisher, 90–110. Philadelphia: University of Pennsylvania Press.

Bruckner, Pascal. 2010. *Perpetual Euphoria: On the Duty to Be Happy*. Princeton: Princeton University Press.

Calestani, Melania. 2013. *Anthropology Journal in Well-Being: Insights from Bolivia*. Southampton: Springer.

Carr, Alan. 2004. *Positive Psychology: The Science of Happiness and Human Strengths*. London: Routledge.

Chang, Shu-Sen, David Stuckler, Paul Yip, and David Gunnell. 2013. "Impact of 2008 Global Economic Crisis on Suicide: Time Trend Study in 54 Countries." *British Medical Journal* 347: 1–15. https://doi.org/10.1136/bmj.f5239.

Christopher, John Chambers, and Sarah Hickinbottom. 2008. "Positive Psychology, Ethnocentrism, and the Disguised Ideology of Individualism." *Theory & Psychology* 18 (5): 563–89. http://doi.org/10.1177/0959354308093396.

Cieslik, Mark. 2017. *The Happiness Riddle and the Quest for a Good Life*. London: Macmillan.

Cleveland, Kyle. 2014. "Hiding in Plain Sight: Minority Issues in Japan." In *Critical Issues in Contemporary Japan*, edited by Jeff Kingston, 213–22. New York: Routledge.

Cooper, Davina. 2014. Everyday Utopias: The Conceptual Life of Promising Spaces. Durham and London: Duke University Press.

Coulmas, Florian. 2008. "The Quest for Happiness in Japan." Working Paper 09/1, German Institute for Japanese Studies, Tokyo, 2008. https://www.dijtokyo.org/wp-content/uploads/2016/09/WP0901_Coulmas.pdf.

Csikszentmihalyi, Mihaly. 1997. *Creativity: Flow and the Psychology of Discovery and Invention*. New York: Harper Collins.

Csikszentmihalyi, Mihaly. 1990. *Flow: The Psychology of Optimal Experience*. New York: Harper Collins.

Davies, William. 2015. *The Happiness Industry: How the Government and Big Business Sold Us Well-Being*. London: Verso.

Dolan, Paul. 2014. *Happiness by Design: Change What You Do, Not How You Think*. New York: Hudson Street Press.

Dolan, Paul, Tessa Peasgood, and Matthew White. 2006. "Review of Research on the Influences on Personal Wellbeing and Application to Policy Making." London: Defra. randd.defra.gov.uk/Document.aspx?Document=SD12005_4017_FRP.pdf.

Ehrenreich, Barbara. 2009. *Bright-Sided: How the Relentless Promotion of Positive Thinking Has Undermined America*. New York: Henry Holt.

Ferguson, Iain. 2007. "Neoliberalism, Happiness, and Wellbeing." *International Socialism* 117 (December): 7–13. http://isj.org.uk/neoliberalism-happiness-and-wellbeing/.

Fernández-Ríos, Luís, and J.M. Cornes. 2009. "A Critical Review of the History and Current Status of Positive Psychology." *Annuary of Clinical and Health Psychology* 5: 7–13.

Fischer, Edward F. 2014. *The Good Life: Aspiration, Dignity, and the Anthropology of Wellbeing*. Stanford: Stanford University Press.

Foucault, Michel. 1980. *The History of Sexuality*, vol. 1. Translated by Robert Hurley. New York: Vintage.

– 1979. *Discipline and Punish: The Birth of the Prison*. Translated by Alan Sheridan. New York: Vintage.

Gable, Shelly, and Jonathan Haidt. 2005. "What (and Why) Is Positive Psychology?" *Review of General Psychology* 9 (2): 103–10. https://doi.org/10.1037%2F1089-2680.9.2.103.

Geertz, Clifford. 1975. "On the Nature of Anthropological Understanding." *American Scientist* 63: 47–53.

Gibson-Graham, J.K. 2006. *A Postcapitalist Politics*. Minneapolis: University of Minnesota Press.

– 1996. *The End of Capitalism (As We Knew It): A Feminist Critique of Political Economy*. Oxford, UK: Blackwell.

Goodman, Roger. 2012. "Shifting Landscapes: The Social Context of Youth Problems in an Ageing Nation." In *A Sociology of Japanese Youth*, edited by Roger Goodman, Yuki Imoto, and Tuukka Toivonen, 159–73. New York: Routledge.

Hage, Ghassan. 2011. "Dwelling in the Reality of Utopian Thought." *Traditional Dwellings and Settlements Review* 23 (1): 7–13.

Harvey, David. 2000. *Spaces of Hope*. Berkeley: University of California Press.

Hitokoto, Kidehumi, and Yukiko Uchida. 2015. "Independent Happiness: Theoretical Importance and Measurement Validity." *Journal of Happiness Studies* 16 (1): 211–39. https://doi.org/10.1007/s10902-014-9505-8.

Horiguchi, Sachiko. 2012. "Hikikomori: How Private Isolation Caught the Public Eye." In *A Sociology of Japanese Youth*, edited by Roger Goodman, Yuki Imoto, and Tuukka Toivonen, 122–38. New York: Routledge.

Izquierdo, Carolina. 2009. "Well-Being Among the Matsigenka of the Peruvian Amazon: Health, Missions, Oil, and 'Progress'." In *Pursuits of Happiness: Well-Being in Anthropological Perspective*, edited by Gordon Mathews and Carolina Izquierdo, 67–87. New York: Berghahn Books.

Jackson, Michael. 2011. *Life Within Limits: Well-Being in a World of Want*. Durham and London: Duke University Press.

James, Wendy. 2008. "Well-Being: In Whose Opinion, and Who Pays?" In *Culture and Well-Being: Anthropological Approaches to Freedom and Political Ethics*, edited by Alberto C. Jiménez, 69–79. London: Pluto.

Jiménez, Alberto Cosín, ed. 2008. *Culture and Well-Being: Anthropological Approaches to Freedom and Political Ethics*. London: Pluto.

Johnston, Barbara Rose, et al. 2012. "On Happiness: Vital Topics Forum." *American Anthropologist* 114 (1): 6–18. https://doi.org/10.1111/j.1548-1433.2011.01393.x

Joshanloo, Mohsen, and Dan Weijers. 2014. "Aversion to Happiness Across Cultures: A Review of Where and Why People Are Averse to Happiness." *Journal of Happiness Studies* 15: 717–35. https://doi.org/10.1007/s10902-013-9489-9.

Keefe, Janie, Melissa Andrew, Pamela Fancy, and Madelyn Hall. 2006. *A Profile of Social Isolation in Canada*. Halifax: Nova Scotia Centre on Aging and the Department of Family Studies and Gerontology at Mount Saint Vincent University.

Keenan, John. 2016. "Dubai Wants to Be the 'World's Happiest City.' Report Says It Has a Long Way to Go." *The Guardian*, March 16, 2016. https://www.theguardian.com/cities/2016/mar/16/world-happiest-city-dubai-happiness-index-report.

Kingfisher, Catherine. 2013. "Happiness: Notes on History, Culture and Governance." *Health, Culture and Society* 5 (1): 67–82. http://doi.org/10.5195/hcs.2013.145.

Kingfisher, Catherine, ed. 2002. *Western Welfare in Decline: Globalization and Women's Poverty*. Philadelphia: University of Pennsylvania Press.

Kingfisher, Catherine, and Jeff Maskovsky. 2008. "Introduction: The Limits of Neoliberalism." *Critique of Anthropology* 28 (2): 115–26. https://doi.org/10.1177/0308275X08090544.

Kingwell, Mark. 1998. *Better Living: In Pursuit of Happiness from Plato to Prozac*. Toronto: Penguin.

Kitanaka, Junko. 2012. *Depression in Japan: Psychiatric Cures for a Society in Distress*. Princeton: Princeton University Press.

Klein, Naomi. 2017. *No Is Not Enough: Resisting the New Shock Politics and Winning the World We Need*. Toronto: Random House.

Lambek, Michael. 2015. "*Le Bonheur Suisse*, Again." *HAU: Journal of Ethnographic Theory* 5 (3): 111–34. http://doi.org/10.14318/hau5.3.007.

Layard, Richard. 2005. *Happiness: Lessons from a New Science*. London: Penguin.

Leheny, David. 2014. "What's Behind What Ails Japan." In *Critical Issues in Contemporary Japan*, edited by Jeff Kingston, 288–99. New York, Routledge.

Levitas, Ruth. 2013. *Utopia as Method: The Imaginary Reconstitution of Society*. New York: Palgrave Macmillan.

Linley, P. Alex, Stephen Joseph, Susan Harrington, and Alex M. Wood. 2006. "Positive Psychology: Past, Present, and (Possible) Future." *Journal of Positive Psychology* 1 (1): 3–16. http://doi.org/10.1080/17439760500372796.

Lutz, Catherine A. 1988. *Unnatural Emotions: Everyday Sentiments on a Micronesian Atoll and Their Challenges to Western Theory*. Chicago: University of Chicago Press.

Mageo, Jeannette M. 1998. *Theorizing Self in Samoa: Emotions, Genders, and Sexualities*. Ann Arbor: University of Michigan Press.

Malinowski, Bronislaw. 1926. *Myth in Primitive Psychology*. London: Norton.

Manzenreiter, Wolfram, and Barbara Holthus. 2017. "Introduction: Happiness in Japan Through the Anthropological Lens." In *Happiness and the Good Life in Japan*, edited by Wolfram Manzenreiter and Barbara Halthus, 1–21. London and NY: Routledge.

Markus, Hazel Rose, and Shinobu Kitayama. 1991. "Culture and the Self: Implications for Cognition, Emotion, and Motivation." *Psychological Review* 98 (2): 224–53. https://doi.apa.org/doi/10.1037/0033-295X.98.2.224.

Mathews, Gordon. 2017. "Happiness in Neoliberal Japan." In *Happiness and the Good Life in Japan*, edited by Wolfram Manzenreiter and Barbara Halthus, 227–42. London and New York: Routledge.

– 2012. "Happiness, Culture, and Context." *International Journal of Wellbeing* 2 (4): 299–312. http://doi.org/10.5502/ijw.v2.i4.2.

– 1996. *What Makes Life Worth Living? How Japanese and Americans Make Sense of Their Worlds.* Berkeley: University of California Press.

Mathews, Gordon, and Carolina Izquierdo, eds. 2009. *Pursuits of Happiness: Well-Being in Anthropological Perspective.* New York: Berghahn Books.

McDonald, Matthew, and Jean O'Callaghan. 2008. "Positive Psychology: A Foucauldian Critique." *The Humanistic Psychologist* 36 (2): 127–42. https://doi.apa.org/doi/10.1080/08873260802111119.

McMahon, Darrin M. 2006. *Happiness: A History.* New York: Grove Press.

Moore, Henrietta. 2011. *Still Life: Hopes, Desires, and Satisfactions.* Cambridge: Polity.

Moore, Henrietta. 1990. "Visions of the Good Life: Anthropology and the Study of Utopia." *Cambridge Journal of Anthropology* 14 (3): 13–33.

Nussbaum, Martha C. 2011. *Creating Capabilities: The Human Development Approach.* Cambridge: The Belknap Press of Harvard University Press.

Ortner, Sherry B. 2016. "Dark Anthropology and Its Others: Theory Since the Eighties." *HAU: Journal of Ethnographic Theory* 6 (1): 47–73. https://doi.org/10.14318/hau6.1.004.

Peterson, William. 2016. *Places for Happiness: Community, Self, and Performance in the Philippines.* Honolulu: University of Hawai'i Press.

Robbins, Joel. 2013. "Beyond the Suffering Subject: Toward an Anthropology of the Good." *Journal of the Royal Anthropological Institute* 19 (3): 447–62. https://doi.org/10.1111/1467-9655.12044.

– 2015. "On Happiness, Values, and Time: The Long and the Short of It." *HAU: Journal of Ethnographic Theory* 5 (3): 215–33. https://doi.org/10.14318/hau5.3.012.

Sargisson, Lucy. 2007. "Strange Places: Estrangement, Utopianism, and Intentional Communities." *Utopian Studies* 18 (3): 393–424.

– 2012. "Second-Wave Cohousing: A Modern Utopia?" *Utopian Studies* 23 (1): 28–56. https://doi.org/10.5325/utopianstudies.23.1.0028.

Schulz, Evelyn. 2014. "Beyond Modernism." In *Future Living: Collective Housing in Japan*, edited by Claudia Hildner, 11–26. Basel: Birkhäuser.

Seligman, Martin. 2002. *Authentic Happiness: Using the New Positive Psychology to Realize Your Potential for Lasting Fulfillment.* New York: The Free Press.

– 2006. *Learned Optimism: How to Change Your Mind and Your Life.* New York: Vintage.

– 2012. *Flourish: A Visionary New Understanding of Happiness and Well-being*. New York: Free Press.

Seligman, Martin, and Mihaly Csikszentmihalyi. 2000. "Positive Psychology: An Introduction." *American Psychologist* 55 (1): 5–14. http://doi.org/10.1037/0003-066X.55.1.5.

Sen, Amartya. 1999. *Development as Freedom*. New York: Anchor Books.

Stiglitz, Joseph E., Amartya Sen, and John-Paul Fitoussi. 2010. "Report by the Commission on the Measurement of Economic Performance and Social Progress." Special Report commissioned by President Nicolas Sarkozy. https://ec.europa.eu/eurostat/documents/8131721/8131772/Stiglitz-Sen-Fitoussi-Commission-report.pdf.

Sugimoto, Yoshio. 2014. *An Introduction to Japanese Society*, 4th ed. Melbourne: Cambridge University Press.

Taylor, Charles. 1989. *Sources of the Self: The Making of Modern Identity*. Cambridge, MA: Harvard University Press.

Thin, Neil. 2012. *Social Happiness: Theory into Policy and Practice*. Bristol: The Policy Press.

Throop, C. Jason. 2015. "Ambivalent Happiness and Virtuous Suffering." *HAU: Journal of Ethnographic Theory* 5 (3): 45–68. https://doi.org/10.14318/hau5.3.004.

Tiefenbach, Tim, and Florian Kohlbacher. 2013a. "Happiness from the Viewpoint of Economics: Findings from Recent Survey Data in Japan" (Working Paper 13/1, German Institute for Japanese Studies, Tokyo). https://www.dijtokyo.org/wp-content/uploads/2016/09/WP1301_Tiefenbach_Kohlbacher.pdf.

– 2013b. "Happiness and Life Satisfaction in Japan by Gender and Age" (Working Paper 13/2, German Institute for Japanese Studies, Tokyo). https://www.dijtokyo.org/wp-content/uploads/2016/09/WP1302_Tiefenbach_Kohlbacher.pdf.

Toivonen, Tuukka. 2012. "NEETs: The Strategy within the Category." In *A Sociology of Japanese Youth*, edited by Roger Goodman, Yuki Imoto, and Tuukka Toivonen, 139–58. New York: Routledge.

Turner, Edith. 2012. *Communitas: The Anthropology of Collective Joy*. New York: Palgrave Macmillan.

Uchida, Yukiko, and Shinobu Kitayama. 2009. "Happiness and Unhappiness in East and West: Themes and Variations." *Emotion* 9 (4): 441–56. https://doi.org/10.1037/a0015634.

Uchida, Yukiko, and Yuji Ogihara. 2012. "Personal or Interpersonal Construal of Happiness: A Cultural Psychological Perspective." *International Journal of Wellbeing* 2 (4): 354–69. http://doi.org/10.5502/ijw.v2.i4.5.

Uchida, Yukiko, Yuji Ogihara, and Shintaro Fukushima. 2015. "Cultural Construal of Wellbeing: Theories and Empirical Evidence." In *Global*

Handbook of Quality of Life, edited by Wolfgang Glatzer, Laura Camfield, Valerie Meller, and Mariano Rojas, 65–78. New York: Springer.

United Nations. 2011. "Happiness Should Have a Greater Role in Development Policy." *United Nations News Center*, July 19, 2011. http:// www.un.org/apps/news/story.asp?NewsID=39084#.WW35TdPyvq0.

Vaillant, George E. 2015. *Triumphs of Experience: The Men of the Harvard Grant Study*. Cambridge: Belknap Press: An Imprint of Harvard University Press.

van Uchelen, Collin. 2000. "Individualism, Collectivism, and Community Psychology." In *Handbook of Community Psychology*, edited by Julian Rappaport and Edward Seidman, 65–78. New York: Springer.

Walker, Harry, and Iza Kavedžija. 2015. "Values of Happiness." *HAU: Journal of Ethnographic Theory* 5 (3): 1–23. http://doi.org/10.14318/hau5.3.002.

Zevnik, Luka. 2014. *Critical Perspectives in Happiness Research: The Birth of Modern Happiness*. New York: Springer.

8 Mental Health, Recovery, and Prevention: Rethinking the Governance of Mental Abnormality in Canada

JANET PHILLIPS

Introduction

Canadian mental health policy is at a transformative juncture, marked by three overlapping shifts. First, after centuries in the closet, the topic of mental health is widely engaged in everyday conversation, ranging from workplace and campus initiatives to celebrity testimonials. Second, after various provincial and federal commissions' investigations identified a crisis in Canada's mental health system in the early 2000s, it became apparent that a growing demand for mental health services was confronting a fragmented, underfunded, and inadequate service system. Third, in response to the demand, crisis, and the dearth of services, mental health policy discussions and their prescriptive solutions have shifted away from service provision and towards the development of personal resiliency. Taken together, these shifts reflect a unique and interesting moment in the governance of mental abnormality,* which has very real consequences for "those categorized as mentally abnormal" (TCAMA).

This chapter mobilizes Janine Brodie's method of social enquiry, diagnosing the present moment in Canadian mental health policy by locating it alongside past approaches to the governance of mental

---

* This project relies on a Foucauldian conception of abnormality (1965; 2003a). It uses the term "mental abnormality" to refer to what at different times has been called lunacy, insanity, feeblemindedness, mental illness, and now, mental health problems. Consequently, it refers to those who have been labelled as lunatics, insane, feebleminded, and mentally ill as "those categorized as mentally abnormal" (TCAMA). This explanation was taken from my dissertation: "From Containment to Resilience: A Genealogy of the Governance of Mental Abnormality in Canada" (PhD thesis, University of Alberta, 2017).

abnormality. In doing so, it demonstrates that although mental abnormality is not a new policy problem, it *is* being approached in new ways. Specifically, while mental health has come out of the closet and into everyday conversation as a pressing public issue, the ways it is being talked about indicate a shift towards a resilience mentality. This mentality responds to increasing demands on a fragmented and inadequate mental health service system by suggesting that mental abnormality can be prevented, by drawing on one's inner strength and bouncing back in the face of life's challenges. As Brodie's work shows, neoliberalism moves the responsibility for those who suffer from a collective responsibility based on a sense of shared fate, towards a resilience mentality that effectively downloads responsibility for mental health to the individual (Brodie 2007, 159–60). In light of what Brodie also documents as neoliberalism's erosion of a social safety net, this revised approach to the governance of mental abnormality has potentially dangerous consequences for those least equipped to bounce back.

Building on Brodie's application of a governmentality lens to Canadian state forms and public policy, this chapter undertakes a genealogy of the present to unearth three distinct mentalities, or ways of thinking about mental abnormality, espoused between the 1830s and 1990s, which it subsequently locates alongside resilience: containment, medicalization, and deinstitutionalization. Governmentality denotes a method of governance unique to the liberal state, providing a grid through which to analyze multiple relations of power, including power and conduct beyond the state (Brodie 2007; 2008; Brown 2015; Dean 2010; Foucault 2008, 186; Miller and Rose 2008; Walters 2012). Here, mentalities constitute rationalities, or "ways of rendering reality thinkable in such a way that it [is] amenable to calculation and programming" (Miller and Rose 2008, 16). Mentalities guide the ways we think about social problems, opening them up to social intervention. They are traceable through an analysis of the language used to categorize and problematize social phenomena – in this case, mental abnormality. Here, discourse is productive, making "reality amenable to certain kinds of action" (Miller and Rose 2008, 31). It defines and limits potential solutions. Mentalities, in turn, inform programs and technologies. Categorizations and problematizations of mental abnormality inform solutions to it, otherwise known as programs. Programs translate an ethos, or what should be, into a *techne*, or the mechanisms needed to reach that end (Barry, Osbourne, and Rose 1996, 8). Technologies, on the other hand, put programs into action (Miller and Rose 2008, 63). They constitute the tools used to operationalize solutions. This is not to say that mentalities translate perfectly into programs, nor that programs translate perfectly into technologies. As Miller and Rose remind us, "whilst we inhabit a world of programs, the world is not itself programmed" (2008, 71). Governance is a messy and complicated process, wherein mentalities, programs, and technologies shift and respond to one another, and where "solutions for one program tend to be problems for another" (Miller and Rose 2008, 71). These mentalities informed various programs and technologies advanced to manage mental abnormality. They were coded as lunacy, insanity, feeblemindedness, and mental illness, and, notably, each of these programs and technologies were considered progressive and "in the best interests" of TCAMA in their time.

As I will elaborate, a governmentality analysis reveals that the public transcripts of the twenty-first century are grounded in prevention and recovery discourses, which are emblematic of resilience, an emergent fourth mentality surrounding mental abnormality. Consistent with broader neoliberal discourses, resilience is a way of thinking about mental abnormality that downloads responsibility for one's mental well-being onto the individual, regardless of one's capacity to cope. Resilience informs prevention and recovery programs, which responsibilize and individualize TCAMA to prevent the development of mental illness by bouncing back from life's stressors in the first place, or for those who have already succumbed to mental illness, to adapt to life despite it. Hence, resilience draws a new line between mental normality and abnormality, not based on mental illness but, rather, on one's personal capacity to bounce back.

In 2006, an investigation by the Standing Senate Committee on Social Affairs, Science and Technology (SSCSST) into the state of mental health in Canada tabled its groundbreaking report *Out of the Shadows at Last: Transforming Mental Health, Mental Illness and Addiction Services in Canada* (Kirby Report), documenting an ever-increasing demand on an underfunded, fragmented, and inadequate mental health service system. To be sure, these problems had already come to light in a series of Ontario inquiries in the 1980s and 1990s, including the "Heseltine Report," or *Towards a Blueprint for Change: A Mental Health Policy and Program Perspective* (1983), the "Graham Report," or *Building Community Support for People: A Plan for Mental Health in Ontario* (1988), and *Making It Happen: Implementation Plan for Mental Health Reform* (1999). All of these investigations pointed to the failures of deinstitutionalization and the mass release of thousands of ex-patients without sufficient mental health supports in the community. The Kirby Report, however, marked a turning point: at the same time that it documented Canada's failing mental health system, it demonstrated a need for new approaches.

These approaches would find articulation in two key reports at the provincial (Ontario) and national levels, respectively: *Open Minds, Healthy Minds* (2011), and *Changing Directions, Changing Lives* (2012).

As identified above, resilience was preceded by three dominant mentalities: containment (1830s–1920s), medicalization (1930s–50s), and deinstitutionalization (1960s–90s). I centre my analysis on Ontario (Upper Canada) due to the fact that the care of TCAMA falls under provincial jurisdiction, and the province's long history of mental health policy reform. I begin with containment by outlining the context within which, in the 1830s, lunacy came to be understood as a political problem for Upper Canada. I then map three containment programs: lunacy reform, mental hygiene, and eugenics. Following this, I introduce medicalization as a new way of thinking about what became mental illness in the 1930s. This approach supported invasive treatment programs such as lobotomy and electroshock. Next, I chart the shift away from medicalization and towards deinstitutionalization, which informed the emptying out of both psychiatric wards and large-scale psychiatric hospitals. The final portion of the chapter discusses the outcomes of deinstitutionalization programs, which opened a space for new mental health policy directions in the 2000s – most notably, resilience.

Containing Lunacy, Insanity, and Feeblemindedness in 1830s–1920s Ontario (Upper Canada)

In 1830s Upper Canada, mental abnormality was understood as lunacy. "Lunacy" and "lunatic" were used in Europe as far back as the 1200s, with etymological origins in Roman mythology (Reaume 2002, 407–8). Rooted in the Latin *lunaticus*, meaning "moon-struck," use of the word "lunatic" implied a connection between lunar cycles and mental abnormality (*Online Etymology Dictionary*, s.v. "lunatic"). Uncontrollable yet cyclical, an association with lunar cycles ascribed a sense of fatalism and incurability to lunacy. This mentality thus framed lunacy as incurable but containable.

Official legislative discussions surrounding lunacy reform began in Upper Canada in the 1830s (Brown 1984, 30–4; Dear and Wolch 1987, 74–5; Moran 2000, 49). Until then, lunatics fell under the care of their families, but many ended up in district jails (Brown 1984, 27–9). By the 1830s, however, districts complained that lunatics had become a financial burden, with even prisoners protesting that lunatics were a nuisance. For example, an 1830s prisoners' petition from the Home District Gaol disputed an insufficient dietary allowance, as well as the presence of lunatics (Brown 1984, 35). District authorities felt that lunatics were "an unwanted drain on district funds," not to mention "a dangerous moral contagion that might infect others, even criminals and debtors" (Brown 1984, 35–6). On the other hand, private charities pressured the government for greater public aid, and a "rising tide of protest (especially from judicial quarters) focused attention on the plight of the insane" (Dear and Wolch 1987, 74, 81). Effectively then, lunatics had become a "social problem." This concept, as Brodie observes, was introduced in the early 1800s and prompted interventions on problem groups – such as lunatics – in order to provide "the salvation of wayward or broken people," and, the "strengthening of the collective" (Brodie 2008, 26). Hence, as a social problem, and an emerging crisis, lunatics required intervention "for their own good," as well as for the good of society.

On May 11, 1839, the Legislative Assembly of Upper Canada asserted its new responsibility for lunatics by passing "An Act to authorize the erection of an Asylum within this province for the reception of Insane and Lunatic persons" (Brown 1984, 32; Dear and Wolch 1987, 81; Frankenburg 1982, 172). Issues with site selection delayed construction, but finally, on January 26, 1850, Upper Canada's first asylum opened at 999 Queen Street West, Toronto (Reaume 2000, 6). Asylums quickly multiplied across Upper Canada, opening in London (1870), Mimico (1890), and Cobourg (1902), to name just a few (Mitchinson 1988, 92).

Lunacy reform was not limited to the construction of asylums, but also included moral treatment, a program comprised of work therapy, religion, and recreation (Brown 1984, 45, Moran 2000, 92–6; Reaume 2000, 14; 2006, 69–70; Scull 1984, 26; Shortt 1986, 128–9). Moral treatment was considered a humane alternative to the chaining up of lunatics in jails, and its purpose was to reform lunatics and return them to society (Brown 1984, 45; Dowbiggin 2003, 6). The problem, however, was that more lunatics were admitted than discharged, and moral treatment proved ineffective. In its 1876 annual report, the Asylum for the Insane, Toronto, reported that 87.5 per cent of admissions were considered chronic (Reaume 2000, 7).

While asylums filled, lunacy slowly became an outdated term, to be supplanted by insanity. Thus, in 1871, 999 Queen Street West, the "Provincial Lunatic Asylum, at Toronto" was renamed the "Asylum for the Insane, Toronto" (Reaume 2002, 409). "Insane" was rooted in the Latin *insanus*, which loosely translated into "unsound," and insanity was an "unsoundness of mind" (Reaume 2002, 409; *Online Etymology Dictionary*, s.v. "insanity"). "Unsoundness" could be applied to multiple levels of affliction, and therefore, "insanity" referred to various levels of disturbance. Those who "fell short of the criteria necessary for [...]

asylum admission" were treated via private neurology clinics – if they had the resources (Dowbiggin 2003, 10–11; Shortt 1986, 139). Moreover, following the extensive professional reorganization of psychiatry towards medical and scientific legitimacy in the late 1800s, asylums were renamed hospitals. In 1907, 999 Queen Street West was renamed "Hospital for the Insane, Toronto" at the urging of its superintendent, Daniel Clark (Reaume 2000, 6). For Clark, "hospital" implied treatment, conveying optimism, whereas "asylum" sounded custodial and fatalistic (Reaume 2002, 410–411).

The perceived failures of moral treatment, and the subsequent overcrowding of asylums/ hospitals, presented a crisis for a containment mentality. Mental hygiene emerged as the solution to this crisis in the early 1900s. "Mental hygiene" referred to a science of mental health and was part of a broader public hygiene movement centred on disease prevention (Richardson 1989, 1). Essentially, the logic ran that if insanity could not be reformed, it could be prevented. The Canadian National Committee on Mental Hygiene (CNCMH), today known as the Canadian Mental Health Association (CMHA), was established in 1918, and its members, many of them psychiatrists, were dedicated to the prevention of insanity (Dowbiggin 2003, 19; McLaren 1990, 59).

In keeping with the branding of the twentieth century as "the century of the child," mental hygiene programs were directed at children (Richardson 1989, 2). Implemented in schools, which provided "an unprecedented opportunity for large-scale public intervention into child life," programs were designed to properly socialize children (Richardson 1989, 2, 14). Programs were comprised of both moral and physical training, and mental testing (Richardson 1989, 14). Parenting was also a site for intervention, with many psychiatrists attributing insanity to poor parenting (Martin 1928, 6).

Eugenics, a much more radical containment strategy, developed alongside mental hygiene. Eugenics was grounded in hereditarian knowledges, which suggested that genetic predispositions to mental afflictions were attributable to the reproduction of the mentally unfit. The development of hereditarianism was entwined with the discursive production of "feeblemindedness," a lesser form of insanity that was harder to detect (Dowbiggin 2003, 161). The feebleminded were considered a "menace" (Martin 1928, 4; Reaume 2000, 31–2), and were blamed for everything from physical threats, such as the spread of disease, to moral threats, such as the perceived breakdown of traditional Anglo-Saxon values (McLaren 1990, 27).

Like their mental hygienist counterparts, eugenicists sought to contain insanity, as well as feeblemindedness, through prevention. In order to achieve this, however, eugenicists went beyond socialization to call for interventions into the reproductive capacities of the feebleminded. Most infamously, eugenicists advocated for the sterilization of the mentally unfit (Dowbiggin 2003, 167). Although sterilization laws were never passed in Ontario, the practice was used unofficially (Dowbiggin 2003, 187–8; McLaren 1990, 25). Such laws were passed, however, in Alberta and British Columbia, and were not abolished until 1972 (Dowbiggin 2003, 133–4; 2006, 179; McLaren 1990, 107).

Medicalizing and Deinstitutionalizing Mental Illness in 1930s–1990s Ontario

Mental hygiene and eugenics did not contain mental abnormality, but they did contribute to a medicalization mentality. Medicalization reframed mental abnormality as mental illness, where those "who formerly were described as 'insane and dangerous to be at large' ... were now described as 'mentally ill'" (Frankenburg 1982, 173). The medicalization of mental abnormality made room for new interventions. Since mental illness was an illness like any other, medicalization programs took the form of physical treatments, which were directed towards the pursuit of a cure. Treatments were largely experimental, and, indeed, were labelled "heroic" because the "'dramatic' attempt to relieve a person of his or her affliction was, in itself, a sign of the 'valour' of this approach" (Reaume 2000, 18). Such treatments included insulin shock, metrazol shock, and lobotomy (Reaume 2000, 19–20).

By the 1970s, interventionist medical treatments were deployed far less frequently due to their inefficacy, legal hoops influenced by an emerging patients' rights movement, and the discovery of psychopharmaceuticals (Reaume 2000, 20; Scull 1984, 80). Following years of experimental procedures, experts realized that mental illness was incurable but manageable using psychopharmaceuticals. Moreover, psychopharmaceuticals also offered a means to address public concerns regarding overcrowding in provincial psychiatric hospitals (PPHs) (Dear and Wolch 1987, 16). These sentiments, in addition to the financial demands of PPHs on provincial coffers, contributed to a shift away from medicalization, and towards a deinstitutionalization mentality.

A deinstitutionalization mentality asserted that the mentally ill no longer constituted a threat, and that with the right community supports, they could assimilate into society. It dealt with two old problems – incurability and overcrowding – by moving patients outside of hospital walls and into the community. The problem, however, was that a comprehensive community service system was never put in place.

Few of the dollars from PPH operating budgets followed patients into the community. For example, just $1.15 million of Lakeshore Psychiatric Hospital's $13 million annual budget was transferred into community services (Dear and Wolch 1987, 108). Absent sufficient supports, ex-patients found themselves in precarious situations. Many ended up in "psychiatric ghettos" (Nelson 2012, 234), made up of "poor quality and unregulated housing" (Hartford et al. 2003, 67). A meagre monthly welfare allowance barely covered the costs of housing, let alone clothes, transportation, and personal items (Dear and Wolch 1987, 109). Many more "wandered the streets dressed in rags, living in doorways and barely able to fend for themselves" (Simmons 1990, 256). Others ended up in prisons, which quickly filled with ex-patients following the emptying out of PPHs (Chaimowitz 2012, 3).

By the 1980s, deinstitutionalization had precipitated a crisis in Ontario, prompting a series of reports, each making recommendations towards the completion of the deinstitutionalization process through the implementation of a comprehensive community service system. However, by the 2000s, this system was still lacking, creating room for new mental health policy directions, and more broadly, new ways of thinking about mental abnormality.

Promoting Mental Health to Prevent Mental Illness in Canada

These new ways of thinking are evident in the recent public transcripts identified in The Kirby Report (2006), *Open Minds, Healthy Minds* (2011), and *Changing Directions, Changing Lives* (2012). In these reports, "mental illness" shifted to "mental health." Unlike mental illness, which denotes an individual, specific affliction, mental health refers to a more commonly experienced state of mental well-being. This shift is consistent with what Catherine Kingfisher points to elsewhere in this volume as positive psychology's movement away from "what is wrong" – in this case, mental illness, and towards "what is right" – in this case, mental health. For example, *Open Minds, Healthy Minds* stated that "We will create an Ontario where all people have the opportunity to thrive, enjoying good mental health and well-being throughout their lifetime" (4). It expressed the need to "identify standards and best practices that improve mental health and reduce addictions – and help everyone in the province reach their full potential" (5). It defined mental health as follows:

> Good mental health is a resource for living. It enhances physical health and helps people succeed in school, at work and in their relationships and to contribute to our communities. People who feel good about themselves

and their lives are more productive and less likely to take sick days. To improve their mental health, Ontarians must know how to manage stress and enjoy work-life balance. They need constructive ways to deal with negative emotions such as anger, sadness, fear and grief. They also need activities and interests that help them feel more self-confident and form supportive friendships. (10)

Similarly, *Changing Directions, Changing Lives* defined "positive mental health" as "feeling well, functioning well, and being resilient in the face of life's challenges" (20). Mental health was even likened to physical health and, thus, something that everyone should strive for. *Open Minds, Healthy Minds* explained that

Ontarians do many things to maintain their physical health – like eating healthy foods, staying active, and not smoking. When people do become physically ill, our health system is there to provide treatment and support. It's time to take the same approach to mental health and addictions, from prevention, to identification, to treatment. (5)

Notably, "mental health" is a wide-ranging definition. As a category, it broadens the parameters for intervention to include everyone, not just those with diagnosed mental illness.

A recovery-oriented system was one of the most significant program proposals offered by the documents. The guiding vision of the Kirby Report's recommendations, and one of six strategic directions in *Changing Directions, Changing Lives*, recovery was

built on the principles of hope, empowerment, self-determination, and responsibility. In a recovery-oriented system, people who experience mental health problems and illnesses are treated with dignity and respect. To the greatest extent possible, they control and maintain responsibility for their mental health and well-being, and they make their own choices about which services, treatments and supports may be best for them, informed by the advice of professionals, as well as family and peers. (16)

Changing Directions, Changing Lives presented recovery as the ability to live the best life possible despite symptoms. Specifically, it defined recovery as "living a satisfying, hopeful, and contributing life, even when there are ongoing limitations caused by mental health problems and illnesses" (15). The Kirby Report was broader in its conceptualization of recovery, leaving it to the individual to define: "*Recovery* is not the same thing as being cured. For many individuals, it is a way of living a satisfying, hopeful, and productive life even with limitations caused by the illness; for others, recovery means the reduction or complete remission of symptoms related to mental illness" (42, italics in original). However, even when defined as the amelioration of symptoms, the Kirby Report used the descriptors "reduction" and "remission," suggesting that mental abnormality was incurable. The recommendation towards a recovery-oriented system, offered by both the Kirby Report and *Changing Directions, Changing Lives*, was significant because it was informed by a fatalistic logic that suggested that mental abnormality was incurable, and therefore, that TCAMA had to make do and live the best life possible despite ongoing problems.

A person-centred system was important, the documents suggested, because it empowered TCAMA to make their own choices in accordance with their self-determined recovery plans. *Open Minds, Healthy Minds* argued that "mental health and addictions services must be centred around the person and better integrated with each other and with other health care services to provide supports that are necessary" (16). Similarly, the Kirby Report recommended a "system that puts people living with mental illness at its centre, with a clear focus on their ability to recover" (37). *Changing Directions, Changing Lives* likewise explained that

> To the greatest extent possible, [TCAMA] control and maintain responsibility for their mental health and well-being, and they make their own choices about which services, treatments and supports may be best for them, informed by the advice of professionals, as well as family and peers. (16)

Because the documents put the individual at the centre of their proposals for service integration, the community was framed as a market of services, as opposed to a shared identity or collectivity.

The location of a person-centred recovery model alongside a social determinants model of mental health within both the Kirby Report and *Changing Directions, Changing Lives* is, at first glance, one of their most glaring contradictions. At its outset, the Kirby Report notes that "There has been a complete lack of attention to the social determinants of health as they relate to people with mental health or addiction issues" (6). Further into the Report, a diagram locates the individual at the centre of five social determinants of health, including income, social status, education, employment, and housing (53). *Changing Directions, Changing Lives* observes that social determinants impact mental health, and similarly identifies poverty, housing precarity, and lack of access to education and employment opportunities as determinants that may increase one's risk for mental illness (80). Despite references to these structural forces, however, the documents responsibilize the individual rather than the collective. Here, as Brodie explains in her description of individualization, "Responsibility for social crises that find their genesis in such macro processes as structural unemployment, racism, or unequal gender orders is shifted onto the shoulders of individuals" (2008, 41). Hence, the use of "social" to describe determinants of one's mental health functions to demarcate non-biochemical contributors, rather than as a rally cry to the public, as a collective, to transform inequitable social conditions.

Another key recommendation offered by the documents was the prevention of mental illness via the promotion of mental health. The idea of promotion suggested that good mental health, including personal resiliency, could prevent mental illness later in life. The Kirby Report explained that

> Mental health promotion focuses on the foundations of good mental health. Broadly speaking, it emphasizes positive mental health, as opposed to mental illness. It addresses the determinants of mental health – the many personal, social, economic and environmental factors that are thought to contribute to mental health, and to the overall health and well-being of the population. Such factors include healthy childhood development, income and social status, and education. (411)

Similarly, *Changing Directions, Changing Lives* suggested that although "it is not possible to know in advance which individuals will experience the symptoms of a mental health problem or illness," that "we can enhance factors that are known to help protect people" (20). It identified such "protective factors" as "having a sense of belonging, enjoying good relationships and good physical health, feeling in control of one's life, and possessing good problem-solving skills" (20). In short, the solution offered by prevention programs was to limit, to the greatest extent possible, future demand on service systems. *Open Minds, Healthy Minds* suggested that "Ontarians are happier, more resilient, and more likely to succeed in school, work and life when they are able to cope with stress and manage the ups and downs in life. Programs will be available for all ages to help Ontarians develop the skills they need early in life to improve their mental well-being and to lead healthier lives" (7). The "happiness imperative," theorized by Kingfisher in this volume, provides a helpful framework for identifying and calling into question the normalization of happiness evident in these prevention and promotion discourses. As Kingfisher explains, this imperative is intertwined with preventative approaches to mental health that disregard structural impacts and places the onus for well-being on the individual, rather than the collective.

Resilience and Its Early Cracks

As noted at the beginning of the chapter, resilience suggests that mental illness can be prevented by learning to bounce back rather than succumb to life's stressors. Those who do not bounce back can learn to live a meaningful life despite mental illness, through recovery. From unemployment to natural disasters, we are told that we can overcome anything that life throws our way provided we work hard enough and have the right attitude. Bookstore shelves are lined with a seemingly infinite supply of self-help guides, and resilience training is now being written into public school curriculum and university wellness initiatives.

Contemporary mental health care reform discussions are increasingly informed by a resilience mentality. The term "resilience" is rooted in the latin *resilire*, meaning to jump back (Bourbeau 2013, 6; Sehgal 2015). It refers to the ability to adjust to, or recover from, adversity, misfortune, and change (Bourbeau 2013, 6). The resilient individual is one who "suffers some insult or disturbance, but whose integrity is held to have been maintained, or even enhanced, by its resistive or adaptive response" (Munro 2013, 1). In short, resilience refers to the capacity to bounce back from, rather than succumb to, life's unpredictable challenges.

Resilience downloads collective problems onto the individual (Beck and Beck-Gernsheim 2002, 3; Welsh 2013, 8). It responsibilizes the individual subject for one's successes and failures, reframing the latter as a reflection of individual, personal character (Sehgal 2015). Resilience displaces the victim, instead attributing misfortune to individual will (Schott 2013, 211). This logic absolves the state of an obligation to provide the supports necessary for our survival. As Brodie points out, those who are not self-sufficient are told to take responsibility for their own bad choices (2007, 159–60). Hence, rather than offer any concrete supports, the state targets interventions in the form of resiliency training to those deemed to be at risk, offering them "a 'hand-up' to the labour force and to entrepreneurialism rather than a 'hand out' to a certain life of dependency" (Brodie and Phillips 2014, 7). The neoliberal state is not held accountable for its lack of social supports when it is up to the individual to ensure one's own well-being: "'Resilient' people do not look to states to secure their well-being because they have been disciplined into believing in the necessity to secure it for themselves" (Reid 2012, 69). At the same time, the resilient subject knows that one's well-being will never be secured, and that one must continually adapt to new threats and dangers (Evans and Reid 2013, 85).

Resilience informs "mental health," the preferred *mot de jour*. The new mentally abnormal are those who do not work to improve their mental health. Unlike past approaches, mental illness and mental health are not binary categories. There is no longer a neat dichotomy between those who are lunatics, insane, and mentally ill, and those who are not. Rather, as *Changing Directions, Changing Lives* argued, "there is no 'us' and 'them' when it comes to mental health and well-being" (2012, 12). As Brodie and Phillips argue, "There is no longer anything special or unique about the experiences of the chronically mentally ill" (2014, 18). Instead, those with mental illness are at the extreme negative end of a continuum, and they can return to equilibrium if they so choose. The problem with this approach, however, is that it invisibilizes the unique needs of those with chronic mental illness, for whom returning to equilibrium presents far more challenges than for others. The shift towards mental health draws a new line between normal and abnormal. Mental illness does not make you abnormal, but the inability to keep going despite it, does.

Open Minds, Healthy Minds (2011), the Kirby Report (2006), and *Changing Directions, Changing Lives* (2012), put forward a variety of solutions, which I loosely grouped under recovery and prevention. Scholars point out that recovery has been deployed to responsibilize TCAMA for their own well-being, while simultaneously covering over the social inequities that contribute to mental illness in the first place (Battersby and Morrow 2012; Morrow 2013). Battersby and Morrow argue that

> Although recovery models encompass social supports (like housing and income) for people with mental illness, our findings demonstrate that, in practice, an individualistic view of mental illness persists that works against recognizing the contribution of systemic social and structural inequities to people's experiences of mental illness and to their recovery journey. (2012, 104)

Similarly, Morrow and Weisser argue that dominant notions of recovery overlook additional structural barriers along the lines of race, gender, sexuality, and age (2012, 28). They note that dominant recovery discourses overlook neoliberal cuts to social supports, arguing that "recovery without a full recognition of the current social and political context which has eroded social welfare supports will be impotent to foster real systemic change" (2012, 40). As Morrow argues, "For people experiencing mental distress, who in the course of 'treatment' may lose certain citizenship rights and who may rely on and off on the social service system for most of their lives, the emphasis on private solutions to social problems is particularly reprehensible" (2013, 328). Recovery situates every TCAMA at the same starting line, disregarding that fact that some people face additional hurdles. When those hurdles interfere with their ability to recover, this is perceived as a personal moral failing – that is, they did not recover because they did not work hard enough.

The final documents fell short on prescriptive prevention programs. This silence is indicative of a broader problem with resiliency discourses, which as Brodie and Phillips point out, lack "concrete programs that are actually aimed at building resilience" and are "[silent] about the role of social programs …" (2014, 8). Over the past ten years, a plethora of promotion programs have sprung up in multiple sites, ranging from the home, to the public school, to the university, to the workplace. These programs offer tips on building personal resiliency but lack concrete guidance.

Alberta Health Services' *Bounce Back Book* series is one such program. One of its workbooks, *The Bounce Back Book: Building Resiliency Skills in Your Preschooler* (2010), recommends a variety of activities to parents to help develop resiliency in their children. The introduction claims that "Helping children develop self-confidence, problem solving skills, emotional regulation and empathy skills will equip them to be successful in life" (3). It encourages parents to "Get silly with your kids! Build resiliency in your children that will last a lifetime" (3). The activity book is sub-divided into four resiliency skills, including self-confidence, problem solving, emotional regulation, and empathy, each with multiple activities (5). To build self-confidence, the book recommends building a wall of fame for one's two-year-old, because "Children thrive on adult attention and approval" (8). The "Little Shopper activity" builds problem solving skills by having three-year-olds fetch grocery store items. Parents can instill emotional regulation in their three-year-old through the "Double bubble the fun" activity that teaches relaxing breathing techniques (26). Empathy can be instilled in four-year-olds by having them act out scenarios with puppets (36). This program authorizes the parent, who is, in turn, charged with the responsibilization of their preschooler.

Resilience logics have informed a discursive shift away from mental illness, and towards mental health and, in short, a subsequent shift away from the treatment of the few, and towards the mental health of all. Resilience is not a new concept, having long served as a popular area of study in ecology and engineering. However, it is now being taken up in new ways, coopted by neoliberal logics and inserted into multiple policy domains. One such domain is mental health. This chapter located two overarching mental health policy directions – recovery and prevention – within a broader resilience mentality. Both directions individualize and responsibilize TCAMA for their own fates. None of the reports and strategies analyzed in this chapter provided concrete recovery recommendations. Rather, recovery is first and foremost a subjective concept, meaning that recovery journeys should be individually planned and defined, rather than imposed. In contrast, promotion programs, such as Alberta Health Services' *Bounce Back Book Series* (2010) and the University of Alberta's mental wellness initiatives, are targeted at entire constituencies. The purpose of these programs is to teach students the skills needed to cope with life's challenges.

Only time will tell if resilience is successful as a mental health policy direction, however, cracks in its logic have already begun to reveal themselves in the face of both the COVID-19 pandemic, as well as updates to Canada's Medical Assistance in Dying (MAiD) legislation. COVID-19 and its associated stressors, such as heightened feelings of isolation, have shone a light on the early failures of resilience to respond to the mental health needs of pandemic magnitude. A resilience logic suggests that anyone with the right skill set can bounce back from an unforeseen disruption. However, in the face of such a disruption not everyone is bouncing back, and once again in the history of Canadian mental health policy, a spotlight has been shone on a lack of state-funded mental health services. For example, the federal minister of health's updated mandate letter, issued January 15, 2021, states that "[…] COVID-19 has intensified the health inequities and barriers to care across the country […]," following which the prime minister directs the minister to accelerate work with federal, provincial and territorial partners "to ensure that all Canadians, including vulnerable populations and those living in rural and remote areas, have access to a family doctor or primary health care team, as well as critical health and mental health resources and services […]" (Justin Trudeau to Patty Hajdu, January 15, 2021). Furthermore, the federal government delivered funding for Wellness Together Canada, a website that those with mental health and substance use needs brought about by the pandemic can visit to access supports, including counselling via phone, video, or text. The website explains that "Wellness Together Canada was created in response to an unprecedented rise in mental health and substance use concerns due to the COVID-19 pandemic [...]" (Wellness Together Canada 2021). Ultimately, the pandemic is providing the unforeseen disruption that the concept of resilience hinges upon. However, society is not bouncing back – and those who were struggling prior to the pandemic are especially suffering.

One of neoliberalism's most troubling features, noted throughout this volume, is its capacity to adapt itself in response to crises of its own making. Although resilience is still in its early infancy as a policy approach, it too has already begun the process of rewriting itself in response to its inherent crises. Notably, COVID-19 has come with a slew of mental health tips grounded in resilience at the same time that the state is scrambling to fill large-scale service gaps made worse by the failures of resilience as a mental health strategy. A tip sheet released by the MHCC, "Cultivating Resilience in the Wake of COVID-19," reminds us that "we can all cultivate resiliency by focusing on the actions and attitudes that strengthen our mental health" (MHCC 2021). In its "Mental Health First Aid COVID-19 Self-Care and Resilience Guide," the MHCC provides instruction for tailoring a "self-care and resilience plan," inviting readers to select from a curation of "self-care practices and resilience-building strategies" (MHCC 2020). The list contains options such as "Make a gratitude list"; "Take a nap"; "Lay in the grass"; "Create a poster with images of a positive vision"; and "Wear something that makes you feel confident" (MHCC 2020). Notably, in addition to lacking concrete mental health supports, these tips, practices, and strategies require a certain amount of leisure time that is inaccessible to many. A single mother balancing shift work with remote learning for her children, for example, may not have time to take a nap or lay in the grass.

Perhaps one of the biggest failures of resilience as a mental health policy response is reflected in Canada's recent changes to its MAiD legislation, passed by the Senate on March 17, 2021. As of March 17, 2023, those living in a constant state of suffering on account of mental illness will be eligible for MAiD. Bill C-7: An Act to Amend the Criminal Code (Medical Assistance in Dying) broadens the eligibility criteria for MAiD beyond those whose deaths are reasonably foreseeable, to include those whose deaths are not reasonably foreseeable, but who "have a serious and incurable illness, disease or disability" that comes with "enduring and intolerable physical or psychological suffering that cannot be alleviated under conditions the person considers acceptable"

(Government of Canada 2021). Prior to coming into effect in 2023, the Ministers of Justice and Health have been tasked with undertaking an "expert review" to "[consider] protocols, guidance and safeguards [...] for persons suffering from mental illness, and to make recommendations within the next year (by March 17, 2022)" (Canada 2021).

The extension of MAiD eligibility to include mental illness demonstrates the failure of resilience as the latest policy response to mental abnormality. Not everyone is bouncing back from life's challenges, and in the end, no amount of naps in the grass will protect someone from a manic episode, catatonic depression, or from hearing voices. Resilience as a mental health strategy is hardly adequate to address the needs of those living in chronic mental distress, yet death is an extreme alternative. As of March 17, 2023, MAiD eligibility criteria will make possible the "letting die" (Foucault 2003b, 241) of those with chronic mental illness, and consequently, the individualization of eugenics. Furthermore, by framing MAiD as a personal choice, and in the absence of sufficient services and supports, the legislation potentially absolves the state and society of any responsibility for providing TCAMA with a future beyond their suffering.

Conclusion

The failures of deinstitutionalization programs made room for new ways of thinking about the governance of mental abnormality. Resilience is one such mentality. It prescribes recovery and prevention programs that individualize and responsibilize TCAMA for their own fates, who in turn are expected to bounce back from, or adapt to, life's challenges. Under a resilience mentality, a mental illness diagnosis does not mean one is mentally abnormal. However, the inability – perceived as the refusal – to bounce back, or adapt to it, does. Prevention and recovery are appealing ideas – it is easy to be seduced into the idea that after hundreds of years, we have found the solution to mental abnormality. However, this chapter demonstrated that captivating and convincing discourses can translate into dangerous technologies, and that new inclusions result in new exclusions. If prevention and recovery centre the individual, who do they marginalize? Who is silenced when we talk about our mental health? If promotion campaigns bolster the mental health of all, what about the mental illness of the few? Who will catch those who do not bounce back and recover when they fall? Lastly, and perhaps the most important question inspired by Brodie's work – how do we catch them?

REFERENCES

Alberta Health Services. 2010. *The Bounce Back Book: Building Resiliency Skills in Your Preschooler*. Edmonton, Alberta: Alberta Health Services.

Barry, Andrew, Thomas Osborne, and Nikolas Rose. 1996. *Introduction to Foucault and Political Reason: Liberalism, Neo-liberalism and Rationalities of Government*, edited by Andrew Barry, Thomas Osborne, and Nikolas Rose, 1–17. Chicago: University of Chicago Press.

Battersby, Lupin, and Marina Morrow. 2012. "Challenges in Implementing Recovery-Based Mental Health Care Practices in Psychiatric Tertiary Care." *Canadian Journal of Community Mental Health* 31 (2): 103–17. http://doi.org/10.7870/cjcmh-2012-0016.

Beck, Ulrich, and Elisabeth Beck-Gernsheim. 2002. *Individualization: Institutionalized Individualism and Its Social and Political Consequences*. London, ON: Sage.

Bourbeau, Philippe. 2013. "Resiliencism: Premises and Promises in Securitisation Research." *Resilience: International Policies, Practices and Discourses* 1 (1): 3–17. https://doi.org/10.1080/21693293.2013.765738.

Brodie, Janine. 2007. "The New Social 'isms': Individualization and Social Policy Reform in Canada." In *Contested Individualization: Debates about Contemporary Personhood*, edited by Cosmo Howard, 153–85. New York: Palgrave Macmillan.

– 2008. "The Social in Social Citizenship." In *Recasting the Social in Citizenship*, edited by Engin F. Isin, 20–43. Toronto, ON: University of Toronto Press.

Brodie, Janine, and Janet Phillips. "Resilience, Crisis and Precariousness: The Case of Mental Health Policy Reform in Canada." Paper presented at the Annual Convention of the International Studies Association, Toronto, Canada, March 26–29, 2014.

Brown, Thomas E. 1984. "The Origins of the Asylum in Upper Canada, 1830–1839: Towards an Interpretation." *Canadian Bulletin of Medical History* 1 (1): 27–58. https://doi.org/10.3138/cbmh.1.1.27.

Brown, Wendy. 2015. *Undoing the Demos: Neoliberalism's Stealth Revolution*. Brooklyn, NY: Zone Books.

Canada. 2021. "Canada's New Medical Assistance in Dying (MAID) Law." Accessed April 3, 2021. https://www.justice.gc.ca/eng/cj-jp/ad-am/bk-di.html.

Canada. 2003. "Proceedings. (Issue No. 9, February 26) 2nd sess., 37th Parliament, 2002-03." https://sencanada.ca/Content/SEN/Committee/372/SOCI/pdf/09issue.pdf.

– 2006. *Standing Senate Committee on Social Affairs, Science and Technology. Out of the Shadows at Last: Transforming Mental Health, Mental Illness and Addiction Services in Canada*. Ottawa: Parliament of Canada.

Chaimowitz, Gary. 2012. "The Criminalization of People with Mental Illness." *The Canadian Journal of Psychiatry* 57 (2): 1–6.

Dean, Mitchell. 2010. *Governmentality: Power and Rule in Modern Society*, 2nd ed. London: SAGE Publications.

Dear, Michael J., and Jennifer R. Wolch. 1987. *Landscapes of Despair: From Deinstitutionalization to Homelessness*. Princeton: Princeton University Press.

Dowbiggin, Ian Robert. 2003. *Keeping America Sane: Psychiatry and Eugenics in the United States and Canada, 1880–1940*. Ithaca and London: Cornell University Press.

Evans, Brad, and Julian Reid. 2013. "Dangerously Exposed: The Life and Death of the Resilient Subject." *Resilience: International Policies, Practices and Discourses* 1 (2): 83–98. https://doi.org/10.1080/21693293.2013.770703.

Foucault, Michel. 1965. *Madness and Civilization: A History of Insanity in the Age of Reason*. Translated by Richard Howard. New York: Vintage Books.

– 2003a. *Abnormal: Lectures at the Collège de France, 1974–1975*. Edited by Valerio Marchetti, Antonella Salomani, François Ewald, Alessandro Fontana, and Arnold I. Davidson. Translated by Graham Burchell. New York: Picador.

– 2003b. *Society Must Be Defended: Lectures at the Collège de France, 1975–1976*. Edited by Mauro Bertani, Alessandro Fontana, François Ewald, and Arnold I. Davidson. Translated by David Macey. New York: Picador.

– 2008. *The Birth of Biopolitics: Lectures at the Collège de France, 1978–1979*. Edited by Michel Senellart, François Ewald, Alessandro Fontana, and Arnold I. Davidson. Translated by Graham Burchell. Houndmills, Basingstoke, Hampshire, NY: Palgrave Macmillan.

Frankenburg, Frances. 1982. "The 1978 Ontario Mental Health Act in Historical Context." *HSTC Bulletin: Journal of the History of Canadian Science, Technology and Medicine* 6 (3): 172–7. https://doi.org/10.7202/800144ar.

Hartford, Kathleen, Ted Schrecker, Mary Wiktorowicz, Jeffrey S. Holch, and Crystal Sharp. 2003. "Four Decades of Mental Health Policy in Ontario, Canada." *Administration and Policy in Mental Health* 31 (1): 65–73.

Heseltine, G.F. 1983. *Towards a Blueprint for Change: A Mental Health Policy and Program Perspective*. Toronto, ON: Ontario Ministry of Health.

Martin, Charles F. 1928. "The Mental Hygiene Movement in Canada." In *Mental Hygiene of Childhood*, edited by the Canadian National Committee for Mental Hygiene, 1–7. Toronto and Montreal: Canadian National Committee for Mental Hygiene.

McLaren, Angus. 1990. *Our Own Master Race: Eugenics in Canada, 1885–1945*. Toronto: McClelland & Stewart.

The Mental Health Commission of Canada. 2012. *Changing Directions, Changing Lives: The Mental Health Strategy for Canada*. Calgary, AB: The Mental Health Commission of Canada.

– 2020. "Mental Health First Aid COVID-19 Self-Care & Resilience Guide." Accessed April 4, 2021. https://www.mhfa.ca/sites/default/files/mhfa _self-care-resilience-guide.pdf.

– 2021. "Cultivating Resilience in the Wake of COVID-19." Accessed April 4, 2021. https://www.mentalhealthcommission.ca/sites/default /files/2020-09/covid_19_tip_sheet_resilience_eng.pdf.

Miller, Peter, and Nikolas Rose. 2008. *Governing the Present: Administering Economic, Social and Personal Life*. Cambridge: Polity.

Mitchinson, Wendy. 1988. "Reasons for Committal to a Mid-Nineteenth Century Ontario Insane Asylum: The Case of Toronto." In *Essays in the History of Canadian Medicine*, edited by Wendy Mitchinson and Janice Dickin McGinnis, 88–109. Toronto: McClelland and Stewart.

Moran, James E. 2000. *Committed to the State Asylum: Insanity and Society in Nineteenth-Century Quebec and Ontario*. Montreal and Kingston: McGill-Queen's University Press.

Morrow, Marina. 2013. "Recovery: Progressive Paradigm or Neoliberal Smokescreen?" In *Mad Matters: A Critical Reader in Canadian Mad Studies*, edited by Brenda A. LeFrançois, Robert Menzies, and Geoffrey Reaume, 323–3. Toronto: Canadian Scholars' Press.

Morrow, Marina, and Julia Weisser. 2012. "Towards a Social Justice Framework of Mental Health Recovery." *Studies in Social Justice* 6 (1): 27–43. http://doi.org/10.26522/ssj.v6i1.1067.

Munro, Andrew. 2013. "Discursive Resilience." *M/C Journal: A Journal of Media and Culture* 16 (5). https://doi.org/10.5204/mcj.710.

Nelson, Geoffrey. 2012. "Mental Health Policy in Canada." In *Canadian Social Policy: Issues and Perspectives*, 5th ed., edited by Anne Westhues and Brian Wharf, 229–52. Waterloo, ON: Wilfred Laurier University Press.

Online Etymology Dictionary. s.v. "insanity." http://www.etymonline.com /index.php?term=insanity&allowed_in_frame=0 (accessed October 27, 2016).

Online Etymology Dictionary. s.v. "lunatic." http://www.etymonline.com /index.php?term=lunatic (accessed October 26, 2016).

Ontario. 2011. *Open Minds, Healthy Minds: Ontario's Comprehensive Mental Health and Addictions Strategy*. Toronto: Queen's Printer for Ontario.

Ontario Ministry of Health. 1998. *The Provincial Community Mental Health Committee. Building Community Support for People: A Plan for Mental Health in Ontario*. Toronto, ON: Ministry of Health.

Ontario Ministry of Health and Long-Term Care. 1999. *Making It Happen: Implementation Plan for Mental Health Reform*. Toronto, ON: Ministry of Health.

– 1999. *Making It Happen: Operational Framework for the Delivery of Mental Health Services and Supports*. Toronto: Ministry of Health.

Phillips, Janet. 2017. "From Containment to Resilience: A Genealogy of the Governance of Mental Abnormality in Canada." PhD diss., University of Alberta. University of Alberta Education and Research Archive. https:// doi.org/10.7939/R3Q81572P.

Reaume, Geoffrey. 2000. *Remembrance of Patients Past: Patient Life at the Toronto Hospital for the Insane, 1870–1940*. Oxford: Oxford University Press.

– 2002. "Lunatic to Patient to Person: Nomenclature in Psychiatric History and the Influence of Patients' Activism in North America." *International Journal of Law and Psychiatry* 25 (4): 405–26. https://psycnet.apa.org/doi /10.1016/S0160-2527(02)00130-9.

– 2006. "Patients at Work: Insane Asylum Inmates' Labour in Ontario, 1841– 1900." In *Mental Health and Canadian Society: Historical Perspectives*, edited by James E. Moran and David Wright, 69–96. Montreal and Kingston: McGill-Queen's University Press.

Reid, Julian. 2012. "The Disastrous and Politically Debased Subject of Resilience." *Development Dialogue* 58 (58): 67–80.

Richardson, Theresa R.1989. *The Century of the Child: The Mental Hygiene Movement & Social Policy in the United States & Canada*. New York: State University of New York.

Schott, Robin May. 2013. "Resilience, Normativity and Vulnerability." *Resilience: International Policies, Practices and Discourses* 1 (3): 210–18. https:// doi.org/10.1080/21693293.2013.842343.

Scull, Andrew. 1984. *Decarceration: Community Treatment and the Deviant – A Radical View,* 2nd ed. Cambridge: Polity.

Sehgal, Parul. 2015. "The Profound Emptiness of 'Resilience.'" *The New York Times,* December 1, 2015. https://www.nytimes.com/2015/12/06 /magazine/the-profound-emptiness-of-resilience.html?_r=0.

Shortt, S.E.D. 1986. *Victorian Lunacy: Richard M. Bucke and the Practice of Late Nineteenth-Century Psychiatry*. Cambridge: Cambridge University Press.

Simmons, Harvey G. 1990. *Unbalanced: Mental Health Policy in Ontario, 1930– 1989*. Toronto: Wall & Thompson.

Trudeau, Justin. Mandate Letter, Justin Trudeau to Patty Hajdu, January 15, 2021. https://pm.gc.ca/en/mandate-letters/2021/01/15/minister -health-supplementary-mandate-letter.

Walters, William. 2012. *Governmentality: Critical Encounters*. London: Routledge.

Wellness Together Canada. 2021. "About Wellness Together Canada." Accessed April 3, 2021. https://wellnesstogether.ca/en-CA/about/.

Welsh, Marc. 2013. "Resilience, Risk, and Responsibilisation: Governing Uncertainty in a Complex World." Online Paper, Department of Geography and Earth Sciences, Aberystwyth University, 2013.

9 Situating Non-citizenship: Humanitarian Aid, Self-Reliance Schemes, and Migrant Agency

SUZAN ILCAN

Introduction

Despite the development of international human rights conventions and practices, non-citizens, such as asylum seekers and refugees, face limits to their rights, mobility, security, and employment prospects, and experience vulnerabilities and insecurities on an international scale (Goldring and Landolt 2013; Ilcan 2018). This chapter considers non-citizenship in the context of humanitarian aid and self-reliance schemes for refugees. I engage with critical migration and citizenship studies literature (e.g., Brodie 2012; Darling 2017; Goldring and Landolt 2013; Hovil and Lomo 2015; Johnson 2015; Lecadet 2016; Nyers and Rygiel 2012; Pascucci 2017) and ethnographic research on issues of refugee governance and self-reliance with refugees and representatives of government and humanitarian organizations in the Nakivale Refugee Settlement (hereafter Nakivale) in Southwest Uganda. The notion of self-reliance, as advocated by organizations such as the UNHCR, requires more analytical and empirical attention in critical migration scholarship. The term "self-reliance," among other things, embraces practices and initiatives that embolden individuals to take greater responsibility for themselves, involving them in supporting the values of enterprise and free markets, and in becoming active participants in small-scale entrepreneurial initiatives to meet their essential requirements. It obliges them to integrate into market economies and to take greater responsibility for meeting their own needs and those of their families. As a neoliberal governing technology, self-reliance sets in motion a particular political dynamic among diverse actors, including state and humanitarian actors who deem certain individuals, such as refugees, as having the capacity to become self-reliant. It is an approach that, I argue, individualizes refugees through its discourses and strategies, failing to recognize the complexity of social and economic relations, insecurities, and situated non-citizenship. As a result of such governing efforts, structurally disadvantaged groups can be "collectively individualized" in citizenship discourses and public policy (Beck and Beck-Gernsheim 2002 in Brodie 2008, 41) and recaptured by new orientations that raise crucial issues for "citizenship politics" (Brodie 2008, 43).

I view non-citizenship as a political status that, as Tonkiss and Bloom (2015) contend, is not simply the absence of citizenship, but shapes people's positioning and abilities. Non-citizenship can regulate peoples' lives through international, national, and local policies and practices; link non-citizens to certain social and economic relations; be crosscut by gender, racialization, social class, language, skills, and other dimensions (Goldring and Landolt 2013); and contain political agency (e.g., Isin 2008; Johnson 2015; Nyers and Rygiel 2012; Sigona 2015). I refer to these processes as *situating non-citizenship*, which highlights the various acts, activities, and social relations involved in producing, negotiating, and contesting non-citizenship at various scales. Situating non-citizenship in the migration field may entail, among other things, its links to diverse governing programs within and across states; the practices of international, national, and local actors; market-based schemes, such as neoliberal self-reliance expectations directed towards refugees, and varied forms of political action.

In the context of neoliberal self-reliance for Uganda's refugees, I argue that these schemes emphasize the entrepreneurial and self-reliant participant, encourage refugee non-citizens to acquire the conduct and skills to participate in livelihood and income-generating initiatives, and connect refugee non-citizens to local market economies, to new relations with the land, and to urban environments. Refugees, and those who advocate on their behalf, can respond through their situated political voices, underscoring a dimension of non-citizenship that can effect change while simultaneously demonstrating the irregularity of neoliberal governing initiatives. In other words, the political subjectivities of refugees can, potentially, foreground the complex power relations underpinning humanitarian aid and self-reliance schemes. These activities are enacted by other precarious non-citizen migrants who challenge relations of power through their participation in rights-claiming, community mobilization, or solidarity-building activities (e.g., Goldring and Landolt 2013; Casas-Cortes 2019; Ilcan 2022).

The qualitative field research informing this chapter (interviews, field observations, informal conversations) was carried out in Kampala, Uganda, and in the Nakivale Refugee Settlement in the summer of 2014. With the aim of exploring contextualized relations between aid organizations and refugee non-citizens in Uganda, 25 in-depth interviews and informal conversations were conducted with representatives of international and non-governmental organizations, and government officials in Kampala and in Nakivale. Fifteen in-depth interviews and informal conversations were conducted with refugees living in Nakivale. Like other studies that reveal refugees as engaged subjects rather than victims (e.g., Casas-Cortes 2019; Lecadet 2016; Moulin and Nyers 2007), this study emphasizes refugee accounts of their status and living conditions in a manner committed to a contextual understanding of their views. Bearing similarity to other refugee camp research (e.g., Holzer 2012; Pascucci 2017), refugees in Nakivale emphasize concerns with their living conditions and self-reliance schemes.

The chapter proceeds as follows. The first part provides a framework for understanding how refugee camps are shaped by humanitarian aid and neoliberal self-reliance schemes that are primarily directed to and mediated by refugee non-citizens. The schemes were formulated in the late 1990s and early 2000s with the downsizing of international aid budgets, prompting aid interventions to focus on creating less aid dependency. As such, aid organizations encouraged refugees to take greater responsibility for their own social welfare by engaging in market relations to bring about self-reliance, in turn, producing other kinds of insecurities. Mobilizing this framework, the second part examines the introduction of self-reliance schemes in Uganda, notably, the country's 2006 Refugee Act and UNHCR's Handbook for Self-Reliance. The third part focuses on the Nakivale Refugee Settlement and how these schemes are directed to refugee non-citizens by encouraging them to learn new forms of conduct that hinge on their participation in the market while also enacting their situated political subjectivity. Refugee responses to the schemes underscore their non-citizenship agency in effecting change while concurrently raising questions about the constancy of neoliberal governing initiatives.

Humanitarian Aid, Neoliberal Self-Reliance Schemes, and Situating Refugee Non-citizens

The liberal democratic values that framed planning in the aftermath of the Second World War gave rise to the international refugee regime, both the legal apparatuses and the Office of the United Nations High Commissioner for Refugees (UNHCR) (Hyndman 2013, 12). At this time, UNHCR would coordinate and administer refugee camps in the Global South and monitor state compliance with the 1951 United Nations Convention Relating to the Status of Refugees, which was responsible for distributing and managing humanitarian aid relating to forced migration (Ilcan and Rygiel 2015).

With the establishment of UNHCR in 1950 and the 1951 Refugee Convention, a new understanding of the refugee emerged: namely, a person fleeing political persecution from Communist regimes in Eastern Europe. These refugees were viewed as courageous freedom fighters, easily integrated into European countries (Lui 2004, 128–9). Those who met the criteria for refugee status were highlighted as "heroic, political individual(s)" (see Johnson 2011, 1016).

In the 1960s and 1970s, refugee camps were flourishing in the Middle East and Asia and, from the late 1980s, intensifying in Africa. As the movements of refugees shifted from the Cold War context of Eastern Europe to those from the Global South to the Global North, Western countries gradually introduced restrictive asylum and migration policies. During this time, refugees came to be viewed as "nameless," "undifferentiated victims," "poverty-stricken masses" (Johnson 2011, 1016), and environmental and economic burdens (Crisp 2003, 3–4). Support for these mobile populations was provided by international organizations through humanitarian aid – an assemblage of actors, programs, and practices that aims to promote human welfare while also governing aid recipients. Such aid was not viewed as mere charity; it became framed through neoliberal governing discourses that were developing in the early 1980s. As Brodie (2015) insightfully reveals, such discourses commonly reframed key relationships between public and private, and government and citizens; shifted the attention of government away from the primary concerns of Keynesianism (such as economic stabilization and social protection) to market and market relations; and advanced new ways to shape peoples' conduct, political identities, and everyday experiences, which in turn transformed the practice of government (Brodie 2015, 7–8). As such, these governing activities rely less on governing through society and more on cutting the welfare state; depending on markets to solve political and social problems; and identifying individuals as active participants in solving their own social and economic challenges (see Buire and Staeheli 2017; Haughton, Allmendinger, and Oosterlunck 2013). It is worth noting, though, that neoliberal governance encompasses variation, diverse interventions, and counter discourses, agendas, and imaginaries operating on international, national, and local scales (Brodie 2010, 1567). Thus, according to Brodie, neoliberal governance is "marked by instability, contradiction, and experimentation" (2010, 1568).

Despite important differences in international refugee policy reform, the neoliberal governance of refugee camps extended market logics to a vast array of organizations and refugee populations and attempted to transform refugees' relationships to the market and reframe their relationships with the state. It consisted of rationalities, strategies, and techniques to shape the comportment of refugees and to encourage them to be self-sufficient market actors who should bear greater responsibility for themselves and their families as public services diminished. Much like the happiness imperative discussed by Kingfisher and resilience prescriptions for mental health outlined by Phillips in this volume, self-reliance was a crucial element of these schemes, including efforts to encourage individuals to take greater responsibility for their choices, and for their ability to be economically autonomous (e.g., Brodie 2015; Ilcan and Rygiel 2015; Milner and Loescher 2011; Omata and Kaplan 2013; Slaughter and Crisp 2009; UNHCR 2011; 2013).

As I discuss below, the individualization of refugees through self-reliance efforts demands that they become active participants in neoliberal markets that are commonly understood as "natural, self-governing, and the primary source of individual well-being, choice, and freedoms" (Brodie 2008, 39). Thus, through individualization processes targeting refugees, humanitarian organizations, partner organizations, and states are released from responsibility for eliminating refugee insecurities that are generated through power relations of inequality and injustice such as capitalism, racism, and sexism. In this way, humanitarianism reveals its governmental features. Studies have demonstrated humanitarianism's ability to establish zones of governance along territorial edges of nation states by diverse agents and towards multiple ends (Walters 2015); to create hierarchies (Fassin 2010); to participate in the removal of rights; to withhold the "acknowledgement of life and loss" (Ticktin 2016, 261); and to recast refugee identities through neoliberal ideas of empowerment that shape how individuals are thought of as deserving or undeserving of care and aid.

Beginning in the 1990s, many humanitarian organizations asserted that the prolonged availability of aid to refugees undermined their resilience and autonomy, and that refugees need to achieve economic and social self-reliance. By the late 1990s and early 2000s, international aid budgets had been downsized, leading to the re-organization of aid into interventions that were understood to create less aid dependency (see Hyndman 2001; Pascucci 2017). For example, UNHCR has been increasingly engaged in promoting refugees as active participants by emphasizing the discourses and practices of self-reliance, of "helping refugees help themselves" (UNHCR 2011), and of sustainable livelihoods (Omata and Kaplan 2013, 10). It has also been involved in viewing refugees as active participants by "grounding protection within communities" (UNHCR 2013, 6). Such self-reliance activities are, however, a way to govern vulnerable and marginal populations such as refugee non-citizens. For example, Ilcan and Rygiel (2015) suggest that refugee self-reliance underscores a global trend to "reimagine camps from temporary spaces for housing refugees as aid recipients to more permanent spaces of settlement aimed at developing a new form of community and more entrepreneurial and responsible populations" (2015,16). Similarly, Pascucci's (2017) study on refugee community shelters in Cairo, Egypt, views community as an informal and precarious infrastructure in which refugees' social relations are mobilized as substitutes for humanitarian aid in the broader context of shrinking aid budgets. She conceptualizes community-based shelter provision as a relational bordering practice in which new universal humanitarian values of empowerment and resilience produce old exclusions. There is little doubt that self-reliance and similar initiatives permeate different policy fields, frame new views of community, empowerment, and responsible populations and, in so doing, recast refugee identities and their situated non-citizenship.

While refugee non-citizens may be framed within self-reliance schemes, they are not determined by them; they can respond to them as political subjects, in the same vein as the Indigenous refusal that Isabel Altamirano discusses in this volume (see, for e.g., Hakli, Pascucci, and Kallio 2017; Ilcan 2018; Johnson 2015; Rygiel 2011). For example, Pascucci (2017) convincingly demonstrates that the informal "camps" frequently set up by Sudanese and Ethiopian refugees near the UNHCR premises in Cairo expose the limits of self-reliance policies. She argues that these improvised encampments are a protest against the lack of substantial assistance and underscore the tension between UNHCR's non-material reformulation of refugee governance and people's persistent need for a basic physical infrastructure of protection. In this regard, as we will see in the context of Uganda's self-reliance schemes below, political responses not only point to the instability and variations of neoliberal governance, they emphasize the complexities of refugee lives. In particular, refugee non-citizens who stay in refugee camps for several years, sometimes decades, can use their own situated contexts for enacting political subjectivity, which raises crucial issues about the constitution of non-citizenship.

In challenging the foundationalism of citizenship, which is a strictly legal, institutional product of state authority and rationality, Tonkiss and Bloom (2015) emphasize non-citizenship as heterogeneous and complex. As they claim, it is "an amalgamation of different categories according to status, both official and not, and cutting across different social divisions and relationships" (2015, 848). Importantly, non-citizenship can be constituted in situated contexts (legal, social, economic, solidarity movements) in which non-citizens interact, and through which they navigate and can be constructed by multiple actors (Johnson 2015; Landolt and Goldring 2015; Tonkiss and Bloom 2015). As this scholarship shows, there are many examples of non-citizenship, including statuses such as refugee, asylum seeker, and undocumented migrant (e.g., Tonkiss and Bloom 2015), which can also enable connections to states and civil society organizations, to certain rights and forms of belonging, and to international, national, and local programs. In other words, non-citizenship is situated in and through diverse transformations in the organization of work, humanitarian aid, and the relationship between states and citizens, which in turn are connected to neoliberal agendas as well as other governing initiatives.

In what follows I emphasize that upon their arrival to Uganda, refugees have a legal relationship with the host state and ties to humanitarian organizations through programs such as UNHCR's Self Reliance Strategy (SRS). The SRS aims to connect refugee non-citizens to market-oriented lifestyles, new relations with the land, and urban environments. Given that most refugees living in refugee camps in the Global South are non-citizens in host states, the SRS is one site for mediating non-citizens and constituting them in ways that can make them more market-oriented and sometimes more vulnerable, while creating the conditions for them to respond politically to their situated experiences. That is, refugee non-citizens may be framed by the SRS but they are not determined by it, as they can engage in political actions that have effects on governing practices and social relations. Paying attention to the voices of refugees, and those who advocate on their behalf avoids reproducing perspectives that highlight "migrants as passive and helpless beings" (Walters 2008, 188), or that universalize the effects of governance in the migration field, and can account for the ways in which refugee non-citizens are speaking, participating, and creating a visible presence (see Johnson 2015, 958), notwithstanding their lack of access to the rights and protections of citizenship.

Self-Reliance Schemes for Non-citizen Refugees in Uganda

Uganda hosts the highest number of asylum seekers and refugees in Africa and third highest globally, after Pakistan and Turkey (Matovu and Chrispus 2021; RLP 2021). It is currently home to over 1.4 million refugees and asylum seekers, with the majority originating from South Sudan (UNHCR 2018). It has provided asylum for many mobile groups, notably Rwandans fleeing the 1994 genocide, Congolese evading ongoing armed conflict, Sudanese escaping the SPLA/M struggle (Sharpe and Namusobya 2012, 561), and South Sudanese fleeing the civil war. Uganda is also recognized as having implemented an open-door policy and self-reliance approaches since 1999 and permitting refugees a plot of land and the opportunity to move, work, and trade elsewhere (Bjørkhaug 2020).

Uganda's Refugee Act of 2006 marks a crucial legislative move towards the greater protection of refugee rights. The Act explicitly allows recognized refugees the right to work, to move freely within the country, to live in the local community (rather than in camps or settlements), and to remain in Uganda. However, Uganda's approach does not entitle refugees, or their Ugandan-born children, to formal citizenship, and therefore underlines the preferential treatment of Ugandan citizens over non-citizen refugees, an arrangement common in most refugee-receiving countries (e.g., Agier 2011).[1] While refugees living in settlements are eligible for humanitarian assistance (Sharpe and Namusobya 2012, 566–77), those residing in urban areas receive no or little aid and can only remain in these areas if they are able to verify "self-sufficiency" through proof of residency or proof of employment (Bernstein and OKella 2007, 51; Interviews, RLP, 2014). Here, non-citizen refugees have rights as a consequence of their relationship with the Ugandan state: they have the right to occupy urban spaces under certain conditions such as holding the status of self-sufficiency, while others residing in settlements are considered aid dependent, and therefore in need of having their conduct transformed so that they can become responsible market actors. A representative of a prominent, activist-oriented, Kampala-based NGO, Refugee Law Project, emphasizes that under the Act refugees "can stay in any urban areas so long as they can take care of themselves because … according to UNHCR policy, a refugee in the camp is given assistance but once you are out of the camp you don't get any assistance" (Interview, RLP, July 2014).

Although the Act provides for "equal" opportunities, such as access to paid employment, non-citizen refugees confront social and economic challenges. An RLP representative emphasizes that they face immense struggles around employment and discrimination: "If you are qualified and you are able to do the work, you have the opportunity, but many times you see jobs specifying Ugandans only, where refugees are not allowed to do those jobs." She also commented on how refugees can be viewed as undeserving, which, in part, relates to their non-citizenship status. In her words: "When it comes to actual [job] interviews, they [employers] get to know you are a refugee; however qualified you are there is ... xenophobia, which gives birth to that kind of discrimination." She also claims that there are key sentiments associated with this discrimination, including the following views: "'Refugees – you are the ones that bring us Ebola;' 'You are the ones that bring us HIV/AIDS;' 'You are the ones on the street promoting bad culture'" (Interview, RLP representative, Kampala, July 2014). Based on interviews with refugees and NGO representatives, it is clear that non-citizen refugees face persistent challenges in urban centres (and in camps), including insufficient employment income, various forms of discrimination and racialization, and limited access to education and affordable and safe housing. Some refugees, however, have been able to engage in alternative forms of belonging through the establishment of migrant and NGO solidarity networks in centres, such as Kampala, and through the support of organizations such as the Refugee Law Project. Such activist networks illuminate some of the critical issues in the emerging scholarship on migrant activism in urban environments (see, for example, Bauder 2016; Darling 2017; McNevin 2011; Squire and Darling 2013).

The Refugee Act operates alongside the Ugandan government's support of UNHCR's Self-Reliance Strategy (SRS), the latter of which is a move away from long term "care and maintenance" programs, focusing on self-reliance and local solutions for refugees (see Milner and Loescher 2011, 12). The UNHCR's "Handbook for Self-Reliance" defines "self-reliance" as "the social and economic ability of an individual, a household or a community to meet essential needs (including protection, food, water, shelter, personal safety, health and education) in a sustainable manner and with dignity. Self-reliance, as a program approach, refers to developing and strengthening livelihoods of persons of concern, and reducing their vulnerability and long-term reliance on humanitarian/external assistance" (2005, 1; see also UNHCR 2018). It is clear from this passage that the SRS targets groups that have an aid dependency, including non-citizen refugees who rely on humanitarian and other forms of assistance for their survival. One UNHCR representative notes: "When you live in a camp, it becomes difficult for you to even economically grow or develop because you are used to distribution. Every time you sit there and wait [for] the end of the month for UNHCR or World Food Programme to give you food ... it creates that dependence syndrome" (Interview, UNHCR, Nakivale, July 2014). This representative continues:

At Nakivale [...] the refugees for a very long time they've had this kind of dependency thing, they just know UNHCR is supposed to give them everything [...] so they sit and wait for handouts. And we want this attitude to change. The attitude of refugees is something we really need to work on. They are so used to handouts, some of them just don't want to work. (Interview with UNHCR, Nakivale, 23 July 2014)

Viewing refugees as people who "don't want to work," need an "attitude" change, and wait for "handouts" equips governing authorities to manage them as non-citizens through discourses and practices that grant them limited rights and entitlement in state law, and shape and represent them in and beyond the politics of migration and citizenship. Indeed, emphasizing the problem of refugees' aid dependency allows UNHCR, in this case, to encourage refugees to activate their capabilities to attain self-sufficiency and become responsible for their own social welfare (see Ilcan, Oliver, and Connoy 2017).

Dating back to 1999, the government of Uganda and UNHCR introduced the SRS as a way to integrate assistance for both non-citizen refugees and their hosts, with its main objective to foster the self-sufficiency of refugees (Hovil 2007; Hovil and Lomo 2015; Ilcan, Oliver, and Connoy 2017). Under the SRS, land is allocated to each refugee household in every refugee settlement in Uganda to facilitate refugees' economic independence through agricultural livelihoods, income-generating interventions, and small-scale local trade and minor businesses (Kaiser 2006, 603). Eventually "refugees would be able to grow or buy their own food, access and pay for basic services, and maintain self-sustaining community structures" (Dryden-Peterson and Hovil 2003, 8). The assumption that refugees need to alter their conduct not only reflects ideas embedded in migration management practices (see Geiger and Pécoud 2010; Scheel and Ratfisch 2014), but it also circumscribes a connection between the SRS, particularly UNHCR and its partners, and non-citizen refugees. In other words, it is assumed that after a period of time, refugees would become self-sufficient and be "phased off" food and other humanitarian forms of aid. Due to the hardships and restrictions associated with living in settlements, thousands of refugees in Uganda have "self-settled" among the national population, particularly in border areas and the capital city, Kampala (Interview, RLP, July 2014; see also Hovil 2007, 600–1). However, most self-settled refugees, who are not under UNHCR's protection mandate, face difficulty in finding formal employment and adequate housing, accessing social services (see also Hammond 2014), and acquiring a sustainable living, especially in cases where they relocate to urban centres without sufficient means to support themselves. Uganda's adoption of the UNHCR's neoliberal, self-reliance approach raises crucial questions about the ways that refugees are to become active participants in the market economy and engage in livelihood activities in settlements such as Nakivale.

Nakivale: Self-Reliance Schemes and Political Responses

Nakivale is Uganda's largest and oldest refugee settlement. Located in Mbarara District in Southwest Uganda on 86 square kilometres of land, some 60 kilometres from the town of Mbarara, it was created in 1960 in response to an influx of Tutsi refugees fleeing the Hutu regime that had taken power in Rwanda. Since its inception, it has hosted numerous non-citizen refugees, including those from the Congo (almost half), and other groups from Somalia, Rwanda, and Burundi. It consists of three large zones – Juru, Rubondo, and Base Camp – each containing small markets and trading centres. It is co-managed by the Office of the Prime Minister of Uganda (OPM) and the UNHCR and consists of several of UNHCR's implementing and operating partners, such as Windle Trust Uganda, Nzamizi, and Uganda Red Cross Society. Throughout Nakivale, refugees are able to sell and trade their surplus crops to residents and those outside the settlement, and shop for goods and exchange services with each other, but they are still highly dependent on humanitarian aid, such as monthly food rations, which are in limited supply.

Refugees in Nakivale are typically provided with one acre of land per family for housing and agricultural purposes. Agriculture is the primary livelihood activity, but inadequate space, seeds, food, health care, housing, and farming know-how creates uncertainty in refugee lives. Through Uganda's SRS, they are encouraged to generate income through small business activities, including selling crops (maize, beans, sorghum, cassava, and potatoes), fish from the lake, meat, goats, chickens, and other goods (Interviews with Congolese refugees; interview with UNHCR representative, Nakivale, July 2014). An official from Uganda's Department of Refugees stated that the SRS was "a strategy to strengthen and focus our policy," particularly "local integration, settlement policy, where people have land" (Interview, OPM, Kampala, July 2014).

Through livelihood programs, refugees in Nakivale are encouraged to be responsible, entrepreneurial actors, and to engage in commercial relations in the camp and with other nationals in nearby markets. For example, Nsamizi, a prominent livelihood programming organization and partner of UNHCR, offers refugees training to achieve self-reliance and to "empower" themselves. Its activities promote agricultural expansion, and training on the knowledge of seeds, crop rotation, and sustainable animal rearing for refugees, some of whom (such as Somalis) have little prior farming experience. Nsamizi also fosters vocational training programs that promote practical and professional skills development, including butchery, goat rearing, tailoring, hair cutting, mobile phone repair, and restaurant management (Interview, Nsamizi, Nakivale, July 2014). Such programs aim to provide refugees with skills to create small businesses within Nakivale and sell goods and offer services outside of the camp (see also Svedberg 2014, 15–16). More specifically, Nsamizi's livelihood programming initiatives involve the formation of agricultural groups for selling crop goods to attain refugee self-reliance. The goal here is to foster the development of active participants who will care for and support themselves in new economic situations. Such initiatives are thought to embolden refugee self-reliance by reducing the costs of international humanitarian aid for refugees (see Slaughter and Crisp, 2009; see UNHCR 2014), and promoting responsible refugees who can change their behaviour by supporting the values of enterprise and self-sufficiency (Ilcan, Oliver, and Connoy 2017). A representative from the RLP stresses that such programs can be "successful" as refugees can sell their surplus crops to neighbouring Ugandan communities and markets (Interview, RLP, July 2014; see also Svedberg 2014, 12). These programs have limitations, however, in that refugees in Nakivale do not receive any training on how they, as market sellers, or their marketed goods will be perceived by others in market economies outside of Nakivale. Additionally, refugees in Nakivale are not informed of the lack of evidence regarding the impact of livelihood projects in generating self-sufficiency among significant numbers of refugees in Uganda, nor that such projects can cultivate social and economic insecurities for them.

While the neoliberal approach to empowering refugees through the SRS has been touted as beneficial to refugees by humanitarian and state actors, they are often associated with social and economic injustices. Part of the overarching strategy to make refugees self-sufficient involves the premature withdrawal of food rations, which not only obstructs refugees' prospects of reaching self-reliance but can also worsen their living conditions. Refugees often face enormous discrimination, isolation, and xenophobia as they participate in self-reliance schemes that encourage them to sell urban market goods or make a life for themselves in urban centres outside of Nakivale. As non-citizens, they confront a growing ethos of exclusion expressed by some local groups and organizations that question the Ugandan state's support for the care of non-citizens. On this point, an RLP member emphasizes: "[As a refugee], you are free to choose where you want to stay, but if you choose to stay in town, in urban centres, whatever happens to you, you take care of yourself. You have to fend for life like any other normal resident in your area (Interview, RLP, Kampala, July 2014). Another RLP member, who engages in community police training to create awareness about the rights and duties of refugees and asylum seekers, comments on the problems refugees face: "[W]hen refugees come [to Uganda] they are exploited. You find people giving them higher rent ... and if they don't pay they evict them without anything. There is no ... tenant's agreement. There are a lot of issues. And of course, that's why we are doing community training with the police." She goes on to emphasize that the implementation of self-reliance needs to be done "very carefully" and "communities ... need to be sensitized thoroughly before you can bring a policy to people. And if you don't do that, then the refugees may not be safe. If you are calling for self-reliance and the society where they are going to stay is not sensitized, it will bring a lot of discrimination ..." (Interview, RLP, Kampala, July 2014). More recently, through its gender and sexuality program, the RLP is involved in conducting training for the Uganda Police Force on issues addressing conflict-related sexual violence, mental health, and access to justice related needs for forced migrants (RLP 2021: https://www.refugeelawproject.org).

When asked about whether the SRS is a positive outcome for refugees, an RLP member stressed that it works well for those who are citizens. In her words: "Well, it's [the SRS] a good idea for refugees who have been nationalized. If Uganda nationalizes refugees, they are given land and they do activities just like Ugandans. We stay with them, we marry each other, we share. We share medical services, we share water sources, without discrimination" (Interview, RLP, Kampala, July 2014). Contributing to the tensions between humanitarian actors and non-citizen refugees, the SPS enables those who have Ugandan citizenship to access resources and form certain social and economic relationships but leaves non-citizen refugees and others in Uganda vulnerable to inadequate employment and racial discrimination and therefore less likely to establish long-term social and economic networks and a sustainable way of living.

Based on field research in Nakivale, the SRS is never wholly circumscribed, as some refugees not only acknowledge the difficult and marginalized circumstances in which they live but they also articulate concerns about self-reliance strategies. Some exercise their agency by choosing to engage or not engage in these strategies, and to voice concerns about them. Such political engagements are, I argue, one way to redefine or decentre the practice of self-reliance. Some refugees assert their own rights to political agency and to protect the spaces where they can speak out as non-citizen refugees. For example, one DRC refugee critiqued the UNHCR-supported livelihood initiatives of Nsamizi on the grounds that they are "limited; the services reach very few people" with very little benefit. He also recognized the negative outcomes of livelihood programs, such as not acknowledging recurrent drought problems or the issues they face when selling agricultural products in nearby markets. As another person from the DRC stated: "When they do give seeds, they plant, then they die. When you bring goats ... there is a difficulty of diseases which come and attack the goats, then they die. When they were given chickens, they also die. So, they [livelihood programs] are failing to help ..." (Interview with DRC refugee, Nakivale, July 2014).

Likewise, some refugees cited their unwillingness to participate in the UNHCR-supported SRS because they felt the organization had not provided sufficient help for them and their families, while always demanding something from them. These refugees spent the little money that they received from UNHCR's livelihood programs to meet other survival needs such as purchasing food. For example, one male refugee exclaimed: "Of course I cannot keep one hundred thousand [Ugandan Shillings] in my pocket when I sleep with an empty stomach. So, this money will not go for business; I would rather it go for food" (Interview with Congolese refugee, Nakivale, 23 July 2014). Their refusal to participate in the SRS conveys their political subjectivity as non-citizens, though such refusals vary and may be ambiguous. Nevertheless, acts of refusal challenge the rules of engagement associated with non-citizen refugees and generate shared exchanges, rights, or ways to defy control of mobile peoples, creating a "mobile commons" (e.g., Trimikliniotis, Parsanoglou and Vassilis 2017). Indeed, one NGO representative recalls times when refugees had a "sit down at UNHCR. They went there and refused to leave... And some of them have also been lodging complaints before the Uganda Human Rights Commission" (Interview, NGO representative, July 2014). In this way, refugees' political actions are about transforming their limited rights and precarious status as non-citizens by altering their connections to the land and market relations in Nakivale, their relations with humanitarian organizations and the Ugandan state, and their ties to others, thus enabling them to act as political subjects with the potential to reshape settlement experiences in and beyond the SRS.

Some key organizations in Uganda advocating on behalf of refugees assess the SRS critically. The Refugee Law Project is a noteworthy NGO located in Kampala that aims to promote the protection, well-being, and dignity of forced migrants and their hosts; encourage national and international debate on issues of forced migration, justice, and peace, and inspire forced migrants, communities, and diverse actors to "challenge and combat injustices in policy, law and practice" (RLP 2018). It has field offices in the western districts of Mbarara and Hoima and provides, among other activities, legal assistance to forced migrants in several refugee settlements, including Nakivale. It not only advocates on behalf of refugees but also raises serious concerns about the country's SRS, particularly the inability of subsistence agriculture to realize self-reliance for refugees. In the words of one RLP representative: "the strategy's narrow focus on subsistence agriculture and inadequate provision for freedom of movement for encamped refugees leaves them impoverished and dependent" (RLP April 2007, 1).

On a larger scale, the Refugee Law Project repoliticizes and rearticulates the spaces and conditions of life for refugees in Uganda. It foregrounds the struggles that refugees experience and express, fosters support groups to overcome mutual challenges, and encourages these groups to be active participants in demands for social justice and social and economic transformations. Its advocacy work involves communicating refugee rights to refugees, recognizing the inequalities, hierarchies, and exclusions they face, whether in refugee settlements or urban centres. Through language instruction, research and advocacy, and consciousness-raising activities, it aims to integrate refugees by challenging the injustices facing them, such as the unsustainability of self-reliance programs and state views of citizenship and belonging (Interviews, RLP, July 2014). For example, its Access to Justice Program "seeks to bring legal aid services closer to forced migrants, to empower forced migrants to advocate for their rights, to strengthen the capacity of justice institutions to deliver justice, and to improve the legal and policy environment for forced migrants in Uganda" (RLP 2018). It is though such critical training and grassroots engagement, that refugees can bring their experiences, views, and histories to the transformation agenda and advocate for unconventional perspectives on their livelihoods, rights to employment, and alternatives to self-reliance schemes.

These and similar developments raise questions about the broader role of refugee activism and citizenship politics in and outside of Uganda (see, for e.g., Agier 2008; Holzer 2012; Ilcan 2014, 2022; Lacadet 2015).[2] In this regard, one NGO representative commented: "Refugees have spoken out several times about the living conditions in the camps, even during celebrations, national celebrations, like World Refugee Day … They come up and air out these issues to the government." This representative went on to say that they have demanded change by voicing their concerns and articulating that "we don't get enough food, we are starving, the services are not good, help us" (Interview, NGO representative, July 2014). More recently, in 2018, South Sudanese refugees in Bidibidi Settlement Camp in northern Uganda held peaceful demonstrations to protest delays in food distribution and the relocation of food distribution centres, and demanded change. They were met by army and police intervention, which, in turn, spurred much media coverage. Indeed, refugees in Uganda continue to engage in a multitude of strategies and practices of protest, including public discussions and information campaigns, marches, political speaking events, and solidarity mobilizations.

Conclusion

While there are many examples of non-citizenship that emerge from the field of migration and that give rise to statuses such as refugee and asylum seeker, in this chapter I have argued that non-citizenship connects to humanitarian and state actors, to certain rights and forms of belonging, and to international, national, and local programs. I refer to these and other similar processes as "situating non-citizenship," a term that connotes relationships between individuals, states, and civil society organizations and that operates through expectations about the conduct of non-citizens as well as responses to these expectations. Through a focus on complex, diverse, and contradictory neoliberal governance programs (Brodie 2010; Haughton, Allmendinger, and Oosterlunck 2013), the chapter has paid analytical attention to the establishment of self-reliance in the context of Uganda's non-citizen refugees. It has shown that self-reliance strategies permeate different policy fields, frame new views of empowerment and responsible populations, and, in so doing, recast refugee identities and their situated non-citizenship. Within this situated non-citizenship context, refugees articulate their vulnerabilities and lack of full rights and formal citizenship, as well as their engagement in settlement life as political subjects, challenging neoliberal self-reliance initiatives. On a variety of scales, much more critical attention needs to focus on and provide meaningful support towards the activities of refugees, civil societies, and social movements that challenge the limited rights of refugees, inclusive/exclusive logic of citizenship, and the empowerment promises of self-reliance schemes. Such challenges can foster projects of social, legal, and political justice that can influence local government, humanitarian bureaucracies, and public policy, and contribute to the lives of people on the move in ways that are collective, transformative, and sustainable.

ACKNOWLEDGMENTS

The research for this chapter was supported by a Centre for International Governance Innovation (CIGI) research grant to Suzan Ilcan (PI) and Marcia Oliver (CI). I am grateful for the collaboration of my colleague, Marcia Oliver, on the project, and thank Laura Connoy for her research assistance. I acknowledge with great appreciation the refugees, the NGO and civil society personnel, and Ugandan government officials who participated in this study. I thank the editors of this book for their valuable feedback on an earlier version of this chapter.

NOTES

1 Although refugees and refugee rights organizations in Uganda have called for naturalization for refugees living in the country, refugees have not been able to acquire citizenship. This situation encouraged the Refugee Law Project and the Centre for Public Interest in 2010 to apply to Uganda's Constitutional Court in an attempt to clarify that refugees can acquire citizenship under the law. There is a disagreement on the interpretation of the constitutional provisions regarding whether refugees can acquire citizenship in Uganda. For more on this issue, see: Citizenship Rights in Africa Initiative 2016; Matovu and Chrispus 2021.

2 From camps across sub-Saharan Africa and elsewhere, much scholarly attention has focused on refugees as recipients of humanitarian aid, living in protracted situations, and facing desperate living conditions. Less attention has focused on refugees as non-citizens who have a political voice. Refugee activism in camps is diverse and includes demands for better living conditions (Ilcan 2014; Lacadet 2015), adequate food and health care (e.g., Agier 2008), and sustainable social, economic, and legal support. It also includes challenges to humanitarian management (e.g., Agier 2008; Holzer 2012), opposition to state policies (e.g., Holzer 2012), appeals for regularization, and the right to claim the protection of the state and to remain (e.g., Lecadet 2015; Rygiel 2011).

REFERENCES

Agier, Michel 2008. *Gerer les indesirables: des camps de refugies au gouvernement humanitaire*. Paris: Flammarion.

Bauder, Harold. 2016. "Possibilities of Urban Belonging." *Antipode* 48 (2): 252–71. https://doi.org/10.1111/anti.12174

Bernstein, Jesse, and Moses Okello. 2007. "To Be or Not to Be: Urban Refugees in Kampala." *Refuge* 24 (1): 46–56. https://doi.org/10.25071/1920-7336.21367

Bjørkhaug, Ingunn 2020. "Revisiting the Refugee–Host Relationship in Nakivale Refugee Settlement: A Dialogue with the Oxford Refugee Studies Centre." *Journal on Migration and Human Security* 8 (3): 266–81. https://doi.org/10.1177/2331502420948465

Brodie, Janine. 2008. "The Social in Social Citizenship." In *Recasting the Social in Citizenship*, edited by Engin Isin, 33–56. Toronto: University of Toronto Press.

– 2015. "Income Inequality and the Future of Global Governance." In *Critical Perspectives on Global Governance: Reimagining the Future*, edited by Stephen Gill, 45–68. Palgrave Macmillan.

– 2010. "Globalization, Canadian Family Policy, and the Omissions of Neoliberalism." *North Carolina Review* 88 (5): 1559–91.

– 2012. "White Settlers and the Biopolitics of State Building in Canada." In *Shifting the Ground of Canadian Literary Studies*, edited by Smaro Kamboureli and Robert Zacharias, 106–27. Waterloo: Wilfrid Laurier Press.

Buire, Chloé, and Lynn Staeheli 2017. "Contesting the 'Active' in Active Citizenship: Youth Activism in Cape Town, South Africa." *Space and Polity* 21 (2): 173–90. https://doi.org/10.1080/13562576.2017.1339374

Casas-Cortes, Maribel. 2019. "Care-tizenship: Precarity, Social Movements, and the Deleting/Re-Writing of Citizenship." *Citizenship Studies* 21(1): 19–42. https://doi.org/10.1080/13621025.2018.1556248.

Citizenship Rights in Africa Initiative. 2016. "The Eligibility for Refugees to Acquire Ugandan Citizenship." March 22, 2016. http://citizenshiprightsafrica.org/the-eligibility-for-refugees-to-acquire-ugandan-citizenship/

Crisp, Jeff. 2003. "No Solution in Sight: The Problem of Protracted Refugee Situations in Africa." Centre for Comparative Immigration Studies. http://escholarship.org/uc/item/89d8r34g

Darling, Jonathan. 2017. "Acts, Ambiguities, and the Labour of Contesting Citizenship." *Citizenship Studies* 21 (6): 727–36. https://doi.org/10.1080/13621025.2017.1341658

Dryden-Peterson, Sarah, and Lucy Hovil, 2003 "Local Integration as Durable Solution: Refugees, Host Populations and Education in Uganda." Working paper 93, New Issues in Refugee Research, UNHCR, 2003.

Fassin, Didier. 2010. "Inequality of Lives, Hierarchies of Humanity: Moral Commitments and Ethical Dilemmas of Humanitarianism." In *In the Name of Humanity: The Government of Threat and Care*, edited by Ilana Feldman and Miriam Ticktin, 238–55. Durham: Duke University Press.

Goldring, Luin, and Patricia Landolt.2013. "The Conditionality of Legal Status and Rights: Conceptualizing Precarious Non-citizenship in Canada." In

Producing and Negotiating Non-Citizenship: Precarious Legal Status in Canada, edited by Luin Goldring and Patricia Landolt, 3–30. Toronto: University of Toronto Press.

Häkli, Jouni, Elisa Pascucci, and Kirsi Pauliina Kallio, 2017. "Becoming Refugee in Cairo: The Political in Performativity." *International Political Sociology* 11 (2): 185–202. https://doi.org/10.1093/ips/olx002

Hammond, Laura. 2014. "History, Overview, Trends and Issues in Major Somali Refugee Displacements in the Near Region." Research Paper 268, New Issues in Refugee Research, UNHCR, Geneva, 2014.

Haughton, Graham, Phil Allmendinger, and Stijn Oosterlunck. 2013. "Spaces of Neoliberal Experimentation: Soft Spaces, Postpolitics, and Neoliberal Governmentality." *Environment and Planning A: Economy and Space* 45 (1): 217–34. https://doi.org/10.1068/a45121

Holzer, Elizabeth. 2012. "A Case Study of Political Failure in a Refugee Camp." *Journal of Refugee Studies* 25 (2): 257–81. https://doi.org/10.1093/jrs/fes006

Hovil, Lucy. 2007. "Self-Settled Refugees in Uganda: An Alternative Approach to Displacement?" *Journal of Refugee Studies* 20 (4): 599–620. https://doi.org/10.1093/jrs/fem035

Hovil, Lucy, and Zachary Lomo. 2015. "Forced Displacement and the Crisis of Citizenship in Africa's Great Lakes Region: Rethinking Refugee Protection and Durable Solutions." *Refuge* 31 (2): 39–50. https://doi.org/10.25071/1920-7336.40308

Hyndman, Jennifer. 2001. *Managing Displacement. Refugees and the Politics of Humanitarianism*. Minneapolis: University of Minnesota Press.

– 2013. "A Refugee Camp Condundrum: Geopolitics, Liberal Democracy, and Protracted Refugee Situations." *Refuge* 28 (2): 7–15. https://doi.org/10.25071/1920-7336.36472

Ilcan, Suzan. 2014. "Activist Citizens and the Politics of Mobility in Osire Refugee Camp." In *Routledge Handbook of Global Citizenship Studies*, edited by Engin F. Isin and Peter Nyers, 186–95. London: Routledge.

– 2018. "The Humanitarian-Citizenship Nexus: The Politics of Citizenship Training in Self-Reliance Strategies for Refugees." *Geografiska Annaler: Series B, Human Geography* 100 (2): 97–111. https://doi.org/10.1080/04353684.2018.1453754

– 2022. "The Borderization of Waiting: Negotiating Borders and Migration in the 2011 Syrian Civil Conflict." *Environment and Planning C: Politics and Space* 40 (5): 1012–31. https://journals.sagepub.com/doi/abs/10.1177/2399654420943593

Ilcan, Suzan, Marcia Oliver, and Laura Connoy. 2017. "Humanitarian Assistance, Refugee Management, and Self-Reliance Schemes: Nakivale Refugee Settlement." In *Transnational Social Policy – Social Support in a World on the Move*, edited by Luann Good Gingrich and Stefan Köngeter, 152–78. London and New York: Routledge.

Ilcan, Suzan, and Kim Rygiel. 2015. "'Resiliency Humanitarianism': Responsibilizing Refugees through Humanitarian Emergency Governance in the Camp." *International Political Sociology* 9 (4): 333–51. https://doi.org/10.1111/ips.12101

Isin, Engin. 2008. "Theorizing Acts of Citizenship." In *Acts of Citizenship*, edited by Engin F. Isin and Greg M. Nielsen, 15–43. London: Zed Books.

Johnson, Heather. 2015. "These Fine Lines: Locating Non-citizenship in Political Protest in Europe." *Citizenship Studies* 19 (8): 951–65. https://doi.org/10.1080/13621025.2015.1110287

– 2011."Click to Donate: Visual Images, Constructing Victims and Imagining the Female Refugee." *Third World Quarterly* 32 (6): 1015–37. https://doi.org/10.1080/01436597.2011.586235

Kaiser, Tanya 2006. "Between a Camp and a Hard Place: Rights, Livelihoods and Experiences of the Local Settlement System for Long-Term Refugees in Uganda." *Journal of Modern African Studies* 44 (4): 597–621. https://doi.org/10.1017/S0022278X06002102

Lui, Robin. 2004. "The International Government of Refugees." In *Global Governmentality: Governing International Spaces*, edited by Wendy Larner and William Walters, 116–35. London: Routledge.

Matovu, Fred, and Mayora Chrispus. 2021. "A Synthesis of Key Aspects of Health Systems and Policy Design Affecting the Refugee Populations in Uganda." CHE Research Paper 180, University of York, February 2021. https://www.york.ac.uk/media/che/documents/papers/researchpapers/CHERP180_refugee_population_uganda.pdf

McNevin, Anne. 2011. *Contesting Citizenship: Irregular Migrants and New Frontiers of the Political*. New York: Columbia University Press.

Milner, James, and D. Loescher. 2011. "Responding to Protracted Refugee Situations: Lessons from a Decade of Discussion." Force Migration Policy Briefing 6. Refugee Studies Centre, Oxford Department of International Development. Oxford, University of Oxford.

Moulin, Carolyn, and Peter Nyers, 2007. "'We Live in a Country of UNHCR' – Refugee Protests and Global Political Society." *International Political Sociology* 1 (4): 356–72. https://doi.org/10.1111/j.1749-5687.2007.00026.x

Nyers, Peter, and Kim Rygiel. 2012. "Introduction: Citizenship, Migrant Activism, and the Politics of Movement." In *Citizenship, Migrant Activism, and the Politics of Movement*, edited by Peter Nyers and Kim Rygiel, 1–19. London: Routledge.

Omata, Naohiko. 2017. *The Myth of Self-Reliance: Economic Lives Inside a Liberian Refugee Camp*. New York and Oxford: Berghahn Books.

Omata, Naohiko, and Josiah Kaplan. 2013. "Refugee Livelihoods in Kampala, Nakivale and Kyangwali Refugee Settlements: Patterns of Engagement with the Private Sector." Working Paper Series No. 95. Oxford: Refugee Studies Centre.

Pascucci, Elisa 2017. "Community Infrastructures: Shelter, Self-Reliance and Polymorphic Borders in Urban Refugee Governance." *Territory, Politics, Governance* 5 (3): 332–45. https://doi.org/10.1080/21622671.2017.1297252

Refugee Law Project (RPL). 2014."Giving out Their Daughters for Their Survival: Refugee Self-Reliance, 'Vulnerability,' and the Paradox of Early Marriage." 2007. Working Paper No.20. RLP, Kampala. Accessed February 6, 2014. http://www.refugeelawproject.org/files/working_papers/RLP .WP20.pdf

– 2021. "A Window of Hope for Survivors of Conflict-Related Sexual Violence Living in Nakivale Refugee Settlement." February 12, 2021. https://www .refugeelawproject.org/index.php?option=com_content&view=article&id =241:a-window-of-hope-for-survivors-of-conflict-related-sexual-violence -living-in-nakivale-refugee-settlement&catid=26&Itemid=101

– 2018. "Access to Justice for Forced Migrants" https://www .refugeelawproject.org/our-work/access-to-justice-for-forced-migrants

Rygiel, Kim. 2011. "Bordering Solidarities: Migrant Activism and the Politics of Movement and Camps at Calais." *Citizenship Studies* 15 (1): 1–19. https:// doi.org/10.1080/13621025.2011.534911

Sharpe, Marina, and Salima Namusobya. 2012. "Refugee Status Determination and the Rights of Recognized Refugees under Uganda's Refugees Act 2006." *International Journal of Refugee Law*. 24 (3): 561–78. https://doi.org/10.1093 /ijrl/ees036

Sigona, Nando. 2015. "Campzenship: Reimagining the Camp as a Social and Political Space." *Citizenship Studies* 19 (1): 1–15. https://doi.org/10.1080 /13621025.2014.937643

Slaughter, Amy, and Jeff Crisp. 2009. "A Surrogate State? The Role of UNHCR in Protracted Refugee Situations." Research Paper 108, UNHCR EPAU.

Squire, Vicki, and Jonathan Darling, 2013. "The 'Minor' Politics of Rightful Presence: Justice and Relationality in City of Sanctuary." *International Political Sociology* 7 (1): 59–74. https://doi.org/10.1111/ips.12009

Svedberg, Erik. 2014. "Refugee Self-Reliance in Nakivale Refugee Settlement, Uganda." George Washington University, International Affairs. SIT Study Abroad (Spring).

Ticktin, Mariam. 2016. "Thinking beyond Humanitarian Borders." *Social Research: An Interdisciplinary Quarterly* 83 (2): 255–71. https://doi.org /10.1353/sor.2016.0030

Tonkiss, Katherine, and Tendayi Bloom. 2015. "Theorising Noncitizenship: Concepts, Debates and Challenges." *Citizenship Studies* 19 (8): 837–52. https://doi.org/10.1080/13621025.2015.1110278

Trimikliniotis, Nicos, Dimitris Parsanoglou, and Vassilis Tsianos. 2017. "Introduction: Mobile Commons and/in Precarious Spaces: Mapping Migrant Struggles and Social Resistance." In *Politics of Precarity: Migrant Conditions, Struggles and Experiences*, 224–44, Leinden: Koninklije Brill NV. https://doi.org/10.1163/9789004329706_012

UNHCR. 2005. "Handbook for Self-Reliance." Reintegration and Local Settlement Section Division of Operational Support UNHCR, Geneva. http://www.unhcr.org/44bf3e252.html

– 2013. "Community-Based Protection." Executive Committee of the High Commissioner's Programme, Standing Committee 57th meeting. http://www.unhcr.org/51d19cb79

– 2014. "Nakivale Fact Sheet." UNHCR Uganda.

– 2018. "Uganda – Fact Sheet." https://reliefweb.int/sites/reliefweb.int/files/resources/UNHCR%20uGANDA.pdf

Walters, William. 2008. "Acts of Demonstration: Mapping the Territory of (Non)Citizenship." In *Acts of Citizenship*, edited by E. Isin and G. Neilson, 182–206. London: Zed Books.

PART FOUR

Producing Neoliberal Citizens

10 Apologies and Raids: Public Sex, 2SLGBTQ Communities, and Neoliberalism in the Detention State

ALEXA DEGAGNE

Introduction

North American 2SLGBTQ[1] history has been shaped by hostile relations with police organizations and the criminal legal system. Riots against police surveillance, criminalization, and abuse have been galvanizing moments in which queers and gender-nonconforming people fought back against the regulatory bodies of the state. In transformative resistances against police targeting and killing of Black and Indigenous people – including George Floyd and Breonna Taylor in the United States, and Andrew Loku, Abdirahman Abdi, Eishia Hudson, and Chantel Moore in Canada – anti-racism 2SLGBTQ activists have confronted ongoing police incursions in queer spaces and events, demanding accountability, reform, defunding and/or abolition of police organizations and prisons. In these calls, activists appropriated neoliberal austerity language to argue that police organizations are over-funded and perpetuate state violence against marginalized people. Calls to defund and abolish the police are not actually neoliberal, however, as activists argued that funding should be rerouted to social programs and community-based organizations. At the same time, privileged and influential members of 2SLGBTQ communities are cooperating with police organizations by inviting them into queer and trans spaces in exchange for social acceptance and protection of themselves and their private property. This chapter considers how neoliberalism functions through these thorny and precarious relationships between 2SLGBTQ communities and police organizations, observing both the operation of historical and ongoing divisions and hierarchies but also, following Jyoti Puri, by examining how these categories reproduce, change, and challenge neoliberalism (2016).

Three events in Toronto in 2016 provide a rich empirical source from which to demonstrate this changed relationship between police and the queer community and its consequences.

1. In June 2016, the Toronto Police Service officially apologized for Operation Soap – the 1981 bathhouse raids – in which 160 police officers arrested 304 people.
2. Black Lives Matter Toronto (BLM-Toronto) walked in Pride Toronto's 2016 parade as an honoured group. After initiating a sit-in, BLM-Toronto members presented a list of demands to Pride Toronto including support and event funding for queer people of colour at Pride, and the removal of police floats from future Pride Toronto events. These actions sparked protests and discussions across Canadian 2SLGBTQ communities about police organizations in queer spaces.
3. Two months later, the police initiated Project Marie, an undercover operation that surveilled, arrested, and charged men who sought out and engaged in sex with men in Etobicoke's Marie Curtis Park (Draaisma, November 11, 2016).

The timing of the three events was not accidental. Rather, I argue that Project Marie was initiated to reinforce the role of police in Toronto's 2SLGBTQ communities and spaces, and the boundaries and regulation of sexuality, sex in public, and private spaces. Moreover, as BLM-Toronto and Queers Crash the Beat activists argued, the protests, discussions, and the police action were enabled by mainstream LGBT people's incorporation into neoliberal institutions and relations, and their accession to the criminal legal system and police.

The first two sections of the paper outline three neoliberal political projects pursued by the mainstream LGBT movement: (1) focusing on private spaces to secure police-free sexual activity; (2) prioritizing domestic confinement through same-sex marriage; (3) gentrifying gay private and public spaces to profit from urban renewal. Through these projects, homonormative people have sought state and police protection, reinforcing neoliberal marginalization and criminalization of poor and street-involved people, trans people, Indigenous people, Black people, people in mental distress, activists, sex workers, and people who engage in public sex. The second section examines how the mainstream LGBT movement's changing relationship with police and the criminal legal system has been facilitated through this turn towards neoliberalism. The third section analyzes the events of 2016, focusing on police regulation of public and private spaces; the meaning of public sex; and the criminalization and exclusion of marginalized people.

Theoretical Framework: Neoliberalism and the 2SLGBTQ Movement in Canada

Since the 1980s, the LGBT mainstream has pursued political and social goals in line with neoliberal principles of privatization, individualism, and personal responsibility, thereby exacerbating divisions, inequality, and hierarchies within the 2SLGBTQ community (see Smith 2005). Janine Brodie observes that successive Canadian governments have "abandoned the vision of social citizenship, social security, and social justice, offering in their place a new social imaginary that pinpoints the market, one buoyed by the logics of neo-classical economics, as the primary, if not 'natural' source of both individual well-being and freedom, and political legitimacy" (2007, 99). Governments are largely silent in the face of structural inequality and social injustice, arguing, instead, that citizens will be better off if they are left to "live in the mythical econometric space where all other things are equal" (Brodie 2007, 100). Citizens are, accordingly, constructed and disciplined by governments into self-governance and self-sufficiency, denying "identity markers" that differentiate them from the norm, "ris[ing] above systemic barriers," and taking personal responsibility for their successes and failures in the "natural" and "equal" market (Brodie 2007, 104).

Lisa Duggan adds that neoliberalism functions by denying structural inequality in order to obscure the redistribution of wealth to those at the top, reinforcing divisions according to racialized, sexual, gender, class, and national identities and hierarchies (Duggan 2003, 14). This phenomenon can be seen in Canada's 2SLGBTQ movement in which relatively privileged constituents have pursued political and social goals that perpetuate the injustices of neoliberalism. Duggan developed the term "homonormativity" to describe this form of engagement with neoliberalism: "a politics that does not contest dominant heteronormative assumptions and institutions, but upholds and sustains them, while promising the possibility of a demobilized gay constituency and a privatized, depoliticized gay culture anchored in domesticity and consumption" (Duggan 2003, 50). Each of these concessions relegates more of life to the private, shrinking public responsibility and engagement with community and the state. In so doing, homonormative people gain at the expense of 2SLGBTQ people who cannot succeed within neoliberalism, and thus legitimize and sustain the institutions and perspectives that reinforce marginalization.

The 2SLGBTQ movement's fight for privacy from state intervention into sexual actions and spaces preceded the adoption of distinctly neoliberal strategies and goals. As Duggan notes, since the 1950s, the LGB movement in the United States was consistently focused on "the expansion of a right to sexual privacy against the intrusive, investigatory labeling powers of the state, and the simultaneous expansion of gay public life through institution building and publicity" (Duggan 2003, 51). Thus, the fight for privacy was not initially associated with private space, but rather with freedom from state surveillance, harassment, violence, and criminalization.

Police organizations in Canada have long intervened in and regulated the lives of queer and gender-non-conforming people through various sodomy, obscenity, bawdy house, and gross indecency laws (Everitt and Camp 2014, 228). Indigenous, racialized, gender-non-conforming and poor people within 2SLGBTQ populations were more likely to be targeted by police and charged and convicted for such crimes (Cole 2020; Mogul et al. 2011).[2] In Canada, the Criminal Law Amendment Act (1968–9) changed, but did not repeal, two provisions in the Criminal Code relating to buggery and gross indecency. Thus, activists and academics have argued that the 1969 Criminal Code changes did not "legalize homosexuality." Rather, the 1969 Omnibus Bill only protected homosexual sex acts if they occurred in private, between two people over the age of 21 (Hooper 2017). In reference to the 1969 Omnibus Bill, Prime Minister Pierre Trudeau famously declared, "There's no place for the state in the bedrooms of the nation" (CBC Digital Archives 2017). Public sex, however, was distinctive. As Trudeau elaborated: "What's done in private between adults doesn't concern the Criminal Code, when it becomes public it's a different matter" (CBC Digital Archives 2017). While the changes to the law were celebrated by many LGB advocates, others warned that those who engaged in sex in public remained vulnerable.

The conflation of privacy and the domestic was subsequently articulated in the fight for same-sex marriage. For same-sex marriage advocates, marriage was understood as a vehicle for privacy, social acceptance, and recognition, legal protection, emotional fulfilment, and economic stability. The fact that neoliberal governments are relatively ambivalent towards the private, domestic affairs of economically self-sufficient citizens made it possible to extend state recognition to homonormative gay couples. "Privatization, a hallmark of neoliberalism, aligns well with sexuality's affinities to privacy and concealment from the public" (Puri 2016, 309). Further, Duggan notes that homonormative gay couples received privacy in exchange for "domestic confinement" as opposed to the freedom that was once assumed to come with privacy from the state (Duggan 2003, 65–6). With the domestication of homonormal citizens' sexual and familial lives, the state can sharpen its focus on regulating public, "deviant" sex and sexuality, as I discuss in relation to public sex and police raids.

The fight for privacy and the implementation of privatization were also produced through the gentrification of the gay neighbourhoods that had emerged in the latter twentieth century across North America. Gentrification ushered neoliberalism into urban spaces through development and renewal, corporate investment, and privatization. Public spaces, affordable housing, and local organizations and businesses were squeezed out by corporate and public investors (Doan and Higgins 2011). While gay neighbourhoods became unaffordable for many 2SLGBTQ people, middle- and upper-income gay people, predominantly white gay couples, perpetuated neoliberalism by either buying and investing in property in the neighbourhood or by moving to suburban areas (Nash and Gorman-Murray 2014).

While some have argued that the development of gay neighbourhoods displaced racialized, immigrant, and poor marginalized people, Sarah Schulman observes that many 2SLGBTQ people were racialized, immigrants, poor and/or in need of safe(r) space and protection that the dense, tight-knit urban neighbourhoods could provide (2013). In their pre-gentrification form, these neighbourhoods were often seen as dilapidated and dirty, and as harbouring society's poor, sexually deviant, violent, criminal, and undesirable people. The concentration of 2SLGBTQ people and establishments, therefore, meant that the public, governments, and police were better able to identify, target, and intrude, often violently, in the daily public and private lives and spaces of 2SLGBTQ people (Nash 2014). 2SLGBTQ activist and advocacy organizations responded to such attacks by guarding gay businesses and community spaces; by establishing safety patrols to ward off homophobic and transphobic attacks; by creating communities of care; and by advocating for 2SLGBTQ people who were arrested and charged by police for a host of offences (Hooper 2017). By providing relative safety and protection, gay neighbourhoods provided select 2SLGBTQ people with public and private spaces for community building, art and cultural development, political organizing, and sexual activities.

As Puri states: "Privacy becomes a matter of privilege, a right contingent on one's access to resources, especially those attached to class status" (2016, 311).Through the focus on privacy as freedom from state intervention, the prioritization of the private and the domestic through same-sex marriage, and the gentrification of gay private and public spaces, particular homonormal citizens ascended to self-sufficient and rights-bearing citizens, while those who could not seek shelter, safety, and connection within the terms of private provision were further excluded and exposed to state and public condemnation and regulation.

Public Sex in the Detention State

The privatization of gay life took place at the same time as governments in Canada and the United States were dismantling the welfare state and individualizing responsibility. In both countries, state agencies simultaneously deregulated the market while expanding their regulation of the public through intensified policing of everyday life, the criminalization and incarceration of more people, and the development of more prisons. Dean Spade calls this neoliberal project the "detention state" (Spade 2009). Building from Spade, Kaplan-Lyman notes that the detention state increasingly regulates those "realms where individual and collective actions are, for whatever reason, not subject to the forces of the market and therefore not naturally efficient – crime being the most egregious form of inefficient behavior" (Kaplan-Lyman 2012, 189). Crime and criminality were understood as violations of the "natural order" of neoliberalism wherein those who cheat or fail were outside of the regulatory reach of the wage labour system, and were therefore subject to state discipline through the criminal legal system (Kaplan-Lyman 2012). Welfare became "prison-fare" as law-and-order government interventions in the lives of the poor, racialized, marginalized, and deviant were designed to render people docile, to create economic and social stability, and thus to maximize market functioning (Johnson 2014; Kaplan-Lyman 2012). Poverty, marginalization, and crime, which were largely caused by the shrinking welfare state and market deregulation, were blamed on individual choices within the "fair" market. As Doug Meyer observes, "the state concerns itself not with reducing the economic causes of crime but with punishing individual offenders" (Meyer 2014, 118).

Police organizations in North America adopted new modes of policing in the 1990s which "emphasize[d] the policing of low-level disorder" in order to ward off higher level criminality (Kaplan-Lyman 2012, 181). Initially, disorder policing focused on stopping people for lesser infractions who were suspected of more serious crimes. The tactic progressed, however, to stopping, carding, and frisking people who were thought to be potential offenders. Many police forces, including the Toronto Police Service, have faced resistance to these practices (Yunliang 2017).

Carding/street checks, surveillance, harassment, and displacement continue to disproportionately target people who are Black, Indigenous, unhoused, poor, disabled, in mental distress, neurodivergent, and un-documented within 2SLGBTQ populations (Cole 2020). These mar-ginalized people are thus more likely to be charged and convicted of crimes, to receive harsher and longer sentences, and to experience dis-crimination, sexual assault, and violence from police and correctional officers (Maynard 2017). Carding and street checks often focus on of-fences that emerge from poverty and marginalization, including pan-handling, selling legal and illegal substances, sex work, homelessness/loitering, having large objects (mattresses, furniture, tents) in public spaces, riding public transportation for free, public drinking, and pub-lic sex (Kaplan-Lyman 2012). Such activities are regarded as disordering public spaces. Thus, disorder policing contributes to the privatization of public spaces by criminalizing poor and marginalized people for ex-isting in public spaces (Spade 2009).

The effort to bring order to public spaces facilitates neoliberal gentri-fication and efforts to "clean up" public spaces for the comfort, safety, visual consumption (Kennelly 2015), and profits of developers, busi-ness and domestic property owners, and consumers. The language of cleanliness has long been used in reference to sexuality, sexual acts, and sexually transmitted diseases. Yet while efforts are made to secure, depoliticize, and ensure economic stability, governments are careful to appear "liberal, tolerant, and welcoming," in order to avoid criticism and dissent from citizens, and divestment from domestic and foreign corporations (Kennelly 2015, 12). Police organizations, therefore, are represented as sanitizing public space to ensure that the city is welcom-ing and tolerant of those who choose to abide by the rules of neoliberal order. As Puri states, "Rather than a pattern of reduced governance, looking at the intimacies between sexuality and neoliberalism brings home the Foucauldian paradox of intensified and expanded regulation at the very moment of states' retrenchment" (Puri 2016, 317–18).

While the mainstream LGBT community has a history of rebelling against discriminatory sex and obscenity laws, and police raids, sting operations, violence, and incarceration, contemporary mainstream LGBT organizations have not mobilized against neoliberal govern-ments' establishment of a detention state or the criminalization of various "sexually deviant" people such as people living with HIV/AIDS and sex workers (Meyer 2014; Spade 2009). Indeed, economically self-sufficient white gay men and women are, in fact, making alliances, asking for protection, and ultimately legitimizing police and prisons in their communities. The state and police's willingness to protect certain segments of previously targeted populations is celebrated as a "symbol of social inclusion and care for sexual diversity" (Lamble 2013, 230).

The state is no longer seen as the perpetrator of homophobic violence (for some people), but is, instead, a "neutral arbiter of injury" and a protector against violence at the hands of deviant citizens (Lamble 2013, 240, 248). Moreover, certain LGBT people are measuring their citizenship statuses, inclusion, and freedom not just by whether the state will protect them, but also by whether the state will incarcerate other citizens on their behalf (Lamble 2013, 230). As Chandan Reddy (2011) argues, the expansion of freedom, protections, and rights for some, is often accompanied by more severe violence for others.

In this context, public sex represents a violation of neoliberal norms and the power relations of the detention state. Not all public sex is equal, however, as the public, government, and police generally understand and treat particular kinds of public sex differently on the basis of the sexuality, gender identity, class, housing status, race, indigeneity, and occupation of those involved (Woods 2009). Particular gay people attempted to strike a deal with the state in which they promised to assimilate to heteronormal marriage standards in exchange for an end to government and police intervention in their (private and privatized) sex lives. Yet despite their homonormativity, marriage did not afford gay people the same discretion that is given to (white) heterosexuals who have public sex. Rather, heteronormative sensibilities still require "dirty," "diseased," "dangerous," and "deviant" queer sex, and sex work to remain out of public sight (Catungal and McCann 2010).

While sex occurs in many public spaces, public parks – the venue of the 2016 Project Marie sting and raid – have been of particular meaning making and concern to the public and police. John Paul Catungal and Eugene McCann argue that parks were segregated spaces which represented a colonial mastery over nature, the maintenance of civility, and the reproduction of proper moral citizens (2010). Public sex certainly represented a taboo for "wholesome and moral publics" (Catungal and Eugene McCann 2010, 77–8). In the context of neoliberal sexual regulation, public sex represents a subversion of dominant meanings of urban spaces, both gentrified and yet-to-be gentrified, and a contestation of heteronormative orders within and beyond the 2SLGBTQ community.

Public Apologies and Police Raids: Toronto Police Service's Official Apology for Operation Soap, June 2016

As part of Pride Month 2016, Toronto Police Chief Mark Saunders issued an official apology for the 1981 Operation Soap[3] bathhouse raids, and unveiled a mural recognizing the 1981 raid, the 2000 raid on Pussy Palace,[4] and a host of other historical, police-involved injustices against

2SLGBTQ communities in Toronto and beyond. This section takes up the discourses of the apology and mural, arguing that, on the 35th anniversary of the Operation Soap raids, particular gays reached a place of neoliberal respectability, entitling them to an official apology from the Toronto Police Service (TPS), and obscuring the continued criminalization of marginalized 2SLGBTQ people by the TPS.

Chief Saunders opened his address saying, "Thank you for coming to police headquarters. We hope that every time you come here you feel more than accepted" (Xtra News, June 23, 2016). He then offered the following apology:

> We cannot let this evening go without historic acknowledgment. The Toronto Police Service recognizes that February 5 of this year marked the 35th anniversary of one of the largest mass arrests in Canadian history. The Toronto police raids on Toronto bathhouses did not occur on just one evening, but the February 1981 event was the most dramatic in its destructiveness and in the number of men arrested, some 300. An extraordinary community response led to the eventual acquittal of almost everyone arrested that night. The 35th anniversary of the 1981 raids is the time when the TPS expresses its regret for those very actions. It is also an occasion to acknowledge the lessons learned about the risks of treating any part of Toronto's many communities as not fully a part of society. Recognizing diversity requires consistently renewed practice strategies, and reaching out to communities and vigilance in challenging stereotypes. Policing requires building mutual trust, and that means forging links with the full range of communities that make up this extraordinary city. The TPS recognizes that the lessons from that period have continuing relevance for the creation of a more inclusive city. While the TPS has made real progress in relations with the mainstream LGBTQ2S communities, we recognize the need for renewed commitment to work together cooperatively and respectfully with other marginalized groups and still disadvantaged sexual minorities. (Ibid.)

The apology contained many standard ingredients. First, it acknowledged an historical injustice without specifically naming the affected community, in this case men who were targeted for being in a space where homosexual sex was occurring. Second, it mentioned the police insofar as they arrested 300 people but offered no discussion of police officers' use of violence, property damage, public shaming, sexual and verbal assaults, and arrests to target, humiliate, and silence the gay community. Third, it applauded the community in question for fighting back so valiantly without mentioning that such rebellion came with a new wave of police violence, harassment, and arrests. Fourth, it claimed that lessons had been learned about the "risks of treating any part of Toronto's many communities as not fully a part of society," while continuing to surveil, target, and criminalize those on the margins. Fifth, it implored the affected community to work with and trust the police, a strategy that has historically resulted in the justification of more police in the community and more arrests of community members. Finally, it counted as a win that "mainstream 2SLGBTQ communities" had fallen in line with the police and pledged to work towards incorporating those who remained "disadvantaged."

Following his apology, Saunders announced two initiatives that he hoped would "further our relationship with the LGBTQ2S communities, specifically the trans communities" (ibid.). First, a gender-neutral washroom had been designated at the TPS headquarters, and all new TPS buildings and major renovations would include gender-neutral washrooms. Second, TPS developed a police service guide for the transgender community. Saunders stated: "We know that hate crimes against trans persons happen at an alarming rate. We also know that for many reasons, including negative experiences with the police, trans people have generally not reported these crimes to the police. This must stop" (ibid.). Transgender peoples' fear of engaging with the police was not explicitly attributed to transgender peoples' experiences of police harassment, sexual and physical assault, targeting, surveillance, and criminalization. Instead, the solution to violence against transgender people was to educate them on how to report a crime, the supports available for victims of crimes, and how the court process works. 2SLGBTQ and anti-racism activists have been regulated disproportionately by the criminal legal system, and consequently have long educated each other on police and legal systems, creating organizations to support and represent 2SLGBTQ people through the criminal legal system. Yet it was the transgender community, not the police, that needed an education. Here transgender people were implored to integrate into the detention state in order to access the benefits of state protection.

Police Chief Saunders closed his speech by referencing the 2016 shooting at the Pulse Nightclub in Orlando, Florida, assuring those in attendance that "this year I can promise you, we will have a great parade, it will be a safe parade" (ibid.). The TPS solution to violence against the 2SLGBTQ community was to take ownership of the Pride parade, to promise more police in 2SLGBTQ spaces and events, and to encourage transgender people to use the police against others. Black Lives Matter Toronto responded to the apology stating:

As a movement comprised of and led by LGBT Black folks, we are invested in a queer and trans community safe from police violence, harassment, and brutality. Police violence in our communities is real, disproportionately impacting Black, Indigenous, and Brown Trans women, sex workers, undocumented, street-involved people, youth, etc. This violence is enabled by increased police presence at Pride, cushy relations between police and LGBT orgs, and events like this. We denounce Toronto Police's apology. We reject their attempts at pink washing. Their attempts at portraying cops as friendly to the LGBT community. We give a big fuck you to increased police presence in LGBT spaces. We demand accountability for their continued terrorizing of LGBT Black, Indigenous, migrant, street-involved, or sex-working peeps. TPS, Mark Saunders, we see through you. (BLM Toronto, June 27, 2016)

In her analysis of a police apology for raiding a gay event in Australia in 1994, Emma Russell states that the case "highlights how state institutions navigate and avoid accountability to a specific and historically targeted group" (2015, 122). BLM Toronto stated that Pride Toronto and other LGBT groups in the city were giving the police a platform and legitimacy to ignore and deny police violence against Black, Indigenous, street-involved, and trans people: "Can we talk about how the Toronto Police are using Pride in an attempt to erase their racism problem? Can we talk about how Pride is letting Toronto Police do this at the expense of trans folks & racialized queers?" (BLM Toronto, June 23, 2016).

In addition to the apology, the TPS unveiled a mural in commemoration of the 1981 raids. Located on the north wall of 425 Church Street, the mural featured many historical symbols of LGBT identity and community. An invitation to the unveiling was sent to LGBTQ community members, stating: "The mural acknowledges the history of the community and the Service; it also promotes the Toronto Police Service as being LGBTQ inclusive. Most importantly, not only will this mural beautify the neighbourhood, but it will educate people. It tells a story about our history and where we have been as LGBTQ people" (ibid.). BLM Toronto members interrupted the TPS and Police Chief Saunders' press conference at the mural unveiling. One BLM Toronto member stated to the crowd:

If you haven't paid attention, the vast majority of the Black Lives Matter movement is made up of queer and trans people. We are the people on the front-lines. We are the people who have been most impacted by police brutality. We are not going to condone a hollow apology while sex workers are still traumatized at the hands of TAVIS [Toronto Anti-Violence

Intervention Strategy]. Where is that apology? Where was the mural for Sumaya Dalmar? (BLM Toronto, June 27, 2016)[5]

Janaya Khan, a co-founder of BLM Toronto, posted a response to the apology, mural, and press conference in which they recounted that members of the crowd started chanting "All Lives Matter" as Black Lives Matter Toronto members spoke (Khan, June 25, 2016). Khan writes:

> In all of our actions, from shutting down highways, to occupying the police headquarters, to having actions in schools in support of Black students, never once have people tried to chant that. this is important. these people who i am meant to share my queer and trans identity with, who have an experience of oppression, used their white privilege and ignorance in an effort to silence us. white supremacy is white supremacy no matter the gender or sexuality. their racism and narcissism surrounding their experience of oppression, combined with white supremacy, makes a toxic and dangerous reality. a reality that requires my silence, the erasure of my Blackness, in order to achieve their liberation. remember, white Pride is still White Pride. some of y'all will be waving that gay flag as quickly as the confederate. some of y'all gon' get it this pride though. (Khan, June 25, 2016)

While white LGBT people were actively focused on gaining the acceptance of the state and the police, BLM Toronto argued that police acceptance reinforced their white supremacy. As Khan stated, in order for these respectable white people to reach and maintain their privilege, they distanced themselves from racialized, Indigenous, street-involved, poor 2SLGBTQ people, and legitimized the state's continued regulation of the "deviant" in their community. The neoliberal detention state compels people to aspire to be accepted, successful, and self-sufficient, and many white gay people have complied. As we will see in the next section, though, at any moment that privilege can be revoked.

Toronto Police Service's Project Marie, September–October 2016

Three months after the Toronto Police Service officially apologized for the 1981 Operation Soap raid, Project Marie was initiated, wherein undercover police officers from 22 Division surveilled Etobicoke's Marie Curtis Park for sexual activity and arrested and/or charged people "who allegedly solicited the officers for sex" (Mann, November 11, 2016). Using tactics from past raids and sting operations, police officers augmented their public presence, warned community members about alleged public sex, surveilled the areas in question, and interacted with community members engaging in or seeking to engage in sexual activities (Reason, November 10, 2016). While the tactics were unchanged, the regulation of public and private sex had altered over 35 years. Project Marie reveals the vulnerability that remains for particular kinds of people engaged in public sex.

As discussed, not all public sex is treated equally. Amid accusations from media and the 2SLGBTQ community that Project Marie was targeting gay men, Constable Kevin Ward of 22 Division stated:

> I want to make it very clear, that the purpose of this project is not to target any one specific orientation or anything like that ... But there have been a lot of unacceptable occurrences going on down there for quite a long time ... and the community's had enough. They're not going to tolerate it anymore. (Reason, November 10, 2016)

Meaghan Gray, a Toronto Police Service spokesperson, similarly stated:

> Engaging in sexual activity period is not allowed in public spaces and that's why we were there responding to those complaints [...] Whether it's men engaging in sexual activity, men and women, two women – it does not matter. (Mann, November 11. 2016)

The grassroots group Queers Crash the Beat (QCB), formed in resistance to fight "back against homophobic, racist, and discriminatory policing in public space" (Queers Crash the Beat 2017). QCB discussed the complexity of sexual activity, identity, and public spaces, arguing that sexual activities do not determine sexual identities:

> For many men who don't identify as gay, aren't out of the closet, or are not connected to the LGBT community because of where they live or who they are, discreet cruising in parks is a way to meet other men. Some also enjoy cruising for other reasons. Most men who cruise don't want to be seen or caught, and want consensual sex. (December 12, 2016)

While it seems like the police and QCB were both promoting a sexual future where people were not defined or regulated by their identities, the two groups differed in their intentions. The police, I argue, maintained that they were targeting certain behaviour, rather than certain men, for fear of violating liberal rights. They evoked neoliberal detachment of people from their marginalized identity, community, and systems of oppression, and thus from claims to systemic inequality by focusing on the sexual actions, and the location at which those sexual acts occurred. QCB, on the other hand, pointed to the incongruence between some people's identities and their actions in order to assert that many people engaging in public sex were discreet, and thus non-threatening, precisely because they feared punishment.

Advocates, including QCB, maintained that while men who have sex with men may not identify as gay, Project Marie was intended to target gay men and specifically marginalized gay men, and men who have sex with men. A protester stated that marginalized men were most likely to be arrested in such stings:

> That this sting is happening in Etobicoke and not the downtown core speaks volumes [...] This is a community with lots of folks from racialized communities, a lot of folks that are new to Canada that might not have access to the larger LGBT community. (Mann, November 19, 2016)

Marcus McCann, the lawyer defending many of the accused likewise stated:

> It's a large park in the southwest end of Toronto that straddles Toronto and Mississauga. There's a playground, a bicycle trail and wooded areas. Because it's so secluded, it has long been a park in which gay men meet. The recent gentrification of the neighbourhood has put pressure on that. (Shea, November 18, 2016)

The park and surrounding community represented many of the historic and ongoing effects of gentrification: the area was home to racialized and newcomers to Canada; and racialized and newcomer 2SLGBTQ people used the park, in part, because they were unable or unwilling to access the downtown 2SLGBTQ community and neighbourhood. The police then perpetuated (white) gentrification of the area in the name of family, public safety, and quality of life.

Toronto Police Service spokesperson Meaghan Gray said that the operation was initiated by community complaints and reports of sexual assault, indecent exposure and sexual activity in the park (Mann, November 11, 2016). Thus, the Toronto Police Service could represent its actions as responding to the local community's demand for the protection of women, children, and families in the park. Similar discourses have a long history in attacks against queer and racialized people, and were seen in discussions about transgender rights and public facilities such as bathrooms and change rooms. Muriel Draaisma of *CBC*

News reported that Gray "said the community wants the park to be a family-friendly place where adults and children can enjoy the outdoors without fear of witnessing sexual acts. There have also been complaints about litter left behind, including condoms" (November 11, 2016). The elicitation of fear in relation to sexual acts, and disgust in relation to condoms, rested on the discursive association of queers and men who have sex with men with promiscuity, dirt, disease, contamination, and violence.

Calls to police gay public sex "are often accompanied by the invocation of the middle-class heterosexual family as the appropriate user of local greenspace" (Catungal and McCann 2010, 78). Steven Maynard states:

> It is an issue of sexual orientation, only the orientation is heterosexuality. It's about heterosexual families (and, no doubt, some of their homonormative counterparts) and their right to enjoy public park space free from the disturbing sight of undomesticated sexual pleasure. This, of course, is not how they'd put it. They are much more apt to say it's about protecting children from unwanted sexual activity and its [waste] in the form of used condoms. (Maynard, November 30, 2016)

Gay public sex counters the image that mainstream homonormative people have tried to advance through same-sex marriage. It was the heterosexual and homonormal white families that claimed offence, danger, and injury, and accordingly used the police to seek protection from, and intervention in, the lives of those who are already subject to heightened police surveillance and violence. Marcus McCann, a lawyer who defended many of the accused, discussed the repercussions: "We know these kinds of charges can have very severe consequences. Not because of the legal repercussions – many of the charges are just bylaw infractions – but because of the shame and stigma attached. There is the risk of outing these people to their families, and there are potential employment consequences. The Toronto Police have now admitted that all of the charges relate to consensual sexual activity between adults. That's important, because there has been misinformation on that" (Shea, November 18, 2016). Moreover, the identity, community and legitimacy of heterosexuality and homonormativity was maintained through the regulation of these deviant public sexualities and the simultaneous erasure of homosexual identity and community through a professed targeting of sex acts as opposed to sexual identity groups.

Despite the fact that none of the charges involved offences against women or children,[6] the Toronto Police Service and several community organizations held an event to "Take Back the Park" and "Walk the Beat" following the Project Marie operation on 19 November 2016 (Tovey, November 19, 2016). Jim Tovey, Councillor for Ward 1 in Mississauga, invited constituents to the event, stating: "Your community officers and City officials will be present to discuss the issues plaguing Marie Curtis Park. Officers will discuss "Project Marie," the Toronto Police Service's response to these issues" (November 19, 2016). The language of "taking back the park" comes from feminist efforts to "take back the night" in relation to sexual and physical assaults in public areas. In this case, though, the "re-taking" was appropriated to target the "plague" of non-heterosexual men who were an alleged threat to heterosexual women and their families. To do so, the invitation stated that community members could "walk the beat" with police officers in the areas where the public sex had allegedly taken place. Declan Keogh of *Now Toronto* reported that the event

> featured free hot dogs and hot chocolate, a picnic, park cleanup and "fun activities for the kids." The highlight: a candlelight walk through the areas where police say men have been engaging in public sexual activity. It was all part of a wider police initiative, according to Tovey, to 'foster community support and involvement. (2016)

Heterosexual and homonormal families, in sum, were invited to simulate being police officers, to build better relations with the police, to gawk at the salacious and dangerous locations of the alleged gay public sex, to participate in "fun family activities," and then to hold a solemn candlelight vigil – an emotional rollercoaster of white hetero- and homo-normal affirmation.

A group of LGBTQ women wrote an open letter to Toronto Police Chief Saunders, the chair of the Toronto Police Services Board, the mayor, and City Councillors Shelley Carroll, Chin Lee, Kristyn Wong-Tam, Mike Layton, and Joe Cressy. In the context of historical police raids, including the Pussy Palace raid, and police racial profiling:

> Men who have public sex with other men are members of our communities and deserve to have a say in how public spaces are used. The Project Marie sting was unwarranted and damages public safety for people who are targeted by police. We demand that you immediately stop targeting men who have sex with men at Marie Curtis Park, and immediately disclose and cease any other similar operations currently underway in Toronto public spaces. Policing public sex is an important issue for queer, transgender and sex working women because increased police presence

compromises the safety and livelihood of those who do sex work, and poses a danger to homeless and underhoused LGTBQ people, two spirit and gender non-conforming people. Women of all orientations, transgender people, sex workers, and our gay brothers experience high levels of gender-based violence in public spaces, and we have a sincere and vested interest in advancing nuanced and responsive strategies for creating safe(r) civic multi-use spaces. We wholeheartedly reject the contention that safety for some women and children trumps the needs of LGBTQ and racialized communities – especially when it is clear that TPS does not consider protecting the safety and best interests of the trans women and sex workers as part of their responsibility. (*Xtra News*, December 5, 2016)

The authors of the letter challenged dominant systems of police regulation of sex in public, calling for LGBTQ, racialized and Indigenous people, and sex workers and street-involved people to be central to determining how public spaces are used, and how the safety of all users is prioritized.

In response to Project Marie and the Walk the Beat event, Queers Crash the Beat held a protest against the "large-scale police investigation with homophobic undertones that they [felt] targeted a marginalized community" (Mudhar, November 19, 2016). QCB "spoke and debated with local residents and police officers about Project Marie [...] and [stood] in support of the men charged in Project Marie while condemning the sting, especially in light of the Toronto police's apology for the 1981 bathhouse raids only five months ago" (Mann, November 19, 2016). In May 2017, QCB invited "queer folks" to a ribbon cutting ceremony at Queen's Park, the site of the Ontario Legislative Building, to "celebrate the beginning of cruising season," stating "for thousands of years, humankind has celebrated the warming spring by gathering in the bushes, shrubs, and glorious trees of our lovely parks and fields after dark, seeking the company of likewise carnally inspired cruisers for mutually sensual and consensual encounters" (BlogTO 2017). Thus, honouring traditions of community-building and sexual freedom, QCB invited queer folks to unabashedly engage in sexual activities in the city's most political, public-serving park.

Conclusion

This paper has considered how social divisions and inequalities have reproduced, challenged, and shaped neoliberalism, and examined the connections among the neoliberal domestication, individualization, and privatization of gay life; police and community surveillance and regulation of private and public spaces; LGBT people's participation in the criminalization and exclusion of marginalized people; and the enabling of police to enhance their image by claiming to be open and tolerant of well-behaved, cooperative LGBT citizens. Canada's mainstream LGBT communities have contributed to the perpetuation of neoliberal institutions and incorporation within the detention state. Particular members of the 2SLGBTQ community were deemed worthy of a police apology and acceptance, while others were not deserving because of their perceived inferiority, deviance, and culpability in their own persecution. BLM Toronto stated that Pride Toronto and other LGBT groups in the city were willfully ignoring and denying police violence against Black, Indigenous, street-involved, and trans people.

While neoliberalism transforms in these times of crisis and resistance, and, as John Clarke argues in his chapter in this volume, its form is contingent on local forces, it is also true that the 2SLGBTQ community has been fundamentally shaped by the effects of neoliberalism. These effects include the shrinking of public space and engagement, the continued exposure of vulnerable people to police intervention, and dependence on regulatory institutions, including marriage, the "free" market, and the detention state. Yet, those homonational citizens who bought into the project of neoliberalism for its promises of freedom and safety are never fully protected from state intervention. Access to the relative safety or privileges of neoliberalism is contingent on people's ability to reinforce, and thus legitimize, inequality and exclusion. The terms of inclusion shift as new crises develop, and the priorities and tactics of the neoliberal detention state reconfigure. BLM Toronto's warning was realized when Toronto Police surveilled and charged men for having sex in a public park outside of Toronto's downtown gay neighbourhood. Homonormativity thus offers precarious safety in exchange for the constriction of public space, community engagement, and political action.

Since the summer of 2016, in reaction to ongoing violence against and murders of Black, Indigenous, and 2SLGBTQ people in Canada, calls to defund and abolish the police have intensified. The Toronto coalition No Pride in Policing has called on the Toronto City Council to defund the Toronto Police Service, and on Pride Toronto to hold an anti-racism march in place of their 2020 pride parade. The Vancouver Pride Society announced it supports defunding police organizations, and that police would not be allowed to participate in the 2021 digital Pride parade or in future pride parades. Several Canadian city councils have considered motions to significantly cut police budgets, and to divert the funds to community-based social programs. Activists are not calling for neoliberal austerity against a state institution: they are calling for collective futures rid of the neoliberal detention state. 2SLGBTQ community organizers, such as BLM Toronto and Queers Crash the Beat, continue to queer public spaces – roads, neighbourhoods, parades, and parks – using their bodies to sit in, build shelter, have sex, and grow community.

NOTES

1 Throughout this chapter, I shift among "LGB," "LGBT," "2SLGBTQ" and other initialisms to refer to various organizations and communities. I have respected the identification that specific groups use to describe themselves. In the absence of such identification, I chose an initialism that seemed to suit a group's politics, location, and time period.

2 Indigenous, racialized, and poor queer, trans, and gender-non-conforming women were most often targeted for gender-non-conforming violations. While cisgender women were rarely involved in sodomy law cases, their sexuality was regulated under marriage, adultery, sex work, and obscenity laws (Mogul et al. 2011).

3 In 1981, during *Operation Soap,* Toronto police targeted four bathhouses. At the culmination of a six-month undercover operation, 160 police officers inflicted violence, verbal abuse, and property damage, and arrested 304 men (Guidotto, 2011).

4 In September of 2000, the Toronto Women's Bathhouse Committee (TWBC) hosted a bathhouse event, "Pussy Palace," for self-identified queer women. Five male plainclothes police officers entered the event under the pretence of evaluating the event's liquor licence. The officers observed and questioned some of the 350 female attendees and recorded the names and addressed of the organizers. Charges were eventually laid against two of the volunteer organizers for a number of liquor violations (Bain and Nash, 2007).

5 Sumaya Dalmar was a Somali-Canadian transgender activist and model whose death was considered a homicide by community activists but the TPS stated that they were not treating her death as suspicious and would therefore not investigate the case.

6 "Meaghan Gray, spokesperson for the Toronto Police Service, reported that the criminal charge that has been laid is failure to comply. The other charges are provincial or municipal offences, involving such infractions as trespass to property, accessing restricted areas and engaging in a prohibited activity." (Draaisma, November 11, 2016)

REFERENCES

Bain, Alison L., and Catherine J. Nash. 2007. "The Toronto Women's Bathhouse Raid: Querying Queer Identities in the Courtroom." *Antipode* 39 (1): 17–34. https://doi.org/10.1111/j.1467-8330.2007.00504.x.

Black Lives Matter Toronto. 2016. "As a movement comprised of and led by LGBT Black folks ..." June 27, 2016. *Black Lives Matter Toronto Facebook page.* https://www.facebook.com/blacklivesmatterTO/videos/516654378530057/.

Black Lives Matter Toronto. 2016. "Can We Talk about How the Toronto Police Are Using Pride ...?" June 23, 2016. http://archive.is/hKIfA#selection -6297.1-6294.2.

BlogTO. 2017. "Cruising Season Ribbon Cutting with Queers Crash the Beat" https://www.blogto.com/events/cruising-season-ribbon-cutting-with -queers-crash-the-beat/.

Brodie, Janine. 2007. "Reforming Social Justice in Neoliberal Times." *Studies in the Social Justice* 1 (2): 93–107. http://doi.org/10.26522/ssj.v1i2.972.

Catungal, J.P., & McCann, E.J. 2010. "Governing Sexuality and Park Space: Acts of Regulation in Vancouver, BC," *Social & Cultural Geography* 11 (1): 75–94. https://doi.org/10.1080/14649360903414569.

CBC Digital Archives. 2017. "Trudeau: 'There's No Place for the State in the Bedrooms of the Nation'" http://www.cbc.ca/archives/entry/omnibus -bill-theres-no-place-for-the-state-in-the-bedrooms-of-the-nation.

Cole, Desmond. 2020. *The Skin We're In: A Year of Black Resistance and Power.* Toronto: Doubleday Canada.

Draaisma, Muriel. November 11, 2016. "Toronto Police Lay Charges after Etobicoke Residents Complain of Public Sex Acts in Park." *CBC News.* http://www.cbc.ca/beta/news/canada/toronto/toronto-police -marie-curtis-park-indecent-acts-etobicoke-1.3847878.

Doan, Petra L., and Harrison Higgins. 2011. "The Demise of Queer Space? Resurgent Gentrification and the Assimilation of LGBT Neighborhoods," *Journal of Planning Education and Research* 31 (1): 6–25. http://doi.org /10.1177/0739456X10391266.

Duggan, L. 2003. *The Twilight of Equality: Neoliberalism, Cultural Politics, and the Attack on Democracy.* Boston: Beacon.

Everitt, Joanna, and Michael Camp. 2014. "In versus Out: LGBT Politicians in Canada." *Journal of Canadian Studies* 48 (1): 226–51. https://doi.org /10.3138/jcs.48.1.226.

Guidotto, Nadia. 2011. "Looking Back: The Bathhouse Raids in Toronto, 1981." In *Captive Genders: Trans Embodiment and the Prison Industrial Complex*, edited by Eric Stanley, Nat Smith, 63–76. Oakland, CA: AK Press.

Hooper, Tom. 2017. "Policing Gay Sex in Toronto Parks in the 1970s and Today." http://activehistory.ca/2017/02/policing-gay-sex-in-toronto/.

Johnson, Andrew. 2014. "Foucault: Critical Theory of the Police in a Neoliberal Age." *Theoria* 61 (141): 5–30. http://doi.org/10.3167/th.2014.6114102.

Khan, Janaya. 2016. Facebook, June 25, 2016. https://www.facebook.com /janayafuturekhan/posts/10154242901518119.

Kaplan-Lyman, Jeremy. 2012. "A Punitive Bind: Policing, Poverty, and Neoliberalism in New York City." *Yale Human Rights and Development Law Journal* 15 (1): 177–221.

Kennelly, Jacqueline. 2015. "'You're Making Our City Look Bad': Olympic Security, Neoliberal Urbanization, and Homeless Youth." *Ethnography* 16 (1): 3–24. https://doi.org/10.1177%2F1466138113513526.

Keogh, Declan. 2016. "Panic in Marie Curtis Park." *Now Toronto*, November 23, 2016. https://nowtoronto.com/news/panic-in-marie-curtis-park/.

Lamble, Sarah. 2013. "Queer Necropolitics and the Expanding Carceral State: Interrogating Sexual Investments in Punishment," *Law and Critique* 24: 229–53. http://doi.org/10.1007/s10978-013-9125-1.

Mann, Arshy. 2016. "Protesters, Residents and Police Discuss Park Sex Crackdown at Protest." *Xtra News*, November 19, 2016. http://www .dailyxtra.com/toronto/news-and-ideas/news/protesters-residents-and -police-discuss-park-sex-crackdown-at-protest-210592.

– 2016. "Toronto Police Charge Dozens of Men with Sexual Offences in Etobicoke Park." *Xtra News*, November 11, 2016. http://www.dailyxtra .com/toronto/news-and-ideas/news/toronto-police-charge-dozens-men -with-sexual-offences-in-etobicoke-park-210040.

Maynard, Robyn. 2017. *Policing Black Lives: State Violence in Canada from Slavery to the Present.* Halifax: Fernwood Publishing.

Maynard, Steven. 2016. "Is the Queer Community Ready to Defend Public Sex?" *Xtra News*, November 30, 2016. http://www.dailyxtra.com/toronto /news-and-ideas/opinion/the-queer-community-ready-defend-public-sex -211309.

Meyer, Doug. 2014. "Resisting Hate Crime Discourse: Queer and Intersectional Challenges to Neoliberal Hate Crime Laws." *Critical Criminology* 22 (1): 113–25. https://doi.org/10.1007/s10612-013-9228-x.

Mogul, Joey L., Andrea J. Ritchie, and Kay Whitlock. 2011. *Queer (In)justice: The Criminalization of LGBT People in the United States.* Boston: Beacon Press.

Mudhar, Raju. 2016. "Marie Curtis Park Becomes Centre Point of Debate about Public Space." *The Toronto Star*, November 19, 2016. https://www.thestar .com/news/gta/2016/11/19/marie-curtis-park-becomes-centre-point-of -debate-about-public-space.html.

Nash, Catherine J. 2014. "Consuming Sexual Liberation: Gay Business, Politics, and Toronto's Barracks Bathhouse Raids." *Journal of Canadian Studies* 48 (1): 82–105. http://doi.org/10.3138/jcs.48.1.82.

Nash, Catherine, and Andrew Gorman-Murray. 2014. "LGBT Neighbourhoods and 'New Mobilities': Towards Understanding Transformations in Sexual and Gendered Urban Landscapes." *International Journal of Urban & Regional Research* 38 (3): 756–72. http://doi.org/10.1111/1468-2427.12104.

Puri, Jyoti. 2016. "Sexualizing Neoliberalism: Identifying Technologies of Privatization, Cleansing, and Scarcity." *Sexuality Research & Social Policy: Journal of NSRC* 13 (4): 308–20. doi:10.1007/s13178-016-0236-y.

Queers Crash the Beat. 2017. "About." Facebook, 2017. https://www.facebook.com/pg/QueersCrashTheBeat/about/?ref=page_internal.

Queers Crash the Beat. 2016. "In Advance of Our Big Event TOMORROW!" Facebook, December 12, 2016. https://www.facebook.com/QueersCrashTheBeat/posts/279403289128494

Reason, Cynthia. 2016. "Toronto Police Crack Down on Public Sex in Marie Curtis Park: Walk the Beat Event Aims to 'Take Back the Park.'" *Etobicoke Guardian*, November 10, 2016. http://www.insidetoronto.com/news-story/6958146-toronto-police-crack-down-on-public-sex-in-marie-curtis-park/.

Reddy, Chandan. 2011. *Freedom with Violence: Race, Sexuality, and the US State.* Durham, NC: Duke University Press.

Russell, Emma. 2015. "Revisiting the Tasty Raid: Lesbian and Gay Respectability and Police Legitimacy." *Australian Feminist Law Journal* 41(1): 121–40. http://doi.org/10.1080/13200968.2015.1031931.

Schulman, Sarah. 2013. *The Gentrification of the Mind: Witness to a Lost Imagination.* Oakland, CA: University of California Press.

Shea, Courtney. 2016. "Q&A: Marcus McCann, the Lawyer Who's Defending the Men Accused of 'Lewd Behaviour' in an Etobicoke Park." *Toronto Life,* November 18, 2016. http://torontolife.com/city/crime/marcus-mccann-project-marie-qa/.

Smith, Miriam. 2005. "Resisting and Reinforcing Neoliberalism: Lesbian and Gay Organising at the Federal and Local Levels in Canada." *Policy & Politics* 33 (1): 75–93. http://doi.org/10.1332/0305573052708483.

Spade, Dean. 2009. "Trans Politics: Beyond Law and Order." Lecture delivered at University of Alberta. Edmonton, Alberta.

Tovey, Jim. November 19, 2016. "'Walk the Beat' Will Be in Marie Curtis Park (West Side)," http://www.jimtovey.ca/event/walk-beat-marie-curtis-park/.

Xtra News. 2016. "Why These Queer Women Stand in Solidarity with Gay Men Opposing Project Marie." *Xtra News*, December 5, 2016.

https://xtramagazine.com/paid-post/why-these-queer-women-stand-in
-solidarity-with-gay-men-opposing-project-marie-72582.

Xtra News. 2016. "Toronto Police 'Regrets' Bathhouse Raids." *Xtra News*, June
23, 2016. http://www.dailyxtra.com/toronto/news-and-ideas/news
/toronto-police-regrets-bathhouse-raids-196318.

Yunliang, Meng. 2017. "Profiling Minorities: Police Stop and Search Practices
in Toronto, Canada." *Human Geographies: Journal of Studies & Research in
Human Geography* 11 (1): 5–23. http://doi.org/10.5719/hgeo.2017.111.1.

11 Making Canadians: Citizenship Acquisition and Foreign Adoption

LOIS HARDER

In December 2007, the Government of Canada passed Bill C-14, an amendment to the Citizenship Act that allowed children adopted abroad to be granted citizenship rather than having to become permanent residents and complete the immigration process upon their arrival in Canada.[1] The aim of the bill was to create a more equitable regime of citizenship acquisition between children born abroad and adopted by Canadian parents, and children born abroad to Canadian parents.[2] This amendment was compelled by the Federal Court's decision in *Canada v Dular* (1998), holding that adoption constituted an analogous ground under the Charter's sec. 15 equality rights – that adoptive parentage should be treated the same way as "biological" parentage in immigration and citizenship law. In essence, a birthright claim to Canadian citizenship should be available to children of Canadian parents regardless of whether those children were "biological" or adopted from abroad.[3] Adoption by, like birth to, a Canadian citizen parent should render the location of the child's birth irrelevant. Adoptive parents and international adoption agencies had advocated strenuously for this option for citizenship acquisition, though importantly, they also wanted to ensure that the immigration route remained available.

In 2008, the Canadian government implemented another set of amendments to the Citizenship Act.[4] Many of these changes were designed to reinstate citizenship for people who had been born in Canada or born abroad to citizen parents, but had subsequently lost their citizenship due to the complex loss provisions of the 1947 and 1977 Citizenship Acts. Yet along with the expansion of citizenship entitlement, the 2008 amendments also imposed a hard, second-generation cut-off rule. As of April 17, 2009, Canadians born abroad were no longer able to convey their citizenship to their born-abroad children.[5] The equality of treatment that had led to the *grant* of Canadian citizenship for children adopted abroad as a parallel process to the entitlement to citizenship of *jus sanguinis* children carried over into the second generation cut off rule. Those children adopted through the immigration process, however, would be able to pass along Canadian citizenship to their born abroad children, just as naturalized adult immigrants and *jus soli* citizens do. This reform met with a great deal of opposition from the international adoption community, but their objections went unheeded. Census data from 2016 indicates that a majority of adoptive parents continue to opt for the immigration process.[6]

The Canadian state's approach to the citizenship of international adoptees calls to the fore Janine Brodie's insights into the makings of the Canadian national identity. Brodie's work on the Canadian nation challenges the progress narrative in which citizenship rights are systematically extended to formerly marginalized groups, rewriting Canada's national story "as an ongoing and incomplete project of recognition and accommodation of cultural diversity and represented as a model for other diverse national polities'" (Brodie 2012, 92). Instead, she argues that "multicultural narratives invariably privilege some members of the new post-settler majority, by virtue of their ethnic origins, as being more 'at home' in socio-cultural terms than other segments of the multicultural matrix" (ibid., 94). This conceptualization of Canadianness in terms of relative "at homeness," gains further normative force in its association with what it means to be a "genuine" or "authentic" Canadian; proximations to Canadian national identity that are the purview of citizenship officials and judges in their adjudications of the validity of international adoptions. In this assessment process, genuineness combines with the differential incorporation of racialized subjects within the Canadian nation and maps on to who is doing the adopting and who is adopted. In the situation in which a Canadian parent(s) adopts a child who has been abandoned in her home country and comes to her new family unencumbered by ties to her birth family, the veneer of Canadian multicultural inclusivity adheres quite securely. Following Howell, I argue that this is possible because the sending state, the Canadian state, and the adoptive parent(s) regard this child as "socially naked" and "denuded of meaningful relatedness" (2006, 4). Indeed, one of the requirements for the grant of citizenship to a child adopted from abroad is a "full adoption"– the creation of a "genuine parent-child relationship," the proof of which lies in a complete severing of ties to the child's biological or previous parents.[7] Racial difference may exist within the adoptive family, and the social intelligibility of the family may require some interpretive work on the part of both the adoptive parent(s) and the community, but when the parents understand themselves as part of the dominant Canadian cultural norm, their adopted children are incorporated into that norm as well (see Dorow and Swiffen 2009; Dorow 2006).

Notably though, there is a second category of inter-country adoptions in which Canadian citizens – often racialized – seek to adopt relatives whose parents are unable to care for their child/children due to poverty, civil strife, or ill health. Here, Brodie's work on the precarity of "the social" under conditions of neoliberal governance, as well her analysis of the interaction of national identity and security discourses is especially apposite (see Brodie 2008; 2009; 2010). In the case of inter-country relative adoptions, we find families heeding neoliberalism's admonition that people in need should rely on "their own." In a globalized context, though, this responsibilization may well require some flexibility in national borders. And at the same time these adoptive families are also facing the requirement that their care for their relative constitutes a genuine parent-child relationship. It is true that the strictures of severing are less stringently applied in the case of relative adoptions, but as the judicial record clearly shows, the "genuineness" of the parent-child relationship is a key point of interrogation for Canadian immigration officials. The transnational relative adoption confronts a securitized Canadian state, with prospective adoptive parents facing the presumption that they are engaging in an "adoption of convenience," attempting to take advantage of Canada, and that a child still encumbered by kin relations in her country of origin might one day seek to sponsor remaining family members. The tensions within the white European concept of "authentic" Canadian identity confronts Canada's multicultural and multiracial past and present, as well as the racial and geographic diversity of contemporary Canadian immigration policy.

In every country in the world, citizenship – political membership – is determined by criteria of birth. As political theorist Jacqueline Stevens vividly demonstrates, the story of consent that undergirds liberal democracies is a fiction (1999). Instead, we rely on laws that govern parentage (*jus sanguinis*) or that define the boundaries of the nation state (*jus soli*) to name who belongs in a political community. Of course, immigration is also an important source of membership, but naturalization – an evocative descriptor – is the means to citizenship for only a small portion of the population. Moreover, once naturalized, citizens are able to pass on their new citizenship to their children, realizing the full power of that ecological metaphor – to integrate a foreign species within a new environment, complete with the capacity of that species to reproduce in its new surroundings (Somerville 2005, 667 and 669).

Inter-country adoption is located in a liminal space between immigration and birthright (though much closer to immigration than to birthright). Children, in their innocence, vulnerability, and futurity, are irresistible slates for meaning-making.[8] Children adopted from abroad are a particularly rich symbolic source, offering up an invigorated citizenship narrative, the virtue of child rescue and, often, the invocation of inclusive, multicultural values (see Strong-Boag 2006). Yet despite the opportunity for national re-enchantment that inter-country adoption brings, the legal requirements that surround it belie Canada's suspicion of "outsiders" and thus the Canadian state's deeply paradoxical relationship to its settler origins. Children adopted from foreign lands are simultaneously welcomed into the family – both nuclear and national – yet the completeness of their kinning is surrounded by ambivalence. These children can be made Canadian – and in turn, make Canada – but the genuineness of their connection to the country is a site of national anxiety.

Drawing from parliamentary debates around adoption amendments to the Citizenship Act, published guidance to citizenship and immigration officials for handling inter-country adoption applications, and judicial decisions adjudicating inter-country adoption and Canadian citizenship, this paper focuses on four key themes emerging from the implementation and adjudication of the grant of Canadian citizenship: a remembering and forgetting of the distinction between adoptive and "biological" kinship; the emphasis on connection as a basis for citizenship; the creation of a genuine parent-child relationship; and, relatedly, the assurance that the adoption was "not entered into primarily for the purpose of acquiring a status or privilege in relation to immigration or citizenship."[9] These themes are replete with assumptions about the proper relationship between family and nation, contestation about the form of the normative family, the work of kinship rules in policing national boundaries and the relationship between race and nation. Moreover, their empirical instantiations show us how Canadians are made.

The Canadian Inter-country Adoption Regime

The legal process surrounding international adoption in Canada is complicated. Provincial and territorial governments have constitutional authority over parentage and adoption, while the federal government is responsible for citizenship and immigration. For a child adopted through the international process to receive citizenship or permanent resident status, the adoption must be legal in the child's country of origin and approved in the parent(s)' usual province of residence (or country of residence if they are not currently residing in Canada). As well, if the child's country of origin is party to the Hague Convention on the Protection of Children and Co-operation in Respect of Intercountry Adoption (Hague Convention),[10] the central authority in that country must "determine that the child meets the Hague Convention eligibility criteria for an international adoption and that there are no suitable families in the child's country who are willing and able to adopt the child."[11]

On the Canadian side, the provinces and territories are responsible for establishing the suitability of the adoptive home, and the federal government's citizenship process assesses the prospective placement to determine whether the adoption

1. is in the best interests of the child;
2. creates a genuine relationship of parent and child;
3. takes place in accordance with the laws of the child's country of origin and the laws of the country of residence of the adopting citizen;
4. has not be entered into primarily for the acquisition of a status or privilege in relation to immigration or citizenship.[12]

These criteria also apply to parents who choose the immigration route, through applications for permanent resident visas made in the family class category for adopted children, children to be adopted in Canada, and orphaned relatives, and are outlined in the regulations to the Immigration and Refugee Protection Act.[13]

It is important to observe that both the grant of citizenship and the immigration route attract the same level of scrutiny by state officials and, moreover, how very distinctive this scrutiny is from the experiences of parents accessing derivative/*jus sanguinis* citizenship for their children. Obviously, it is important that the legal safeguards surrounding adoption are followed and that Canada upholds its international obligations under the UN Convention on the Rights of the Child and the Hague Convention. Care must be taken to ensure that adoptive children are placed in suitable homes and that their best interests are fully considered. But the point I want to emphasize here is the alleged equality between a grant of citizenship and a birthright claim. Not only does birth within a presumptively biological family not attract determinations of best interests, genuineness, or rationale, the entitlement to family privacy and the benefit of the doubt regarding parental motives also translates directly into national membership. The "natural" – and national – family walks a preferred path to the political community. To be clear, my argument is that the law is fully engaged in both adoptive and "biological" family formation. What I want to foreground is how the "natural" and the "artificial" family are constituted in law, and how that translates into political membership.

Bill C-14 (2007)

The tension in the distinctive treatment of adoptive parents and biological parents in their capacity to extend Canadian citizenship to their born-abroad children is rife in parliamentary debate and judicial decisions. The desire to mitigate the distinction was the clear motivation for the statutory amendment of Bill C-14 (2007),[14] but the process of deriving the appropriate approach reveals a simultaneous forgetting and remembering of how membership is constituted through kinship rules. For example, Monte Solberg, the Conservative Minister of Citizenship and Immigration who was ultimately responsible for introducing the legislative amendment, rose in the House of Commons on the bill's second reading to wax eloquent on its many virtues. He stated that the intent of the legislation was to "ensure there are no distinctions between naturally born children and adopted children. This is a Canadian value. People want to show this generosity to everyone, and it is reflected in the legislation."[15] He went on to describe babies "as people just starting out with a blank slate" (ibid.). But he was also careful to reassure the House that the legislation included safeguards against adoptions of convenience by ensuring the "existence of a genuine parent-child relationship is demonstrated, that the best interests of the child are being met, that a proper home assessment has been made, that the birth parents have given their consent to the adoption, and that no person will achieve unwarranted gain as a result of the adoption" (ibid.).

When the legislation went to Committee, this alternation between collapsing and reinforcing the distinction between the processes of citizenship acquisition for adopted and birthright citizens continued. In his appearance before the House of Commons Standing Committee on Citizenship and Immigration, Mark Davidson, the Director and Registrar of Canadian Citizenship, began his presentation on the proposed legislative changes by stating that

> this bill is intended to minimize the difference in treatment between children adopted outside of Canada by a Canadian parent and those born outside of Canada to a Canadian parent. It's a matter of principle and equity to make these amendments in order to ensure that children adopted by a Canadian citizen have immediate access to citizenship as soon as the adoption is completed.[16]

He then went on to describe the distinction between the immigration process and the proposed grant process as "no longer resembl[ing] the criteria for permanent residents seeking citizenship. Instead, it will be limited to ensuring that a full legal adoption has taken place and that the best interests of the child are protected" (ibid.). In truth, though, this was a misrepresentation. The process of securing permanent residency for adopted children has long been distinguished from that of family class adults, particularly with regard to medical conditions. And as his presentation went on, the distinctiveness between the grant of citizenship and permanent residency criteria for adopted children that he celebrated at the outset collapsed into a discussion of the similarities in the processes of determining the validity of the adoption. Even if Mr. Davidson wanted to hold fast to the distinctiveness of the approaches, the official guidance to citizenship and immigration officers offered in operations manuals on adoption clearly notes their parallels. As stated in *CP 14: Grant of Canadian Citizenship to Persons Adopted by Canadian Citizens*, "The criteria for granting Canadian citizenship to foreign-born adopted children of Canadian citizens under the Citizenship Act and Citizenship Regulations are similar to those for granting permanent resident status to adopted persons under the IRPA/IRPR."[17]

The amendment to the Citizenship Act was undertaken in the first instance as a result of court rulings finding that adoption constituted an analogous ground of discrimination under the Charter's section 15 equality rights and that parents of adopted children should be treated the same as "biological" parents. It is clear from the judicial record that the federal government was not always supportive of this view. In *Canada v Dular* (1998, 1997) and *Canada v McKenna* (1999) for example, the federal government advanced the view that strict conditions on eligibility determination were necessary in international adoption cases in order to prevent "misuse of the adoption provisions for the purpose of immigration" (*Canada v Dular*, 1998, 1997). The courts, however, adjudged that the goal of "keep[ing] the immigration system honest could be accomplished without discriminating against adopted children." Moreover, "as long as citizenship is granted as of right to children of citizens, in the belief that their status as children of citizens gives them sufficient connection to Canada, then that right must be granted without discriminating between adopted children and non-adopted children" (*Canada v McKenna*, 1999).

The fact that the Government[18] subsequently found a means to meet the equality expectation by folding the immigration requirements into the citizenship grant requirements, passing this off as a long-overdue righting of injustice, should offer pause. One might argue that the legislative amendment produced equality of result. It certainly did not produce equality of process. Again, this is not to argue that home studies and assessments of parental suitability to care for a child are inappropriate. Rather, it is to observe that when we move from the adequacy of the family to the realm of political membership, the state makes the process of inclusion a great deal easier for those with a "biological" connection to the state than those deemed obliged to rely on formal adjudications of worthiness. Thus, as Brodie notes, the imagined distinction between "nationals" and "foreigners" is naturalized, settlers and their reproductive capacities are rearticulated as Canadians, Canada's colonial past is disappeared, the demarcation between citizens and aliens is reinforced (Brodie 2009, 691). The one notable exception to this process appears in the development of the second-generation cut-off rule.

Bill C-37 – The Second-Generation Cut-Off

When Bill C-14 was passed, legislators and adoption advocates were untroubled by the decision to equate born abroad adopted children with born abroad, or *jus sanguinis,* children. The consequences of being born abroad were not especially dire, nor, importantly, were they particularly well known. That dispassion abated promptly, however, with the Harper Government's introduction of Bill C-37. As noted in the introduction, Bill C-37 introduced a second-generation cut-off rule. Children born abroad to *jus sanguinis* Canadian parents would not acquire their parents' citizenship, and children adopted abroad who acquired their citizenship via grant fell under the same limitation. The legislation did include a stopgap for children who would otherwise be stateless, but this provision was limited to people who had a bloodline connection to a Canadian citizen parent.[19]

The government's justification for instituting the second-generation cut-off rule was framed in terms of strengthening the meaning of Canadian citizenship by ensuring a substantive connection to the country. According to the government,

> Under the old rules, it was possible for Canadians to pass on their citizenship to endless generations born outside Canada. To protect the value of Canadian citizenship for the future, the new law … put a limit on citizenship by descent to one generation born outside Canada …[20]

This was, in fact, an overstatement, as the Citizenship Act had required second generation born-abroad children to reside in Canada for a year and affirm their citizenship by the age of 28.[21] There were a number of difficulties administering this affirmation provision, however, resulting in a series of bureaucratic errors and embarrassments. More politically significant to the hardening of the second-generation cut-off, though, was the development of a discourse of "citizens of convenience" in the wake of the evacuation of Canadian citizens from Lebanon after the Israeli bombings of 2006.[22] This concern about convenient citizenship had a parallel iteration in the adoption context, where "adoptions of convenience," as we have noted, were already established as a potential threat to the integrity of Canadian citizenship via the inter-country adoption process.

The second-generation cut-off rule has attracted a great deal of criticism from both "biological" and adoptive parents who are primarily concerned about the inequalities this provision generates between *jus soli* and *jus sanguinis* acquisition of citizenship, and the restrictions on life choices that such an imposition may make. Effectively, the argument is that the second-generation cut-off rule is over-inclusive (see Shachar 2004). It denies Canadian parents who were born or adopted abroad and have a strong connection to Canada, even if they are also living and working abroad, to convey their citizenship to their born- or adopted-abroad children. For example, Dorinda Cavanaugh, representing an international adoption placement agency and appearing before the Standing Committee on Citizenship and Immigration observed that "if any of these people dare to take jobs overseas, move there temporarily, and either have or adopt a child while in that foreign country, their child will be deprived of his or her full citizenship rights."[23] If a *jus sanguinis* Canadian wants to gain some educational, employment and/or life experience overseas, the argument runs, they should not have to worry about the citizenship consequences of their reproductive decision-making.

Andrew Bilski, appearing before the committee as a concerned adoptive parent, challenged the presumption that a second-generation birth abroad was necessarily reflective of a lack of connection or commitment to Canada.

> [W]hat's the evidence that the second group of children, the foreign adopted ones who acquired citizenship through the direct route, will not have an enduring presence or commitment to Canada? Are they more likely than other Canadians, such as Liberal Party of Canada Leader Michael Ignatieff, to live abroad for vast periods of their lives? Are they less likely than other Canadians, such as the 40 per cent or so who don't even both[er] to vote in federal elections, to be committed to this country?" (Ibid.)

Bilski's argument is particularly telling in its problematization of birthright citizenship entitlement and active democratic engagement. Yet while he clearly feels that citizens have duties to the country, the core of his argument is that children adopted abroad by Canadian citizens should have the same right to exercise, or indeed, disregard, their citizenship obligations as Canadians with a blood or soil claim to political membership. Criteria of birth – "biological" or adoptive – are what make citizens. Democratic engagement comes later or perhaps not at all.

In response to the representations of adoption organizations and parents – including Members of Parliament whose children would be affected by the amendment – the Standing Committee on Citizenship and Immigration recommended that the legislation be revised so that children adopted from abroad to parents normally resident in Canada would have the same legal status as *jus soli* children, and that *jus sanguinis* Canadians who could prove residence in Canada for a specific period of time prior to the birth of their child would be entitled to pass on their Canadian citizenship to their born-abroad children.[24] The Conservative Government was unmoved. In his response to these recommendations, the Minister of Citizenship and Immigration, Jason Kenney, was unwilling to consider further amendments that would create equality of status between *jus soli* children and children adopted from abroad. In the \Government's view, a residence requirement for the adopted child's parent(s) would be "difficult to administer and enforce in the absence of exit controls to verify residence."[25] A similar objection was advanced in response to the minimum residency recommendation for *jus sanguinis* citizenship transmission. Yet the government does find a way to ensure that permanent residents can account for their physical presence in Canada sufficiently to meet their status renewal requirements and citizenship requirements. It was certainly within the power of policy-makers to devise a more elegant and effective means to assess connection and communicate the legal requirements to those affected. Instead, the Conservative Government chose a very blunt instrument – the hard, second-generation cut-off. Ironically, however, because adoptive parents still have the option of securing citizenship for their children via the immigration route, they have a way around the second-generation cut-off that is not available to the "biological" children of born abroad Canadians. And, of course, naturalized Canadians are also able to pass their Canadian citizenship on to their born abroad children. When it comes to the second generation then, consent trumps blood while place of birth serves as a proxy for (dis) connection.

Genuine Parent-Child Relationships and Adoptions of Convenience

In the effort to bridge the gap between blood and adoption in the context of birth and political membership, the existence of a genuine parent-child relationship is a fundamental criterion for eligibility. So what *is* a genuine parent-child relationship? According to the citizenship manual providing guidance on the grant of citizenship for children adopted by Canadians, such a relationship must exist in law and in fact, and, in the first instance, is created through a "full" adoption. A full adoption "completely sever[s] the adopted person's legal ties with his or her biological parents or previous legal parents and create[s] a new legal and factual parent-child relationship between the adoptive parents and the adopted person."[26]

From the perspective of citizenship and immigration officials and lawmakers, the severing of "biological" ties fulfills two purposes. It serves the best interests of the child, and it ensures that "immigration program integrity is upheld by preventing the future sponsorship of the biological parents by the adopted person ...." (ibid., 48). Despite the growing emphasis on the benefits of "open adoption" for the mental health and adjustment of the adopted child, the international context of adoptions remains tied to an older conception of the adoptive relationship in which the biological parents are effectively disappeared from the child's life and legal existence. This severing seems all the more pernicious when read against the conflation of child's best interests with a ban on future sponsorship of a biological parent. There is some softening of this stance with regard to adoptions by relatives, wherein an ongoing relationship and contact may still occur. Nonetheless "the new parent-child relationship between the adopted person and the adoptive parents should be evident and not simply exist in law" (ibid., 51). Tellingly, the vast majority of adoption cases contested in the courts involve relative adoptions and the question of a "genuine parent child relationship."

The fact that the Canadian state regards the future sponsorship of a "biological" relative by a child adopted from a foreign country as unacceptable exemplifies what Brodie has identified as the "paradox of the social" in the contemporary context of neoliberal governance and globalization. Also discussed by Bakker in this volume, this paradox entails an increased obligation to rely on family members to meet social needs in the absence of a robust social architecture that can support people in times of economic and personal crisis (Brodie 2010: 1581). But when those family members reside across international borders in places that are disadvantaged by the workings of global markets, the

Canadian state has deemed that such support must be circumscribed. This situation also exposes the contradictions of blood-based membership forms. In the absence of a legal severing, membership in the Canadian polity might have to be extended to a "biological" relative of a Canadian residing outside of Canada. The adopted child, in her youth and promised futurity, might merit inclusion in the Canadian national community, but the prospect of extending that welcome to her birth parent(s) is, as the law makes clear, unthinkable.

While immigration officials seek evidence of a "genuine parent-child relationship" in the new adoptive arrangement through the clarity of a complete severing of the relationship between the "biological" parents and the child, the courts and adoptive parents often have a more complex understanding of a genuine parent-child relationship. Judicial decisions have contemplated the question of *when* a genuine parent-child relationship must be established relative to the adoption. In *Perera v Canada (2001)*, for example, Justice Dubé held that the relationship was necessarily prospective. In this case, an aunt and uncle – naturalized Canadians – sought to adopt their nephews from Sri Lanka. The boys' mother was widowed and unable to care for them, and the children were subsequently placed with another uncle, but he too was unable to maintain his responsibilities for the boys. Nonetheless, the visa officer and the IRB appeal division had regarded this as a non-genuine adoption because, at the time of the hearing, the boys were again living with their natural mother and regarded her as their mother. By contrast, in the judicial review of this decision, Justice Dubé's position was that

> the words "genuine parent and child relationship" do not require that there existed a fully developed parent and child relationship between the adoptive parents and the children at the time of a sponsored application. More often than not, the genuine relationship is created as a result of the adoption. The mere fact that adoptive parents want to bring their adopted children with them to the country where they live is not a presumption that they are attempting to create an adoption of convenience. Canadian parents fly all over the world to find and adopt children. Surely, visa officers will not close the door to these children because genuine parental relationships have not yet been created. (Ibid., at para 12)

Other justices, however, have disagreed, finding that whether a relationship was genuine and whether that determination must consider the future state rather than the present condition was a determination that could only be made on the facts, rather than a general condition that one would presume from an adoptive relationship.[27] Nonetheless, in more recent decisions, the future state argument has been applied.[28]

Justice Dubé's argument draws a parallel between "stranger" and "relative" adoptions and challenges the fact that immigration officials are more willing to see the prospects of a genuine parent-child relationship when there are no other family members in the picture. Yet as the conflation of child's best interests with a ban against future sponsorship would suggest, when immigration officials go looking for a "genuine parent-child relationship," the future they are interested in concerns subsequent family sponsorship applications – future claims to Canadian political membership by people the Canadian polity has already adjudged as unworthy for inclusion. Children are one thing. After all, they are "blank slates." But parents who gave them up are beyond the pale.

Representatives of immigrant-serving agencies have also flagged concerns about determinations of genuine parent-child relationships and presumptions of adoptions of convenience. Appearing before the Standing Committee on Citizenship and Immigration in 2003, the director of the Metro Toronto Chinese and Southeast Asian Legal Clinic observed that while the adoption of orphans posed no difficulties with obtaining immigration status for adoptive children, relative adoptions involving children whose parents are still alive are often denied by immigration officials, even when the adoption is approved by the provincial adoption agency. Like Justice Dubé, her view was that the appropriate test of a genuine parent-child relationship should be future-oriented, which would be more consistent with the way these adoptions evolve.[29] In response, a Canadian Alliance MP offered the consummate summation of the "adoption of convenience" argument replete with racist overtones.

> You mentioned that a lot of your people are family. Do they have no parents? There is some fear that people might send their children here to have better lives by having them adopted. I don't know about your country, but it has been brought to my attention that this is done, that people here will adopt them just so they will have a better life, not because they're parentless or because the people here are childless.[30]

The person making the case for the genuineness of relative adoptions was a Canadian citizen, a graduate of the U of T Faculty of Law, living and working in Toronto.[31] Rather than recognizing her efforts to support Canadian families, and expanding membership in the Canadian polity, the implication here, and in the text of the regulations and implementation guidance, is that certain racialized categories of people (*your* people; *your* country – which is not Canada) are engaged in systematic immigration fraud via adoption and, moreover, that seeking a better life for a child is a duplicitous rationale for adoption. Yet as Justice Kane would later argue, "an adoptive parent's intent of providing a better quality of life for an adopted child in Canada is a 'legitimate goal.'"[32] Further, "the fallacy of the reasoning employed is best revealed if the proposition is inverted; what parent would give up a child if they knew it faced a more difficult life with fewer opportunities?"[33]

Having reviewed 40 recent cases in which a "genuine parent-child relationship" was at issue before the courts, the characteristics of the complainants are remarkably consistent. The cases overwhelmingly involve naturalized citizens, presumptively racialized, seeking permanent residence or a grant of citizenship for an adopted relative – niece, nephew, cousin, grandchild – from their country of origin. And most of them fail. Sometimes the appeal does not succeed on the basis of technicalities that might subsequently be overcome. Sometimes the evidence that an extended family is seeking a way to access an international education for a young person rather than a more wide-ranging relationship of care is also fairly clear. But there are also numerous instances in which an on-going connection between a child and a biological parent – despite the existence of a legal adoption in the child's country of origin and the adoptive parent's clear intention to establish a new life with the child in Canada – is turned back. In yet another paradox of birth and adoption, then, whereas blood ties provide a kind of sanctity to the integrity of a nuclear family and the basis for national connection that underpins citizenship, when blood appears in the extended family form, mediated through international adoption, suspicions of instrumental rationality and, I would assert, a white conception of Canada, come to the fore. The genuineness of a parent-child relationship requires a break between the Canadian national and the foreigner.[34]

Conclusion

Reading Canada's laws governing *jus sanguinis* citizenship alongside the citizenship provisions for inter-country adoptions provides a rich opportunity to interrogate the practices of nation-making and national identity formation in Canada. Even as successive Canadian governments represent the country as a space of liberal rights and inclusion, selective membership rules are devised and deployed to restrict that inclusion. Janine Brodie's engagements with national identity formation and the imaginative work of making the Canadian nation are resonant in this contradiction. As Brodie notes, the idea of a nation requires both a remembering and a forgetting (Brodie 2002, 162). Canada, in its self-representation, advances itself as "a peaceful kingdom, an orderly society, and a cultural mosaic which values accommodation, diversity, and collectivity" (ibid.). But in order to make such claims, Canada must also forget – its history of colonialism; its hierarchy of racialized belonging. In the governance of inter-country adoption, the reticence to extend birthright entitlement to adopted children and limit its inter-generational operation, to ensure a severing of ties to birth families, and valiantly guard against adoptions of convenience, belies a deep anxiety about who should constitute the members of the Canadian polity. And what would the Canadian polity be if we did remember? If we did choose to think long and hard about what it means to be a member of a political community. But more importantly, what would it mean to be barred from that community? If we engage with these questions seriously, it is also incumbent upon us to consider why we place bounds around political membership, what the limits and exclusions of those bounds should be, or alternatively, what other forms of social organization might support our flourishing.

NOTES

1   An Act to amend the Citizenship Act (adoption), S.C. 2007, c. 24.
2   House of Commons, Standing Committee on Citizenship and Immigration, *Evidence,* No 79 (22 November 2005), online:<https://www.ourcommons.ca/DocumentViewer/en/38-1/CIMM/meeting-79/evidence> [https://perma.cc/J5FZ-B2B7]
3   I am using scare quotes around "biological'"to signal that parentage is, in fact, a product of law. The law defines who constitutes a 'biological' parent, but as the long history of the paternal presumption makes clear, it is heterosexual marriage (and more recently common law relationships) that turns men into fathers, at least in the first instance. That is, a child's father is presumed to be the husband or common-law partner of the woman who gives birth to the child. There is no requirement of a DNA test to ensure that the child and the father are, in fact, related. Rather, a biological relationship is read off the social relationship. This presumption can certainly be contested, but in the absence of legal action, the presumption *makes* a biological relationship. Notably, the parental presumption has not been extended to same-sex partners. Certainly, the non-birth or non-genetically related partner may achieve legal standing as a parent, but, in most provinces, this only happens when a child is

conceived with the help of assisted reproductive technologies and an agreement on parentage is reached prior to conception, through adoption or through a legal declaration of parentage. See, for example: Ontario, Children's Law Reform Act, 2016, c. 23 s. 4-s. 11; Alberta, Family Law Act, S.A. 2003, c F-4.5 s. 7–9; and, British Columbia, Family Law Act, SB 2011, c 25 s. 23–31.

4 An Act to Amend the Citizenship Act, SC 2008 c.14.

5 Citizenship Act, R.S.C. 1985, c C-29 s 3.3. Canadians working abroad in the public service, broadly defined, are exempt from this provision.

6 This finding was determined through a combination of the data reported by Statistics Canada on "sponsored intercountry adoptions" (the immigration route), subtracted from Hague convention data on the total number of intercountry adoptions in Canada. Stats Can reports that between 2011–16, 3,305 children were sponsored through the intercountry adoption route. See Statistics Canada, 2017, "Admission Category and Applicant Type (46), Period of Immigration (7), Age (12) and Sex (3) for the Immigrant Population Who Landed Between 1980 and 2016, in Private Households of Canada, Provinces and Territories, 2016 Census – 25% Sample Data." Subtracting that figure from the information provided to the Hague Convention by the Canadian government (and which does not include 2016 data), 2713 children would have accessed a grant of citizenship. See Selman, Peter. 2017. *Global Statistics for Intercountry Adoption: Receiving States and States of Origin 2004–2015.*

7 Citizenship and Immigration Canada, *CP 14 Grant of Canadian Citizenship to Persons Adopted by Canadian Citizens* 2015, 36.

8 Canadian law also allows for the adoption of adults, often in circumstances in which the child has been fostered by a Canadian period for an extended period.

9 Citizenship Act, R.S.C. 1985, c C-29 s.5.1(1)(b) and (d).

10 *Hague Convention on the Protection of Children and Co-operation in Respect of Intercountry Adoption*, 1993.

11 Alberta, *International Adoption*, 2014, online: <https://www.alberta.ca /international-adoption.aspx> [https://perma.cc/YU9X-TH29] Although this text is taken from the province of Alberta, the same rules apply in all provinces and territories. The Hague Convention requires that the child is legally free for adoption, that necessary consents have been given freely, in the required legal form and in writing, that the birth parents have consented and understand the consequences for their parental rights, the decision to place the child for adoption is not motivated by financial gain and the child's consent to the adoption, where such consent is required, has been given freely, in the required legal form and in writing. See Citizenship and Immigration Canada, *OP 3 Adoptions*, 2015, online:

<http://www.cic.gc.ca/english/resources/manuals/op/op03-eng.pdf>
[https://perma.cc/G7Y3-MKKS]

12 Citizenship Act, RSC 1985, c C-29, s. 5.1.

13 *Immigration and Refugee Protection Regulations*, SOR 2002. See especially: Part 7, Division 1, s 117.

14 Note that this is a different Bill C-14 amending the Citizenship Act from the provision passed in 2014.

15 *House of Commons Debates*, 39–1, vol. 141 (June 13, 2006).

16 House of Commons, Standing Committee on Citizenship and Immigration, *Evidence*, No 79 (22 November 2005), online: <http://www.parl.gc.ca/HousePublications/Publication.aspx?DocId=2139842&Language=E&Mode=1&Parl=38&Ses=> [https://perma.cc/J5FZ-B2B7]

17 Citizenship and Immigration Canada, *CP 14 Grant of Canadian Citizenship to Persons Adopted by Canadian Citizens*, 2015, 11, online: <https://www.canada.ca/content/dam/ircc/migration/ircc/english/resources/manuals/cp/cp14-eng.pdf> [https://perma.cc/E2EF-QM9S]

18 While it might be tempting to read this approach as characteristic of the Harper Conservatives' restrictive attitude towards immigration, virtually identical legislation had been introduced by the Martin Liberals in the previous sitting but had died on the order paper with the 2006 election call.

19 Citizenship Act, R.S.C., 1985, c. C-29, s 5(5).

20 *House of Commons Debates*, 40–3, No 49 (26 May 2010) at 1905 (Hon. Joe Preston), online: <https://www.ourcommons.ca/DocumentViewer/en/40-3/house/sitting-49/hansard> [https://perma.cc/Z7PA-QVR6]. This same explanation was provided by Citizenship and Immigration Canada 2009, *Frequently Asked Questions: New Citizenship Rules*, Question #4 'Why is Government Doing This?' Cited in Lois Harder and Lyubov Zhyznomirska. 2012. "Claims of Belonging: Recent Tales of Trouble in Canadian Citizenship." *Ethnicities* 12 (3): 293.

21 Citizenship Act, SC 1976, c. 108 s.7.

22 In a classic political deflection, the government covered over its shoddy evacuation response by casting suspicion on the national commitment of Canadians – presumed ethnically Arab – who were in Lebanon at the time of the crisis.

23 House of Commons, Standing Committee on Citizenship and Immigration, *Evidence*, No 22 (June 11, 2009), online: <http://www.parl.gc.ca/HousePublications/Publication.aspx?Language=e&Mode=1&Parl=40&Ses=2&DocId=3979528> [https://perma.cc/99M4-8VYQ]

24 House of Commons, "Review of the Subject-Matter of Bill C-37, An Act to Amend the Citizenship Act, Enacted in the second session of the 39th Parliament: Report of the Standing Committee on Citizenship and

Immigration" (June 2009) (Chair: David Tilson), online: <http://www
.ourcommons.ca/Content/Committee/402/CIMM/Reports
/RP3989008/402_CIMM_Rpt11/402_CIMM_Rpt11-e.pdf> [https://
perma.cc/2DQJ-RB7B]

25 House of Commons, "Government of Canada response to the Standing
Committee on Citizenship and Immigration's report entitled Review of the
Subject Matter of Bill C-37, An Act to Amend the Citizenship Act, Enacted
in Second Session of the 39th Parliament" (23 October 2009) (Hon. Jason
Kenney), online: <http://www.ourcommons.ca/DocumentViewer
/en/40-2/CIMM/report-11/response-8512-402-13> [https://perma.cc
/DEB7-8AJM]. Certainly CIC officials had been inconsistent, inattentive
and, at worst, inept in their administration of the affirmation requirements
of the earlier legislation. For example, representations by the Mennonite
Central Committee to the House of Commons Standing Committee on
Citizenship and Immigration relayed cases involving Mennonites who
migrated to Mexico for religious reasons, but understood themselves to
maintain their Canadian citizenship, often moving back and forth across
the border. They would be issued citizenship cards and passports, and
later apply for renewal, only to be informed that they were not, in fact,
Canadian citizens. The case of *Giesbrecht Veleta v Canada*, 2006 FCA 138
offers an especially poignant example.

26 Citizenship and Immigration Canada, *CP 14 Grant of Canadian Citizenship
to Persons Adopted by Canadian Citizens*, 2015, 36, online: <https://www
.canada.ca/content/dam/ircc/migration/ircc/english/resources
/manuals/cp/cp14-eng.pdf> [https://perma.cc/E2EF-QM9S]

27 See *Hurd v Canada*, 2003 FCT 719.

28 See *Mclawrence v Canada*, 2015 FC 867 and *Young v Canada*, 2015 FC 316.

29 House of Commons, Standing Committee on Citizenship and
Immigration, *Evidence*, No 22 (February 11, 2003) at 815–820 (Avvy Yao-Yao
Go), online: <http://www.parl.gc.ca/HousePublications/Publication.
aspx?DocId=696137&Language=E&Mode=1&Parl=37&Ses=2> [https://
perma.cc/JJ52-LV6M] .

30 Ibid., at 910 (Hon Lynne Yelich).

31 See "Avvy Go" <https://en.wikipedia.org/wiki/Avvy_Go> [https://
perma.cc/C2W7-6QDC]

32 *Smith v Canada*, 2014 FC 929, at para 65.

33 *Young v Canada*, 2015 FC 316, at para 24.

34 The tension between form and function is especially acute in situations
involving the adoption of children from Muslim countries. Sharia law
prohibits a complete severing of the child's relationship to her biological
parents, but it does make provisions for a strong form of guardianship
that, arguably, is effectively the same as adoption. And while provincial

courts have demonstrated a willingness to privilege function over form when assessing the genuineness of the caring relationship between parent and child, Canada's federal courts – operating in the context of citizenship determination – are much more attached to formalism. This subset of inter-country adoptions merits a much longer discussion than can be undertaken here.

REFERENCES

Brodie, Janine. 2002. "An Elusive Search for Community: Globalization and the Canadian National Identity." *Review of Constitutional Studies* 7 (1–2): 155–79.

– 2009. "From Social Security to Public Safety: Security Discourses and Canadian Citizenship." *University of Toronto Quarterly* 78 (2): 687–708. https://doi.org/10.3138/utq.78.2.687.

– 2008. "The Social in Social Citizenship." In *Recasting the Social in Citizenship*, edited by Engin Isin, 20–43. Toronto: University of Toronto Press.

– 2010. "Globalization, Canadian Family Policy and the Omissions of Neoliberalism." *North Carolina Law Review* 88 (5): 1559–91. http://scholarship.law.unc.edu/nclr/vol88/iss5/4

– 2012. "White Settlers and the Biopolitics of State Building in Canada." In *Shifting the Ground of Canadian Literary Studies*, edited by Smaro Kamboureli and Robert Zacharias, 87–108. Waterloo: Wilfrid Laurier University Press.

Dorow, Sara, and Amy Swiffen. 2009. "Blood and Desire: The Secret of Heteronormativity in Adoption Narratives of Culture." *American Ethnologist* 36 (3): 563–73. http://doi.org/10.1111/j.1548-1425.2009.01179.x.

Dorow, Sara. 2006. "Racialized Choices: Chinese Adoption and the 'White Noise' of Blackness." *Critical Sociology* 32 (2–3): 357–79. https://doi.org/10.1163%2F156916306777835277.

Howell, Signe. 2006. *The Kinning of Foreigners: Transnational Adoption in a Global Perspective*. New York: Berghahn Books.

Shachar, Ayelet. 2009. *The Birthright Lottery: Citizenship and Global Inequality*. Cambridge: Harvard University Press.

Somerville, Siobhan. 2005. "Notes toward a Queer History of Naturalization." *American Quarterly* 57 (3): 659–75. http://doi.org/10.1353/aq.2005.0054.

Stevens, Jacqueline. 1999. *Reproducing the State*. Princeton: Princeton University Press.

Strong-Boag, Veronica. 2006. *Finding Families, Finding Ourselves: English Canada Encounters Adoption from the Nineteenth Century to the 1990s*. Toronto: Oxford University Press.

Conclusion: Neoliberal Conversations and Contentions

JANINE BRODIE

Introduction

The chapters in this volume testify to the necessity of a vibrant critical social science for our times. This book was initially conceived and written as an exploration of the multiple repercussions of neoliberal governing discourses and practices in our daily lives, public policies, and political imaginations. The term "neoliberal" has been contentious from the moment it first entered our vocabularies in the late twentieth century. It has provoked critical debates about its theoretical parameters as well as its complicity in generating gross social inequalities, eroding the public sector, multiplying democratic deficits, and aggravating environmental perils. In many ways, the novel coronavirus that swept around the globe in 2020 only amplified these debates. It plunged the world into a period of "radical uncertainty," dominated by a public health crisis of unique proportions, and a livelihood crisis that surpassed records set during the Great Depression of the 1930s (Irwin 2020; WEF 2021).

In the early months of the pandemic, public conversations and aspirations revolved around the question of when life would return to "normal." Others, however, argued that the pandemic marked an historic turning point of such magnitude that returning to normal was an impossibility, and that our times would be forever reframed as "before" and "after" COVID (Addley 2021). Neoliberalism, moreover, was identified by many as an unanticipated casualty of the coronavirus. The pandemic devastated its foundational logics and imperatives, including limited and frugal government, global supply chains, open borders, and the supremacy of markets. This random biological mutation also intensified popular demands for a new social contract between governments and citizens, one that would take into account the gendered, racialized, and generational underpinnings of social inequality, precarious life, and essential work. Governments also were challenged to envision a new deal for those born in this century, the so-called pandemials, who are asked to settle for a bleak present, and a postponed or lost future (WEF 2021). The public health crisis ignited by the coronavirus, in other words, has mutated into myriad social and political tensions and uncertainties.

Historians tell us that wars and plagues often trigger demands for greater social equality and launch sustained periods of progressive social change. Yet such outcomes are neither spontaneous nor inevitable. Political responses to calamitous shocks vary with popular perceptions about what government can and should do and with the prevailing balance of power. The realization of fairer societies always requires substantial political mobilization around new visions of social equality and social justice (Spinney 2020). The coronavirus pandemic momentarily suspended the global economy, selectively upended livelihoods, ravaged marginalized communities, and laid bare the racialized and gaping inequalities that neoliberalism cultivated over the course of two generations. Still, it is not clear that neoliberalism will count as yet another victim of the virus. It has been pronounced dead several times in past decades, but it has consistently reinvented itself by "metabolising criticism" and changing the conversation (Plehwe and Slobodian 2020, 21).

As this book goes to press, it remains an open question whether the pandemic will launch a more equitable and sustainable politics. In crisis times, governments typically grasp at familiar policy manoeuvres and immediate, if only piecemeal responses to gaping social needs, leaving deeper social fractures unacknowledged and unresolved. After COVID-19 has been subdued, we may discover that the pandemic did not mark an historic tipping point or neoliberalism's death knell. It is very likely that new global supply chains will be established; economies will re-globalize rather than de-globalize; and governments will revert to austerity to dampen down the massive public debt built up during the pandemic (Haass 2020). Social scientists necessarily must be attentive to what governments are signalling when they talk about "bouncing back," "building back," "economic recovery," "personal responsibility," and "resiliency" in the wake of the pandemic. Do these terms embody new social imaginaries, or reversions of neoliberal's credo of market dominance and market logics?

For better or worse, a good part of my research career might be described as a biography of the neoliberal experiment in Canada, beginning with the Free Trade debates of the late 1980s. My work variously contested neoliberalism's overconfident and fatalistic claims about "no alternatives," unpacked its reformulations of citizen identities, social policy regimes, and equity claims-making, and underlined its legacies of inequality, insecurity, and precariousness. I have always considered research as an intervention in much broader and ongoing conversations about the challenges that confront us. These conversations are nurtured and enriched by legacies of critical thought, diverse perspectives and experiences, and, especially, fellow travellers, accomplished and emerging scholars, students, and activists who continuously refuel research imaginations about "the world as it is" and "the world as it should be." I am especially grateful to the fellow travellers who expertly engage with many of neoliberalism's contentions in this volume.

The editors have asked me to reflect on the ways in which the discipline has changed during my career, my approach to the study of politics, and the research contributions in this volume. In what follows, I try to address each of these themes, but it has been an unexpectedly difficult task. So much of one's personal journey is shaped by extraordinary mentors and teachers, chance encounters, unpredictable political dynamics, and possibilities afforded only to some by prevailing disciplinary cultures. Indeed, we may not even recognize the significance of these influences until years later. Over the course of my research career, I have drawn on many different approaches to the study of politics, because the idea of research orientation rather than research method, specifically assuming a critical posture towards prevailing wisdoms and commonsense, has been more important to me. While so-called eureka moments in the research process are personally gratifying, critical social science research is inescapably both a product of, and a contribution to, much broader conversations about our collective condition and common affairs. At its best, the weight of research interventions is not measured by citation indices and other contemporary forms of academic "likes" but, instead, by their capacity, however fleeting, to disrupt dominant discourses with alternative interpretative tools and literacies, and spark new, more inclusive, imaginaries of what might be.

The contributors to this volume engage with several conversations that animated my research over the past four decades. In this chapter, I reflect on three broad conversations about disciplines and disciplinary boundaries; political economies and governance; and the social in neoliberalism. In so doing, I am reminded that social science research is often predicated on the personal and the conjunctural (see John Clarke in this volume), that is, on one's own social "situatedness" and political/ethical positioning. As novice social scientists, we enter conversations that are already in progress, and already privilege particular interlocutors, idioms, and framings that simultaneously reveal and conceal. As established researchers and teachers, we are indelibly implicated in reproducing these ways of seeing and ways of not seeing. As critical social scientists, we are obliged to disrupt the exclusions implicit in prevailing disciplinary dialogues, especially when we come to see that these exclusions lurk between the lines of our own research contributions. In this way, as Bourdieu prescribes, "all researchers in the social sciences have to free themselves from the things they know" (2014, 106). This process of unencumbering necessarily begins with the formation and reinforcement of disciplinary walls within the social sciences themselves.

Disciplining the Boundaries

Over the course of their doctoral studies and beyond, graduate students are required to successfully navigate three distinct performances of the word "discipline." First, the term refers to a branch of expert knowledge that is institutionalized, generally in post-secondary institutions, and certified through graduate degrees, professional associations, specialized publication venues, and awards and other hierarchies of professional recognition. Academic disciplines regularly police the boundaries of their expertise and generate a rolling consensus among its practitioners about applicable theories, appropriate research methodologies, and germane research questions. Although each has its own history of contentious politics, all professional disciplines are political constructs that are invested in maintaining and reproducing claims to disciplinary terrains and expertise (Bourdieu 2014, 88). A good part of this disciplinary work involves "ruling in" research questions (and questioners) that embody the discipline, and "ruling out" those that do not. The net effect of disciplinary expertise thus is to make certain things unthinkable both within disciplinary boundaries, but, invariably, this is a vain and impossible task (Bourdieu 2014, 126).

In a second sense, discipline describes proficiency in regulating one's own behaviour in order to master a skill or realize a specific goal. Acquiring certification in a professional discipline such as political science, at a minimum, requires the self-discipline to read vast literatures, pay "homage to the great questions" and canons of the discipline, conform to the implicit censorship of disciplinary boundaries and generate original research questions within these constraints (Bourdieu 2014, 106, 126). Certification also requires the self-discipline to meet the escalating demands of various stages of apprenticeship from research assistant, teaching assistant, and sessional lecturer to postdoctoral fellow and untenured professor. Each stage of apprenticeship cultivates firmer allegiances to the methods and conceptual parameters of the discipline as well as compliance with unstated disciplinary norms of conduct that subtly configure "who fits in" and "who advances."

In all these ways, the aspiring disciple of political science demonstrates discipline, but certification also entails a third operationalization of the term – "being disciplined" by disciplinarians, who gain this role precisely because they have been disciplined themselves. They are empowered to guard the boundaries of the discipline and administer forms of exclusion, penalty, or punishment to those variously deemed as undisciplined subjects. The activities and venues of the disciplinarian vary from the professor in the classroom, to the examiner on thesis boards, to members of hiring or granting agency committees. Within these and many more contexts, disciplinarians are empowered to open and shut doors, and to be gateways or gatekeepers (Smith 2017). It took me many years on the job, acting both as an avid disciple of political science and as one of its disciplinarians, to appreciate the subtle ways in which these three instances of discipline – professionalization, self-regulation, and penalty – work together to demarcate the substance, ethics, and demographics of disciplinary expertise.

These disciplinary processes of "ruling in" and "ruling out" were integral to the early partitioning of the broad ambitions of social science to improve the human condition into specialized and professionalized disciplines, chief among them economics, political science, and sociology/anthropology. Although this division of analytic labour began in the nineteenth century, it intensified after the Second World War when vast public investments in the post-secondary sector made university education accessible to the baby-boom generation. At risk of oversimplification, the parameters of these ascendant academic disciplines mirrored and reproduced the liberal imaginary of separate spheres, which asserted the relative independence (rather than interdependence) of the economic, political, and social.

The task of understanding markets fell to the discipline of economics which progressively expanded and refined specialized knowledges about the dynamics of production, exchange, and consumption as well as the idioms of micro and macro theory, mathematical modelling, and rational choice (and its construction of economic man). As Isabella Bakker's chapter in this volume explains, mainstream economics focused on the behaviour of markets, thus ruling out critical dimensions of human activity that did not conform to or were not counted by market metrics. The discipline of economics thus propagated "false economies" that discounted and concealed the daily and intergenerational reproduction of individuals, communities, and societies and the unpaid care work of women. As Bakker (2003) and other distinguished feminist economists repeatedly highlight, the gendered labour, time, and skills associated with biological and social reproduction are inescapable preconditions for all market activity, but these factors were discounted, until very recently, by the mainstream of economic theory, and rarely prioritized in economic analyses or policy making. Feminist economists, moreover, underline that women typically pay a motherhood penalty, whether in the form of lower pay, part-time work, or dead-end jobs, because they have to balance the demands of labour force participation with care work. The COVID pandemic tipped this precarious balance for many women as the multiple demands of remote work, home-schooling, and daycare closures have exacerbated existing gender inequalities, forcing some out of the paid labour force altogether.

The new discipline of political science fortified its disciplinary terrain by disavowing its interdisciplinary roots in political economy (that asserted a synergetic relationship between states, markets, and the distribution of scarce resources), political sociology (that saw power operating in all social relations), and political philosophy (that focused on competing imaginaries of the real, the possible, and the good). Preferring parsimonious definitions of power and the political, political science asserted expertise in structures and systems of governance, institutional processes and behaviours, and relationships both among citizens and the national state, and among national states. Although both economics and political science made claims to universal theories and concepts, both of these disciplines embodied the broader demographics of wealth and power in the West where they initially flourished. The economy and formal politics were indisputably masculine domains and, thus, its disciples and disciplinarians alike were predominately male, and white, and Eurocentric in focus.

Almost everything else in this arbitrary division of disciplinary power, not the least, intimate life, families, communities, and difference, fell under the broad mandates of sociology and anthropology. These disciplines were charged with realizing a science of culture, social relations, and human behaviour writ large. Much of the terrain of these sciences of society was more feminized and diverse, and this was reflected, however marginally, in the concerns and demographics of its practitioners. The variegated and expansive boundaries of sociology/anthropology also created greater space for boundary contestation and innovations in theory and approach. In this century, non-conforming economists and political scientists, such as feminist, postcolonial

Indigenous, and anti-racism scholars, have regularly hopped over arbitrary disciplinary walls to take up more insurgent strains of sociological theory and method. In response, the disciplines also have relaxed the "taboo" of boundary-crossing (Bourdieu 2014, 106) or yielded to pressures to create subfields to accommodate inquiries that have been habitually concealed or ruled out of the disciplinary mainstream. For example, the American Political Science Association (APSA), arguably the pinnacle of professionalization in political science, hosts over forty organized specialized sub-sections, including women and politics, new political science, race and ethnicity, and sexuality. The Canadian Political Science Association (CPSA) houses twelve sub-sections, among them women, gender, and politics, and race, ethnicity, and Indigenous peoples and politics.

Although admittedly rough, I want to underscore three points in this disciplinary origins story: first, social science disciplines are political constructs and firmly situated in Western liberal imaginaries; second, their boundaries are both sites of discipline and contestation; and third, their institutionalization and professionalization are relatively recent phenomena. In Canada, this professionalization has largely coincided with my academic career. For example, the CPSA launched its own flagship journal, the *Canadian Journal of Political Science*, in 1968, a year after it ceased sharing a journal with economics (CJEPS). Economics created its own disciplinary journal a year earlier, while the *Canadian Journal of Sociology* appeared a few years later.

Being Disciplined

Always being interested in politics and current events, I was an eager recruit to the discipline of political science in the early 1970s. As I recall, my early training was especially focused on disciplinary boundaries and methods as prescribed by the disciplinary approach *de jour* – American behaviouralism. As budding disciples, we students were told that politics was appropriately conceived as a stable system of feedback loops where a vast array of groups pressed the political system with demands to advance their desired outcomes. The state (although this term was rarely used at the time) was neither biased nor unduly exclusionary but, instead, accumulated and weighed competing demands and converted them into outputs (public policies), whereupon the cycle of inputs-conversion-outputs begins again.

In this model of politics, things were settled: there was no prognosis of rupture or crisis (although already in the mid-1970s, conservative think tanks began talking about democratic demand overload). We disciples were captured by the idea that we were part of a new science of politics that eschewed the dusty musings of ancient political philosophers, institutional and constitutional formalism, and the siren calls of ideology. Instead, we were dedicated to observable and measurable facts, testable hypotheses, and statistical correlation. This new science would explain (perhaps even predict!) political events by building up the discipline brick by brick, one confirmed or refuted hypothesis at a time. We were told that political science properly studied the "what is," the hard and objective facts of politics, while questions of "what if" or "what should be" were best left to ideologues and philosophers.

I wish I could say that I contested these disciplinary credos: I did not see them as doctrinaire at that time. Instead, I was an eager apprentice – coding, computing, and "discovering" new facts about all manner of things deemed properly "political." Whatever dissonance I experienced came from accumulating messages that the discipline did not have room for me. I was the only woman in my MA cohort, with all the gendered micro-aggressions that entailed in the 1970s. But those experiences did not bother me as much as the resistance that my research questions provoked. I wanted to compare the political attitudes of men and women political party activists, using a readily accessible large-N data set. The problem, it seemed, was neither my conceptual framing nor method, both rooted in behaviouralism, but rather my use of gender as an independent variable. "Why is gender relevant?" I was pressed, and, besides, I was told, "There is no literature to build on, only suspect anecdotes and slim biographies." But I knew from personal experience that, although rarely candidates for public office, there were a lot of women working within party organizations. Occasionally, I had been one of them. Wasn't it valid to ask about their attitudes and behaviours, especially when they were effectively excluded from party leadership? Ultimately, it was agreed that I could proceed if I had a sociologist (the feminized discipline) on my supervisory committee. Discipline, disciple, and disciplinarian thus aligned.

A second encounter with disciplinary walls occurred a few years later when, as a doctoral student, I submitted my first abstract to the annual meeting of the CPSA. My very conventional treatment of women candidates was rejected because, as explained, no other proposals on gender were submitted and thus a panel could not be created (although I might add there were plenty of panels on political parties). After much protest and on my second try, I was put on a Canadian political party panel with a discussant who was a well-known specialist, indeed, a co-author of one of only a handful of books on Canadian party organizations at the time. I sweated through his commentaries, as he carefully combed through each of the three other papers on the panel. Then, it was my turn, and this is what he said, "And now for the Brodie paper. What can I say? Girls, be patient." That was it! And then the panel was opened to questions from the audience. I think one was thrown my way perhaps as a gesture of simple kindness. In 1985, nevertheless, I published *Women in Politics in Canada*, the first book on this topic.

I recount these early encounters with disciplinary walls for a several reasons, most obviously to underline that social science disciplines are sites of contestation, which can shift disciplinary boundaries and disciplinary practices. Women in the profession in these years can readily attest to the struggle to get political science to recognize the politics of gender, let alone feminist critiques of the "political," political representation, and public policy. I was privileged to have had women professors and mentors, to whom I owe so much, who opened doors for me. Many other women, Indigenous peoples, and people of colour hit disciplinary walls that excluded research questions, degraded expertise, slowed careers, and shut doors. In the intervening years, many more women have entered the profession but too often this shift in the demographic of political science only represents the "diversification of whiteness" (Smith 2018). Indigenous scholars and people of colour remain notably underrepresented in the discipline.

Diverse and ongoing struggles within social science disciplines, as in broader society, have different outcomes: some segments of border walls crumble, others segments are converted into anterooms, while still others are jealously guarded and reinforced. Opening borders to more diverse scholars and scholarship typically unsettles disciplinary denizens and disciplinarians who periodically rally on the borders, calling for a return to fundamentals, more "balanced" perspectives, renewed enforcement of proper methods, and the containment of so-called identity politics. It is perhaps the inevitable logic of professional disciplines that habitually marginalized groups will always be told to "be patient," but as good social scientists we also have to ask, "Who is doing the telling" and "who is doing the waiting"? Contentious conversations in all social science disciplines are enriched and transformed precisely when they turn their critical gaze back onto themselves.

Political Discourses and Political Economies

Maybe I missed the crucial lecture in my undergraduate years when it was explained that behaviourism was only one among many competing interpretations of the mission and method of political science. That message became abundantly obvious, however, when I entered a doctoral program at another Canadian university in 1976. Thereafter, I was bombarded with alternative approaches and very contentious conversations about the conceptual framings and skill set that I had carried into my doctoral studies. For the first time, I was introduced to critiques of behaviouralism for its myopic methodological individualism, indifference to deeply embedded structures of disadvantage, and reproduction of liberal myths of democratic pluralism. I came to understand, as the late Robert Cox reminds us, that "theory is always for someone, and for some purpose" (Cox 1981, 128). These formative conversations stretched my research imagination and a reevaluation of my own ethical orientations and obligations as a political scientist and citizen.

One question that vexed students of Canadian politics in these years was why Canada seemed so similar and yet so different when compared to other Western democracies. Canada was a rich nation with a modest welfare state but its economy relied on resource extraction rather than manufacturing, and its citizens clung to so-called pre-modern identities and social divisions such as religion, ethnicity, and region, rather than social class. In *Crisis, Challenge and Change*, Jane Jenson and I undertook a historical analysis of the federal party system to try to explain why class-based identities and voting were so fragile in the Canadian context (1980, 1988). We concluded that political parties did not simply express voter preferences and aggregate them into winning coalitions one election at a time, as existing literatures maintained. Instead, we argued that political parties, in many ways, created voter preferences and alignments by formulating a "definition of politics." Among an infinite range of social identities and tensions, this definition specified which identities would be considered political and amenable through democratic politics, and thus how electorates divided among themselves into stable partisan alignments.

In retrospect, our contentions about the cultivation of particular kinds of political identities and social cleavages through the electoral process appear tentative, even innocent, especially in light of the subsequent "discursive turn" in the social sciences, and the broad embrace of Foucauldian conceptions of power/discourse and governmentality in political science in this century. But we were intervening in conversations that understood political identities as already being "out there," as antecedents to political processes and the products of particular stages of economic development. This early collaboration with Dr. Jenson, nonetheless, fundamentally shifted my perspectives on the ways political identities and political cultures are shaped, resisted, and reshaped through discourse. It prompted me to be more attentive to political conflicts over the dominant framing of political problems both in political speech and in public transcripts, not the least because states "never stop talking" (Corrigan and Sayer 1985, 3).

Political science has become much more adept at listening to what states say about nation, citizenship, and governance, as several chapters in this volume skillfully attest. Brent Epperson, for example, tracks media reports and America state legislative debates (Utah and Massachusetts) to demonstrate how neoliberal idioms continue to frame and limit national and subnational debates in the United States about access to basic health care. Despite the obvious failures of market-based approaches to provide health care to poor and marginalized communities, legislators continue to rely on market-based metrics such competition, choice, and personal responsibility to assess health care reforms. Similarly, Lois Harder uses parliamentary debates, policy documents, and judicial decisions to scrutinize Canada's inter-country adoption policies. She points out that, in neoliberal times, responsibility for the vulnerable has been increasingly downloaded onto families that are obliged to look after their own. Naturalized, often racialized citizens often want to adopt children who are family members from other countries because they are threatened by poverty, civil war, or inadequate medical care. Public policy and the courts, however, demand proof of a "genuine parent-child relationship" before they approve of such adoptions, even though one would expect such a relationship to develop only after the endangered child came to Canada, and only after an adoption was officially approved. This legislative hurdle that applies primarily to naturalized and racialized citizens, as Harder points out, betrays Canadian national narratives about cultural recognition and accommodation, and the progressive expansion of equal citizenship rights to ever more diverse populations.

Other chapters in this volume pick up on my previous engagements with such concepts as National Policies, governing philosophies, and political rationalities. While each term invites different assumptions and methods, all highlight the ways in which, historically, Canadian public policies, national narratives, and citizenship identities typically have congealed around overarching, reinforcing, and always contested ways of thinking about the political economy of governance, and its insistent questions about who benefits and to what effect. I was first introduced to Canadian political economy (CPE) during my doctoral studies and especially was drawn to Harold Innis's meticulous historiographies of successive "staples" extraction projects (for example, 1927; 1940). Innis insisted that economic theories developed in old societies did not account for the dynamics of development in new societies. White settler societies such as Canada, he argued, prospered and consolidated around resource extraction for markets located in an imperial centre, but this form of dependent development was inherently uneven across regions and inherently unstable. Abrupt shifts in international demand locked such new societies in a perpetual boom and bust cycle: the exploitation of each staple required new investment, new infrastructures, and labour at proximate points of extraction. However, when international markets disappeared, as they invariably did, each staple left in its wake massive public debt, abandoned communities, ravaged landscapes, and regional grievances.

I was especially taken by Innis's ways of seeing the imprints of successive developmental strategies on physical, social, and political geographies, one layered upon the other across time, and used this perspective as a springboard to explore the cumulative impacts of national development policies on recurring regional divisions in Canada. *The Political Economy of Regionalism* (1990) argued that Canada's uneven topographies of possibility, identity, and culture were artefacts of public policy, of successive national development strategies or National Policies (Fowke 1957; Smiley 1975). Alexandra Dobrowolsky's chapter in this book demonstrates that these imprints continue to shape contemporary immigration and settlement policies in Manitoba and British Columbia. The legacies of these development strategies weave through formal governmental scales, distinct histories of migration, and more recent constructions of the "ideal" entrepreneurial immigrant as a quick fix for deeply embedded and uneven economic development and resulting demographic dilemmas.

Yet, for all that the political economy approach revealed to me, in hindsight, I am bewildered by what it concealed. Canadian political economy, similar to all disciplines, has its own history of boundary-setting, of the personal and the situational. Although Innis died the year I was born, his work was revived by a stream of Canadian political economy in the 1970s because it spoke to then contentious conversations about American imperialism, Canadian identity, and the need for Canadian Studies. However, this movement to "tell our own stories" failed to see what was concealed in such tropes as "new world," "settler societies," and "national identity." For example, my focus on National Policies pursued settler imaginaries – tales of the new world that reiterated the doctrine of *terra nullius* and ignored how Canada's landscapes also bore the imprints of Indigenous ways of being and colonial plunder. Political economy, for the most part, did not consider Canada's irreducible and formative dispossession of Indigenous lands and peoples, recognize settler colonialism as a distinctive genre of statecraft, or interrogate the cumulative discourses and practices that continue to hold this distinct form of colonialism in place. As Isabel Altamirano-Jiménez underlines in her chapter, the very possibility of a new world or Europeans could only be realized by rendering Indigenous territories empty, all resources potentially extractable, and Indigenous bodies and communities dispensable. Turtle Island, once a diverse archipelago of Indigenous nationhood, she elaborates, continues to be a site of both ongoing waves of dispossession and displacement and accumulating social and environmental risks for Indigenous peoples. Our hegemonic new world stories are inextricably connected to the suppression of Indigenous stories of the new world.

The transformative critiques and scholarship of new generations of Indigenous academics and activists have progressively exposed the conceits of the settler imagination, not only with respect to new worlds, empty lands, and exploitable resources, but also critically about our relationships with the land, water, and other species. Global warming, now widely recognized as an existential crisis, betrays Eurocentric illusions about Dominion (as in the Dominion of Canada) over diverse peoples, all other forms of life, and nature. The story of Canadian Studies and Canadian social science thus begs a major edit with new plot lines that foreground colonial discourses of white supremacy and control, ongoing settler territoriality and the logics of elimination, and the compounding injuries of extractive mentalities and economies (see for example Altamirano-Jiménez 2013; Dhillon 2017; Smith 2018; Wolfe 2006). Such long-concealed plotlines in stories of the new world will necessarily generate "unsettling" and contentious conversations that have the potential to transform our disciplines at their core.

Neoliberalism and the Social

The chapters in this volume demonstrate the multiple and complex ways in which neoliberal governing ideas have transformed diverse policy terrains and everyday life over the past forty years. Its core tenets were initially formulated in relative obscurity in the mid-twentieth century by a handful of conservative philosophers and economists who decried socialism and the welfare state as a threat to individual freedom. In the 1980s, however, many international financial institutions and advanced democracies embraced neoliberalism as a plausible solution to the economic stagnation of the previous decade. It promised to restructure the postwar social state and unleash the power of market forces and entrepreneurship to create new markets, more jobs, and economic prosperity for all. Its early adopters, including UK Prime Minister Margaret Thatcher and US President Ronald Reagan, argued that eliminating red tape, selling off public assets, implementing market-friendly rules to expand global markets and supply chains, and reducing the tax load on so-called job creators would benefit everyone. In fact, Thatcher famously argued at the time that "there was no alternative" to this governing formula.

My initial engagements with neoliberalism began in the early 1990s, when it travelled as a loose but invested amalgam of market-enhancing governing strategies under such aliases as "trickle-down economics," "economic globalization," and, in Canada, "restructuring." Restructuring discourses of the time pronounced that the welfare state had promised more than it could deliver, and that innovations such as trade liberalization, privatization of public infrastructures and services, and deficit reduction (largely aimed at social spending) were necessary precisely in order to ensure the sustainability of core social programs. "Short-term pain," we were told, had to be endured to ensure "long-term gain." In contrast to the United States, where at the time government was framed as "the problem," Canada's strands of neoliberal dogma were ushered in through the back door as way to ensure the ongoing viability of the social state.

These ideas generated immediate and sustained resistance, especially from the Canadian women's movement. It had long insisted that the postwar welfare state was inherently gendered, extending social security to male breadwinners, and minimal, conditional, and often degrading welfare schemes to women, especially single mothers (Brodie 1998; Brodie and Bakker 2008; Brodie 2010). But the movement also was primed to write gender equity into the postwar welfare state by extending its reach to include universal child care, extended parental leave, pay equity, reproductive rights, and better legal protections and pensions for homemakers. The women's movement had built up its political muscles in federal politics over two decades, and, finally, had a seat at the federal cabinet table devoted to "women's issues" (Brodie 2007a; 2008c). It was prepared to fight the idea of restructuring and, especially, continental free trade agreements, on the grounds that they would invariably "ratchet-down" Canadian social programs to lower North American standards, and prohibit the federal government creating new ones in the future.

In *Politics on the Margins* (1995), I focused on Canada's restructuring agenda as a strategy to redefine the public and private and radically reduce spaces for political contestation by expanding the autonomy and responsibilities of market and the family. Privatization, a core theme in restructuring discourse, for example, involved two distinct processes: first, commodification transformed existing and future public goods into marketable products, thus increasing financial burdens on families and pressures on mothers to enter the work force; and second, re-familialization downloaded greater burdens of social care and social reproduction onto women and families with the growing expectation that they should look after their own. Restructuring did not simply divert things from the public sector to the market or the domestic sphere; it transformed and magnified the burdens of everyday life.

As Alexa DeGagne rightly argues in her chapter, however, shifting constructions of the public and private resonate differently among those who do not conform to heteronormative assumptions about families and gendered divisions of labour. LGBT and racialized communities experience the private sphere both as a site of personal relationships and social care, and as a space of freedom from state intervention, violence, and criminalization. As neoliberalism progressively stretched the terrain of the private in the early twenty-first century, the mainstream of the LGBT movement prioritized the legalization of same-sex marriage as a political goal, not the least, to shield some community members and their intimate lives from ongoing police surveillance and harassment, and the always lurking threats of public condemnation and interpersonal violence. This private zone of protection and social inclusion for homonormative members of the LGBT community, however, only reinforced the harassment and criminalization of "street-involved" people who do not have safe private spaces to live their lives. DeGagne explains that homonormative members of the LGBT community were extended public protection and public apologies, while others were re-inscribed as inferior, deviant, and targets for ongoing exclusion, punishment, and violence.

In the early twenty-first century, market-friendly discourses and policy innovations proliferated across scales, national borders, and policy sectors. Rather than simply reconfiguring the public-private divide, neoliberalism aspired to extend and disseminate market values to all institutions, social action, and individual conduct (Brown 2005, 42–3). Neoliberal rationalities privileged specific vocabularies, styles of truth telling, and expertise that progressively reshaped governing programs and instruments, political identities, and common sense (Miller and Rose 2008; Dean 1999). At the time, I struggled to find a concept that would help me think through these larger cultural and political shifts and, especially, the progressive erosion of the identities and grammars of post-war citizenship. I eventually settled on the idea of the social (Kingfisher 2002; Clarke 2004).

The social is not an easy concept to grasp or define. On one hand, it is part of our common vocabulary and experience: we use this term to name society writ large; to categorize things generally regarded as non-economic or non-political; and to specify public policies that directly connect us to the state as recipients of various entitlements and benefits. On the other hand, the social is also a notoriously amorphous and contested terrain in political life and scholarly research. As John Clarke describes in his chapter in this book, it has several scholarly cadences, including relations and practices of social reproduction, a field constituted and reformed by governmental practices (that seek either to make better people or people better), and an imaginary that helps frame common understandings of self, mutual obligations, and relationships between economic and political forces.

Rather than assume that the social is an inherent property of collective life, my work focused on its emergent, generative, and contingent properties, especially in neoliberal times. I was struck by Mitchell Dean's keen observation that the social "did not arise from the implementation of a theoretical model of society," but, instead, is "a condition of such a model" (1999, 53–4). Rather than being part of the original blueprint, the social was an addition to liberalism's political architecture.

I returned to Karl Polanyi's pivotal work, *The Great Transformation*, and his account of the emergence of the idea of a social in nineteenth century Britain when the prevailing doctrine of laissez-faire violently upended the previous governing order with unconstrained exploitation, rampant poverty, and (then unimaginable) environmental degradation. Polanyi argued that the laissez-faire governing experiment enabled "the market mechanism to be the sole director of the fate of human beings and their natural environment" (2001, 76), and that "no society could stand the effects of such a system of crude fictions, even for the shortest time" without taking steps to protect itself (2001, 76–7). It was in this context, he argued, that people "discovered society," explored "the meaning of life in a complex society," named "social problems" and undertook collective measures to protect itself. As important, the collapse of laissez-faire in the early twentieth century generated the "spontaneous eruption" of all manner of counter-movements that offered competing solutions to the shifting but endemic tensions between democracy and markets (2001, 89, 124). For Polanyi, the social was an emergent condition and a site of ongoing contestation about the capacities of extant institutions, including markets, to allocate goods and protect society (Brodie 2008b).

In this formulation, the idea of the social stretches beyond portrayals of social policies as mechanisms to ameliorate glaring systemic failures, regulate perceived problem populations, or satisfy the biopolitical instincts of the state. The social may variously contain these elements but it is also generative of much more. It fuels competing social imaginaries about formative questions of political collectivity, such as where and how the state should intervene, and for whom. It also informs social literacies that specify a problem as a "social problem" and authorize specific forms of political claims-making and claims-makers (Brodie 2007b). Postwar social literacies in Canada and elsewhere, for example, understood that markets required state regulation, framed many social vulnerabilities as collective rather than individual risks, and committed to the expansion of social rights and citizen equality (Brodie 2012). To be clear, postwar welfare states differed greatly in the expression and implementation of these goals. There were different mutations that embodied the institutional and political traits of their hosts. The postwar social imaginary, nonetheless, opened new spaces for excluded and marginalized groups to make claims on the state for protection, equity, and inclusion precisely because it "harbored ideals in excess of itself" (Brown 2015, 206). These immanent dynamics generated waves of equity-based identity formation and claims-making in the second half of twentieth century, including various configurations of the anti-racist, feminist, LGBT, and resurgent Indigenous movements.

Specific configurations of the social are profoundly conditional upon local/national histories and path dependencies, the relative strength of competing social forces, state capacities, and, most critically, as this volume attests, pronounced shifts in governing philosophies. With the ascendency of neoliberalism, core elements of the postwar settlement, including common understandings of the public interest, public ownership, common goods, equality, [and] the redistribution of wealth progressively became "unspeakable" (Hall and Massey 2012, 59). It was not that neoliberalism, in its formative moments, did not advance ideas about justice and the good society – it did. The problem was that its vision was profoundly anti-social, as citizens had come to understand the term, prioritizing markets over governments, decollectivizing and privatizing responsibility for shared social risks, and celebrating market metrics of fairness, equity, and justice. In this imaginary, market mechanisms were neutral and rightly distributed rewards to those making the greatest economic contributions to society, whether through hard work, investments-in-self, innovations, or entrepreneurship. It followed that it was unjust for the state to confiscate and redistribute the individual rewards of entrepreneurial citizenship. Moreover, neoliberal individualization, as several chapters in this volume underline, dictated that individuals were themselves responsible for designing "biographic solutions" to risks that were often beyond their personal control (Beck and Beck-Gernsheim 2002, 22–6; Bauman 2002, 69).

Citizens Are Thus Summoned to Be Self-Reliant

Several chapters in this volume describe how this imperative of self-sufficiency has been interwoven into public policy and personal life. Suzan Ilcan's chapter on the governance of refugee populations in Uganda, for example, demonstrates how international non-governmental organizations and government policies aim to "to help refugees to help themselves" through labour force participation. These organizations equate self-sufficiency with the capacity to integrate into local labour markets; indeed, this is a requirement for refugees to escape the confinements of refugee camps and move into cities, at which point, they are phased off food and other forms of humanitarian aid. While these refugees, in the broadest terms, may achieve the status of "market citizen," they, nonetheless, remain non-citizens because they are often prohibited from applying for good jobs that are solely reserved for Ugandan citizens. "Successful resettlement" thus creates an urban underclass and ongoing marginalization, exclusion, and containment.

Similarly, Janet Phillips explores contemporary Canadian approaches aimed at another routinely marginalized population – those categorized as mentally abnormal. She combs through successive government inquiries from this and the past century to track how "mental abnormality" has been variously identified and regulated. She argues that the current goal of building "resiliency" among those with mental health challenges is a neoliberal response to the failures of previous deinstitutionalization programs and the progressive erosion of funding for mental health care services. Talk about "bouncing back" from personal crises, "coping" with personal and societal barriers, and embracing strategies for self-care, in the absence of institutional supports, only intensifies the already precarious lives of affected individuals and families.

Phillips's critique of resiliency resonates with Catherine Kingfisher's incisive analysis of the contemporary Western obsession with happiness and myriad new technologies that aim to help everyone to enhance their inner selves and overall well-being. Evocations of the happiness imperative, she explains, echo through popular culture, pharmaceutical marketing, and a burgeoning self-help industry. Contemporary Western discourses about happiness, however, cannot be separated from the progressive disassembling of the social supports and the isolation and alienation engendered by multiple processes of neoliberal individualization. The happiness imperative is both an artifact of the crisis of neoliberalism and a technology for the production of proper neoliberal subjects who are challenged by intensifying economic, political, and environmental precariousness. Kingfisher demonstrates that the idea of happiness is not self-evident but is, instead, a profoundly cultural construct. This prescription to turn to one's inner life in the face of these multiple and encroaching systemic crises amounts to little more than the vacuous adage "don't worry, be happy."

Concluding Conversations

Academic conversations about neoliberalism have grown increasingly contentious in recent years, not least because neoliberalism in theory has not aligned well with neoliberalism in practice. Looking back, I think it is fair to say that early research on neoliberalism, including my own work, was too willing to accept this governing philosophy on its own terms, as a coherent political ideology, rather than as a grab bag of vested ideas variously calculated to empower markets and dismantle the postwar social state. In effect, we granted neoliberalism more disciplinary and transformative power in our theoretical imaginations than it actually possessed, or ultimately could achieve in the face of governing realities and its own contradictions. In the past thirty years, neoliberalism has abandoned many of its founding premises, mutated to conform to local or national contexts, and invented new conceptual framings that are only indirectly connected to its initial commitments to minimal government and unleashed entrepreneurialism.

Justin Leifso's account of the adoption of Lean management in fields very far flung from its origins in Japanese auto manufacturing – including public sector governance – underscores both the inventiveness and fragility of neoliberal ambitions in local contexts. The Lean industry promised untold efficiencies in the delivery of public goods, if only adopters conformed to its hodgepodge of quirky idioms, rituals, and templates. Jurisdictions have subsequently abandoned this experiment in public management after it collided with local political cultures, subject-matter expertise, and entrenched bureaucratic practices, and without producing tangible efficiency gains.

Neoliberalism's inventive and disjointed track record has prompted many researchers to question whether it is accurate or even useful to continue using this term to frame our analyses of contemporary social and political life. They variously argue that the terms "neoliberal" and "neoliberalism" have been vastly overused and should be replaced by more exacting concepts such as neoliberalization or assemblage, if not jettisoned altogether (Fink 2017, 156). Neoliberalism, moreover, has been declared "dead" several times in the past decade, most recently when the coronavirus shut down the global economy and triggered massive government intervention to ease the economic shock and protect public health.

Does neoliberalism's recurring shape-shifting and its meanderings from the script provide reason enough to discard the concept altogether? Are researchers applying expectations of efficacy, uniformity, and consistency to neoliberalism that have not been applied to other governing philosophies in the past? As Plehwe and Slobodian remind us, the histories of other "isms," including Marxism, liberalism, and conservatism, typically have been marked by "kaleidoscopic refraction, splintering, and recombination." Avoiding the term neoliberalism, or rejecting it, they argue, "does little to address the ideology it was coined to describe" (2020, 3).

Admittedly, I am conflicted on this question, but the political economist in me is reluctant to lose sight of the enduring imprints that neoliberalism has carved into our collective condition, not the least an unprecedented concentration of wealth and power among a handful of global plutocrats, unsustainable income inequalities, the erosion of democratic processes, and an accelerating climate crisis. These imprints will persist long after the coronavirus is subdued, informing the focus, limits, and possibilities of post-pandemic politics. If anything, the pandemic has only further exposed and accelerated conditions of uncertainty and extreme precariousness.

John Clarke's chapter in this volume provides constructive advice about how we might think about neoliberalism in such moments of disruption, especially when competing political forces and political voices have assembled around new versions of populism, nativism, and racism. While Clarke underscores that "neoliberalisms" provide an indelible backdrop to the contemporary politics of uncertainty, he cautions scholars of the "here and now" to avoid interpreting this moment either as another stage in the long march of neoliberalism, or as a break with neoliberalism and the beginning of a new era. Instead, he challenges social scientists to adopt a different "way of telling time," one that focuses on the "moment" or "conjuncture" – spaces of intersection in lived experiences, which combine and recombine the old and new, the transnational and local, and strains of many other "isms," including colonialism, racism, and nationalism. Our times are roiling with competing social imaginaries: some portend amplified violence, insecurity, and ecological disaster; others cast light on thinkable futures, realizable futures, better futures. Social scientists are challenged to unpack these competing imaginaries of the here and now, expose their deceits, and illuminate the hard choices that beckon on our immediate horizon.

Before the pandemic struck, there had been many signs that neoliberal imperatives were losing their hold on public and policy imaginations. Massive street demonstrations, anti-racist and climate action groups, and new political parties all suggested, as Clarke observes, that people wanted "the social back." In truth, few wanted it taken away. Sometime in the future, however, historians may well recount that it took a random zoonotic mutation to ultimately unmask the neoliberal myths of self-sufficiency and market governance. The pandemic shattered the neoliberal axiom that "there is no alternative" to market-based governance. Governments met the speed and scale of the pandemic with the greatest expansion of the welfare state "in living memory." In 2020 alone, governments around the world launched over 1,600 new social programs and allocated unprecedented public funding to sustain livelihoods and provide basic income support to the millions who lost their jobs overnight (*The Economist* 2021).

Governments have insisted that this exceptional social spending was a necessary response to an unexpected and unprecedented catastrophe, rather than a long-term commitment to reverse the staggering inequalities in income, security, and well-being that distinguish the neoliberal paradigm from previous governing strategies.

Predictably, these emergency responses were immediately opposed in certain political quarters, whether because the pandemic supports were too generous, discouraging people from working, or such levels of public investment were unsustainable, only inviting a harsh reckoning with public austerity once the crisis subsides. It is difficult to assess how these familiar neoliberal tropes will resonate in a post-pandemic world. Social supports, once established, are always difficult to withdraw from people with demonstrable need. More critically, however, the pandemic shifted public expectations about what governments can and should do for ordinary people struggling to pay their bills and get ahead. Although ideas about universal basic incomes and a new social contract have circulated in policy circles for some time, they gained traction during the pandemic. Indeed, a few political parties have begun to recalibrate their platforms to tap into growing public demands for concrete policies to address inequality, exclusion, eroding public infrastructures, and the climate crisis. As one prominent advocate for a new social contract explains, "the politics of turmoil we observe in many countries is only a foretaste of what awaits us if we do not rethink what we owe each other" (quoted in *The Economist* 2021; Shafik 2021). The case for a rigorous critical social science for our times could not be more immediate or compelling.

REFERENCES

Addley, Easther. 2021. "A Very Dangerous Epoch: Historians Try to Make Sense of Covid." *The Guardian*, February 13, 2021. https://www.theguardian.com/world/2021/feb/13/a-very-dangerous-epoch-historians-try-make-sense-covid.

Altamirano-Jiménez, Isabel. 2013. *Indigenous Encounters with Neoliberalism: Place, Women, and the Environment in Canada and Mexico.* Vancouver: UBC Press.

Bakker, Isabella. 2003. "Neoliberal Governance and the Reprivatization of Social Reproduction." In *Power, Production and Social Reproduction*, edited by Isabella Bakker and Stephen Gill, 66–82. London: Palgrave Macmillan.

Bauman, Zygmunt. 2002. *Society Under Siege.* London: Polity Press.

Beck, Ulrich and Elizabeth Beck-Gernsheim. 2002. *Individualization: Institutionalized Individualism and Its Social and Political Consequences.* London: Sage.

Bourdieu, Pierre. 2014. *On the State: Lectures at the College de France, 1989–1992.* Cambridge: Polity Press.

Brodie, Janine. 2012. "Social Literacy and Social Justice in Times of Crisis." *The Trudeau Foundation Papers* 1, 117–46.

– 2010 "Globalization, Canadian Family Policy and the Omissions of Neoliberalism." *North Carolina Law Review* 88 (5): 1559–92.

– 2008a. "The New Social 'isms': Individualization and Social Policy Reform in Canada." In *Contested Individualization: Debates about Contemporary Personhood*, edited by Cosmo Howard, 153–70. Routledge.

– 2008b. "Rethinking the Social in Social Citizenship." In *Rethinking the Social in Citizenship*, edited by Engin Isin, 22–50. Toronto: University of Toronto Press.

– 2008c. "We Are All Equal Now: Contemporary Gender Politics in Canada." *Feminist Theory* 9 (2): 145–64. https://doi.org/10.1177%2F1464700108090408.

– 2007a. "Canada's Three Ds: The Rise and Decline of the Gender-Based Policy Capacity." In *Remapping Gender in the New Global Order*, edited by Marjorie Cohen and Janine Brodie, 166–84. London: Routledge.

– 2007b. "Reforming Social Justice in Neoliberal Times." *Studies in Social Justice* 2 (1), 93–107. http://doi.org/10.26522/ssj.v1i2.972.

– 1998. "Restructuring and the Politics of Marginalization." In *Women and Political Representation in Canada*, edited by C. Andrew and M. Tremblay, 19–38. Ottawa: University of Ottawa Press.

– 1990. *The Political Economy of Canadian Regionalism.* Toronto: Harcourt Brace Jovanovich.

– 1995. *Politics on the Margins: Restructuring and the Canadian Women's Movement.* Halifax: Fernwood Publishing.

– 1985. *Women and Politics in Canada*. Toronto: McGraw-Hill.

Brodie, Janine, and Isabella Bakker. 2008. *Where Are the Women? Gender Equality, Budgets and Canadian Public Policy*. Ottawa: Canadian Centre for Policy Alternatives.

Brodie, Janine, and Jane Jenson. 1988. *Crisis, Challenge, and Change: Party and Class in Canada Revisited*. Toronto: McGill-Queen's University Press.

– 1980. *Crisis, Challenge, and Change: Party and Class in Canada*. Toronto: Methuen.

Brown, Wendy. 2015. *Undoing the Demos: Neoliberalism's Stealth Revolution*. New York: Zone Books.

– 2005. *Edgework: Critical Essays on Knowledge and Power*. Princeton, NJ: Princeton University Press.

Clarke, John. 2004. *Changing Welfare, Changing States: New Directions in Social Policy*. London: Sage Publications.

Corrigan, Philip, and Derek Sayers. 1985. *The Great Arch: English State Formation as Cultural Revolution*. New York: Basil Blackwell.

Cox, Robert. 1981. "Social Forces, States, and World Orders: Beyond International Relations Theory." *Millennium* 10 (2): 126–55. https://doi.org/10.1177%2F03058298810100020501.

Dean, Mitchel. 1999. *Governmentality: Power and Rule in Modern Society*. London: Sage.

Dhillon. Jaskiran. 2017. *Prairie Rising: Indigenous Youth, Decolonization, and the Politics of Intervention*. Toronto: University of Toronto Press.

The Economist. 2021. "Shelter from the Storm: The Future of the Welfare State." *The Economist*, March 6, 2021. https://www.economist.com/briefing/2021/03/06/covid-19-has-transformed-the-welfare-state-which-changes-will-endure.

Fink, Ben. 2017. "How Neoliberalism Got Organized: A Usable History for Resisters with Special Reference to Education." *The Good Society* 25 (2–3): 158–71. https://doi.org/10.5325/goodsociety.25.2-3.0158.

Fowke, Vernon. 1957. *The National Policy and the Wheat Economy*. Toronto: University of Toronto Press.

Haass, Richard. 2020. "The Pandemic Will Accelerate History Rather Than Reshape It: Not Every Crisis Is a Turning Point." *Foreign Affairs*. April 7, 2020. https://www.foreignaffairs.com/articles/united-states/2020-04-07/pandemic-will-accelerate-history-rather-reshape-it.

Hall, Stuart, and Doreen Massey. 2012. "Interpreting the Crisis." In *Soundings on the Neoliberal Crisis*, edited by Jonathan Rutherford and Sally Davidson, 55–69. London: Soundings.

Innis, Harold. 1927. *The Fur Trade in Canada*. Toronto: University of Toronto Press.

– 1940. *The Cod Fisheries*. Toronto: University of Toronto Press.

Irwin, Neil. 2020. "It's the End of the World Economy as We Know It." *New York Times*, April 16, 2020. https://www.nytimes.com/2020/04/16/upshot/world-economy-restructuring-coronavirus.html.

Kingfisher, Catherine, ed. 2002. *Western Welfare in Decline: Globalization and Women's Poverty*. Philadelphia: University of Pennsylvania Press.

Miller, Peter, and Nikolas Rose. 2008. *Governing the Present: Administering Economic, Social, and Personal Life*. Malden, MA: Polity Press.

Plehwe, Dieter, and Quinn Slobodian. 2020. "Introduction." In *The Nine Lives of Neoliberalism*. Edited by Dieter Plehwe, Quinn Slobodian, and Philip Mirowski. New York: Verso Books.

Polanyi, Karl. 2001. *The Great Transformation: The Political and Economic Origins of Our Time*, 2nd ed. Boston: Beacon Press.

Shafik, Minouche. 2021. *What We Owe Each Other: A New Social Contract for a Better Society*. Princeton, NJ: Princeton University Press.

Smiley, Donald. 1975. "Canada and the Quest for a National Policy." *Canadian Journal of Political Science* 8 (1): 40–62. doi:10.1017/S0008423900045224.

Smith, Malinda. 2018. "Diversity in Theory and Practice: Dividends, Downsides, and Dead-Ends." In *Contemporary Inequalities and Social Justice in Canada*, edited by Janine Brodie, 143–68. Toronto: University of Toronto Press.

– 2017. "A Dirty Dozen: Unconscious Race and Gender Biases in the Academy." In *The Equity Myth: Racialization and Indigeneity at Canadian Universities*, edited by Frances Henry et. al., 263–96. Vancouver: UBC Press.

Spinney, Laura. 2020. "Will Coronavirus Lead to Fairer Societies: Thomas Piketty Explores the Prospect." *The Guardian*, May 12, 2020. https://www.theguardian.com/world/2020/may/12/will-coronavirus-lead-to-fairer-societies-thomas-piketty-explores-the-prospect.

Wolfe, Patrick. 2006. "Settler Colonialism and the Elimination of the Native." *Journal of Genocide Research* 8 (4): 387–409. https://doi.org/10.1080/14623520601056240.

WEF. World Economic Forum. 2021. "Pandemials: Youth in an Age of Lost Opportunity." https://reports.weforum.org/global-risks-report-2021/pandemials-youth-in-an-age-of-lost-opportunity/.

Contributors

Isabel Altamirano-Jiménez is Binizá from the Isthmus of Tehuantepec, Mexico. She is a professor of Political Science and Canada Research Chair in comparative Indigenous feminist studies at the University of Alberta. Her research investigates how different modalities of resource extraction are operationalized and experienced at different scales (the body, community, the non-human world).

Isabella Bakker is Distinguished Research Professor in the Department of Politics, York University. Her research examines the interplay between feminist perspectives and international public policy, with a focus on how macroeconomics and fiscal policy affect questions of gender equity, and social and intersectional justice.

Janine Brodie is Distinguished University Professor Emerita at the University of Alberta. Over the past four decades she has contributed to many critical conversations in Canadian political science relating to partisanship, regionalism, gender politics, social policy, and neoliberal governance.

John Clarke is Emeritus Professor in the Faculty of Arts and Social Sciences in the Open University, UK. He has written on a wide range of subjects, centred around changing formations of nation, state, and welfare. He is working on a book on the current conjuncture in the UK, provisionally titled "The Battle for Britain," to be published by Bristol University Press in May 2023.

Alexa DeGagne is Associate Professor in Women's and Gender Studies at Athabasca University. Her current research, funded by the Social Sciences and Humanities Research Council, examines the changing relationships between 2SLGBTQ communities and police organizations across Canada.

Alexandra Dobrowolsky is Professor of Political Science at Saint Mary's University and teaches in the areas of Canadian and comparative politics, and women's and gender studies. She has published in a variety of national and international journals and has written, edited, and co-edited six books on issues related to social policy, representation, constitutionalism, and citizenship broadly conceived.

Brent Epperson is Assistant Professor of Conflict Studies at Saint Paul University in Ottawa and a practising ombudsman in Europe, Canada, and the United States. His research interests involve ombudsman practice and the growth of the ombuds profession, public sector governance and the development of administratively fair and equitable policy and procedure, and issue representation and (re)framing in public policy debates – in particular, debates on health care, higher education, and minority rights.

Lois Harder is Dean of Social Sciences and Professor of Political Science at the University of Victoria. Her research explores the intersections of political belonging, citizenship, and reproduction. She is the author, most recently, of *Canadian Club: Birthright and Belonging* (University of Toronto Press, 2022).

Suzan Ilcan is University Research Chair and Professor in the Department of Sociology and Legal Studies at the University of Waterloo. Her key research areas are forced migration, critical border studies, and citizenship and social justice.

Catherine Kellogg is a professor of Political Science at the University of Alberta, where she teaches political theory. Her research concentrates on contemporary critical political theory, especially feminist theory, psychoanalysis, and deconstruction. She is the author of *Law's Trace: From Hegel to Derrida* (Routledge 2010) and is currently working on a book-length study of cruelty in politics.

Catherine Kingfisher is Professor Emerita of Anthropology at the University of Lethbridge. She is the author of *Women in the American Welfare Trap* (UPenn 1996), *A Policy Travelogue: Tracing Welfare Reform in Aotearoa/New Zealand and Canada* (Berghahn 2013), and *Collaborative Happiness: Building the Good Life in Urban Cohousing Communities* (Berghahn

2021). She is the editor of *Western Welfare in Decline: Globalization and Women's Poverty* (UPenn 2002). She lives in Quayside Village Cohousing Community in North Vancouver.

Justin Leifso is Assistant Professor in Political Science at the University of Victoria. His research and teaching focuses on critical engagements with public policy, specializing in discourses of efficiency and innovation and the affective dimensions of policy in Canada.

Steve Patten is a professor of Political Science at the University of Alberta, where he teaches and researches in the field of Canadian politics, with a focus on the political party system and public policymaking. In addition to his scholarly articles and chapters, he is co-editor of *The Chrétien Legacy* (McGill-Queen's 2006) and *Patriation and Its Consequences* (UBC Press 2015).

Janet Phillips holds a PhD (2018) in political science from the University of Alberta, and a MA (2010) and BA (2009) in political science from Western University. Her interests include mad studies, governmentality, Foucault studies, and disability studies.